THE SCOTTISH CHATEAU

THE COUNTRY HOUSE OF RENAISSANCE SCOTLAND

CHARLES McKEAN

SUTTON PUBLISHING

First published in 2001 by
Sutton Publishing Limited · Phoenix Mill
Thrupp · Stroud · Gloucestershire · GL5 2BU

British Library Cataloguing in Publication Data
A catalogue record for this book is available from the British Library

ISBN 0-7509-2323-7

Typeset in 10/13 pt Sabon.
Typesetting and origination by
Sutton Publishing Limited.
Printed and bound in England by
J.H. Haynes & Co. Ltd, Sparkford.

Contents

Preface

This book was born by accident. The Royal Incorporation of Architects in Scotland planned an exhibition for the Edinburgh Festival in 1990 on the subject of the architecture of the Scottish Renaissance. It was led by Deborah Howard and designed by Alexander Fairweather. During the assembly of exhibits, it was a source of despair that so many of the relevant buildings – and almost all the major ones – lay in ruins. To convey an adequate impression of the time, some reconstructions became essential. Simon Montgomery made models of the Parliament House and of Pitsligo, but better visuals were needed of places like Huntly. Those best skilled to undertake the task claimed that they were too busy (they were probably doubtful about the enterprise) so, *faute de mieux*, I undertook to attempt one or two. It was a revelation to me. An architectural language began to emerge from the buildings – or the drawings of them by MacGibbon and Ross or Billings – once roofs and other details of which there were traces were restored. There appeared to be common features, common rhythm, common structure and common proportions. To make such conjectural reconstructions credible, every detail, every odd aperture, had to be explained against the plan, and different sources compared against each other. For example, attempting to synthesise the surviving ruins of the Palace of Boyne into an approximation of what it might have looked like, against the drawings of Grose, Daniell and MacGibbon and Ross, took many hours and repeated abortive versions. It was soon apparent that the vast majority were structures of different periods. A number of further conjectural restorations was displayed in the 'Revelations' exhibition in the RIAS in autumn 1994.

It had become clear that these 'castles' were castles only in name, and that, in many cases, such a name was a modern attribution. They were, rather, largely indefensible stately houses or country seats. Yet what extraordinary passion this interpretation provoked. Whereas I had seen it as a welcome revelation of a hitherto obscured flamboyant culture, it was taken as an attack upon the builders of these houses, on their owners, and as an affront to the honour of the country itself. To remove the warlike overcoat of these great houses was tantamount to robbing them of their dignity and personality. Yet in this respect, architectural history was already lagging far behind mainstream history. While Scotland was loath to accept that many of its fearsome 'castles' were misinterpreted architect-designed Renaissance country seats, it was content to rediscover the glorious Renaissance music of Robert Carver, or contemporary poetry, humanism and philosophy. Architecture was being shunted into a cultural cul-de-sac, with ever more extraordinary interpretations of the one central fact of the time: namely that the Scottish architectural expression refused to follow mainland Europe into classicism.

If the term 'castle' conveyed positive signals of dignity and honour, it also conveyed profoundly negative ones about Scottish Renaissance architectural culture – and thereby about Scotland's Renaissance culture as a whole. The purpose of this book is to introduce those two cultures from the viewpoint that most country houses of this period were 'mock-military' – i.e. *châteaux* – rather than seriously aggressive or defensible.

Many people have participated in this project, and are listed in the acknowledgements. Here I should like to pay particular tribute to the Department of History, Dundee University, to Chris Whatley, James Simpson, and to Neil Grieve. Above all, I should like to thank my long-suffering family – if, that is, they can still recognise who I am.

Charles McKean
Department of History
University of Dundee

Acknowledgements

Many people have contributed to the preparation of this book, although all errors remain mine. People have shared their researches, shown me round their houses, and made their drawings and manuscripts available. I owe them all great thanks.

The book itself owes much to the pioneering work of Deborah Howard. Andrew Nicoll provided invaluable help as research assistant, especially in transcribing much of RH13/1. Chris Whatley, Frank Walker and Alan MacDonald read through the text and gave invaluable advice. Chris Smout generously debated concepts thereon in open forum beneath the rainy walls of Invermark. The Royal Incorporation of Architects in Scotland and its staff have been very supportive. Particular thanks are due to Angus Grossart, Douglas Connell, and the Kintore Charitable Trust for their help in the early stages of this investigation, and to the Department of History at Dundee University – not least for enabling a greater number of illustrations to be included. Dundee University Archives, particularly Pat Whatley and Jan Merchant, provided hardware, material and friendliness. I am grateful, also, to Sarah Reid and Lena Smith for assisting with typing. Jaqueline Mitchell and Sarah Moore have been very understanding editors.

PROVISION OF MATERIAL

I am particularly grateful to those who shared their research with me – notably Michael Bath (the painted interiors of Renaissance Scotland), James Brown (Baltersan), Joe Innes and Blair Brooks (the building history of Innes), Neil Hynd (early seventeenth-century plasterwork), Alan MacDonald (seventeenth-century timber trade), Margaret Stewart (the 6th Earl of Mar), and Charles Wemyss (the later seventeenth-century great houses of Strathearn). The late Annie O'Connor revealed so many of the Society of Antiquaries of Scotland's treasures to me, notably the Riddell Collection. Margaret Wilkes, Diana Webster, Chris Fleet, and the Pont team at the Map Library of the National Library of Scotland have shared five years of enjoyment and information on the Pont project; and Iain Brown introduced me to the drawings of Jean-Claude Nattes, of Major General John Brown and to those collected for Hutton's proposed *Monasticon*, all in the National Library of Scotland. Ian Davidson, Grampian Conservation Manager for the National Trust for Scotland, provided drawings and introduced his buildings to me; and Ben Tindall and James Simpson supplied drawings of the buildings they were working on. Tristram Clarke at the National Register of Archives, Richard Ovenden at Edinburgh University Library Special Collections, Norman

Reid in St Andrews' University Archives and Simon Bennett at Glasgow University Archives were all most helpful.

FOR VISITS TO BUILDINGS

Annie Anderson, Lord and Lady Balfour of Burleigh, Kathleen Dalyell, Marc Ellington, Douglas Forrest, James Grant, Neil Grieve, Nick and Limma Groves-Raines, Dr Hand, Hector Munro, Ken Murdoch, James Simpson, France Smoor, Hermione Tennant, Ben Tindall and Adam Wallace.

FOR INFORMATION AND ADVICE

Malcolm Airs, Jane Anderson, Ian Arrenberg, Ian Begg, David Bowler, Iain Brown, Keith Brown, Peadar Callaghan, Neil Cameron, Kitty Cruft, Ian Cumming, Mike Davis, Pat Dennison, Christopher Dingwall, the late Gordon Donaldson, Peter Donaldson, John Dunbar, George and Nini Fenton, Donald Galbraith, Jane Geddes, John Gifford, Mark Girouard, Andor Gomme, Neil Grieve, Jean Guillaume, Nick Haynes, Bob Heath, Bob Hislop, Robert Knecht, Michael Lynch, Alan MacDonald, Murdo Macdonald, Allan Macinnes, Iain MacIvor, Rosalind Marshall, A. Maxwell-Irvine, Mary Miers, Paul Mitchell, Stuart Mitchell, Atholl Murray, Robert Naismith, John Orr, Tony Parker, Edwina Proudfoot, Denys Pringle, Una Richards, Ted Ruddock, Margaret Sanderson, Cathy Sayer, Hamish Scott, Ian Shepherd, Allen Simpson, James Simpson, Margaret Stewart, Jane Thomas, Sarah Troughton, Robin Turner, Alistair Urquhart, David Walker, Frank Walker, Chris Whatley, Mary Young.

PICTURE CREDITS

I am particularly grateful to a number of institutions for permission to reproduce certain illustrations: The Crown, the Trustees of the National Library of Scotland (NLS), the Trustees of the National Galleries of Scotland (NGS), the Trustees of the National Museums of Scotland (NMS), Her Majesty's Stationery Office, the Royal Commission on the Ancient and Historical Monuments of Scotland (RCAHMS), Historic Scotland (HS), the Royal Incorporation of Architects in Scotland (RIAS), the National Trust for Scotland (NTS), the Scottish National Portrait Gallery (SNPG) and the Society of the Antiquaries of Scotland (SAS). The source of each illustration is credited alongside it.

1
Changing Perceptions

Continue my ride along the curvature of this beautiful bay [Largo] and meet with the cheerful and frequent succession of towns, châteaux, and well-managed farms.

Thomas Pennant, 1772[1]

I sent several drawings of your château and the means of enlarging it.

Robert Mylne to Lord Breadalbane regarding Balloch (Taymouth), 23 November 1789[2]

I am most anxious to introduce the <u>creator</u> of the magnificent château of Murthly to them.

P.B. Ainslie to James Gillespie Graham, Burntisland, June 1830[3]

Until very recently, the case for Renaissance architecture in Scotland was simply put – there was almost none.[4] Instead, the buildings of the period *c.* 1500 to *c.* 1684 were defined by what followed, namely what appeared to be the inevitable triumph of classicism in the late seventeenth century. That was the time when Scottish country gentlemen, blinking like moles in the sunlight, were supposed to have emerged from their strongholds into a countryside enjoying its first real taste of peace. Architectural development in Scotland during the Renaissance centuries was dismissed as anachronistic and unworthy of serious attention.

This conclusion probably derived from the fact that once the Middle Ages were over, Scotland elected to follow a divergent path from the continent. In the fifteenth century, Scots nobles had expressed power and status in a manner not dissimilar to the rest of Europe through the construction of crenellated towers. Although the precise form and material was unique to Scotland, these country houses were essentially recognisable within a European context. But between *c.* 1500 and *c.* 1684, Scots nobles parted cultural company with their peers in France and Italy when they refused to adopt classicism as the Renaissance expression of power.[5]

Bedevilled by how to explain why that happened, scholars constructed a rationale based upon five cultural propositions. First, that all Scots country houses built during the Renaissance remained tower houses;[6] second, that these tower houses were designed *primarily* for defence;[7]

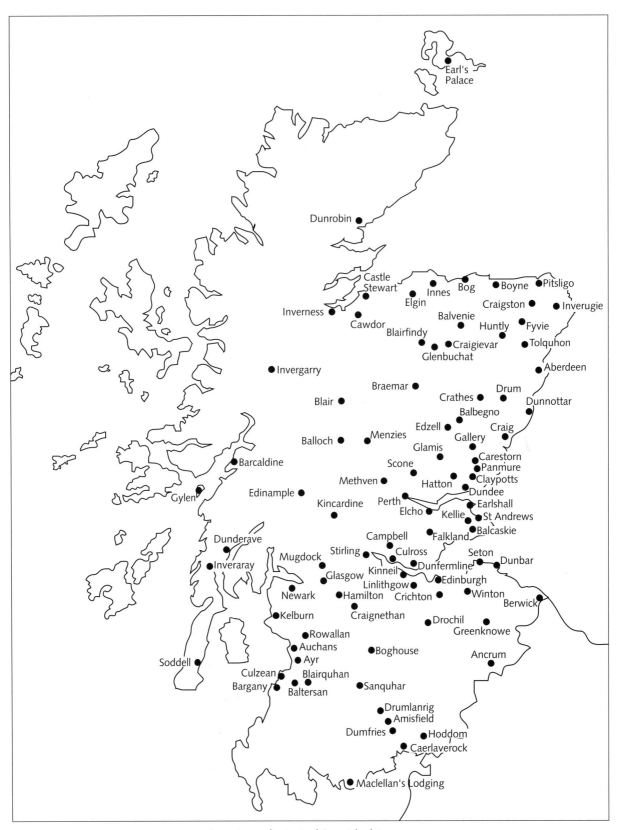

Locations of principal Scottish châteaux.

third, the reason they showed so little classical influence was their remoteness from mainstream Europe;[8] fourth, that Scots were ignorant of architectural movements on the continent;[9] and lastly, that it required the arrival of an architect with knowledge of the classical language to 'design unfortified houses for the first generation of Scottish lairds to realise that the tower house was an anachronism, and to persuade them to abandon corbel and crowstep in favour of cornice and pediment'.[10] So, from an architectural divergence from Europe, much broader conclusions were drawn about the country's Renaissance culture, and about the outlook of its nobility. Scots aristocrats were, it seemed, prevented from enjoying the leisurely architecture of the Loire châteaux or the villas of Palladio by poor communications, a political culture of feuding that required a continuation of castellated building, and an ignorant and introverted building industry.

Each of those retrospective preconceptions is dubious. Contemporaries almost never called these country seats 'tower houses' – and spoke of them as 'castles' almost as rarely (save where the term was desired by a grandee as an added signal of nobility). The word 'tower' was generally restricted to the vertically planned country house of the Middle Ages like, say, Kinnaird in Perthshire. The proposition of isolation from Europe also goes contrary to the facts. Indeed, Scots nobles who had not spent considerable time on the continent felt the need to justify themselves to their peers. Far from there being evidence of Scottish ignorance of contemporary cultural ideas, the truth was rather to the contrary. As for feuding, and the necessity for building for defence (discussed in Chapter 3), suffice it to say that there was probably less need for defensive structures in Scotland than in most European countries, and when considered against the criteria of Renaissance military fortifications, Scottish country houses were woefully inadequate. That is why the use of the word 'château' for the mock-military Scottish Renaissance country seat by the intelligent, well-travelled people quoted at the head of this chapter is so significant. They wished to indicate something nobler than a house, more martial than the classical country seat, possibly something more exotically European than British – certain that it was not a defensible castle. These houses were almost unclassifiable within the normal terminology used for British country house architecture during the eighteenth and nineteenth centuries.

Although also meaning 'castle', 'château' is used in this book according to the Renaissance French meaning of 'the dwelling of the owner of a great property, a large and beautiful pleasure house in the countryside',[11] and its use for this purpose was not unknown in Scotland.[12] The word 'château' avoided both the militaristic implications of the term 'castle', and the patronising domesticity of the phrase 'laird's house', which discounts the displays of chivalric nobility that were, perhaps, the most important aspect of the design. It is simply a different way of expressing the impression such houses made upon visitors at the time – the English traveller, Sir William Brereton, for example, when he passed to Linlithgow in 1636: 'by the way I observed gentlemen's (here called lairds) houses built *all castle-wise* [my italics].[13] 'All castle-wise' is taken to imply *in imitation* of castles rather than the substance of them.

1.1 *The palace of Seton, drawn by John Clerk of Eldin in the later eighteenth century: the 1550s* châtelet *and wing extend north (right); the baroque wing is behind with the old tower in the distance; and the 1630s wing extends west (left).* (Author's collection)

Many of the châteaux that so delighted eighteenth-century naturalist and topographical author Thomas Pennant's eye were greatly altered, reduced to ruins, or vanished within a century of his visit. The rain that washed away their mortar washed away their domesticity, leaving ruins with overemphatic battlements, gunloops and turrets. They were now confirmed as 'castles' and it was as such that the architects David MacGibbon and Thomas Ross categorised them in their exhaustive, five-volumed illustrated survey of the *Castellated and Domestic Architecture of Scotland* over a hundred years ago.[14] It was the first time that Scottish architecture had been examined so thoroughly within its own terms and the effort they expended was prodigious. While earning their living from an architectural practice in Edinburgh,[15] they travelled to every remote neuk of the country by boat, train and horse, to measure, draw, sketch and to watercolour most pre-1700 castles, country houses, sundials, monuments, views, churches and town houses. So exhaustive were they that it is rare to discover a castellated house of the right period that they overlooked. Sometimes, undoubtedly hard pressed for time, they recorded a wrong orientation, or a tower in the wrong place. Their hasty reconnaissance of the Palace of Pitsligo, Buchan, for example, concluded erroneously that it was but a tower surrounded by labourers' dwellings.[16] Perhaps their train was due.

To make sense of what they had seen, measured and carefully researched, MacGibbon and Ross divided Scottish castle construction into four periods[17] with sub-sections according to the shape of the building's plan. They were struck by the similarity in form between the tower house and the early medieval English and Norman keep and assumed that the keep was the standard unit of the Scottish country house. Subsequent developments could be analysed as variations of this basic module: the keep extended into L-plan, U-plan and T-plan and the courtyard. These terms are still used a hundred years later. Since MacGibbon and Ross believed the buildings they were studying were mostly castles in which defensiveness had been the primary consideration, it was scarcely surprising that they looked to somewhere like the Norman keep of Rochester Castle as an appropriate comparator for the Scottish tower house; and failed to include most contemporary houses that were not castellated.

In that, they were simply victims of their time. The predominant Victorian perception of pre-1707 Scotland was of a country isolated from the mainstream European Renaissance, turned in on itself and continuing anachronistically to build castles when mansions, country houses and villas were being constructed elsewhere. That perception remained current well towards the end of the twentieth century. The only distinctive architecture generally acknowledged to be of an international quality was the brief flowering of romance in early seventeenth-century north-eastern Scotland in houses like Craigievar. Even then, in its lack of display of the tenets of classicism this sole Scottish contribution to the Renaissance was portrayed as engagingly odd or – even worse – an expression of a 'Scottish vernacular'. Vernacular implies the lack of an *a priori* design input, and the absence of a skilled designer. The very suggestion that the country seat in Scotland might just be *vernacular*, rather than *designed* like the bulk of country houses elsewhere, demonstrates just how deep-seated had become the perception that the Renaissance had eluded Scotland's architecture. MacGibbon and Ross and their successors found castles because they were looking for them, and interpreted their plans and details accordingly. The principal aim of this book, however, is to examine the Renaissance country seat in its political and cultural context without such a distorting perspective.

1.2 The inner court of Pitfichie, Aberdeenshire, home of a friend of David Bel, mason (see p. 219), painted in typical ruin by James Giles in the early nineteenth century. (NTS)

Many Renaissance sources illuminating this period in Scotland's history and published a hundred years ago would have supported such an unflattering interpretation of the country's architecture – particularly the influential and much quoted volumes of extracts from contemporary documents, *The Domestic Annals of Scotland*. Compiled by that prolific author, architectural enthusiast, antiquarian and early conservationist Robert Chambers, these three volumes of misery heaped upon misery presented a view of sixteenth- and seventeenth-century Scotland that was almost barbaric. Chambers was frank about his prejudice. Mid-sixteenth-century Scotland was a very poor, rude country – a threnody to which he returned again and again, like the chorus of a lamentable Border ballad. 'It is forced upon us that the Scots were, at this very time, a fearfully rude and ignorant people . . . ruder than the England of that day.'[18] He perceived the country as 'bloody and turbulent' and puzzled over the thoughts of the 'polite' French poet Sallust on coming into contact with the royal circle around James VI in 1587, given the 'rude state of the people generally'.[19] Like MacGibbon and Ross, he had a preconception about the country, and there was no shortage of material that he could select to justify it.

And select he did. The *Annals* have a preponderance of material on witchcraft and their trials, upon bloodfeud or rebellion, on plagues, freaks and incredible natural phenomena.[20] This, he claimed, was part of a faithful recording of all 'symptoms of advancing civilisation' or 'anything that illustrates the progress of the arts as worthy of notice'.[21] That was far from true. He omitted almost all of Scottish poetry, painting, architecture, literature and, indeed, material on changing social and living patterns such as inventories. In the context of repeated attempts to explain the tragic fate of 'Marie Stuart' in terms of the defeat of European culture and civilisation by the forces of Scottish primitivism, it cannot be surprising that a notion of Scotland as a brutish country during the Renaissance should have taken root. Furthermore, this perception passed from historical hypothesis into architectural practice in a neat example of life imitating art when country houses undergoing alteration were rendered considerably more 'ancient' than they had been originally. In the late eighteenth century Sir John Dalrymple joked about how, when he had appointed 'Bob Adams' to refashion his ancient seat of Oxenfoord, Midlothian, Adam had 'really made it much older than it was' for the project was really about ratcheting up the romanticism.[22] The nineteenth-century cult of rubblemania, however, was entirely serious. Once majesty and money were deemed to consist in the display of powerful stonework, houses were stripped of the harling that had concealed their joints, strength and the minutiae of their construction. Many of the buildings in this book remained harled long enough to be photographed as such,[23] but when, for example, Robert Lorimer 'restored' Earlshall, Fife, in the 1890s, he removed its coat of harling (*see* Chapter 4) to make it less domestic in character and more *martial*. He likewise removed the plaster from the vaulted Great Hall at Lennoxlove,[24] presumably in conformity to the philosophy that bare stonework added nobility and honour to a 'baronial hall'. Indeed, a contemporary wrote of Blair, Ayrshire (not a Lorimer scheme), 'It is a pity that the vaulted ceiling has been plastered; the

1.3 Earlshall, Fife, drawn pre-1890s restoration for the National Art Survey by Robert Lorimer. The white portions represent harling: this Lorimer stripped off. (Author's collection)

original bare stonework would be so attractive.'[25] If Scottish architecture was to be classified as *primitivism as a work of art*, it was hardly surprising that a belief should grow that 'civilised' qualities only entered the Scottish country seat after James VI had moved down to London – presumably to acquire some polish.[26]

Apart from the classifications by MacGibbon and Ross, the only systematic inventory and analysis of details of the Scottish country house was undertaken from an archaeological perspective, with a preconception firmly focused upon its defensive capability.[27] There has been no attempt to consider it in terms of the four categories suggested by Italian Renaissance architect and theorist Sebastiano Serlio: farm or manor place, fortresses and villas derived from châteaux, small pavilions and 'villas which represent the revival of the Roman "villa suburbana"'.[28] All such categories were to be found in Scotland. Little illumination, moreover, is to be derived from the patterns of English or Irish architecture during the period, since the cultural and technological impulses were so very different. In any case, even early Renaissance architecture in England was considered backward until well after the Second World War, as James Lees-Milne admitted:

It is nowadays usual for knowing connoisseurs to depreciate architecture of the Tudor era as graceless, vulgar and barbaric . . . We . . . are offended by what we consider the Tudors' wilful disregard of the rules of taste and their reliance upon pictorial effect as the end-all of architectural endeavour. That is where we were unjust and wrong. . . .[29]

What was occurring in Scotland was likewise *individual* and likewise misinterpreted.

At least Lees-Milne had plenty of raw material – namely surviving Tudor country houses – with which to redress the balance. Unfortunately, apparently uniquely in Europe, Scotland forswore most of its legacy of Renaissance houses during the eighteenth century. The few that survive reasonably intact architecturally are generally those of families who, through indifference (their principal seat had moved elsewhere), piety or penury, took the unfashionable decision neither to transform nor demolish. The interiors of these properties, however, were likely to have been refurbished with eighteenth- or nineteenth-century material.

The paucity of authentic Scottish Renaissance interiors led to some fine myth-making. The interior of the Provand's Lordship, a 1471 prebendary manse beside Glasgow Cathedral, was 'restored' in 1927 to demonstrate how the house might have been when it was occupied in the late seventeenth century by William Bryson – and was furnished with choice items from Sir William Burrell's great collection.[30] Visitors were presented with a gloomy, stark interior, largely bare-walled and bare-ceilinged, with an occasional bed, tapestry and desultory kist (chest) and one or two items of uncomfortable-looking furniture, the chairs deprived of the elaborate cushions that inventories imply were usual. The harling that had covered the rubble exterior until at least 1901 was removed.[31] It was a tableau of Renaissance Scotland as a place to be tholed (endured). The Renaissance interior presented at Provand's Lordship was a world away from the patterned floors, silks, damasks, piles of furniture, monogrammed cushions, house-clocks, harpsichords, 'little organs', paintings, vividly coloured or plastered ceilings, painted exteriors, the gilt weathervanes and the finials revealed by inventories. One would scarcely imagine its occupier savouring the cosmopolitan fare of capers, olives and anchovies accompanying ptarmigan, followed by chocolate (the paper-brown type rather than the reddish variety) enjoyed by the Campbells of Cawdor.[32] This restoration did Scotland a cultural mischief.

Nigel Tranter's four-volumed *The Fortified House in Scotland*,[33] almost as extensive a survey as that of MacGibbon and Ross seventy years earlier, accepted that most of the buildings described were houses (albeit fortified) rather than castles. Once they were accepted as *houses*, a new distinction began to be drawn: pre-Reformation castles and post-Reformation houses[34] – by implication showing the Reformation as a civilising force. It was the third time people had managed to prove that the Scots always needed some such external agent to reform their ways. First, it was peacefulness settling in the countryside in the later seventeenth century after the Civil War. Then civilising ideas wafted back up north once the king was settled in London after 1603. Now it was the Reformation in 1560 that had managed to transform pre-Reformation castles into peaceable post-Reformation country seats.[35]

In fact, 1560 has no relevance to the developing architecture of the country seat in Scotland, as you shall see. It occurred midway through the Marian period – the time when Scotland was under the influence of Mary of Guise and her daughter Mary Queen of Scots (*see* Chapter 6). This important period in Scotland's cultural evolution has been overlooked through overemphasis upon religion and the absorbingly evil political fortunes of those two monarchs (if the queen regent may be called such).

The principal influence that the date 1560 might have had upon country house design was restricted to the gradual disappearance of the private chapel.

It is impossible to detach architecture from the culture of its time, and the more we know about Renaissance Scotland, the less sustainable the myth of an archaic defensive architecture becomes. The myth would ask us to believe that the sublime harmonies of a glorious Robert Carver ten-part mass[36] – let alone the madrigals, songs, instrumental pieces and clarsach works, the histories of George Buchanan, John Major or Hector Boece, and the volumes of sixteenth-century poetry – were created or enjoyed in buildings of an unnaturally antique character. A distinction of much of the music – notably of Carver's masses – is the extent to which it integrates contemporary European trends with very identifiably Scottish strains. A similar intent to 'lend Scottish public worship a distinctly Scottish accent' underlay the way the 1510 *Aberdeen Breviary* was compiled.[37] If it was accepted in music, poetry and illustration that the Scots had participated in the Renaissance – while adding something of their own individuality – why should those same Scots characteristics reveal backwardness when it came to architecture?

Not least because they were highly valued throughout Europe as good fighting stock, the Scots were enmeshed in European politics and culture. Perhaps Chambers found it difficult to accept the typically Renaissance paradox that somebody could be highly cultured and savage at the same time. Francis Stewart, Earl of Bothwell, for example, a much travelled European Scot with whom Queen Anna liked to converse in French and who had built a fashionable new lodging within Crichton Castle in the 1580s upon his return from Italy, was widely suspected of dabbling in witchcraft if not necromancy. Three times he attempted to separate his kinsman the king, by kidnap, from the malign influence of his adviser Maitland of Thirlestane.[38] Similarly, the Earl of Gowrie, who spent seven years in Padua imbibing the Renaissance, was obsessed with the Cabbala and necromancy, and attempted to murder the king in 1600. Such ambiguities were indigestible to early nineteenth-century rational Presbyterians.

There were European humanists at the Scottish Courts and humanist teaching in Scottish abbeys like Kinloss.[39] There was a distinct Scottish 'nation' at the universities of Orléans and elsewhere from the early fourteenth century, and some of the Scots scholars had stayed.[40] During the mid-sixteenth century, when the French came closest to achieving their goal of making Scotland a French colony, there were substantial numbers of French in Scotland – including an entire French garrison of 100 professional soldiers in Dunbar and the majority of Mary Queen of Scots' personal household (*see* Chapter 6). The Treasurers' Accounts reveal the presence of German mining engineers, Dutch gunners, Spanish clockmakers (and possibly inventors) and Italian trumpeters. One of Montaigne's household was a Scot,[41] and three of James VI's Octavians had been educated in Europe.[42] When King James VI visited Tycho Brahe on his island of Uranienborg on his wedding trip to Denmark in 1590, he must have had a shock to find, staring at him from a prominent position on Brahe's wall, the gaunt features of his old tutor, George Buchanan, with whom Brahe had been corresponding.

The clientele for the Scottish country seat was a largely educated and well-travelled one. It was as intrigued as any other noble society in Europe by the chivalric ideals expressed through jousts and games. It pounced on alterations to status, hierarchy and precedence. Changes to precedence were so sensitive that they could cause a deadly feud. James Melvill recorded in his diary the extent to which James VI had been trauchled by such squabblings during his marriage trip when the Scottish Court was staying in the Kronberg, at Helsingfors, during the wedding trip:

> The Company who were with his Majesty put him to great trouble to agree their continual janglings, strife, pride and partialities. The Earl of Marshall, by reason that he was an ancient Earl . . . thought to have the first place next unto His Majesty, so long as he was there. The Chancellour by reason of his Office, would needs have the preheminence [and so forth].[43]

Precedence remained sufficiently thorny a matter for the king to summon all earls and lords to Holyrood in February 1601 for the purpose of sorting it out. Five years later, the king's *Decreit anent ranking and placing*[44] was designed to put an end to feuds based upon status. None the less, precedence still remained sufficiently problematic that over ten years later the Earl of Montrose entered into a bond with the Earl of Eglinton confirming that a royal commission to Eglinton would not affect the precedence enjoyed by Montrose.[45] Buildings and their emblematic skylines formed one of the principal means by which such preoccupations were expressed.

However, the Scots élite had other preoccupations that lent a distinctive flavour to their architecture. The first was a veneration for ancestors and family. Of David Home of Wedderburn it was written that his love of the House of Home was 'not the least of his virtues',[46] and when remodelling his House of Glamis in the 1670s, the Earl of Strathmore admitted that he was 'inflam'd stronglie with a great desyre to continue the memorie of my familie'.[47] The second preoccupation was the built expression of the first: namely a predilection to reuse and adapt ancient motifs for application to the present. This desire was as evident in royal palaces and churches as it was in the country seat.[48] The turrets and heraldic skylines of the 'nationalist' period in north-east Scotland (*see* Chapter 11) were not at all old fashioned – for they were not turrets but studies in turret form. The principal decorative elements upon Scots Renaissance buildings were not those of the new language of classical architecture, but those of the earlier Scots architecture of defensiveness directed to peaceful purposes, as swords into ploughshares. The medieval gatehouses became *châtelets*, turrets became gazebos, and the fretted silhouette of crenellations would be achieved by the alternation of chimneys and dormer windows (*see* Chapter 9). So the magnificent early seventeenth-century skylines celebrated ancient lineage, the nobility of warfare, and also modernity, clamped together by elaborate cornices designed in echo of ancient machicolations. As was the case throughout Europe, modesty in architectural expression could imply vulnerability, and few Scots aristocrats wished to do that.

Those lonely ruins of free-standing fortified 'tower houses' or (worse) 'keeps', standing like decayed molars, high and dry after their isolation by eighteenth-century landscape planners, are little help in understanding the Scottish Renaissance. They were never keeps, tower houses probably only in the Borders, not fortified, and certainly not solitary. They would have been surrounded by an inner court, and an often extensive establishment of walled yards, gardens, orchards or courtyards. Soaring above all this paraphernalia of the burgeoning rural economy would be the flamboyant, mock-heraldic superstructure, whose turrets provided delightful many windowed, brilliantly lit small chambers with excellent views (*see* Chapter 4).

The machicolations were decorative and unusable, and the cannon-mouths were only water-spouts because Scotland was a country largely at peace by comparison with contemporary Europe. Beyond the frontier lands with England, it had been largely at peace for centuries. Unused to the passage of armies, the country had adopted subtler and more effective methods of deterring the rare predator, feudster or casual brigand than using artillery, moats, drawbridges and beetling defences,

1.4 The châtelet *(or mock-gatehouse) at Rowallan, drawn by MacGibbon and Ross in the 1880s.* (Author's collection)

namely by surrounding houses with a *cordon sanitaire* of walled gardens and extensive yards (*see* Chapter 3). So the sense of outrage caused by the savage destruction of houses and property during the civil war in 1640 may partly be explained by the fact that the country was unaccustomed to such uncivilised behaviour (*see* Chapter 12).

Country house building was probably influenced by considerations of family loyalty and kinship. The drawings on the maps of Timothy Pont, *c.* 1586–1606, imply that the scale and ornamentation of houses reflected the local or regional hierarchy (*see* Chapter 2). The largest houses he drew in Strathearn were Kincardine (Earls of Montrose), Drummond (Lord Drummond) and Tullibardine (Earl of Atholl), and this is illustrative of the extent to which a district might be dominated by the principal local

1.5 Emblematics: these remarkable designs come from the ceiling painted in the House of Prestongrange, East Lothian, for Mark Kerr in 1581. The wilder motifs have been traced by M.R. Apted and W.N. Robertson to the Les Songes drolatiques de Pantagruel *(Pantagruel's Droll Dreams) published in Paris by Richard Breton in 1565. (SAS)*

families. The extravagant constructions of early seventeenth-century north-east Scotland, for example,[49] may be attributable to the leadership of the Earls and Marquesses of Huntly, and of the Earls Marischal. Whereas in Ayrshire 'Kyle was full of gentlemen free to act on their own initiative . . . in Cunninghame such men appear in the followings of nobles'.[50] There was great emphasis not just upon family,[51] but upon how many of the family name a lord could call to his support; and relationships were often underpinned by bonds of manrent – a form of mutually beneficial bond of allegiance.[52] Status would be demonstrated by how many gentlemen might be kept by a lord to ride with him (*see* Chapter 4). Buildings sharing the same features are as likely to reflect kinship patterns as the work of putative architects.[53]

Kinship – sixteenth-century networking – was celebrated by the carved and once gilt marriage stones that adorn so many houses. They recorded an alliance to the wife's father, and probably wealth and new property to the husband (it was often her dowry that funded the new construction). The marriage stone (which always records the wife's maiden initials, identifying for onlookers and posterity the family to which the husband was now allied) celebrates both marital bliss and social advancement – 'being planted in the stock of honour' – by the male in the partnership.[54] A laird marrying an earl's daughter and rebuilding upon the proceeds – as did James Menzies of Weem in 1571 after his marriage to Barbara Stewart, daughter of the Earl of Atholl – would install the record proud, painted and triumphant, facing the entrance.

Such symbols were part of what was an extensive visual culture. When Mary of Guise retook Edinburgh in 1558 after its brief occupation by the Lords of the Congregation, she found that they had had the original mural decoration in St Giles' church painted out, and replaced it with 'the Lord's Prayer, the Belief and the Commandments . . . patent on the kirk-walls'.[55] It is difficult to imagine, in its largely deplastered current gloom, how St Giles was once vividly painted with improving religious texts. Mary of Guise had this propaganda swiftly blotted out.[56] Visual mementos, paintings, banners and posters were customarily deployed for political purposes, particularly by those seeking redress. In 1593, for example, 'there came certain poor women out of the south country, with fifteen bloody shirts, to compleen to the king that their husbands, sons, and servants were cruelly murdered by the Laird of Johnston' – a ritual that was neither infrequent nor effective. Two years later the Earl of Mar had displayed in procession around the district a picture of the corpse of one Forester, a member of his entourage accidentally murdered in a large-scale lover's battle, 'on a fair canvas, painted with the number of shots and wounds, to appear the more horrible to the behalders'. The most famous example was the Dowager Countess of Moray's response to the murder of her son the 'Bonnie Earl' in February 1592: 'The Earl's mother caused draw her son's picture, as he was demained, and presented it to the king in a fine laine cloth, with lamentations, and earnest suit for justice.'[57] By far the most extensive and astonishing residue of this visual culture is the painted decoration of the principal rooms, galleries and bedrooms of country seats. It suggests that Scottish culture was 'deeply infused with an emblematic mentality, and its material culture . . . was deeply impregnated with applied emblematics'.[58] There are only slight remnants of what was probably an equally extensive culture of timber screens, doors, wainscotting and cornices carved with visual messages.

That visual culture embraced the buildings in totality. So, given the relative lack of ornamentation on the lower floors of a country house and the extravagance on the upper floors, the composition of the building's silhouette was probably symbolic in intent. There are no pattern books to help decode the array of gables, turrets, chimneys and dormer windows, so in most cases, their interpretation remains conjectural. However, the symbolic significance of the crown steeples of the great parish churches of Scotland – St Michael's, Linlithgow, St Mary's, Dundee[59] and St Mary's, Haddington; of King's College, Aberdeen; and those of the Tolbooths of Glasgow and Linlithgow[60] – has been unlocked. These were visual representations of the imperial crown, signifying that the King of Scotland was an emperor – that is, a ruler free to rule in his own domain without interference. The imperial crown 'was the most potent available symbol not only of regional solidarity but also of the complete jurisdictional self-sufficiency – effectively the independent national sovereignty – aspired to by the new monarchies of Renaissance Europe'.[61] On the north-east corner of the Palace of Stirling, there is a lion above the statue of King James V, holding an imperial crown on a cushion above the king's head. The use of the crown by the Stewarts – by James IV on his coinage, and by his son on his palaces – was directed particularly at the ancient English claims of sovereignty over Scotland.

Once James VI left for London in 1603, visual messages of independence from England enjoyed a paradoxical resurgence. They varied from the widespread use of the royal arms on the exterior, to vast plaster armorials above the principal fireplace. Frequently attached to the inscription in stone or plaster was the vainglorious motto *Nobis haec invicta miserunt CVI proavi* – which might be translated as 'a line of 106 kings have left us this unconquered' (*see* Chapter 11). To judge from paintings still on display during the eighteenth century, it was also fashionable for the aristocracy to commission portraits of monarchs and fellow members of the nobility when ordering paintings of themselves and their family for their state rooms. In 1628, the Earl of Winton commissioned three such portraits from Adam the painter in addition to his own for the walls of Winton.[62] Much more extravagant were the Campbells of Glenorchy. In 1633 Sir Colin Campbell commissioned an unnamed German artist (perhaps Adam of Koln) to paint a picture of all his predecessor lairds. He then commissioned George Jamieson not only for an extravagant family tree, but also for 16 separate portraits at 20 merks each, each rising to £100 if a gilt frame were to be included.[63] By 1640, the Glenorchys had 24 paintings of the kings and queens of Scotland, and 34 other portraits of the lairds and ladies of Glenorchy and of fellow aristocrats. Indeed, the sheer quantity of paintings in Scottish

1.6 Statue of James V on the corner of the Palace of Stirling. Above his head, a lion holds a cushion with the monogram IV (for JV). On the cushion sits an imperial crown. (HS)

1.7 The Royal Lodging or King's Tower at the north end of the west (entrance) façade of Holyrood Palace, drawn in 1647 by James Gordon of Rothiemay. Note the imperial closed crowns capping each 'round'. (Author's collection)

Renaissance country houses has probably been grossly underestimated. There were 59 paintings in the Glamis seat of Castle Lyon in 1684, and a further 94 in Glamis itself – excluding framed maps and 73 tailledouce pictures. Finavon had 59, and Fetteresso well over 100. Scaled up from these examples to cover the entire country, the number of paintings in Scotland in the late seventeenth century could have been somewhere between 12,000 and 25,000.[64]

Focus upon royal construction has unbalanced perceptions of the evolution of the Scottish country house, and this is indicated by MacGibbon and Ross's conclusions about the penetration of Renaissance architectural ideals into the country:

> There were indications in the architecture of Stirling and Falkland Palaces of the approach of the Renaissance style. But these . . . were exceptional cases, and during the following half-century, the encroachments of that style on the native art of the country were not very considerable.[65]

The measure they used to determine the spread of Renaissance ideas in architecture was the extent that such classically inspired façade detailing had been emulated. They had little sense of any coherent architectural evolution of the country house between 1540 and 1590 – a time when construction was at its peak. But there are other measures for evaluating how far the Renaissance influenced a country: 'More impressive than any superficial imitation of antique or foreign precedent, however, was the dynamic display of virtuosity, both technical and rhetorical, within the framework of what one might call tradition.'[66] So this book also seeks to explore whether, by using those other yardsticks, different conclusions might be reached.

The tendency to treat the sixteenth and seventeenth centuries as though the architecture was relatively homogeneous – save that split at the Reformation – is a principal source of the myth. Such an approach simply cannot be sustained and a more sensitive categorisation is needed. So this book also examines whether architectural evolution matched the reigns of the monarchs. Even though broad, the classifications of English architecture into Tudor, Elizabethan and Jacobean have proved useful. Comparable period divisions might likewise prove useful for Scotland.

Unfortunately, categorising periods of architecture works best where they can be associated with recognisable forms. Pure form was in short supply in Renaissance Scotland. Principally as the result of the country's mass-stone technology and shortage of long-span timber, we developed into, and remained, *a nation of adaptors*. A landowner seeking to improve his house in fashionable mode in the mid-sixteenth century would no doubt find that he had inherited a sturdy building with walls between 6 and 10 feet thick. It making no sense to waste all this masonry, his impulse would be to retain the old building and extend from it, or to build something new within the inner court. The occasional, courageous decision to refashion the entire building complex into a single composite design occurred rarely before the early seventeenth century, and was largely restricted to the north-east. So most Scottish Renaissance country houses lack the easily comprehensible shapes of Azay le Rideau or of Chambord, or the instant recognisability of Compton Wynyates, Montacute, Longleat or Blickling Hall. Instead, most appear as an agglomeration of structures of different ages and different heights, dominated by the tower house from which all else was derived.

Whereas the medieval house had indeed been 'pure form' in the shape of a rectangle or L-plan tower, smaller chambers and stairs compressed within the thickness of the walls, the Renaissance country house burst out of such constraints. Scottish architects threw off the straitjacket of pure form just when the architects of other countries were rediscovering the pleasures of its constraints. The resulting highly expressionist architecture that remained the Scottish fashion until the late seventeenth century stood in counterpoint to the growing formalities of plan and tight expression of the Italian-influenced Renaissance. *That* was another Scottish particularity. But from the very earliest days of the Union, as the very different cultures of Scotland and England began the process of assimilation, this national characteristic was misinterpreted. Take the Revd Thomas Morer, a minister in London who was, for a while, an army chaplain, in which capacity he visited Scotland in 1689:

> The houses of their quality are high and strong, and appear more like castles than houses, made of thick stone walls, with iron bars before their windows, suited to the necessity of those times they were built in, *living in a state of war and constant animosities between their families*. [my italics]. Yet they now begin to have better buildings, and to be very modish in both the fabrick and furniture of their dwellings.[67]

1.8 The datestone recording the building of Craigston: one of the few credible ones. (RCAHMS)

Visitors from England found it impossible to accept that unconscionably tall buildings with turrets and gunloops were the equivalent of their own large-windowed, peaceable, low-slung, moated, Tudor and Elizabethan manor houses. Parapets, crenellations and gunloops would only fit into a British architecture if they were taken to be real rather than metaphorical.

Two English perspectives of Scotland began to emerge. The one, like Sir Anthony Weldon's, determined to overpraise James VI by comparing his great achievements in England to his ghastly origins, and the other a more neutral role of a curious visitor in a foreign country. Weldon's squiffy account of his visit in 1617 described a barbarous country devoid of trees, whose beasts were small ('their women only excepted, of which sort there are none greater in the whole world'), habits revolting and food inedible. He concluded: 'I do wonder that so brave a prince as King James should be borne in so stinking a town as Edinburgh in lousy Scotland.'[68] To set against that there is John Taylor, His Majesty's 'Water Poet' from London,[69] who recorded his splendid visit the following year, and his narrative *Pennyless Pilgrimage* provides a corrective. Even though he too found the houses 'like castles for building',[70] Taylor enjoyed continuous hospitality, praised almost everything, and ended with a little doggerel:

> Yet (arm'd with truth) I publish with my pen
> That there th'Almighty doth his blessings heape,
> In such abundant food for beasts and men
> I never saw more plenty or more cheape.

We have lost so much of our built history (*see* Chapter 2) that any attempt at categorising the Renaissance houses of Scotland has to be tentative. The lack of building records, astonishing by comparison with England or France, can make it difficult to be definite about either dates or designers. Because datestones were so easily moved, their credibility sometimes extends only to recording the date on which they were carved.[71] However, charters sometimes reveal when a building might have been constructed. For example, between receipt of charters in 1517 and May 1541, Michael Scott had made 'an honest mansion with a tower and other policies in the Forest of Ettrick, at the place, steading and lands of Aikwood [Oakwood]'.[72]

Over 1,000 country seats, their extensions or their ruins are attributed to the period 1500–*c.* 1680, and, as you shall see, this represents probably only a fraction of those that once existed. A study of their attributed dates indicates how the quantity of building work varied from period to period,

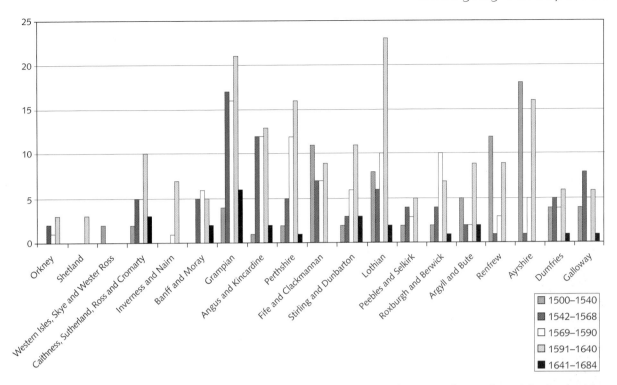

Graph 1 New-build château construction, 1500–1684. The dates are taken from M. Salter's volumes The Castles of Scotland *(Malvern, 1993–6). Only those given sufficiently precise dates are included in this graph and the graphs in the following pages. An equally large number are attributed more approximately. Since Salter's books focus necessarily upon 'castles' (as do so many), rather than upon country houses as a whole, they convey an increasingly unbalanced perception of Scottish country house construction. Extensions have been identified from the same source by datestones or dated dormer windows later than the presumed principal construction period.*

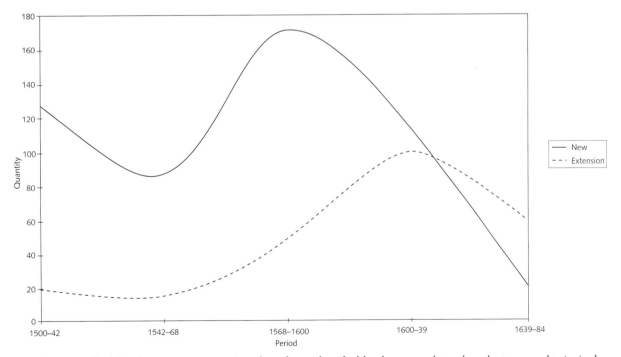

Graph 2 New build and extensions: extensions have been identified by datestones later than the presumed principal construction period.

and from region to region (*see* Graph 1).[73] Since Scottish builders defy classification almost wilfully, both dates and titles for each period are loose, and for guidance only. The period of Mary's influence, for example, lasted beyond her political deposition, and that of her son James a good decade after his death.

In this book, the **Early Renaissance** period is defined as lasting from *c.* 1500 to 1542, during which time a large number of country seats appear to have been constructed. It embraces the latter part of the resplendent reign of James IV until his death at Flodden in 1513, and the entire reign of his son James V. The courts of both were cultured and humanist, explicitly encouraging the arts of architecture, poetry and music. In an era of noble competitiveness and changing lifestyles, magnates were as likely to have been rebuilding as the court, but – with the exception of Sir James Hamilton of Finnart and his entourage – records are scanty. The tower, albeit substantially modified, remained the principal feature of the house.

The **Marian period**, *c.* 1542–*c.* 1568, was one of French-influenced transformation. James V's marriage to Queen Madeleine and, after her death in 1537, to Mary of Guise in 1538 began a period of some thirty years of French-educated female influence or rule. It can best be called the *Marian* period, after Mary of Guise and her daughter Mary Queen of Scots. Writing retrospectively (about 1572), Bishop Lesley was concerned at the costs of conspicuous consumption:

> Here is to be remembered that thair was mony new ingynis and devysis, alsweill of bigging of paleicis, abilyementis, as of banqueting and of menis behaviour first begun and used in Scotland at this time, after the fassione quhilk thay had sene in France. Albeit it semit to be varray comlie and beautifull, yit it wes moir superfluows and volupteous nor the substaunce of the realme of Scotland mycht beir furth or susteine.[74]

> [Here it is to be remembered that there were many new inventions and devices, as well as building of palaces, attire, equipment and fittings, as of banqueting and of men's behaviour, first begun and used in Scotland at this time after the fashion which they had seen in France. Although it seemed to be very comely and beautiful, yet it was more superfluous and voluptuous than the realm of Scotland might bear or sustain.]

Lesley dated the French influence to the king's wedding, *c.* 1536, but architectural change only became evident in the early 1550s. The most extensive construction of the period was in Aberdeenshire. After Mary's deposition in 1567, the country was divided between the queen's (largely Catholic) supporters and the baby king's (largely Protestant) supporters. Yet the French influence lingered. Until the end of the century and beyond, nobles continued to be classified according to whether they were pro-French or pro-English.[75] Even as late as 1612, the young Duke Charles (later Charles I) could write to his father that the most civilised foreign nations were those that spoke French.[76]

During the **Early Jacobean** period of James VI's minority – *c.* 1568–
c. 1590 – the building boom reached its peak, not surprisingly perhaps in
view of the damage caused by the raids and campaigns of the civil wars
between 1568 and 1573. Initially, during the regencies, Scottish
architecture shed much of its francophile romanticism, and a different,
more sober form of confidence emerged. But once James VI took control
in 1585, and the country unified behind him, architecture began to assume
a changed flamboyance, perhaps accounted for by influence from
Denmark. The king had been accompanied on his wedding trip in 1590 to
marry Princes Anna by William Schaw,[77] the royal architect and Master of
Ceremonies, who was to become Chamberlain to and a close confidant
of the queen. Whereas it is only sensible to classify the architecture of
c. 1590–*c.* 1639 as **Later Jacobean** (even though it extended fourteen years
into the reign of Charles I), there were two very distinct types. The **Later
Jacobean villa** was the preferred house of a group of clever men associated
with the court in Edinburgh and largely, although not entirely, restricted to
a fairly small region whose focus was Edinburgh. **Jacobean nationalism**
emerged in the shires, particularly in the north-east. Since most of the
latter, so stridently Scots in character, was built *after* the king had departed
for England in 1603, it implies that outside Court circles, Scotland, far
from adapting to the implications of an absentee court, and absorbing the
new fashions from England,[78] went in the opposite direction.

Country house architecture in the aftermath of the wars of 1640–50
evolved from the architectures of the wealthy pre-war years, but the
former heraldic display mutated into new forms and the preoccupation
with height and skyline was addressed in a new manner (*see* Chapter 12).
But what might be termed 'the Scottish difference' survived until it was
rendered picturesque by Robert Adam a hundred years later in places like
Oxenfoord.

This book first explains how some of the evidence was uncovered and
assessed, examines the extent to which the Renaissance country seat was, or
needed, to be defensible, and then introduces common features of the
country house, its structure, components, function and its setting.

These houses were erected in a country that regarded itself as a cultured
European nation participating in contemporary ideas, and an analysis of
their architecture will differ radically according to whether they are
evaluated within a European or a British framework. When interpreted
within a British context, the Palace of Boyne, Banffshire, for example,
appeared to exemplify 'the lengths to which native conservatism could go. . . .
With its high walls of enceinte, massive circular angle towers, and strong
gatehouse, Boyne might well be taken at first glance for a great thirteenth
century castle of enclosure'[79] like, say, medieval Harlech (Gwynedd) or
Bodiam (Sussex). Boyne's plan did indeed echo a medieval one, but rather
than *being* medieval, it demonstrated how both French and Scots culture
continued to embed the past into the present. Considered within the
European architectural culture, Boyne's adventurous plan closely resembled
that of the sophisticated Château du Bury, by Orléans, in which the designer
Florimond Robertet may have been assisted by Leonardo da Vinci.[80] Boyne's
châtelet is not a strong gatehouse (*see* Chapter 9) and its 'massive circular
angle towers' are towers of lavish and largely indefensible chambers.

1.9 The plan of Boyne, Banffshire, taken from MacGibbon and Ross. (Author's collection)

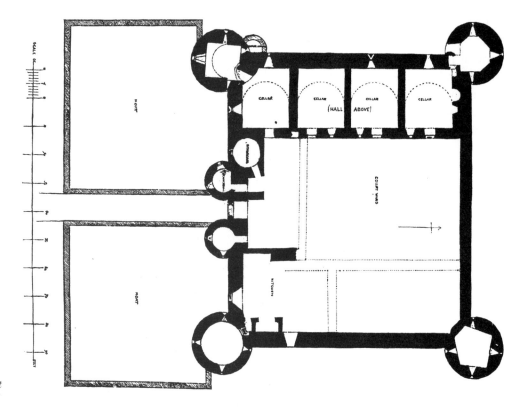

1.10 Boyne drawn from the south-east by William Daniell in 1821. (RCAHMS)

Can Scotland be thought to have had its own architects during this period of staunch resistance against classicism? Hitherto, Scottish Renaissance houses have been dismissed as the product of enthusiastic but untutored masons, rather than the product of skilled design. Their very *irrationality* irritated twentieth-century rationalists, since it went against everything they had been taught that a good architect should do.

> The mason is designing from the wall-head down, not planning. He is thinking of turrets descending from the wall-head, not rising from the ground. . . . In this wayward profusion and irrational importance of secondary features, romantic notions underlying the later tower-houses are most dramatically effected. . . . It is not great art; it achieves no sublimity; it forms no laws and conforms to none. Whimsical and capricious, its creators, mason-architects, depended upon personal inclination, were uncertain on occasion, and were prone to imitate. . . . The architecture of the romantic tower-house . . . is instinctive and arbitrary, the work of skilled artisans.[81]

1.11 *Carvings on the heraldic frontispiece to Mar's Wark, the Regent Earl of Mar's town house in Stirling.* (Author)

That was far from the perception of the times when the country houses were built. Contemporaries considered that they had an architectural culture, and that they had architects. Whether good or bad, contemporaries called their designers 'architectors' or 'architects', and expected an appropriate level of service. Quite what those new skills were (new, because the concept of architect as it now stands first emerges in the late fifteenth century and continued to be modified over the following two centuries) can be inferred from Alexander Montgomery's epitaph to Sir Robert Drummond of Carnock who was Royal Master of Works from 1579 to 1583:

> All buildings brave bid DRUMMOND nou adeu;
> Quhais lyf furthsheu he lude thame by the lave.
> Quhair sall we craiv sik policie to haiv?
> Quha with him straiv to polish, build or plante?
> These giftis, I grant, God lent him by the laiv.[82]

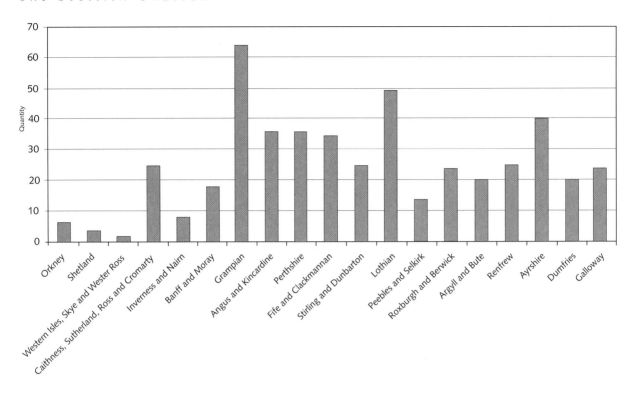

Graph 3 Surviving châteaux by region. The great variation in châteaux construction may well reflect regional variations in wealth, culture or political stability.

[All buildings brave bid Drummond now adieu,
Whose life demonstrated he loved so many of them.
Where now shall we seek building and estate impreovement?
Who with him strove to adorn, build or plant?
These gifts, I grant, God lent him in quantity.]

An architect would be expected to have 'policie' – the ability to conceive of a plan or design, and be knowledgeable about building and landscaping. Above all, he could polish – that is, in Alberti's terms, 'to realise by construction whatever can be most beautifully fitted out for the noble needs of man . . .'.[83] He was no mere administrator.[84]

By reconsidering the buildings and their aesthetic from the position of architectural composition within a structured time frame, this book also intends to investigate whether the perspective of 'untutored masons' is useful any longer. Was Charles Rennie Mackintosh correct in his intuition that each feature of the Scottish château was an act of deliberate design?[85]

2

Sources for Rediscovery

Nothing is scarce here but money
Étienne Perlin, *c.* 1551

Over three-quarters of Scottish châteaux – the prime source for a study of
this kind – have vanished, and most of the remainder are transmogrified
or ruined. Many suffered after their owners' forfeiture in 1715 and 1746 –
grievous among the losses being the great houses of the Earls of Winton
and the Earls Marischal. Most were abandoned during the eighteenth
century, however, once they had begun to seem foreign, inconvenient and
unfashionable to the North British descendants of those who had built
them: a source of embarrassment rather than of pride. Indeed, living in
Scotland itself became increasingly unfashionable as 'the rage of London
depriv[ed] this country of its wealthiest inhabitants'.[1] Once superseded by
a new house, châteaux were consigned to farmers, agricultural labourers,
livestock or ruin. Decay was well set in by the early eighteenth century to
judge by the reports compiled between *c.* 1620 and 1730 which are
contained within Macfarlane's *Geographical Collections*. Of nine country
seats listed in the parish of Kippen, for example, Glentirran, Arnprior,
Garden and Buchlyvie were already ruinous. The proportion was similar
in the parish of Kilmaronock.[2] Of the country seats in the parish of
Leuchars a century later, Leuchars itself was destroyed, Earlshall empty
and unfurnished, Ardit was fast going to ruin, and Pitcullo was
uninhabited and rapidly going to rack.[3] Of the eight named, five have
disappeared, Pitcullo retrieved from ruin in only the last few decades.

Not a single premier seat of the first rank nobility survives even
approximately in its Renaissance condition. Finavon (Earls of Crawford),
Kincardine (Earls of Montrose), Dunkeld (Earls of Atholl), Hamilton
Palace (Earls of Arran), Inchinnan (Earls of Lennox), the Renaissance
portion of Alloa (Earls of Mar) and Douglas Castle (Earls of Angus) are
destroyed, whereas Loudon (Earls of Loudon) and Huntly (Marquess of
Huntly) lie in ruins, and Dalkeith (Earls of Morton), Bog o' Gight
(Marquess of Huntly), Darnaway (Earls of Moray), Inveraray (Earls of
Argyll), Balloch (Earls of Breadalbane) and Terregles (Lords Herries) have
been altered beyond recognition.

Virtually all of the architectural drawings, and most records of building
and construction, that would have helped to unravel the architectural
history of the Renaissance Scotland country house are missing.

Architectural drawings could have tied the form of a building to both date and architect, and – if rooms or dimensions had been indicated – given a great deal of other information. That such drawings *were* in use is revealed in building contracts. The only way client and builder were going to check that Gallery House, Angus, had been built according to contract was that each was to have a copy of the architect's 'draught' against which to inspect the property on completion.[4] Without such drawings, much more will be required of other sources like contemporary records, travellers' accounts, illustrations, engravings and paintings; and the houses themselves demand a revisit to investigate whether they have been misinterpreted.

Travellers do not appear to have considered Scotland too poor to build Renaissance country seats. While it was not as wealthy as nations on the continent, the land being less fertile and the weather less clement, Scotland was none the less relatively prosperous, and continually improving. Etienne Perlin reported to France in 1552 that although short on specie, the country was 'plentiful in provisions, which are as cheap as anywhere in the world'.[5] He was particularly impressed by its state of daily improvement. An English traveller, Fynes Moryson, implied much the same forty years later when commending how the 'stately palace' of Seton was 'beautified with fair orchards and gardens and for that clime pleasant'.[6] Moryson was intrigued at the paradox that although Scotland was largely lacking woods and forests, it was thickly populated with noblemen's and gentlemen's dwellings 'commonly compassed with little groves'. That contrast was expressed much more forcibly in 1641 by the unknown doggerelist, P.J., who had accompanied Montague Bertie, Lord Willoughby, one of Charles I's few attendants on his visit to Scotland in

1641. He found the upland country between Falkirk and Glasgow pretty frightful – a very ill way, with naked rocks, hills and stones – whereas his impression of the policies at Hamilton was entirely different:

> Through fertill Clydsdale we take our way
> The best part of that kingdome most we say
> And Hambleton [Hamilton] we aime at tis our marke,
> Wee'd faine in Scotland see a wood and a parke
> And there we mett with both, the parke well stor'd
> With all such game the clymate could afford . . .[7]

There were so many such descriptions that it would be absurd to discount them.

If contemporary visitors found Scottish architecture backward in a Renaissance context, they never recorded it (the first time such an option appears is in the writings of Englishmen in the later seventeenth century). It has, rather, been our habit to distrust them when they said or wrote the opposite. Lindsay of Pitscottie's description of Mary of Guise's reaction upon her arrival in Scotland, for example, has been treated as partisan – a man hearing what he wanted to hear. What he wrote was this:

> When the queen came to her palace, and met with the king, she confessed, she never saw in France, nor in no other country, so many good faces in so little room, as she saw that day in Scotland: For she said, it was shewn to her in France, that Scotland was but a barbarous country destitute and void of all good commodities that used to be in other countries; but now she confessed that she saw the contrary.

Mary then said of Linlithgow that 'she had never seen a more princely palace',[8] and other visitors reinforced such opinions. Sir Christopher Lowther, who undertook a journey round lowland Scotland in 1629, left us this record of Old Gala House, Galashiels, seat of Sir James Pringle:

> He hath a very pretty park, with many natural walks in it, artificial ponds and arbours now a-making, he hath neat gardens and orchards, and all his tenants through his care, he hath abundance of cherry trees, bearing a black cherry, some of which I see to be about 30 yards high and a fathom thick, great store of sycamores, trees he calleth silk trees, and fir trees.[9]

On the face of it, income from improving estates paid for the prodigious quantity of country house construction during the Renaissance. Visitors were probably unaware that many nobles had another source of income: bribes – bribes from the English, the French and from the Spanish. So long as Scotland remained a theatre of potential war between England and France, gifts were lavished by both sides on their partisans. Indeed, at the end of the century, while King James VI himself was a pensioner of Queen Elizabeth,[10] the Earl of Huntly was enjoying Spanish gold theoretically intended to pay for a counter-reformation.[11]

Visitors sometimes commented on food, dress or social customs, but almost never on the furnishings. For them, inventories are essential. The lavishness and comfort they record in the houses of people well below the grandee level can be surprising. 'Moveable geir' was usually cosmopolitan: Dutch linens, English pewter, carved woodwork partitions from the Baltic, finely chased guns from Dundee, wines from Bordeaux, screens, silverwork from Paris, quantities of tapestry from the Low Countries, silk and velvet cushions, enormously elaborate beds and gorgeous curtains. Scottish society was particularly fond of clothing and jewellery. To judge by the Treasurer's Accounts during James V's reign, you might almost think that the Crown spent most of its money on clothing for courtiers and staff; and the quantities of family jewels in country seats sometimes required inventories of their own.

Fortunately, Scotland's Renaissance buildings were captured in three extensive surveys: the illustrated manuscript maps prepared by Timothy Pont between *c*. 1586 and 1606;[12] the reports on different parts of Scotland collected by Sir Robert Sibbald from the late seventeenth century which form the core of Macfarlane's *Geographical Collections*;[13] and the engravings in *Theatrum Scotiae*, prepared by Captain John Slezer between 1678 and 1690. The contents of the *Collections* vary from early seventeenth-century notes by Timothy Pont, to later seventeenth-century descriptions – like that of Carrick by Mr Abercrummie (Minister at Minibole), or that of Angus by John Ochterlony of Guynd, and early eighteenth-century returns by local ministers. The country seat was undergoing change. Ochterlony's description of the condition, setting and planting of the houses probably records Renaissance seats in the last decades of their original use:

2.2 Palace of Linlithgow from the west, drawn c. 1680 by Captain John Slezer when most of the palace was still occupied, although one tower was roofless. Note the crown steeple on St Michael's Church. (Author's collection)

Without competition, [Kinnaird is] the fynest place, (taking altogether) in the shyre, a great house, excellent gardines, parks with felow-deer, orcheards, hay meadows wherein are extraordinaire quantities of hay. Very much planting, ane excellent breed of horse, catle and sheep, extraordinaire good land. Farnell is lykewayes ane extraordinaire sweet place, delicat yeards, and very much planting.[14]

The 'hudge great lofty Tower in the center of a quadrangular court' that Abercrummie noted at Bargany had been replaced by a 'new house lately built after the modern fashion' standing upon higher ground.[15] Macfarlane's *Collections* contain endless lists of country houses that are not now even a memory – although since the descriptions imply a great continuity of site, many might still lie at the core of later-seeming farmhouses. In many Scottish estates, a site, or residual piece of masonry some 50 feet away from the current house, is held to represent the predecessor to a new-built eighteenth- or nineteenth-century mansion. However, the presence of the occasional vault, a breach of symmetry, or walls of a pre-eighteenth-century solidity inside the current house usually imply that something of the old house probably remains in ghostly form within its successor.

The term 'castle' was very rarely applied to country seats. Sixteenth- and seventeenth-century terminology (although not always consistent) appears to have distinguished between different types and scales of country house. Smaller houses, whose surrounding buildings were entirely subordinate to them, were invariably referred to as houses and usually known simply by their name (e.g. Carnousie). That was also how their owners were addressed. 'Peels' were the houses of even more minor gentry – those worth less than £100 (*see* p. 45). Grander seats, perhaps of a lord or an earl, were referred to as 'the House of' (e.g. Strathbogie). 'Place' or 'palace' implied a formally designed courtyard, like the Palace of Fyvie (*see* Chapter 9). 'Castle' was used ambiguously. *As a description* it was rare, reserved for buildings of serious defensive capability. 'Castle' *as a signal of nobility* was much sought after. Houses often changed names following change of ownership, as when the Bog of Plewlands became Gordonstoun. But the enhanced dignity of 'Castle' for a nobleman's principal seat was something that appeared to require the imprimatur of the Crown. That is why we know when the House of Strathbogie became Castle Huntly at the desire of its earl, the House of Gloume became Castle Campbell for the Earl of Argyll, the great House of Bog o' Gight became Castle Gordon once Huntly had moved to it from Strathbogie, Muchalls became Castle Fraser, and Weem became Castle Menzies. The Perthshire Huntly was renamed Castle Lyon after the family name by the Earl of Kinghorn, and as late as 1696 the Grants obtained consent for Ballachastle or Freuchie to become Castle Grant.[16] These owners regarded the change of title as *adding* the status of their seat. They would have been outraged at the implications of backwardness which later generations inferred from the term castle.

Many plainly named buildings on the maps of Timothy Pont (*see* pp. 28–30) had become 'castles' by the time of General Roy's maps in the 1740s and when the first Ordnance Survey maps of Scotland were published in the

1850s, the term 'castle' was the customary title for any Scottish country house with only a modicum of heraldic achievement. The position today is fluid. Monkton, by Edinburgh, with its remains of a fifteenth-century tower, sixteenth-century palace block and seventeenth-century gallery, is known as Monkton House, perhaps as a reflection of its domestication in the late seventeenth century when its top storeys were sliced off. (A similar homogenisation of a house of different building periods occurred at Invergowrie and Brucefield, and can stand for many others.) Megginch (Perthshire), more obviously a château with its parapet and turret, is called simply Megginch, whereas Ballindalloch, Midmar and Kilcoy – each rather less defensible than Megginch – are all now castles. Such became the prestige attributed to the title 'castle' that houses which were not – Winton, the House of the Binns or Leith Hall – were deemed of lesser status. Yet the lack of 'castle' in their names perpetuates the *ancient* usage. All were once a mock-military country house of the Scots Renaissance. That titles still confer status is implied by the late twentieth-century aggrandisement of delightful Earlshall into Earlshall Castle.

The third principal contemporary source is the wondrous manuscript maps of Timothy Pont, illustrated by myriad minute but sometimes recognisable building elevations. The making of maps was a significant tool for a ruler. On her accession to the English throne in 1558, for example, Elizabeth of England had dispatched a gentleman of her bedchamber to the Scottish border to prepare a map. On his return he fell in with Sir James Melvill of Halhill at Newcastle, who recorded:

> A man well skill'd in the Mathematicks, Negromancy, Astrology, and was also a good Geographer. Who had been sent by the Council of England to the borders, to draw a Map of such Lands, as lye between England and Scotland, which part was alleged to be a fruitful soil, though at the time it served for no other purpose, but to be a retreat to thieves. For Queen Elizabeth of England was lately come to the Crown, and had been advised by her Council to this course *as tending not only to the enlargement of her bounds* [my italics] but rendering those parts civil.[17]

2.3 Weem or Castle Menzies as drawn by Timothy Pont, c. 1590. (NLS)

It may therefore be no coincidence that just when King James VI was entering his own 'personal rule' in 1585, Pont probably began his project of mapping Scotland. James was an unusually well-educated, modernising king, who personally oversaw the end of bloodfeud in Scotland,[18] and the introduction of lairds into the parliament. He would have been well aware of the benefits to the Crown of an accurate survey of the realm.

Although drawings of buildings were not unusual on European or English maps at the end of the sixteenth century,[19] what distinguishes Pont's maps is the frequency of the illustrations, their apparent verisimilitude, and their depiction of the lesser buildings of the countryside, where other maps show only houses of the greatest magnates (if any at all) and then only by notation.[20] Pont's drawings of the larger houses appear to be elevations of their entrance façade to a minute scale: Craignethan[21] to a scale of approximately 1:4,000 and Hamilton Palace[22] 1:3,600. In the key to his drawings on the rear of the Linlithgow

2.4 Balloch (later Taymouth), as drawn by Timothy Pont, c. 1590. (NLS)

manuscript,[23] country seats (to which he refers as towers)[24] are shown as towers – tall freestanding rectangles which would vary in size to reflect the building's scale: 'Tower/series of dots in towers/and other drawings of buildings/showing stages of height of the houses'.[25] However, most of his drawings deviate from the key: very few country seats are shown as freestanding, for around their feet he shows other, lower buildings, providing an indication of 'yards' (*see* Chapter 4). It must have required enormous and painful effort to execute drawings to such a tiny scale while managing to retain some recognisability (never mind finding adequate space at the right location on the manuscript), so each painstaking variation from the notation shown in the key may have been intended to convey information about size and status. The most significant deviation from the key is in the way Pont's drawings elaborate the flat-topped 'tower' symbol to indicate richer detail: silhouette – in Foulis, Perthshire; dormer windows – Weem or Castle Menzies, Perthshire;[26] occasional crenellations – Avendale (or Strathaven), Lanarkshire;[27] turrets – Blair, Perthshire;[28] stairtowers – Pardovan, West Lothian; cupolas – Glamis, Angus;[29] chimneys – Hamilton Palace, Lanarkshire.[30]

How credible are these drawings? Hamilton Palace, on the only dated map, 1596,[31] is portrayed as a main house flanked by two, taller, flat-topped towers, with its entrance in the centre beneath a façade capped by tall chimneys. Isaac Miller's somewhat naïve elevation of the palace eighty years later shows it virtually the same.[32] Pont's depiction of Balloch (later Taymouth), the seat of Sir Duncan Campbell of Glenorchy that his father had built *c.* 1559,[33] can be substantiated by the drawing in William Adam's *Vitruvius Scoticus* (*see* p. 106).[34] So it is likely that these tiny sketches do indeed represent what Pont saw. Where he indicates a location, with or without a building, there was probably a settlement or structure in the late sixteenth century.

The drawings seem to indicate four different scales of higher rank country seats (with a reasonable stab at conveying their appearance) and a standardised notation for lesser rural buildings like mills, windmills, tidemills, farms, fermtouns, cottowns and kilns. The latter all have a chimney, implying that they were more than just peasant hovels – possibly those yeomen's houses to which Pont referred in his description of Cunninghame: 'the duellings of the zeomanrie verry thick poudred over the face of this countrey, all for the most part weill and commodiously planted and granished'.[35] In the earlier manuscripts, a house of the first rank is depicted as never less than four storeys in height, enjoying a full heraldic complement on the skyline surrounded by lesser buildings and usually with an outline of park enclosure. Second-rank homes are of similar scale without the heraldic superstructure. The drawing of Invermay, for example,[36] implies a large, old-fashioned tower with some surrounding yards, well suited to Lord Innermeath who, as a spy reported to Lord Burleigh, was 'of no great power, of indifferent lyvinge, no great vndertakers'.[37] It was nothing to compare with the flamboyance of nearby Kincardine, principal seat of the Earls of Montrose. Lesser houses were shown as smaller-scale versions of Invermay. The implication of a visually expressed hierarchy of Scots Renaissance houses is reinforced by a study of almost any heavily populated district on the Pont maps. The House of

2.5 *Finavon, Angus, seat of the earls of Crawford – by far Pont's tallest and most imposing country house, c. 1590. (NLS)*

Kelly, Angus, is depicted as having two towers, a linking block, yards and a park,[38] by far the largest of the houses of the district. Yet nearby houses like Collieston, Guynd, Cuithly and Cononside were themselves far from insubstantial: only Kelly, however, had the tower.

Pont's drawings can help retrieve pieces of history. The Earls of Crawford, for example, so prominent in the sixteenth century, must have occupied a more imposing seat than the surviving ruin of a small four-storeyed tower, thought to have been built in the early seventeenth century,[39] at Finavon on the banks of the South Esk or the pleasant villa of Balcarres in Fife. Pont's Finavon is a twin-gabled, seven-storeyed giant well worthy of that tempestuous family – the tallest building that he drew, in fact. What survives now was but an appendage. It was another Pont drawing that prompted a review of the architectural history of Innes House, by Elgin, which has fundamentally changed our perception of its history (*see* Chapter 11); and his drawing of nearby Coxton Tower shows it to be at least fifty-three years older than the 1640s date usually attributed to it. (Historians have again been misled by yet another deceiving datestone.) So if there were indeed buildings approximately where Pont placed them in the late sixteenth century, approximately to the scale and heraldic, social or industrial importance that he indicates, Scotland was well provided with country seats, many of considerable splendour.

A visual Domesday Book such as this, accompanied by Pont's descriptions – of which only Cunninghame and those contained with Macfarlane's *Collections* survive – would have provided the king with an invaluable tool of government. It would have complemented the enormously detailed book or *Roll of the names of the Landlordis and Baillies of the landis duelland on the Bordouris and in the Hielandis quhair broken men hes duelt and presentlie duellis* and then the *Roll of landlords in the greater number of the Shires of Scotland* which his Privy Council compiled in 1587.[40] In that same year James also instructed an Assize of Weights and Measures, almost certainly with the intention of increasing royal revenues.[41] All landowners would have been aware of the centralising implications of these innovations. They must have been equally aware of the visits of Pont,[42] for it is inconceivable that he or his team could have penetrated the policies so close to the great houses to make their drawings without leave to do so. Indeed, some of Pont's most detailed drawings might indicate houses in which he stayed. Sir Robert Gordon's dedication to Sir John Scot of Scotstarvet mentions that the king was 'informed of these matters' (of Pont's maps). Perhaps the king himself or one of his great officers of state like Chancellor Seton (*see* Chapter 10) was behind Pont's enterprise.

The fourth principal, almost contemporary, source are the drawings of Captain John Slezer's enterprise, *Theatrum Scotiae* (Sibbald spells his name 'Sletzer' which gives a clue as to how it was pronounced). A soldier, probably from Germany, Slezer had come to Scotland, married there, and rose to be appointed Captain of the Scottish Train of Artillery in 1680.[43] The engravings were originally envisaged as part of Sibbald's great enterprise of an atlas of Scotland[44] comprising the parish descriptions, Slezer's depictions, Gordon of Rothiemay's town drawings, and new maps

by John Adair. The project foundered on government underfunding. Slezer devised a separate project, originally intended to be in two volumes, of illustrating the 'theatre' of Scotland (in military jargon) through large-format, engraved portrayals of the current state of towns, cities, abbeys, castles, fortresses and mansions. Some were published in 1693 with text by Sibbald and poems by Arthur Johnston.[45] Slezer had also made drawings of other towns and houses – such as Burntisland, Stirling, Leith, Glamis, Lyon, the palace at Edinburgh Castle, which may have been intended for the second, unrealised volume. Although his engravers in London and Holland were tempted to interpret and sometimes alter his drawings[46] by adding peasants, orchards, building reflections and rustic scenes, the drawings were none the less remarkably accurate. They confirm the heraldic skylines of the houses and the glories of the walled gardens, show coaches in use and even a military parade in the courtyard of Falkland Palace, which may be the presentation of English colours to the Duke of York.[47] *Theatrum Scotiae* was the last systematic attempt to record Scotland's architecture until *c.* 1850. Until then, we have to rely on soldiers, antiquarians, curious travellers, and the happy accident of a drawing pasted into a book, a château painted on the inside of bedroom shutters, or a sketch hanging unnoticed on the wall of a housekeeper's room.

Soldiers, however, had their uses. Many pictures of Scots towns or buildings were made by them. English soldiers painted Edinburgh during the Rough Wooing invasion of 1544, and Leith in 1547; Francis Place, in the Cromwellian army, sketched Stirling and Dumbarton in the 1650s; and

2.6 A military event in the courtyard of Falkland Palace, drawn by Slezer, c. 1680. (Author's collection)

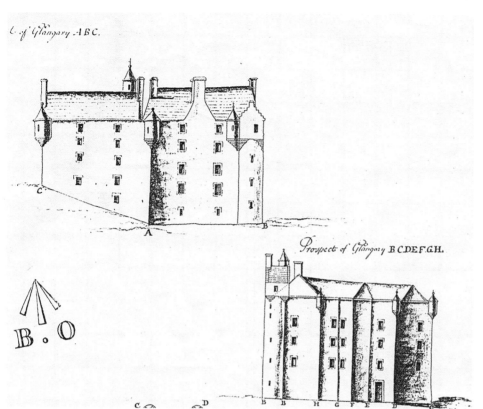

2.7 Invergarry,
Invernesshire, a typical
engineer's unlovely
flattened elevation
drawn by Brigadier
Petit for the Board of
Ordnance in the early
eighteenth century.
(NLS)

2.8 *The court façade of Huntly's palace, Aberdeenshire, drawn 1799 by J.C. Nattes.* (MS 5205.f.30, NLS)

in the late seventeenth and early eighteenth centuries, an anxious government had surveys made of old and new military installations and garrison buildings. So Brigadier Petit, Captain Drury and their colleagues drew perspectives of buildings like Castle Tioram, Duart, Inverness Castle and Invergarry at a time when most were still occupied; and Corgarff and Braemar in their original states.[48] General Roy's map of the entire country prepared in the 1740s almost never illustrated buildings, but was precise about location, parklands, planting and estates. Not long afterwards, Paul Sandby's sketches preserved the appearance of the old House of Inverary, the House of Dean and the Wrichtishousis. Others may similarly be glimpsed in the topographical paintings of Thomas Hearne (Archbishop's Palace, Glasgow), Alexander Nasmyth (the Wrichtishousis), William Simpson (Provand's Lordship and some of the houses on Bute), Horatio McCulloch (Lochaline) and Sam Bough (Mugdock).

Much more focused illustrations appeared accompanying illustrated tours that became fashionable after Bishop Pococke's pioneering trek in the 1760s, and the increasingly frequently published antiquarian volumes. Those most anxious that their volumes should have a strong visual impact brought their own artist. Thomas Pennant was accompanied by Moses Griffith, Dr John Stoddart by Jean-Claude Nattes during the preparation of his *Remarks on Local Scenery and Manners in Scotland*,[49] the Revd Charles Cordiner by W. Mazell, and Captain Francis Grose by his servant Tom Cocking, whose drawings supplemented Grose's own far from inconsiderable ones, and those of his friend Robert Riddell.[50] The rationale was laid out by James Fittler in his introduction to Nattes' drawings:

> Of the utility of works of this nature, little need to be said. To the Antiquary, they afford the means of recording, *in a way no description can ever equal* [my emphasis], those objects which are of the greatest importance. By these means, the possessors of castles, ruins, or even modern buildings or improvements, are able to catch them in their happiest moments of perfection or decay, and transmit them in a manner uninjured by the encroaching hand of time.[51]

Exactly so. It is through them that we may see Craigmillar Castle still partially roofed or Culzean before Robert Adam. Adam de Cardonnel shows Avendale almost complete,[52] and John Clerk of Eldin sketched Lochore environed by water like Kilchurn, the old house of Melvill before it was rebuilt by James Playfair, and the pre-classical Dalvey.[53] The information gleaned during such tours can sometimes solve earlier mysteries. Pont had drawn a curious small house at the far end of the policies high behind Castle Menzies, which has never been found and whose purpose was uncertain. Almost 200 years later, Thomas Pennant learnt of a hermitage built by one of the lairds in an inaccessible chasm to which one of them retired from the world. Perhaps that was what Pont drew. In the early nineteenth century, such drawings became unreliable once Sir Walter Scott's *Border Antiquities* shifted away from antiquarian recording to pandering to romantic sensibilities. Atmospheric pictures of curious maidens creeping with torches round dripping and lichen-covered

Clockwise from top left:
2.9 Avendale, Strathaven, Clydesdale, drawn in the 1780s by Adam de Cardonnel (see p. 98). (Author's collection)
2.10 Balgonie, Fife, drawn by John Clerk of Eldin, c. 1780. (Author's collection)
2.11 Friar's Carse, painted by Alexander Nasmyth. The painting is in the Robert Riddell collection. (NMS Library)
2.12 Peffermill House, Edinburgh, drawn by Francis Grose (see p. 210), c. 1780. (D39. NGS)

ruins were closer to illustrations of fiction than the recording of fact.[54] The delicious and hauntingly beautiful watercolour vignettes of ancient Scotland and its buildings by Scott's friend, the accomplished James Skene of Rubislaw, should not be touched (as the Grant of Ballindalloch motto has it) without a glove, for many of the buildings or scenes had vanished long before Skene's birth.[55]

There was obviously less temptation to heighten the drama where there was no intention of publication. So the sometimes rudimentary paintings, sketches and drawings by Riddell himself, his friend Grose, and Grose's servant Tom Cocking convey valuable information that might have been edited out if they had been prepared for publication – for example, on the use of materials. The three rubble façades of Drumlanrig were harled, and the painting of Comlongon Tower, Dumfriesshire, highlights the visual contrast between the smooth harled tower and the external staircase in well-coursed red sandstone ashlar. Alexander Nasmyth's painting of Riddell's own house of Friar's Carse, Dumfriesshire, shows its principal Renaissance wing to have been thatched – challenging the belief that thatch was necessarily a poor man's material. A less extensive collection of sketches, drawings and notes amassed by Revd John Syme between 1806 and 1841 provides an outline of the vanished seventeenth-century plasterwork in one of the rooms of Abbey House, Culross,[56] and a picture of the seventeenth-century villa added to Cowdenknowes before it was Victorianised.

None the less, historic Scottish architecture had still not been systematically and reliably recorded, and in 1832 George Meikle Kemp, who had prepared conjectural reconstructions of Melrose Abbey and Rosslyn Chapel and was about to prepare plans for the restoration of Glasgow Cathedral for Archibald MacLellan,[57] was duly invited to prepare illustrations of historic Scottish buildings. His publisher[58] withdrew in 1838, just at the time when Kemp developed another preoccupation by winning the competition for the Scott Monument. After his unexpected death in 1844, the Scottish architects William Burn and David Bryce invited the English antiquarian Robert William Billings to undertake a similar survey. Billings' four-volumed *The Baronial and Ecclesiastical Antiquities of Scotland*, which appeared between 1845 and 1852, contained the most comprehensive visual record hitherto available of the architecture of the Scottish Renaissance. The drawings were almost too perfect.[59] He and his exceptional engraver, Le Keux, knowingly dramatised the buildings by overemphasising height, exaggerating perspective and by highlighting important details using sun and shade in parts of the building where direct sun could not reach.

So something of the original state of many châteaux now altered, ruined or vanished may be retrieved from such sources. What new, however, can be learnt from revisiting surviving buildings? Each alteration left its mark, and much of this book is based upon the results of a reconsideration of the houses' fabric and a close scrutiny of their plans. Many hitherto accepted as of one particular construction period emerged as composites of several generations. Craigievar, for example, generally presented as an early seventeenth-century château, is in reality only seventeenth century in its upper storeys, sitting atop a much older tower.[60] Change and alteration may be tracked in the differing thicknesses of its walls, changes in floor level and ceiling height, squint passages, walls that taper or are hollowed, and rooms that are not rectangular. To make sense of them, a working knowledge of the various components of the Renaissance house is an advantage (*see* Chapter 4). Is the passage on the ground floor a tunnel or kitchen corridor? Where are the gallery, guest wing and studies? Clues to be found on the exterior of the building (where it is

2.13 *Kilravock, Nairn, drawn by R.W. Billings. A good example of Billings' technique, with the detail of a dormer window added to the landscape. An equally good example of the conjunction of the vertical medieval tower house, and horizontally planned Renaissance wings.* (Author's collection)

not harled) might include changes in masonry, inconsistencies in window size and placement, and changes in roof level. Where the interpretation of a château in this book differs from the accepted one,[61] it is based upon what these houses still have to tell us.

Those designing and building 500 years ago were skilled and constructed their houses carefully (*see* Appendix 1). They laid them out to a geometric discipline, probably to a set of proportions, and their technology was the most efficient then locally available. Structures were built to constant wall thicknesses (save where enclosing a chimney-stack), and as technology improved, became thinner.[62] The early seventeenth-century upper storeys of Spedlins, Dumfriesshire, have walls 3 feet 2 inches thick, sitting on older, lower walls 9 feet thick. (Walls being made thicker or thinner are quite frequently mentioned in the records.) Since having every wall to a different thickness can be a confounded nuisance, some were thinned and others fattened up, thus concealing the history behind them; and when architects came to draw buildings up for restoration, convenience often tempted them to do the same. James Shearer's initial sketch survey of the House of Brucefield, Clackmannanshire, showed certain features within the building (a turnpike stair and sturdy columns in the hall, for example) and variations in wall thicknesses that implied that it had begun as a small tower, extended in the sixteenth century, reworked in the late seventeenth century, and completed to its current state for Alexander Bruce of Kennet *c.* 1724. However, when Shearer was working up his plans between 1915 and 1922, the received wisdom was that Brucefield had been built all of a piece in 1728. The earlier features contradicted its *persona* as an early eighteenth-century villa on the English model, so Shearer ignored the evidence of his own survey, and re-drew all the walls to a standard thickness.[63] He cannot have been the only one to do so.

The Brucefield case demonstrates that analysis can radically alter its perceived architectural significance. This procedure of 'interrogating the building' can also determine which further places to explore. The video room in Kellie Castle, Fife, has much thinner walls than the room above it: so much is evident on the plans. So the thick walls of the ground floor of the medieval north-west tower had been cloured out (cut or hollowed) but not those of the floors above. It may have happened when a new kitchen was built in what is now called the crypt (those mythologies!) and the north-west stair was used as a service route for food from kitchen to hall above. A constructional peculiarity like this can drive a review of how the house evolved.[64] Likewise, a squint passage (a common feature of many older houses) provides evidence of how a house was changing. These passages had to be cut through mass stone walls, presumably at enormous effort and considerable cost, and the pressing reason behind them was a desire for enhanced privacy. The Renaissance apartment comprised chambers opening in enfilade, one room progressing into the next. Privacy was achieved by the addition of a corridor to the rear (usually to the north) of the state rooms into which they now all opened. Those passages were squint because, having to join a wing to the new corridor through an external wall, they had to avoid a pre-existing feature such as the chimney flue.

Fundamental asymmetries within an allegedly new-built symmetrical composition imply that a house contains some inconvenient remains of an ancestor. The grandly pedimented classical House of Foulis, Ross, is thought to have been largely new-built between 1754 and 1792, albeit incorporating some minor earlier construction in the basement.[65] But Foulis' eighteenth-century classicism is barely skin deep on the upper floors too. The bull's eye or oculus at the centre of the pediment is not at the centre of a room within: indeed it just misses a thick cross-wall. The taller, octagonal, six-storey tower that surges to the rear, capped by library and viewing platform (almost certainly late seventeenth century), rises off-centre to the pediment on the south façade. Foulis' plan reveals its pedimented façade to have been superimposed upon a substantially surviving sixteenth- and seventeenth-century house.

Apply this new scepticism to Melgund, Angus, for example, and you are led to question the received wisdom that it was built from scratch by Cardinal Beaton for his wife Marion Ogilvy from 1542. It comprises a tall tower at the western end and a fine lodging extending to the east. Most texts say of this building (as they do of Carnasserie, Argyll) that it was all built at one time, and that Beaton constructed the tower deliberately in an old-fashioned mode to signify ancient lineage.[66] While the élite characteristically used their country seats to signify ancient lineage, this is insufficient to explain Melgund. Beaton was one of Scotland's most powerful, sophisticated and Europeanised ambassadors. He had been in Rome when the Sistine Chapel was being painted, and was also Bishop of Mirepoix. He would have selected the best designers and builders. So it is curious that Melgund's tower has far thicker walls than the adjoining

2.14 Foulis, Ross and Cromarty. (RCAHMS)

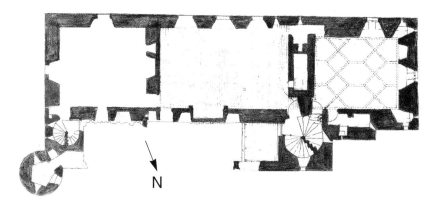

2.15 *Plan of the principal floor of Melgund, Angus, derived from a plan by Benjamin Tindall Architects. The thick-walled tower lying to the west (right) is poorly connected to the palace block extending eastwards, with no direct enfilade room to room. The walls themselves indicate that this was not all built at the same time.* (Author's collection)

palace – thick enough, indeed, to contain mural chambers as they used to in medieval days. Revivalism is usually restricted to the exterior, so to replicate the 'ancient' aspects of thick walls and tiny chambers, both expensive and unsuitable for sixteenth-century living, would have been taking the concept to absurdity. Worse, the tower is not joined to its adjacent towers in enfilade, since its huge kitchen chimney-stack lies in the way. To process from one room to the next requires going out, via the staircase tower, which is hardly sophisticated. Finally, the wall has had to be thinned on its eastern side to allow for the new doors slapped through from the new staircase. The south wall of the palace (probably the original wall of the court) has also had to be thinned to accommodate a new door into the tower. Moreover, during restoration, the masons discovered walls that did not align.[67] Such botch-ups are inconsistent with the finely honed proportional system to which the palace has been designed. To have been built all at the one time, Melgund would have to have been conceived by incompetent designers for an undiscriminating client. That does not sound like Beaton.

So, sufficient sources exist for a rediscovery of the architecture of the Scottish Renaissance château. Now, just over a century after MacGibbon and Ross, it is time to revisit them. There was sufficient money in the sixteenth and seventeenth centuries for fine building, and landowners were proud of their architectural achievements, to judge by datestones, inscriptions, marriage stones and family histories. It is no longer adequate to suppose that a fifteenth-century tower (outside the Borderlands) would be considered an adequate dwelling for a man of substance in the sixteenth century. There were bound to be recidivists – there always are – but peer pressure ensured that landowner would have vied with landowner to be as modern as his wealth allowed.

2.16 *Melgund from the west.* (Author)

3

Real or False Fortifications?

Our histories and experience of all ages teach us that fortresses have never preserved this realm from invasion, yea, the chief cause that we have continued so long a free kingdom has been the lack of them, an enemy finding no place to plant himself.

The Scottish nobles to Queen Elizabeth[1]

My owne opinion [is] when trobblesome times are, it is more safe for a man to keep the fields then to inclose himself in the walls of a house, so that there is no man more against these old fashion of tours and castles then I am.

Patrick, Earl of Strathmore, 1684[2]

The broad perception of the Scottish Renaissance country house is that it is a castle. After all, that is what almost all of them are now called. The purpose of this chapter is to examine the need for defensive structures in Scotland during the sixteenth century, to analyse just how defensive they were, and to question what other reasons there might have been for their apparently warlike appearance and details.

Two opposing perceptions of the sixteenth-century noble country house are the English versus the European. The former holds that the English manor house 'marked the security of English life';[3] whereas the European deployed a warlike language of crenellations, turrets and tourelles to create the 'image of a castle and of power – the castle of dreams'.[4] Both were essentially houses at the peak of fashion: the one evidentially domestic, the other mythically chivalric. The Scottish château comes into the second category; and the misinterpretation to which it has been subjected is the consequence of it having been analysed against the former. Compare solid walls with gunloops to large glass and rather draughty casement windows, and misapprehensions are hardly surprising.

The comparison, however, was invalid. England's architectural impulses were very different from those in Scotland or on the continent. A low-slung manor house with large windows was perceived by Henry VIII to be less of a threat to the state than a mock crenellated castle, and even the use of that new material brick could be taken as a further signal of defortification.[5] Moreover, once the exercise of justice had moved from the magnates to the justices of the peace, the English house no longer had to bear the burden of representing it. In Scotland and in Europe, the exercise of justice remained in the hands of the great magnates (until the eighteenth century in Scotland's case), adding to the dignity and symbolism of authority that they required from their seats of power. Yet symbolism was all it was, even in Europe. Many of the apparent fortifications of European great houses were functionally ambiguous, since they were often quite useless for their apparent purpose. An imposing moat guarding a principal entrance that did not continue round to protect flanks or rear, or gunloops faced in the wrong direction or at the wrong angle to be effective, could only be partially useful. It was at disputed frontiers that the important continental houses were equipped with significant fortification, and sometimes not even then; for it is thought that owners would usually attempt to come to an accommodation with commanders of invading armies to avoid the destruction of their houses and estates. This made sense. One of the principal ways of recouping the expenses of war was through ransom; and it would thus have been perverse to lay waste the potential source of income for the ransom. Commanders of armies were expected to respect this convention, as is implied by a letter of the

3.1 The martial imagery of Glamis' skyline, drawn by R.W. Billings. (Author's collection)

Earl of Mar to his factor after hearing of a potential Jacobite rising in 1708. Mar trusted that its commanders would not be so uncivilised as to damage his great garden at Alloa.[6]

The turreted splendour of some of the early Loire châteaux was created more in deliberate emulation of a distant chivalric past than in response to a threatening present. The Renaissance wing of Ussé sur Loire, for example, imitated the medieval Louvre as it appeared in the drawing within the *Très Riches Heures du Duc de Berry*. Chambord's plan echoes that of medieval Vincennes, and the Château du Berger's roofline details resemble Saumur's – again as depicted in the *Très Riches Heures*.[7] And if the re-creation of a national past proved inappropriate, there were other sources of inspiration. The enormous German schloss of Wittenberg, for instance, may have been conceived in terms of the ideal city.[8] So a symbolic interpretation of Renaissance architecture seems more fruitful than a literal one – as will be shown.

Peaceful England was not altogether immune to the fantasy of medieval pageantry, but it was largely restricted to make-believe, entertainment and caprice rather than being central to the architectural culture. The crenellation, that symbol of martial purpose, was added satirically to the parapets of the enormous, glazed bay windows of Lytes Carey and Compton Wynyates – the very exemplifications of an unwarlike society.[9] In 1607, Lord Howard of Bindon had built Lulworth, Dorset – a 'little pile which he hopes proves pretty' – in the form of 'a castle of the imagination', a three-storeyed crenellated house framed by four-storeyed round corner towers. Its artillery platform faced only the front, to impress visitors.[10] When, ten years later, the Luttrell family rebuilt Dunster as a large-windowed house to designs by William Arnold, they embellished it with towers and crenellations to echo its castle ancestry. Alterations to Kenilworth, Warwickshire, undertaken by Robert Dudley, Earl of Leicester in preparation for a progress by Queen Elizabeth in 1575, were intended to enhance the medieval atmosphere of one of England's greatest medieval castles. Its floor-to-ceiling windows, however, made it glow like a lantern at night in a most unmilitary manner.[11] Yet such buildings were exceptions. The fantasy aspect of the English psyche was generally restricted to the temporary structures required by masques and jousts.

So how did Scottish houses of the same period compare? They followed the European pattern, but in their interpretation naïvety and ingenuousness set in. 'Castles' were taken at face value. Take Sir Lawrence Weaver's analysis of Scotstarvit Tower, Fife, when celebrating the new Scottish National War Memorial:

> The Scottish tower house was no less an expression of the long-continuing element of private warfare which seethed through Scottish life until a far later period. . . . When Sir John Scot of Scots Tarvit Tower, author of that engaging book *The Staggering State of Scots Statesmen*, a man of real culture and of European travel, built himself a home, at a time when Inigo Jones was giving England the subtle refinements of the Banqueting Hall of Whitehall Palace, he merely piled six comfortless rooms one above the other, into a gaunt tower with a single wheel stair: only three of the rooms had fireplaces. The

tower had the refinements of the lair of a robber chieftain, no more and no less.[12]

Even though Sir Lawrence's purpose was to celebrate the martial character of the Scots nation, it was over the top. Yet had he visited Scotstarvit *in that frame of mind*, he would have found ample evidence to support his belief in the backwardness of Scottish seventeenth-century life. Scotstarvit contains rooms without fireplaces, a large chamber lit only by clerestorey windows, and no kitchen. So its owner, Sir John Scot of Scotstarvet, Director of Chancery to the king, Lord of Exchequer and Lord of Session, a man – as he modestly boasted – who had been to London twenty-four times and to the Low Countries twice, who had organised the publication of the *Atlas of Scotland* by John Blaeu (and had also paid Blaeu a hundred double pieces for printing the Scots poets),[13] did not even enjoy cooked food. Historic Scotland has suggested that the kitchen might have been contained within a separate building in the now-missing inner court.[14] Although it was not unknown for a country house to have a distant kitchen in a different building, it was not sophisticated. Scot of Scotstarvet was allowed to have eaten cooked food – but it must have been cold by the time it reached him.

3.2 Scotstarvit Tower, Fife, in the late nineteenth century – splendid as an anachronistic statement of power but unlivable. (RCAHMS)

This is magnificent nonsense. Most towers would have been enfolded within a larger complex of modern buildings by the early seventeenth century, while they themselves took a secondary role as guest quarters, servants' quarters or storage. Scots rarely lived vertically like that any more, except in hunting or seaside pavilions (*see* Chapter 7). A tower like this would have been grossly anachronistic at almost any time during the entire previous century. Moreover, it is expensively wrapped in dressed, squared, polished ashlar stonework – rare in a mere small tower like this, there was an elaborately carved fireplace[15] and a carved armorial panel above the stair doorway at parapet level. Why adorn a building with such costly accoutrements without providing even the basic amenities of a kitchen, or rooms with fireplaces or a view? Almost no part of Scotstarvit Tower fits as it should. The staircase is of a much grander and sophisticated scale than its tiny access passage; its chimney-stacks rise from rooms without fireplaces; the floor levels are wrong, and the parapet crenellations look as though they might have begun life as elaborate window reveals in some great house elsewhere and then been later reset here as ornamental parapet decoration. It was not a seventeenth-century country seat – never mind the lair of a robber baron. Rather, it was a folly, an architectural salvage yard cobbled together by a proud, status-conscious courtier/antiquarian as a statement of historic lineage and nobility. He grafted all this upon a 1475 tower originally called Inglis Tarvit, extended to a manor-place in 1575.[16] When Sir John transformed it into Scotstarvit (note the political implication of the name change) he created almost a pantomime reconstruction of Scotland's medieval past, achieved by widespread serendipity – yet sufficiently *vraisemblable* to deceive unwary foreigners. It did not deceive near-contemporaries like Sir Robert Sibbald, who described it as 'an old [rather than a modern] tower of aisler with a lower house'.[17] Scot may have inhabited the lower house – or one of his other properties nearby – for he could not have lived in what survives today.

The image of Scotland as an irredeemably warlike nation has been utterly pervasive so it is unsurprising that when the House of Auchanachie in Aberdeenshire came recently to sale, it was described as a 'fortified house', built as a stronghold from which to guard the Deveron valley.[18] Analyse the house against its duty, and the concept is revealed as absurd. This prettily harled, crowstepped house comprises a tiny, narrow three-storeyed tower, with a substantial two-storeyed wing extending to the east, with a tight stairtower in the angle (re-entrant) between. The dominant feature is the hardly military stepped kitchen chimney-stack. There are no crenellations, battlements, bartizans nor

3.3 Auchanachie, Aberdeenshire, in the late twentieth century – barely even defensible. (RCAHMS)

wallwalks – not even ground-level gunloops – with which to fulfil such guardianship duties. So four small square apertures at the head of the stairtower are characterised as shot-holes; yet their line of fire covers neither the entrance nor any of the vulnerable windows, and is restricted to less than 15 per cent of the field. Only with extreme difficulty could they even command the ground immediately in front. As shot-holes, they were useless. Nor was the site defensible: although far enough up a slope to enjoy a good view, it was far enough down to be sheltered from the wind, and therefore could be dominated from higher ground. No moat, no portcullis and no fortified gate. None the less, Auchanachie *appears* fortified. In its picturesque and miniature way – with a taller tower, a conically roofed stairtower, romantic openings, and crowstepped gables – it represents what Scots look for now, and probably looked for then, in their houses: height, romantic skylines, and a noble and faintly martial aspect.

So what was the nature of a castle in Renaissance Scotland, and who needed to be defended against whom, how and with what? One would normally begin by looking for sites selected for defence, with probably a moat, gatehouse, portcullis, wallwalks, crenellations, arrow or gunloops, and a general disposition to render attackers vulnerable. Few castles in Scotland match these criteria, and virtually none built during the Renaissance. How, therefore, are the numerous licences to crenellate – the royal warrant seemingly required to construct a fortified building – to be explained? Such licences exist for fewer than 5 per cent of great Scots houses,[19] and there is little reason to believe that the rest have gone missing. This implies either a contemporary acceptance that the majority of the country houses were not fortified, or licences to crenellate had a different purpose.

The phrase 'defensive *ornaments* at the wall-head' stated in a royal warrant of 1430,[20] implies that even in the fifteenth century battlements were decorative, and 'were as much a symbol of lordship and authority as a practical means of defence'.[21] Nor were they restricted to noble houses and military purposes. In 1549, for example, William Ahanny was given full power and freedom to raise his house in the High Gait of Wigton 'with battaling and corbel sailze [projecting] in the maist honest and substantious maner he pleasis', similar to neighbouring town houses which had already received such permission.[22] In 1556, an Edinburgh burgess, Patrick Edgar, was permitted to 'battaill the south syde' of his tenement in the Cowgate to resist not armies, but the violence of wind and weather, and to help conserve his slates and thatch.[23] In some cases, the licence was attached to a grant of privilege, and in others, it might have been issued as a signal of royal favour.[24] The battlement was therefore a symbolic decoration unrelated to military purposes, for which householders desired royal consent.

The image of a tall, grey gaunt tower rising in solitary crenellated defiance is also a romantic confection. The tower was surrounded by ancillary buildings, first and foremost by what was known in the Middle Ages as the 'barmkin' – or the livestock enclosure – the progenitor of the inner court or close. However, the barmkin's reappearance in the Act of Parliament 'For bigging of strengthis on ye bordouris' (building strong houses on the Borders) passed in 1535 has frequently been taken to represent a continuing primitive state of affairs in the Scottish countryside.

> It is statute and ordained for saving of men their goods and gear upon the Borders in time of war, and all other troublous time, that every landed man dwelling in ye inland or upon ye borders, having there a hundred pound land of new extent, shall build a sufficient barmkin upon his heritage and lands, in place most convenient, of stone and lime, containing three score feet of the square, an ell thick, and six ells high, for the receipt and defence of him, his tenants and their goods in troublous time, with a tower in the same for himself, if he thinks it expedient. And that all other landed men of smaller rent and revenue build peels and great strengths as they please, for saving of theirselves, men, tenants and goods. And that all the said strengths, barmkins, and peels, be built and completed within two years, under pain etc. [spelling modernised].[25]

Why was such an instruction (complete with details of wall height, a matter in which one would not normally expect a parliament to be expert) needed? The English had invaded in 1533, and might be tempted to do so again now that a Scottish/French dynastic marriage was being negotiated, and the Act encouraged the construction of enclosures 60 feet square in the frontier lands passively defensible against the country's predatory neighbour. The Act neither applied to the whole of Scotland, nor suggested that the term barmkin was a universal Scottish equivalent for what the French call the *cour d'honneur*. It restricted itself to building barmkins for the protection of beasts in the lands marching with the English frontier, solely in time of war, and they could be located anywhere – with an added tower if the owner chose (implying that there were none there already). The Act had nothing to do with fortifying the country seat.

You will search in vain amid Scots Renaissance châteaux if you seek plentiful portcullises, wet or dry moats, drawbridges, usable *machicolis*, artillery platforms or the flanking bastions of contemporary European great houses. Where they existed, they were notable exceptions: Mugdock had a portcullis, and Dunlop, Glamis and Ardmillan a moat of sorts (most likely a drainage ditch), with some type of movable bridge. Generally, however, the Scottish château lacked such features, which implies a generally settled country. That impression is confirmed by the fact that, virtually alone in Europe, Scotland's towns were not walled for serious defence. The latter was a circumstance reiterated again and again by contemporary chroniclers like George Buchanan and John Spottiswoode,[26] presumably since they understood how curious it would sound to a continental audience. Bishop Lesley tied it to the Scots' dislike of being confined within walls: 'our towns we fortify not with walls, save first the Borders of the realm, thereafter the fields, where need is, they fence about and defend, with the force of their body and armour, according to the laws of their elders [spelling and words modernised].'[27] In 1647, David Buchanan described Edinburgh's city walls as '. . . according to the custom of the nation . . . not so strong as to stand a cannonade, for the Scots are accustomed to defend their cities with men, and not with walls'.[28] Such walls as there were, delineated burgh boundaries. Both Aberdeen and Glasgow developed with virtually two separate unwalled cities – an ecclesiastical/university city and a mercantile one, with open space between, so any army could have cleaved between the two. Sympathetic Europeans found this state of affairs alarming. Impressed by the country and its towns when passing through it in 1548, Jean de Beaugé was shocked at their defencelessness. Restlessly, he offered advice on how to fortify them with bulwarks and citadels; but the need for his advice only occurred during the Civil War almost 100 years later. Scotland's towns had evolved not to combat armies but the wind and rain.[29]

Rather than power residing in a town or city protected by a fortified palace with the most fashionable defences, as in northern Europe and in Italy, power in Scotland lay in the countryside. Most Scots towns and cities had not rebuilt their castle after it had been razed by Robert the Bruce several centuries earlier. The small burghs that clustered at the foot of aristocratic houses like Inveraray, Fochabers and Cullen were in no way comparable. Businesslike fortification was restricted to royal castles and centres of royal power, like Edinburgh and Stirling. Even the Archbishop's Palace in Glasgow could scarce compete with its equivalents abroad: no moat but a herb garden.

So, by international standards, just how violent a country was Scotland during the Renaissance? It was fortunately exempt from the passage of the great armies in pursuit of dynastic wars, religion or territorial aggrandisement that threatened so much of the continent. Conversely, the natural aggression of the Scots, and their desire to win military spurs, was diverted across the North Sea, where Scots mercenaries were much prized and where their rewards could be great. Scotland's principal problem was a predatory neighbour sharing the same island. Considerations of international defence were therefore largely irrelevant – apart from a necessary *cordon sanitaire* along the Border with England, and the fortifications at Eyemouth built by the English 1547–8 and refortified by the French in 1557–8,[30] the English forts at Lauder, Bracenrig (or Balgillo Hill, Broughty) and Haddington, and the French fortifications at Dunbar and Leith. All except Dunbar were transitory.

Since external threat was only occasional and localised, the 'defensive' nature of Scottish country houses has been explained, instead, as a response to internal political instability, the royal minorities of the Stewart dynasty, and to the prevalence of blood feud.[31] Yet by comparison with other countries, Scotland's record was rather good. In most areas there was little question of war and rural threat, save from the bands of broken men of war, reivers and bandits – 'les bandes énormes des gens licencieux' – which plagued all European countries.[32] In only a third of the frequently bitter local disagreements, the 'deidlie feds' (deadly feuds or bloodfeuds) which peaked during James VI's minority in the 1570s and 1580s, was anybody killed,[33] and that usually occurred in a city street rather than in an attack upon a country house. Even the fatal street brawls that resulted from trains of noblemen encountering each other in Stirling or Edinburgh were sporadic compared to the endemic urban violence of Italy. The scale of the latter's ferocity can be gauged by the design of a 'house for a faction leader' by the architect Sebastiano Serlio. Taking it as read that the doors of this great *palazzo* would be smashed down by a rival faction, the inner hall within was raked by sixteen concealed gunloops. Indeed, a nobleman's palace in Rome was required to have both armoury and guardroom.[34] The great castle/palaces of northern Germany, Poland and Denmark were enfolded in multiple moats or canals, and protected by drawbridges, gun emplacements, bastions, outer barbicans, inner gateways and *glacis*. There was nothing like that in Scotland. Most feuds arose from conflicts between equals, inspired by territorial issues, and were complicated by notions of lordship and dependency that could be settled only under certain conditions – until, that is, the king took a hand and virtually extirpated bloodfeuds by the early seventeenth century. They occurred most frequently in the sophisticated heartland of Scotland.

A concerted attack on a country house, rather than the harrying of tenant farmers (in the manner that the Venetian *jeunesse dorée* or 'roaring boys' would harry and beat up tradesmen and craftsmen)[35] was relatively rare. So the seizure of Sanquhar-Hamilton in Ayr (otherwise known as Newton) in 1558, the burning of Corgarff by Edom o'Gordon in the civil war, and the Earl of Huntly's burning of Donibristle when murdering the Earl of Moray in 1591 were unusual. In his introduction to *Minstrelsy of the Scottish Border*, Walter Scott observed that he had not identified a single example 'of a distinguished baron made prisoner in his own house'.[36] The protection – not much use in Corgarff – was for wife and household. The theatre of Scottish feuds tended to be the High Street (for periodic assassination), the countryside (for occasional ambush), or rural settlements (for the sacking of unfortunate tenants or cottars). In 1601, for example, the recidivist William Gordon of Gight harried the tenants of Mowat of Balquolly by breaking doors and windows, and violently dinging one of them within his own house before carrying him off to Gight.[37] Grim though that sounds, life was still nothing like as dangerous as it was in contemporary Italy. It strains credibility, therefore, to conclude that Scotland needed to maintain a culture of defensible building as the consequence of its culture of feuding[38] whereas Italy did not.

The country's internal political record was reasonable by international standards. As Gordon Donaldson has put it: 'In Scotland, the era of the Reformation had involved no massacres or wars of religion as in France, no wholesale executions or uprisings cruelly suppressed as in England, nothing parallel to the brutalities in Germany and the Low Countries.'[39] A gauge of the inherent peacefulness of the country was that James V in 1536–7, Mary of Guise in 1550–1, and James VI in 1589–90 all felt that they could make lengthy visits to France or Denmark, lasting many months, in the reasonable certainty that the country would remain stable during their absence. The Scottish nobility and their monarch tended to collaborate in the general maintenance of the peace, and the principal internal problems that occurred during the half century or so of royal minorities generally arose when there was neither consistently strong nor fair nor stable nor continuous regency government. Only during the civil war of 1568–72 (the king's men versus the queen's men), and the subsequent regency of the Earl of Morton, did factionalism lead to extensive property destruction. It was sufficiently unusual for king, queen or regent to besiege a noble in his own territory that when they did – the Regent Albany threatening Hamilton

Palace with his brass guns in 1515, James V besieging his former captors the Douglases in their fortress of Tantallon in 1528, the Regent Moray destroying country seats belonging to the queen's supporters in south-west Scotland during 1567,[40] and James VI slighting the houses of the Earls of Errol and Huntly in 1591 – such expeditions were all the more striking by their rarity. With the notable exceptions of the Earl of Moray and the Regent Morton, such actions customarily lacked vindictiveness. In 1591, the old towers at Slains and Huntly (homes of two of the principal conspirators, the Earls of Errol and Huntly) were indeed slighted, but the palace at Huntly remained habitable, and Huntly's principal seat, Bog o' Gight by Fochabers, remained untouched.

The frantic efforts of the Earl of Bothwell to distance the king from the malign influence of Chancellor Maitland (which took the form of repeated attempts at armed kidnap in Holyrood and in Falkland)[41] coincided with Sir Duncan Campbell of Glenorchy's land reclamation and planting schemes. Far from the Edinburgh hot-house, Glenorchy was obtaining pine seeds, introducing fallow deer and expanding his horse stud with a new stallion.[42] Too great a focus on political activity has proved distorting. Beyond the Court circles, Scotland was a peaceful, improving country to the extent that when Huntly refashioned his palace from the 1590s, its loggia *faced outwards to the countryside*. The arcaded loggias of Castle Campbell, Crichton and possibly Melgund had faced into the court. That Huntly's faced insouciantly outwards was an expression of supreme confidence in his safety.

Only a limited number of royal fortresses were built or refitted during the Renaissance, and most were down towards the frontier with England. The castle of Dunbar, property of the Albany Stewarts for many generations, had been rebuilt by the Regent Albany with a sophisticated and powerful defensive blockhouse closely following contemporary artillery developments at Berwick. It protected a substantial and favourite royal residence behind.[43] Dunbar governed the sea-borne route round into the Forth, and possibly for that reason it remained garrisoned by 100 seasoned French soldiers for almost twenty-four years after the castle passed from Albany into royal hands.[44] Blackness, likewise projecting into the Forth, had extensive fortifications and casemates added in about 1536 to the inside of the curtain wall facing *inland*. It confirmed Blackness's transformation to the state prison, since a rescue attempt for a state prisoner was more likely to come from within Scotland.

Tantallon, the seat of the Douglas Earls of Angus and thence the Earls of Morton, must have been one of the most intimidating of the private seats.[45] A vignette of it when complete shows the formidable three-towered façade closing off the promontory, with a barbican whose ghostly appearance appears much to resemble the barbican of Saumur as shown in the *Très Riches Heures du Duc de Berry*. Tantallon's skyline is a flamboyance of platforms, parapets and domes.

A fortified structure was probably added to the inner ward of Cadzow (in those days probably known as the castle of Hamilton) in about 1525 by Sir James Hamilton of Finnart (*see* Chapter 5).[46] Not unlike Chinon in having an outer, middle and inner ward, Cadzow lies in the formerly impenetrable Cadzow Forest upon the cliffs of the River Avon. Since its inner ward was cast in upon itself in the late eighteenth century to form a picturesque object for those visiting Châtelherault (the Hamilton family's decorative banqueting house and dog kennel across the Avon gorge), its plan and purpose remain to be uncovered by excavation. Separated from the middle ward by a deep ditch, it comprised a large, single approximately rectangular building with projecting round towers on its two landward corners. Clinging to its cliff, it has the appearance of a place of last resort. One of the towers has a wide-mouthed gunloop facing down the ditch, which contains a large, unexcavated mound.

Two similar, approximately rectangular mounds protect the outer ditch of Tantallon where the wall changes direction. The outer ward was critical to Tantallon's defensive strategy, since it kept hostile gunners out of range. When James V besieged it in 1529, his cannon could not approach sufficiently close to the castle to inflict significant damage, and the siege had to be called off. The purpose of these mounds may have been revealed by the excavation of a comparable one at Craignethan, Lanarkshire, built

Top: *3.4 The caponier at Craignethan, Lanarkshire.* (Author)
3.5 Craignethan from the air. The two wards and the caponier lying between them are clearly visible. (RCAHMS)

3.6 Decorative gunloop beneath the window, possibly by Thomas Leiper, in the summer house of the great garden of Edzell, Angus. Drawing by Billings. (Author's collection)

as his country seat by a noted soldier, Sir James Hamilton of Finnart, from 1531.[47] Like Cadzow, its inner ward is separated from the outer by a deep stone-faced ditch. Once that ditch was excavated, a caponier was revealed – a stone-vaulted musketeer emplacement originally devised by the Italian military engineer and architect Francesco di Giorgio, an idea Finnart may have picked up during a visit to France in 1517. However, since none of its gunloops faces the direction of greatest threat (southwards) the caponier may have been intended more to demonstrate contemporary ideas about fortification to a visiting king than to have any practical effect. Since Finnart was probably responsible for the work at Cadzow, and he was present at the siege of Tantallon and may have undertaken work there afterwards, those other mounds may also be caponiers.

Gunloops form a principal part of the architectural composition of Scottish châteaux, and have been largely responsible for the survival of the 'castle' myth. Their varying shapes have attracted an inordinate amount of attention. Yet whereas their symbolic importance is indisputable, there is much doubt as to their military effectiveness. Guns were expensive, and gunners were rare and valued members of staff. They were not expendable. Yet some of the chambers lying behind gunloops (what the French call *chambres à tirer*) would have been dangerous to use: they were poorly orientated, confined and low in height.[48] The recoil might dash the gunner's head against the vault, even supposing he were not choked with the smoke, or his ear drums blasted by the explosion in what was a confined echo chamber. Gunloops themselves were often wrongly aligned. Those in Craignethan's Lodging face west rather than north towards what is thought to have been the entry gatehouse. They do not command the entrance in Fyvie, and those in Balbegno are at ankle height. A gunner in the Palace of Huntly would be firing dangerously straight into the cobbles of the courtyard[49] and his equivalent in Falkland Palace directly in the buttress facing him. By contrast with the rare, businesslike gunloops that were built with a place for the wooden stock of a gun to rest, a gunner with a sixteenth-century weapon using the typical château gunloop would have had difficulty seeing his enemy, never mind taking a sophisticated aim and being sure that the ball did not hit the sides of the embrasure and ricochet back at him.

If the function of gunloops was not military, what was it? They implied threat and achievement at arms with the same effect as a peacock ruffling its feathers. The massive apertures in the Earl of Atholl's palace block at Balvenie open not from casemates but from smart chambers within, and signify Atholl's position in the aristocratic hierarchy. The delightfully ornate gunloops erected by the peaceable Willie Forbes and his architect Thomas Leiper at Tolquhon (and at Schivas and Fraser as well) were erected not in anger but in irony. Their role was primarily to signify that should the occasion ever arise (which it would not), *of course* the family could defend itself.

The rare purpose-designed *chambre à tirer* is usually easy to recognise. Craignethan's provide adequate space for recoil and fumes, breadth, a gun rest and cupboard for powder and ball. By contrast, how the gunner at Drochil could have taken aim at anything that was not immediately in front at point-blank range is difficult to imagine,[50] and the wooden shutters or glass that kept out draughts at Girnigo's gunloops argue against a military purpose. Guns could presumably be used more effectively from higher up the house, but the fact that so very few châteaux were built with open parapets and crenellations during the sixteenth century suggests that it was not common. The 14 foot thick vulnerable western façade of Craignethan's Lodging was built structurally independent of the principal block behind, with its vaulting in a different direction: a sacrificial wall provided well for artillery protecting the lodging behind. The upper gun emplacements were provided with a large wall cupboard, possibly for powder or ammunition.[51] Craignethan was far from typical, for Finnart had a master gunner on his staff whom he loaned to others from time to time. His collection of guns was eagerly seized by the king upon his forfeiture in 1540.

The more beetlingly formidable the Scottish château, the less defensible it was, whereas the sophisticated, pleasure-seeming villa of Ancy Le Franc, designed in 1544 by Sebastiano Serlio, paradoxically concealed formidable *chambres à tirer* and gunloops. Its military defences – the height and alignment of its cannon emplacements, and its myriad gunloops – were almost imperceptible. So the French approach was to conceal a mailed fist within a silk glove, and the Scottish one to retreat behind yards and yetts, and wait for frenzy to abate.

Many magnates did not even aspire to a gunner, and left the porter to look after the military hardware. In 1600, the porter at the great house of Balloch, seat of Sir Duncan Campbell of Glenorchy – Black Duncan of the Cowl – carefully counted two brass pieces, one cutthroat gun, two hagbuts, ten muskets, some other pieces and a beheading axe. Far from being in a state of readiness, these weapons were all over the place with bits of their operating mechanisms in different rooms, so much so that the porter had to make a plan of where they were to be found. A short gun of brass was inconveniently clogging up the wine cellar.[52] The space in the inventory of Craignbarnet to list the various types of guns (implying that there was a standard format for such records) was left empty. No guns.[53] An inventory of the bankrupt Balquholly in 1699 found only a small sword, a carbine and a fowling piece.[54] Of large guns, even the greatest magnate of them all, the Cock o' the North, the Earl of Huntly himself (that is to say, his corpulent corpse after he suffered a stroke following the Battle – skirmish, rather – of Corrichie on 28 October 1562) could only muster three – two falcons and a cannon.[55] The munitions of a real fortress were of a different order. In 1699, the king's garrison in Dunnottar, for example, had *inter alia* 137 muskets, 17 long and short iron guns, 13 brass guns, 2 iron mortars, 46 hand grenades, 148 small roundshot, 365 great roundshot, and numerous barrels wanting stocks, stocks wanting barrels, matchlocks, and one Standard and Colours.[56]

It has been suggested that the principal reason why châteaux walls became thinner during the sixteenth century was that improvements in gunnery rendered the country house indefensible against brass guns. Cannon were certainly feared: in 1515, Hamilton Palace had surrendered within the day when faced with Albany's brass guns. If there had been any lingering doubt about the consequences of effective artillery bombardment it was dispelled by the destruction of the castle of St Andrews in July 1547. The murderers of Cardinal Beaton had been besieged ineffectively in the heavily fortified castle for the previous fourteen months. Twenty-one galleys carrying the necessary guns, commanded by Leon Strozzi, arrived from France, and on the last day of July, things proceeded shockingly quickly.[57] Nineteen cannon, 'whereof four were cannons-royal, called double cannons', were mounted on the tower of St Salvator's and on the western towers of the Cathedral. This is how John Knox, one of the defenders, described it:

> The cannonade began at four o'clock in the morning, and before ten o'clock of the day, the whole south quarter, betwixt the fore tower and the east block house, was made assaultable. The lower transe was condemned, divers were slain in it, and the east block house was shot off from the rest of it between ten and eleven o'clock.[58]

The castle surrendered that morning.

Conversely, too much can be made of the defensive capabilities of the thick walls of the medieval tower house. Far from being solid, they were perforated and honeycombed with oratories, garderobes, small chambers and stairs. The building form had emerged more from a partiality for compact planning, with the subsidiary chambers and functions contained within the wall thickness, than from the needs of defence. The tower's stability was fundamentally weakened by this burrowing of chambers. It almost certainly caused the collapse of Elphinstone Tower, East Lothian, and, probably, of the east gable of Pitsligo. When Seton's great tower collapsed in 1561, Sir Richard Maitland (who knew it) attributed the crumbling to its age, but also to 'too many windows and easements through it'.[59] Since the seemingly thicker walls of the tower houses were unlikely to have withstood brass guns, improvement in artillery is unlikely to have been a principal reason for the move to a much thinner-walled château.

If Scottish country houses had been located 'primarily for reasons of defence,' you might expect that they would have changed location once defence was no longer as important as the gardens and parterres of the later culture. Most Scottish houses, however, stayed put – *for they were already well situated for such peaceful expansion.* That implies that their original siting was governed much less by defence than has been assumed. Indeed, where such moves occurred, they occasioned remark. The Douglases, for example, abandoned their tower in Loch Leven in the 1560s for Newhouse – a substantial courtyard house on the shore.[60] So when the deposed Mary Queen of Scots was lodged in Loch Leven Castle in 1567, she occupied a mothballed if not abandoned property. Another abandoned island house was that built by the Campbells of Glenorchy when they expanded into Perthshire from their original seat of Kilchurn on a promontory jutting into Loch Awe. Their first move had been to an

3.7 The collapsed gable of the tower of Pitsligo, Buchan, drawn by Nattes, c. 1798. (Author's collection)

island at the east end of Loch Tay, where the third laird had built a hall and chapel some time before 1513.[61] Charters were signed there until such time as their next house – Balloch (later Taymouth) – was completed on the shore to the east in late 1559.[62] Balloch became and remained their principal seat. There was no pretence of anything more than passive defence at Balloch. During the succeeding generation, the Campbells constructed a further house – Finlarig – on low haughland at the western end of Loch Tay, emphasising their control over that entire body of water. Such moves from naturally defensible but inconvenient locations to more congenial ones were relatively rare.

The sixteenth-century country house was not entirely defenceless, for the passive defences of thick walls, restricted entry and grilled windows would certainly keep a sturdy beggar away from the laird's lodging. But an even more effective means of keeping unwelcome predators at bay were the yards. Renaissance Scotland tended to use the generic term 'yards' or 'yairds' for the various walled courtyards, service yards, walled gardens and orchards that spread in every direction around a house (although the term barmkin continued to be used mainly in official documents). Where the inner yard formed a courtyard with the house itself, it tended to be called 'close' or 'court'.[63] In the earlier periods, the court might contain hall, stables, offices, workshops, a smiddy – and perhaps something grander such as round towers at the corners, as did the tight court surrounding the massive L-plan tower of Niddry (West Lothian).[64] More elaborate buildings in the courts of other houses gradually came to replace the tower itself. Once all the functions of Castle Campbell, the Earl of Argyll's principal lowland house, were being satisfied by the horizontally planned buildings surrounding the south and east of its court, its tower may have remained in a ruinous state for much of the sixteenth century.[65] At their simplest, the outer yards beyond provided the great house with much of its food, and a seventeenth-century plan of the Earl's palace at Birsay shows a flower yard, herb yard, kaill yard and plant yard.[66] At their more extensive, they were immensely elaborate (*see* Chapter 4).

So, despite its lack of drawbridge, moat or portcullis, the Scottish Renaissance house would not have been an easy target. Any invader would have had to negotiate these courtyards or walled enclosures containing the stables, smiddies, gardens, bowling alleys, granaries,

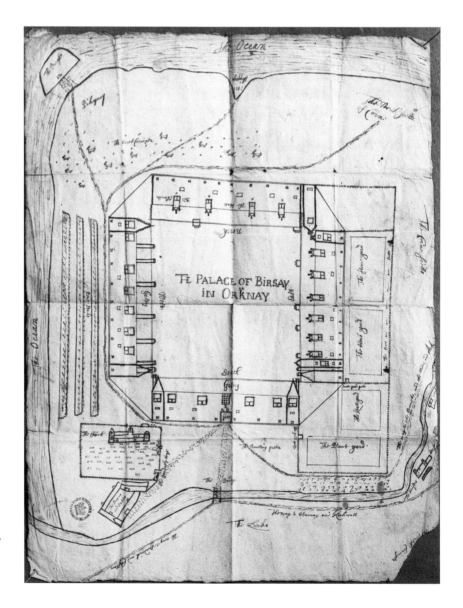

3.8 Seventeenth-century drawing of the Palace of Birsay, Orkney. Note how it is surrounded by yards. (RCAHMS)

orchards and wildernesses. The compensation claim sent to the Court of Session by Sir William Hamilton of Sanquhar-Hamilton in 1559, for damage in one of the rare feuds to involve seizure of a country seat, illustrates this rather well. John Wallace of Craigie had decided to take advantage of the breakdown in law and order caused by the confrontation between the government of Mary of Guise and the Lords of the Congregation to pursue a feud with Hamilton. Sir William was a senior figure at Court, a former colleague of Finnart who had once been captain of Edinburgh Castle; his recent territorial expansion in Ayrshire threatened the Wallaces. So, on 10 November 1559, at 10 p.m., assisted by forty persons 'armed in preparation for violence with coats of mail, steel helmets, spears and hand guns', Craigie assaulted, besieged and scaled the boundary walls of Sanquhar-Hamilton. The invaders had to negotiate, *inter alia*, a stable yard with a hanging iron gate, a brewhouse yard with an iron gate, a large brewery, bakery, another large yard 'containing a double-leaf iron gate and a vaulted passageway with a porter's lodge above it', another yard containing an armoury, a large entrance with a double-leaf gate of wood, two large orchards and yards having three gates and planted with stands of hawthorn trees, gooseberry bushes, redcurrant bushes, rose bushes, apple trees, plum trees, cherry trees, wild plum trees, damsons, almond trees, plane trees, birch trees, ash, hawthorn and other trees, and provided with two ponds and enclosed by a stone wall, capped with lime.[67] That these enclosures performed quite reasonably as passive defence was also discovered by the Earl of Cassilis when he went to uplift his own teinds (rents in kind) from Girvanmains, and found the enclosures 'armed against his entrance'.[68] Soldiers who succeeded in negotiating such formidable obstacles carrying sixteenth-century weaponry probably deserved their prize.

3.9 Sanquhar-Hamilton (or Newton) by Ayr, drawn by Slezer in the late seventeenth century. Note how yards and buildings extend to the west. (Author's collection)

3.10 The gatehouse to Hills, Dumfriesshire. (RCAHMS)

Gatehouses, ceremonial rather than defensive, presented little threat. They tended to be small and scarcely defensible apart from token gunloops, and the room above was neither a portcullis chamber nor an artillery emplacement, but usually the porter's chamber.[69] None the less they remained profoundly important in symbolic terms. In 1535 when the king asked Hamilton of Finnart to move the entrance to the Palace of Linlithgow from the east to the south, with an entry direct from the town, the new processional route passed through two diminutive gatehouses in the form of miniature châteaux. Larger gatehouses were scarcely more militarily effective, and the defensiveness of Falkland's twin towers was fundamentally weakened by a projecting, off-centre oriel window. Indeed, such double-towered gatehouses – particularly those with overtones of a triumphal arch – might be regarded more as a French-inspired fashion accessory than a feature of military significance (*see* Chapter 9).

To contemplate more than 1,000 Scottish country houses of the Renaissance from the perspective of medieval military activity is therefore profoundly misleading. Almost none of them shows evidence of the increasingly sophisticated defensive ideas emanating from the continent. Instead, walls became thinner and windows larger. But, perhaps to compensate for their lack of a genuine military role, they came to be embellished with architectural military metaphors. Round corner towers, hitherto explained by the need to provide flanking or enfilade fire along the walls, are now understood as bedroom or study towers disposed to get the best sunlight, their broad windows indefensible save for grilles.[70] The very scale of those windows was eulogised by the antiquarian Robert W. Billings to the Architectural Institute of Scotland in 1853:

> There is a mistaken notion about Scottish buildings that their windows were small. . . . But are these the real features of our baronial architecture? They are certainly not of the architecture of from 1550–1660. Most of us know Crichton Castle. There the windows are enormous, and in fact, much larger than those we put in houses now.[71]

Nor do the grilles or yetts protecting doors and windows provide evidence of Scotland being more warlike than Germany or Italy, for comparable grilles in the windows of their Renaissance houses were normal.[72]

If almost no aspect of the Scottish château conforms to the requirements for defence, what, then, explains the perception that they are castles? Why should there be such a difference between our understanding of contemporary Scots and French or English houses? The Renaissance châteaux of the Loire are obviously gracious country houses, or hunting seats of the king, nobles and Court officials. Yet even though they share the same plan and are from the same architectural family, the many buildings of the same period in Scotland are classified as fortified structures (what the French call *châteaux forts*). The Loire region is acclaimed as the 'pays des châteaux' whereas Grampian boasts of being 'castle-country'[73] – 'pays des châteaux forts'.

Terminology matters, as was suggested in Chapter 1. Those looking at what is called a castle tend to find a castle. By the mid-eighteenth century, the language of the medieval castle had come to be used to explain the form of Scottish Renaissance country houses and their decoration.[74] Militaria is still embedded in the very title of most books about Scottish Renaissance country houses, and even modest examples have been interpreted in terms of defensive layout and gunloops, using terms like enfilade and artillery emplacement.

It is quite likely that sixteenth-century aristocrats would have been pleased at this misapprehension, for it was important for these houses to appear chivalric. In 1567 the Principal of Aberdeen University commended how 'Robert Arbuthnott, with great expense completed the work [at Arbuthnott], roofed over the same, and decorated the head thereof with eaves galleries and battlement *as is the form of castles* [my italics]'.[75] The belief persisted that a castle – or the nobility implied by a castle – had certain insignia. When Boswell took Johnson to visit diminutive Monboddo, he observed 'two turrets which mark an old baron's residence'.[76] By the seventeenth century, however, fashion was removing those battlements, and it caused a reaction. The continuing symbolic importance *looking like a castle* was emphasised in a 1632 letter from Sir Robert Kerr, a London courtier of a notably conservative family, to his son in Scotland when they were considering modernising the House of Ancrum beside Jedburgh:

> By any means, do not take away the battlement, as some gave me counsel to do, as Dalhousie your neighbour did, for that is the grace of the house, and makes it look like a castle, and hence so noblest, as the other would make it look like a peel.[77]

What Dalhousie – neighbour to Ancrum's other house of Newbattle – had done was to strip away the battlement, leaving some inconvenient corbels, and extend the roof out over the former parapet to provide space for additional rooms and sometimes galleries (*see* Fig. 3.11).[78] A similar view prevailed in France: 'Mais les signes militaires resteront longtemps . . . essential à la définition du château. Simplement, ils deviennent décor.'[79] A decorative resemblance to a castle equalled nobility, whereas a house

3.11 What 'Dalhousie your neighbour' did: Clerk of Eldin's etching of Dalhousie in the later eighteenth century shows that the tower's parapet has been removed (leaving some inconvenient corbels) and the roof extended over it. The ensemble is thoroughly domesticated. (Author's collection)

lacking a battlement signified a lesser status – exactly as implied by the maps of Timothy Pont. In the later Jacobean period, the time had come for the Scottish architectural language to find a means of conveying nobility and lineage without having recourse to battlements, crenellations, machicolations, bartizans and other Crusader-like militaria. The new symbolic devices comprised corbel courses, dormer windows, chimney-stacks, studies,[80] 'a cabinet for your books',[81] and viewing platforms. Old motifs were reworked in a new manner: open machicolations become closed corbels, gunloops become waterspouts decorated as cannon, crenellations become rising and falling corbel courses – all within an asymmetrical but balanced geometry – massing up to a climax upon the skyline. Truly it was *a castle of dreams*.

4

The Scottish Country Seat and its Setting

Every man's proper Mansion House and Home, being the theatre of his hospitality, the seat of his Selfe-fruition, the comfortablest part of his owne life, the Noblest of his sonnes inheritance, a kinde of Private Princedome; nay to the possessors thereof, an epitome of the whole world.

Sir Henry Wotton, 1624[1]

The Scottish country seat, standing high and proud above its yards, plantations and estate, represented the focus of local or regional power ('the chief castle of the sheriffdom' as legalese sometimes put it), the centre of the local economy, locus of justice, and the expression of its owner's standing and cultural ambition. The estate itself was the principal market and focus for skilled trades in those large districts of the country beyond easy reach of the burghs. Here came or congregated the masons, plasterers, painters, joiners, glassinwrights (glaziers), slaters and roofers, gardeners and nurserymen; and it was here you would find smiddies, foundries and kilns, and sawmills and carpenters' workshops. Together with adjacent fermtouns, kirktouns and cottouns, the country estate formed the principal community of rural Scotland, and its population varied from small to substantial. Its study is not just that of the expensive architectural extravagances of the rich, but of the focus of life for the majority of Scots. A middle-sized estate would extend to the 'lands, rents, possessions, tacks, steadings, store places, granges, woods, fishings, mills, multures, houses, mansions, biggings [buildings], males, fermes, and annual rents, corns, cattle, familiar servants, actors, factors, procurators and intromittors with their goods and sundry' that Isobel Henderson's charter listed when she was confirmed in possession of Calderwood on 27 January 1554/5, under Mary of Guise's (and thereby the queen's) *firm protection*.[2] Lesser estates, like the unexceptional House of Moy – the sort implied by Pont's reference to yeoman's houses – had a 'house, onset and biggings', with hall, two chambers, kitchen, stable, barn and other office houses, a barnyard, two great stacks of oats, a stack of wheat, and a great stack of barley.[3]

Most greater country seats would have been occupied only occasionally. With more than one estate, owners were accustomed to travel from house

to house at different times of year, according to the part each property played in their lives. The more distant their estate from Edinburgh, the more likely they were to have one or more lowland seats as well – and town houses as appropriate. So household movables spent much of their time in transit. 'Tapestry in my own chamber in Kincardine', instructed the Earl of Montrose, 'to be taken down, packed well, and moved to Mugdock.'[4] The heavy stuff that was left behind is indicated by a 1621 inventory for Barcaldine, Argyll: long tables, benches, the two standing beds in the chamber of dais, meat chest, iron hooks, doors, shutters, windows and locks.[5] Moving house was a tremendous exercise, and damage to furniture was inevitable. After seven years of transferring from Glamis to Castle Huntly for the summer months (as was the family custom), the first Countess of Strathmore informed her husband that 'nothing contributes soe much to the distraction and utter ruin of furniture as the transportation of it'. The better quality tapestries (or arras) deteriorated each time they were hung up or taken down, and required repeated mending.[6] The Strathmores consequently decided to remain in Castle Huntly until its refurbishment was complete.[7]

The number of inhabitants of a house varied according to rank. The household staff of Wemyss Castle (as distinct from the estate workers) exceeded forty people in 1654. David, 2nd Earl of Wemyss, maintained a chaplain, a lady and two gentlemen-in-waiting for his wife, two gentlemen to ride with him, porter and underporter, coachman and (possibly) under-coachman, a groom, falconer and man, corn grieve, officer, at least seven other males, three washers and perhaps seventeen other female servants.[8] Hugh Rose of Kilravock had but a chaplain, a solitary gentleman, butler, cook, cook's man, porter, coachman, two footmen, two gentlewomen, chambermaid, dairymaid and three byrewomen.[9] Nor did these people all live in the main house. To judge from the Earl of Strathmore's grudging agreement that 'such of the woman-servants as are of best account' might sleep in the attics of the main house with the children,[10] they would normally have slept elsewhere – perhaps above the woman house.[11]

One of the most important roles of the country seat was the 'theatre of hospitality', as indicated in an inscription above the entrance to the inner courtyard of the seat of the Stewarts of Rosyth:

> In due time, draw this cord the bell to clink,
> Whose merry voice [furnishes] meat and drink.[12]

Travellers of rank – or monarchs on their progresses sometimes accompanied by a full Court – stayed in convenient country seats. Seton, Tullibardine, Kincardine (seat of the Earls of Montrose), Alloa (Earls of Mar), Kinneil and Hamilton (Earls of Arran), Dalkeith (Earls of Morton) and Huntly (Earls of Huntly) could expect regular royal visits; and those in the central Lowlands, very frequent ones indeed. James VI had an annual pattern of summer hunting which took him from house to house.[13] Nor was it just the prospect of the Court's arrival that implied heavy duties of hospitality. A non-royal visitation could be equally taxing, since a nobleman's degree and status was partly defined by the number of

Opposite: *4.1 Pinkie inner court and fountain, drawn by Billings.* (Author's collection)

gentlemen who rode with him on attendance. Such relationships were sometimes underpinned by a bond of manrent,[14] like that of William Fairlie who bound himself to Lord Boyd and his heirs, 'truly to serve them upon their retinue and expenses in household and out of household'.[15] According to the family historian Hume of Godscroft, George Home of Wedderburn

> always went with a great number of attendants, kept a great family, about eighteen horsemen, each of whom had two horses. He was likewise attended by his vassals in Kimmerghame. . . . They were about twelve in number. . . . They seldom employed themselves in the country work. . . . They were always ready at command on every emergency to be led or sent where he pleased. . . . Thus he was always guarded with twenty or thirty horsemen.[16]

The Earl of Lennox required twelve gentlemen clad in velvet with chains upon their necks to ride on fair horses in front of him, and thirty who rode behind in grey livery coats.[17] James VI had to limit access to Stirling Castle while his son was being brought up there to 'every earl with four persons only, every lord with two persons, every baron with ane person, every gentleman and other person single'.[18]

Thus when Duncan Campbell of Glenorchy was undertaking some deft regional networking by inviting neighbours to stay in Balloch in

September 1590, his visitors were not just the lairds of Tullibardine, Inchbraikie and Abercairney, the Tutor of Duncrub, the Prior of Perth Charterhouse and the Bishop of Dunkeld, but also what the inventory called 'sundrie uther comers and goers'. If you include gentlemen and appropriate servants, the guests cannot have been fewer than thirty, and the amount they ate implies many more. When Campbell of Glenorchy married his second daughter to Robert Irvine of Fedderat in 1621, the wedding party included the lairds of Drum, Glenbervie, Banff, Pitfodels, Lathes, Inchmartine, Glenlyon, Keillar, Glenfalloch, Glenlyon, Comrie, Edinample and Lady Wemyss – 'with their haill company and boys'.[19] Staying-over guests must have well exceeded fifty.

The Scottish Court and by implication the Scots nobility were much less formal than the English, reflecting the monarch's status as *primus inter pares*. There was little standing upon ceremony (a matter which was to offend Charles I deeply).[20] When James Melvill was about to have his ears boxed (or worse) for the *lèse-majesté* of eavesdropping upon Elizabeth I of England playing on the virginal in her own chamber, he asked her to excuse 'my fault of homeliness, as being brought up in the court of France where such freedom was allowed'.[21] It was the same in Scotland. The practice of perpetually kneeling before the monarch did not commend itself. Conversely, Patrick Gordon of Ruthven held that it was the foreign stateliness emanating from England, disrupting old allegiances, that was a cause of the Troubles of the 1640s: 'For once that English divell, keeping of state, got a haunt among our nobilitie, then began they to keepe a distance, as if there were some divinitie in them.'[22]

Social patterns in the country house may have emulated those at Court. The monarch ate alone, unless he particularly invited somebody to dine with him – as James VI did his favourite the Duke of Lennox, whom he instructed to be placed at the end of his table, to be served of his kitchen and from his cupboard.[23] If Lennox's cupboard held pounds of Barbary dates, crystallised oranges, apricots, peaches and cherries, sweets of violet, rose and caraway, and roast and sugared almonds, what more might the king's have contained?[24] The king would be attended and kept amused by standing nobility, who would eat either afterwards or in a separate chamber. The rest of the household would dine separately again. There might be several kitchens feeding different parts of the household: and once food had been supplied to the principal table, the remainder would be passed down the ranks.[25] When Gilbert Blakhall entered Lady Aboyne's service in 1638 first as chaplain and then virtual chamberlain, he refused to eat at the common table, for the family no longer ate there. His contract stipulated that he ate in his own chamber where he would receive a minimum of four main dishes of meat, accompanied by ale and wine. The relicts (remains) were intended for his servant, but when the latter sold them on instead of eating them, Blakhall supped thereafter with the family.[26] From this separation of eating emerged a new chamber – the 'lettermeat' house or hall (or lottar chamber), a lower hall where the lesser echelons of the household would eat left-over food.

Guests had to be fed, entertained and provided with places to sleep, even if visiting pages and personal servants slept on little cots or truckle beds normally stored beneath the large beds. So guest wings or guest towers – or, perhaps, the conversion of the original tower to guest use once the laird had moved into his new lodging – became inevitable.[27] Guests were received in the inner court, the inner close or *cour d'honneur* (what the Scots, with typical disparagement, and mock-medieval modesty, called a 'barmkin'), which was lined by offices, guest lodgings, woman house and occasionally a chapel. The well was the dominant feature of the inner court, as at Ardmillan,[28] Dunrobin,[29] and the imperially crowned Pinkie[30] (albeit the glories of this august monument are sadly diminished lacking its court enclosure and the fact that it is domesticated by grass). The inner court was a place of arrival and departure, reception and hospitality.

The outer court (base court in England) represented the business side of the estate – the brewhouse(s), stables and farm building, yards, girnals (granaries), byres, hen houses, and estate buildings. General Tam Dalyell provided the House of the Binns with, in addition to its inner court, a foreyard, doocot yard and barnyard, and he distinguished between court stables and workhorse stables. The Earl of Strathmore – an altogether superior figure – maintained separate coach stables, riding stables and hunting stables.[31] 'Forentries' (gatehouses or porter's lodges) at the threshold of the inner court, varied enormously in grandeur, from the couthy entrance of Hills, Dumfriesshire, to the symmetrical towered *châtelet* (or miniature fort) forming the entrance to Tolquhon. For all its strutting, the latter provided only a ground-floor room for the porter, whereas Hills provided the porter with a miniature mansion. Both had the role of welcome.[32]

Most people building or refashioning their country seats had travelled, fought or studied abroad. Not to have continental European experience, it seems, was something of which to be ashamed. So highly was travel regarded as a sign of accomplishment and breeding that Hume of Godscroft felt obliged to over-egg the skills of his kinsman Home of Wedderburn – his knowledge of Latin and French, and his understanding of triangulation – to offset the inconvenient fact that he had never visited the continent.[33] Travellers, scholars, politicians and mercenaries returned to Scotland with ideas and, possibly, publications and engravings. The country was awash with current design information on symbols and motifs for interior painterwork,[34] and there is little reason to believe that there was not comparable information about contemporary architecture (*see* Appendix 1).

Most country seats inhabited the sites of their ancestors. Thick stone walls and vaults provided a reusable resource, and as long as inherited fabric could be adapted to new forms, it was. There was no needless waste. There was similar continuity of site in England,[35] but the extent to which English houses incorporated any older fabric has been little studied.[36] It was rarely otherwise in Scotland. Conversely, those few totally or almost totally new Renaissance country seats, such as the Palace of Boyne[37] or Craigston,[38] probably convey the clearest idea of Renaissance design intentions in Scotland since they were untrammelled by the necessities of retrofit.

Choice of site had largely been dictated by access to drinking water, to quarries of good building stone,[39] and to shelter, sun and fertility. 'Situate', as John Reid advised his readers in 1683, 'your House in a healthy Soyl, near to a fresh-spring, defended from the Impetuous-westwinds, northern colds and eastern blasts.'[40] A favoured location was part way up a slope,

almost invariably surrounded by copses and plantations, sufficiently low to avoid the wind, and sufficiently high to have a prospect. A good number of houses were located in delightful, sunny haughlands, Melville Castle, Midlothian, and Menzies, Perthshire, for example. Its setting suggests that Menzies could never have commanded the strategic route west from Loch Tay with any military effectiveness, for it was vulnerable to any enemy occupying its gardens immediately behind.[41] Moreover, Menzies provided no means by which its occupiers could have exercised that command militarily: no parapet, no wallwalk, and no position for armaments at the wall head. Command was, instead, a matter of presence and stature.

Certain aspects of house design remained consistently important. Architecture conveyed messages of rank, degree, lineage and nobility that were usually realised by exaggerating height, by choreographing the approach, and by the composition of the château's skyline. John Macky's reaction to Glamis in 1723 would have pleased the Earl of Strathmore:

The palace, as you approach it, strikes you with awe and admiration, by the many turrets and gilded ballustrades at the top. It stands in the middle of a well-planted park with avenues cut through every way to the house. The great avenue, thickly planted on each side, at the entrance of which there is a great stone gate, with offices on each side, of freestone, like a little town, leads you in half a mile to the outer court, which has a statue on each side . . . as big as the life. On

4.3 Glamis in the mid-eighteenth century. Note the baroque walls of the inner court. (Author's collection)

the great gate of the inner court are ballustrades of stone finely adorned with statues. . . . The house is the highest I ever saw.[42]

Although height and an emblazoned silhouette were central to the noble aspect of the country seat, the warlike skyline of crenellations was superseded in the sixteenth and seventeenth centuries by an equally impassioned creation of a fundamentally peaceable nature. Crenels and machicolations became decorative design motifs, joined by chimneys, dormer windows, turrets as gazebos, balconies and viewing platforms. The frequency with which tall chimney-stacks – chimneys that could so easily have been relocated by moving the fireplace to the north wall – rise proud above the principal entrance of the country house, implies that they had a symbolic role guarding the principal entrance. A signal of hospitality.

The château differed utterly from the medieval tower house in plan. The customary fifteenth-century house had usually been three and a half storeys tall above a vaulted ground floor of cellars and kitchens, squeezed into the geometric straitjacket of a square, rectangular or L-plan tower. A single main chamber per floor was surrounded by stairs, small bedchambers, garderobe, closet and occasional chapel hidden within the thickness of its wall. The principal chamber or hall lay on the first floor, family chambers on the floor above, and perhaps retainers and servants in the attic or roof space. (The principal apartments of their English equivalents would generally have been at ground level.) The European fondness for a raised *piano nobile* (principal or noble floor) may offer one reason for the difference between the two, but the nature of Scottish construction provides another. The possibility of damp rising up through thick walls of absorbent stone sitting on the ground provided sound technical justification for the cultural preference for placing the principal apartments above its reach.[43] The native structural material for most of Scotland was stone and, until the mid-eighteenth century the customary form of construction remained that of a stone vault with a maximum span rarely wider than 20 feet.[44] That implied both a vertical structure and a compact plan. Additional accom-modation could be provided by building a new module alongside; hence the

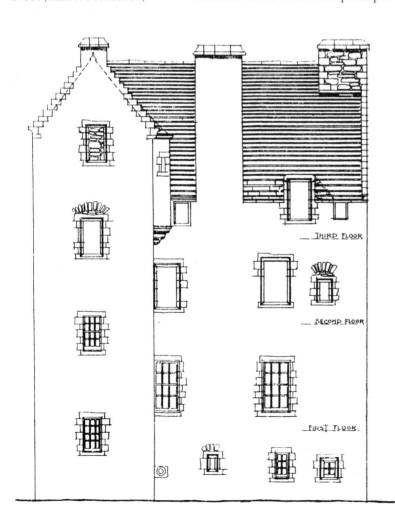

4.4 *The east elevation of the 'chimney of hospitality' at Park O' Luce, Wigtonshire, drawn for the National Art Survey. The preparation of such drawings under the direction of Robert Rowand Anderson began in the 1880s but the only three volumes to be published appeared between 1921 and 1933. (Author's collection)*

THIRD FLOOR

SECOND FLOOR

FIRST FLOOR.

Scots habit of architecture by accretion. Lacking long-span structural timber, Scotland imported it at great expense from the Baltic ('Estland burds' appear in the accounts)[45] or from the Scottish timber colony just south of Bergen in Norway.[46] It was used sparingly, hence the absence of the soaring roofs so characteristic of French Renaissance châteaux. However, the compressions and constrictions of the tower were incompatible with the changes in living patterns that occurred during the sixteenth century.

The principal change was the emergence of the 'state apartment'. The inspiration might have derived from the 1538–40 palace at Stirling, where both king and queen had parallel suites of Guard Hall, Presence Chamber and Bedchamber.[47] There was usually a sequence of three rooms on the principal floor in country houses, sometimes characterised as antechamber, chamber and bedchamber; or Hall, Chamber of Dais and Bedchamber. An identical apartment for the lady of the house

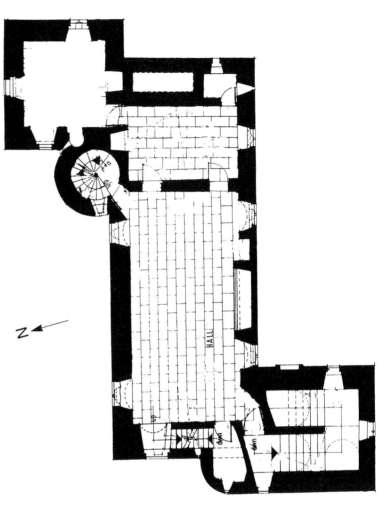

might lie on the floor above. So chambers were no longer stacked in a vertical sequence, but organised in a horizontal one. Liberated from the ordered rectangular rigidities of the tower, Scots designers gloried in their new architectural freedom. The controlled, opaque and austere appearance of the tower was replaced by a flamboyance in which each new accretion – stair, bedroom tower, study, turret, closet, chapel, laird's tower or great chamber – was corbelled onto the main body, its function identified and understood from outside.

Inside some of the larger houses, the hall began to change from its role as the social and communal focus of the great house to a gathering or waiting room, saved for ceremonial occasions, weddings, entertainment or concerts. Although its heraldic purpose remained undimmed, its use for communal meals, which had characterised it during the Middle Ages, may have waned during the sixteenth century. There are scant records of its decoration, although Cromarty's was, apparently, panelled in dark oak.[48] Probably plastered, painted and hung with arras, with wainscotting below, it would be furnished with long tables, benches, some weaponry and a large fireplace. Once halls were converted to upper dining-rooms, or reduced to lettermeat halls, their character became that of their new use. A description of the hall of Fedderate, Buchan, in 1689 oozes neglect. It contained just a principal and a side table, two old green tablecloths,

4.5 The piano nobile *plan of Hatton, Angus, as prepared by J.F. Stephen architects for reoccupation after centuries of ruin. The public stair opens out into a sequence of three rooms – hall, chamber of dais and bedchamber.* (Courtesy of Annie Anderson)

four forms (benches), two of which were fixed, a stool and only four chairs, a chest, wardrobe, two old candlesticks and a container of whisky whose age was not stated.[49]

The next in the sequence of privacy was the chamber of dais – a more private but still formal room, which sometimes contained the principal bed.[50] The term 'chamber of dais' implied throne and signified authority, and it was decorated more sumptuously than the hall. The last room of the state apartment was the bedchamber, where the laird would see only those of high privilege. They would have noticed that the king's gentlemen of the bedchamber (particularly James VI's) exercised even more power than the great state officers. This was so much the case that the Privy Council took steps to reduce 'the confusit nowmer of personis of all rankis quha hes entres in his Majesteis bed chalmer'.[51] The very public nature of the bedchamber is indicated by the number of its chairs (to say nothing of the tables, mirror, brass fire-irons, wall tapestries and the velvet-curtained bedstead of the Velvet Room of Abbotshall).[52]

There is sufficient consistency in planning and construction of these houses that a contract for a three-storey and attic, L-shaped riverside villa may stand for them all. The contract to build the House of Partick, at the junction of the Kelvin and the Clyde by Glasgow (now demolished), was concluded in January 1611 between the Kilwinning master mason William Millar and his client, George Hutcheson, Glasgow merchant and co-founder of Hutchesons' Hospital with his brother.[53] It was a 'very handsome house, well finished and adorned with curious orchyards and gardens, stately avenues and large enclosures, sheltered with a great deal of planting so that it has become one of the sweetest seats upon the River Clyde in this shire'.[54] Complementary contracts would have been required for timberwork (the wright), glasswork (the glassinwright), the plasterer and harler (the pargeoner), and the painter. The unit of measurement for the new house was determined as 'ye said George's awin fute'.

The main body of the building was the 'mayne hous' (in other places called the lodging – in French, *corps de logis*), with walls 3½ feet thick and rising 33 feet high from the ground to the wall head. Partick's main house contained the principal chambers, and was aligned to maximise sunlight, probably slightly north-east/south-west, with the jamb projecting to the north to protect the entrance from the south-westerlies. A 16 foot square wing, called the jamm (jamb), extended to the north-west, with a kitchen in its ground storey. A large circular

4.6 The Earl of Mar's 1628 summer villa of Braemar, drawn by Charles Tarrant in 1741: a house similar in scale to Partick, if rather taller. (NLS)

stairtower with stairs 10 feet wide (the turnpike) rose in the angle (or re-entrant) right up to a gabled wardrobe (sometimes called the cabinet) on the fourth floor. It was not dissimilar to the squatter but more romantic Barcaldine, completed by Sir Duncan Campbell of Glenorchy near Benderloch two years earlier,[55] or to the Earl of Mar's 1628 summer villa at Braemar.

Partick's entrance floor comprised kitchen and two vaulted cellars connected by a vaulted passage (transe).

4.7 The House of Partick, by Glasgow, already greatly ruined when drawn by J.C. Nattes, 1799. (NLS)

On the first floor of the main house lay the four-windowed hall, with a small horizontal window (a 'lying window') presumably above a dresser or some other display. A small pantry, probably screened to keep draughts from the hall, lay between it and the chamber of dais in the jamb. It had a private stair down to the eastmost (presumably wine) cellar. Screens were once common in Scotland, although Craigievar now has one of the few to survive. Fixings for one in the Governor's House in Blackness can be seen cut into the floor, and another is indicated in a drawing of Kinnaird.[56] The second floor of the main house of Partick was divided into two chambers, lit by dormer (storm) windows, with the 'high chamber' in the jamb above the chamber of dais. Thereafter, the turnpike stair carried on up to a fourth storey in the jamb only, the top room of which acted as a wardrobe, likewise lit by a dormer window. The smaller chambers of such wings normally had lower ceilings than the main house, providing four storeys within the same height as the main house's three to allow for the added scale of the hall. Most Renaissance houses, being planned with aesthetics in mind, were probably designed according to a proportional system. In most cases, that still remains to be discovered, although analyses have been undertaken of the Hall at Stirling and of Melgund. Craignethan's façade appears to have been composed to Fibonacci proportions. On a more mundane level, they were probably planned in standardised units – Partick, for example, to a module of 16 feet.[57]

What cannot be ascertained from the contract is the building's appearance, inside or out. It was built of rubble (fine or polished ashlar or 'aislar' would have been specified otherwise) with dressed stone around doors and windows. The rubble would have been coated with harl (a lime-based render) which gave the building a monolithic appearance and highlighted its dressed or carved stonework. By concealing the layers of masonry and the relieving arches above windows and doors, harling transformed the building's proportions from uneasily horizontal to strikingly vertical. Harling was either the colour of local sand, providing a colour-coded regional identity, or had a pigment added to it. (Blue was added to the external plaster of peasants' houses in Holland since they thought it would deter flies.) There is only scant evidence of tinted harling in Scotland,[58] although Sir Robert Sibbald noted approvingly that there was a good ochre mine in Whitehills, Fife.[59]

Harling falls off if unmaintained or unprotected from the rain, and much was stripped off between 1790 and 1850 by apostles of 'rubblemania'. The nineteenth-century fondness for materials 'as found' preferred the 'honesty' of rubble walls to the artificiality of harled ones, and began a still continuing dispute over the extent to which harling was customary.[60] Widespread evidence on the buildings themselves (particularly harling residue in the joints), supported by much visual record and plentiful documentary evidence, indicates that bare rubble was not intended to be seen. Even Edinburgh Castle was harled in the early seventeenth century (stunning to imagine it smooth and glowing brightly),[61] as were Earlshall, the rear three façades of George Heriot's Hospital, Drumlanrig and Pollok House.[62] The modern reharling done in vernacular mode, which highlights the contours of every stone, lacks the geometric precision with which the great houses were once finished.[63]

Decoration in the lower storeys would be restricted to the principal entrance, heraldic gunloop and armorial panel. The focus of the design lay four, five or six storeys upwards. The main body of the building was, in effect, a harled plinth, the purpose of which was to carry what lay above. In the north-east the fashion was to signal that transition by an elaborate, swelling corbelled string-course that wound up and down across the façade, retaining the motif of a machicolation. Turrets (contemporaries called them 'studies') were located on corners for compositional reasons (or for the view). The roofscape would be completed by dormer windows, brilliantly painted finials, sometimes iron weather cocks, and sometimes stone statues. So the silhouette of the Scottish 'castle-wise' country house[64] was formed from a number of vertical elements in collision with each other framed by crowstepped gables.

Rooms, stairs and window embrasures would generally have been plastered and painted, save possibly on the cellar floor – specifically excluded in the Invermay contract[65] – or where there was wainscotting or tapestry. The timber ceilings of the principal chambers would have been painted with motifs gleaned from recently published continental pattern books of emblematics by people like Vredeman de Vries,[66] sometimes political, classical or genealogical, and occasionally biblical, in theme. The full-size portrait of Dame Ely Forbes adorning the wall of Thornton, Kincardineshire, is a rarity in both its subject and its scale.[67] Likewise the mural found beneath later wainscotting in the hall of the house of the Carnegies of Pitarrow in Angus, of

> the city of Rome, and a grand procession going to St Peter's. The Pope, adorned with the tiara, in his full robes of state, and mounted on a horse or mule, led by some person of distinction, was attended by a large company of cardinals, all richly dressed, and all uncovered. At a little distance, near to where the procession was to pass, and nearly in front of it, stood a white palfrey, richly caparisoned. . . . Beyond this was the magnificent cathedral of St Peter.[68]

Overtly religious painting like this appears to have been the exception. None the less, painted decoration was of such significance that it could help identify the chamber. Although rooms might be characterised by their occupant (Lady Chisolme's Chamber) or by their predominant material (Abbotshall's Velvet and Mohair Rooms,[69] or Glamis' Suede Room), they were sometimes known by their painted decoration (Crathes' Nine Muses Room). Most frequently, identification was by colour coding. The principal furnishings of the chamber above the laigh (low) hall at Craigbarnet were all green, for example, whereas those in the chamber above the new kitchen were all blue.[70] Plaster ceilings became customary in the seventeenth century, and extensive wainscotting or full-height panelling brought further comfort (perhaps what was meant when a room was referred to as 'lined').[71] Carpets and 'door curtains' kept out draughts.[72] Once lined with panelling and adorned with cornice, ceiling and overmantle, these rooms proved comfortable, cosy and surprisingly well-lit.

How might a medium-sized villa like Partick have been furnished? Its equivalent two generations earlier was very comfortably fitted out. Kelly Castle, Angus, now a single tall tower with an abbreviated extension and an inner court of lower buildings with circular towers on two corners,

4.8 The 1590s ceiling from Delgatie, Buchan, is an excellent surviving example of what was probably once common. (RCAHMS)

Clockwise from top left: 4.9 *Cabinet once in Linlithgow, drawn for the National Art Survey, which began in the 1880s.* (Author's collection)

4.10 *Bed from Darnick Tower, by Melrose, drawn for the National Art Survey.* (Author's collection)

4.11 *Chair, drawn for the National Art Survey.* (Author's collection)

4.12 *Panels from Baltersan, Ayrshire, drawn for the National Art Survey.* (Author's collection)

was occupied by Cardinal David Beaton's daughter Agnes who had married James Ochterlony of Kelly.[73] A 1562 inventory of her belongings lists hall (sandwiched between kitchens and cellars below and high chamber above), long chamber, gallery chamber, Hollow Chamber (?) under the hall, and the 'new chamber of Kellie'.[74] There were twenty feather beds, some with flowered bedcovers, and the house was awash with napery – Scottish or linen curtains, blankets, tablecloths, and almost ninety table napkins (some embroidered in silk). Most of Agnes's cushions appear to have been in her other house of Balmedie. Kitchens and cellars had their customary brass pots, copper and brass kettles, brewing vats, spits and trenchers, five cheese presses and quantities of pewter plates, beef tubs, fish tubs and brass candlesticks. In one cellar, she also had stored two pavilions or tents, presumably against travel. All rooms except the hall contained beds, and to judge from the oak bedstead, the oak-doored cupboard and the night stool, Agnes's own chamber was probably the 'new chamber of Kelly'. Forty years on, a similar-sized house was much the same. The House of the Byres had a gallery chamber, two beds in the chamber of dais (like Barcaldine), and a hall with long oak tables and benches. Where it differed was in the possession of a gallery (full of tables and buffet stools), a little hall and an enormous wardrobe in a room at the head of the stairs containing cushions, napery, stools, bolsters etc.[75] To judge by the Campbells of Glenorchy, those cushions would be richly embroidered with their owners' monograms.

The House of Partick was a simple villa. More elaborate establishments might have had timber balconies (also called galleries) on which to take the air and enjoy the view. Sometimes they were added (Carsluith and Preston) and sometimes they formed an original feature of the design (Drochil). Craigmillar had two, one looking south over orchard and fish stank, and the other east to North Berwick Law. Those of Dunblane's Bishop's Palace[76] and of Melgund gazed south over their respective rivers, and Girnigo's once looked proudly out over the North Sea.[77] We have underestimated the importance to Renaissance sensibilities of nature and of the view. In an early seventeenth-century description of Roslin, David Buchanan waxed enthusiastic about its 'most agreeable situation on the summit of a steep rock and rejoices in the amenity of a river gently gliding by, and in the pleasant prospect of woods growing all around[78] – sentiments normally associated with the late eighteenth century. Just how significant enjoyment of the view had become is reinforced by the gallery's popularity. Normally, galleries projected from the main house at first-floor level. Judging from inventories, their furnishings were spartan.[79] A significant minority of galleries were 'skied' – that is they were contained within the very apex of the roof space, lit by impressive dormer windows, sometimes provided with balconies themselves like that at Claypotts.

The apogee of this fashion for taking the view was achieved with the viewing platform. Early examples were usually at the top of the entrance tower – the one with the public stair in the ground storey. Adorned with the finest detail – balustrades, finials, parapets, and carvings – the viewing platform was the climax of the design. From between five and seven

4.13 Chairs from Stirling, drawn for the National Art Survey. (Author's collection)

storeys up, a laird and his guests could gaze down upon the yards, plantations and agricultural improvements. Craigievar has two platforms. This preoccupation with the view also expressed itself in the alignment of house and gardens upon some distant object. Although the two best-known are Sir William Bruce's houses – Balcaskie focused upon the Bass Rock, and Kinross upon Loch Leven Castle – a thorough analysis of earlier Renaissance houses is likely to discover others.

English or continental European country houses of the period would almost certainly have contained a large chapel, if not church, sometimes in the inner court, and sometimes integral with the main house itself. Since collegiate churches and chapels were built near to, but not as part of, the country seat, it is rare to find chapels integrated into the inner court in Scotland. The south-east tower at Craignethan, which was almost certainly one,[80] and the seventeenth-century extension to Glamis, containing the impressively panelled chapel painted by Jacob de Wet, were unusual.

A desire for privacy impelled larger houses to separate into different domains toward the end of the sixteenth century. The public domain was becoming differentiated from both the family or private domain, and the guest domain (in a foretaste of how the larger nineteenth-century country house would develop in the hands of William Burn and David Bryce). The key to understanding the change lies in the staircases. Fyvie, Kinneil, Maclellan's Lodging, Kirkudbright, Braemar and Glamis contain some of the few noble staircases that may be compared to the French *escalier d'honneur* running from top to bottom of the building.[81] The entrance to the stairtower became the favoured location for an elaborate armorial frontispiece. However, spacious public staircases with shallow treads usually led only to the public domain on the first floor. If you had leave, other, private stairs, corbelled out from the wall-plane, took you further up: guests' quarters at one (probably the entrance) end, family and household above the main house, and the laird's business room, muniments room, study or closet at the far end. From the 1580s, the circular stair was beginning to be displaced by stairs of straight flights (scale) and landings (platt), and staircases and passages came to contain wardrobes, chests of drawers, napery presses and, in some cases, paintings.

The heights of Elcho contain several tiny, well-lit, well-warmed chambers with excellent views. Sometimes called studies, they might also have been the cabinet for books, or library[82] – which might explain the evident preference for high-level or 'skied' libraries in seventeenth-century Scots houses, Traquair being a noble example. The central high rooms in both the House of the Binns and the House of Dun were also likely to have been libraries; and the amazing fifth-storey octagonal chamber at the apex of the seventeenth-century tower at Foulis most dramatically combines books with a view.

Rooms for washing, or bathrooms, are never identified. Yet there was a bath-house in the south-west corner of the great garden at Edzell, and a rooftop cistern collecting water for unspecified but probably similar purposes at Craigston. A third-floor room with a water-collecting point and drainage holes survives at Glenbuchat,[83] and more probably remain to be identified. Closets have suffered in our perception as a consequence of the later expropriation of the word for lavatories. There would scarcely be a chamber of importance in an apartment of importance that did not have a closet opening from it by the mid-seventeenth century. This was a small and most personal room. It was in her closet that Mary Queen of Scots was dining with the Countess of Argyll and David Riccio when the supper was rudely interrupted by a band of aristocratic murderers who reached it via the private royal staircase. There would be many closets in a large house, and later seventeenth-century mansions sprouted veritable towers of them. Their purpose can be inferred from the 1684 contents of the Countess of Strathmore's closet which opened from her bedchamber: a large Japan chest with a stamped leather cover, four large oval pictures, twelve small pictures, a mirror with a Japan frame, a table with a flowered calico cover, a tortoiseshell strong-box with gilt mounting, and three Dutch chairs.[84] A closet in early eighteenth-century Lochryan was stuffed with fifty-eight old pistols 'many of them wanting locks'; another (perhaps the lady's?) had a tortoiseshell table, two glasses (mirrors), two candlestick holders and a picture. The important one held books, a cabinet and the charter chest – as well as a close-stool (commode).[85] The re-creation of the closet in Argyll's Lodging, Stirling, by Historic Scotland conveys a good impression of the affluent privacy of such rooms.

The principal outdoor room was the private or privy garden (what the French call the *jardin clos*) and its related walled enclosures or yards. The gardens serviced and provisioned the house, and provided passive defence; but they were also showpieces of improvement to be admired once visitors had been hauled up to the viewing platforms. The conceit behind some of the parterre patterns could quite probably only have been appreciated from such loftiness. The garden was a place of great quality, of pleasure to the senses, of symbolism and, sometimes, of a demonstration of the sciences. At its finest, it represented paradise. Most frequently, the garden's function was that of a *Jardin de Plaisir* (the title of a book in Mary Queen of Scots' library).[86] Beyond the necessary function of providing food, vegetables, fruit and herbs, gardens were also used for open-air games like bowls, archery and golf,[87] walking, cosmology, display, the pleasures of love – and for political plotting.[88] With their arbours and private walks, walled gardens offered considerably greater opportunities for privacy than rooms within the house. When the Marquess of Huntly and his kin conspired with the Catholic Father Gilbert Blakhall for the escape of Huntly's niece from Scotland during the Troubles in 1640, they plotted in the garden.[89] Their privacy was ensured by high walls, which formed an enclosure to the parterres, statues and other ornamentation – as may be seen, for example, in Slezer's view of the House of Bog (*see* p. 215).[90]

There were also summer houses, apple houses, banqueting rooms, lodges, sundials and gatepiers.[91] At Glamis, the earl delineated between garden and bowling green by a wall with a 'refreshful' room at the centre, with panelled walls, plaster ceiling and a black and white patterned stone floor.[92] Any hint of a slope was seized for terraces, each level having a different purpose. The narrow flatness of the one nearest to the house implies a bowling green, although it might also have contained a fountain.[93] The corners of the upper terrace were sometimes adorned with small two-storeyed pavilions, latterly

4.14 *The recreated Renaissance garden at Drummond Castle, Perthshire.* (Buxbaum/RIAS Collection)

ogee-roofed like those in the Great Garden at Pitmedden. A pavilion's upper storey, entered from the upper terrace, acted as a summer house, gazebo or parlour offering a good view or 'a small visee to each airth'.[94] The lower, entered from the lower garden, was a gardener's shed or apple house.[95] So far as can be judged, sundials tended to be in the lower garden.

Renaissance gardens formed an important part of overall design, and the type would vary considerably according to site. Many Borders towers – Neidpath, Elibank, Torwoodlee and Hangingshaws, for example – had courtyard gardens in the sixteenth century.[96] The 'jardin clos' at Seton was probably a terrace sandwiched between the palace and the parapet lining the ravine. Few appeared to have the expanse of territory given to the extraordinary gardens of, for example, Gaillon or Bury in France. The head gardener was a man of standing. In 1536, Hugh Rose of Kilravock contracted with Thom Daveson and his man to work and labour his yards, gardens, orchards, avenues, hedgings, fishponds 'and all works perteyning to ane gardener to do, of the best fassoun may be devisit'.[97] In 1536, James V had a French gardener with three assistants busy on the gardens of Holyrood.[98] There are many records of the extent and sometimes of the exotic nature of what was grown in Scottish gardens: many types of apples, cherries and pears, but also peaches and apricots. Dunrobin, for example, was commended in the late seventeenth century both for its commodious situation and 'its gardens and orchards, its varied flowers and thickly planted trees, its excellent crocus, its deep fountain constructed of dressed stone, and its park extending three miles in length and capitally stocked with conies [rabbits]'.[99] A contemporary added that the Dunrobin gardens enjoyed an abundance of excellent fruit, saffron, rosemary – and even tobacco.[100] Even that allegedly savage and wicked Muscovite, Tam Dalyell of the Binns, had two gardening books in his 'bibliotheque'.[101]

The cosmological nature of gardens in Scotland was emphasised by this country's particular fondness for tall, freestanding sundials. These expensively worked ashlar monuments were greatly prized and sometimes moved with the family. In 1712, for example, a new sundial was commissioned for Taymouth at the extraordinary cost of £248, and the condition was that it had to contain '130 dialls or more'.[102] Sundials were the focus of carefully prepared garden plans and probably carried a symbolic meaning largely obscure to us.[103] The most distinctive take the form of an obelisk of ornate cubes piled one upon another: a stack of four or five below supporting a 24-faced dodecahedron centrepiece that resembles a Rubik cube, with five to seven tapering cubes on top. Projecting gnomons are usually on the centrepiece, whereas the other faces are incised with an immense variety of shapes – circles, crescents, hearts, sunbursts – that present as much decoding difficulty as Pictish stones. A simpler plinth or column put commensurately greater emphasis upon the sundial itself, which sometimes took the form of a globe, a faceted globe or a lectern. The plinth of one at Glamis is supported by four lions, each clutching a vertical sundial in its paws. A 24-faced stone sits on the plinth, each face with three or four faceted sundials. An earl's coronet rises upon volutes above. There is an evident preoccupation with the passage of time, and sundials, *and their settings*, were, perhaps, the physical expression of a country fascinated by mathematics, the calendar, the masonic tradition and ancient mythology.

Most Scottish Renaissance gardens exist only in archaeology or in record, making the Great Garden at Edzell a rare survivor. It was completed in about 1604 by Sir David Lindsay. The design of the shot-holes in the summer house and its heavily ornate groined vault imply both an Aberdeenshire influence and the hand of Thomas Leiper working during the previous decade.[104] Lindsay's grandfather had extended north from his tower to form a spacious court in 1553, so the garden was the culmination of a building programme begun some seventy years earlier.[105] His ambition was signified in placing a summer house and a bath-house at the two southern corners of the garden. Ochterlony of Guynd, writing in the later seventeenth century, praised the

> delicat gardine with walls sumptuously built of hewen stone polisht, with pictures and coats of armes in the walls, with a fyne summer house with a hous for a bath on the south corners thereof far exceeding any new work of thir times. Excellent Kitchine gardine and orcheard with diverse kynds of most excellent fruits and most delicat. . . . It is an extraordinaire warme and ear place so that the fruits will be readie there a fourthnight sooner than in any place of the shyre.[106]

4.15 Obelisk sundial at the House of Tongue, Sutherland. (Author)

4.16 Curious face in the lectern sundial at Newliston, West Lothian. (Author)

4.17 Edzell summer house, drawn by Billings. The carefully drawn rubble would once have been harled, and each bay was framed by clasped columns. (Author's collection)

Although Edzell was in straitened circumstances when Lindsay died in 1511, there is no evidence that his penury had been caused by the expense of his new garden. Rather, it was the consequence of fines imposed by the Court for the feuding and other misdemeanors of his eldest.[107] The current planting at Edzell is a twentieth-century representation of what might once have been there, but the walls are original. Although the bath-house has vanished, the two-storeyed summer or banqueting house remains entire in its lustrous red polished ashlar. The composition of the walls is obscured by the lack of harling to cover the rubble, and of the columns that framed the bays into which the gardens were divided. Tall columns grasped by a faceted clasp around the midriff were each probably once capped by a statue. Round-headed niches that penetrate above the parapet appear designed to carry busts. The south wall is divided into ten bays of different widths, each capped by a niche. The horizontally proportioned bays are focused upon a fess-chequy – three layers of recessed, square ashlar-lined holes in a rectangular chequer pattern of solid and void currently filled with flowers echoing the Lindsay colours. It is surmounted by three seven-pointed stars. The alternating bays are almost square, and contain huge oval cartouches like vesicae, of a greyer and more hardwearing stone. These panels are carved with the Deities, the Cardinal Virtues and the Liberal Arts – large and vivid representations of those exemplars of which the Renaissance was so fond, the source of their design being plates engraved in 1528–9 by Georg Pencz,[108] a pupil of Albrecht Dürer. Although the garden at Edzell is now unique, it may not have been then. It can symbolise the extent to which Scottish country landowners were as much absorbed by ideas of antiquity, of culture and of symbolism during the Renaissance as they were with defence or changes in religion.

So although Scottish country houses varied according to when they were built, and to the rank of their builder during the sixteenth and seventeenth centuries, there was broad consistency about their location, and about their evolution from a communal to a more private living pattern. Reviewing such houses without the constraining perspective of considering them primarily defensive makes it easier to discern the substantial changes that took place between the reigns of James IV and Charles II.

5

The Early Renaissance and the Changing Tower House, c. 1500–c. 1542

And now the king, having heirs to succeed him, and by that means becoming more confident of a settled establishment . . . applied his mind to unnecessary buildings.

George Buchanan[1]

In 1507, John Damian, Abbot of Tongland (a man of curious imagination according to Bishop Lesley), attempted to fly from Stirling Castle with feather wings which he had devised, apparently with the purpose of reaching France.[2] Given that there is no real height to the north, east and south of the castle rock, one must surmise that to obtain the best uplift for his long journey, he flew off the west side. To the great merriment of onlookers and the repeated scorn of the poet William Dunbar, the abbot landed in a midden and broke his thigh bone. The story well suited subsequent Protestant historians seeking opportunities to expose the deviousness of the clerics of the previous dispensation, and the gullibility of their audience. It was yet another tale to be used to illuminate how Scotland's Renaissance was, in contrast with the rest of Europe, a provincial, misunderstood and bumbling affair.

All, however, was not what it seemed. Appointed to the abbacy of Tongland by James IV, Damian was an alchemist and inventor, enjoying a royal research grant and research laboratory in Stirling Castle. 'He caused the king to believe that he, by multiplying and otherwise his inventions, would make fine gold of other metal, which science he called the quintessence.'[3] Dunbar's ire may have been prompted by the fact that, despite his continuous lobbying of the king, he had never received the clerical preferment this charlatan received (although Dunbar's pensions were adequate enough).[4] Having such people at Court was virtually *de rigueur* in the Renaissance, and Damien was neither the sole alchemist, nor indeed sole inventor there. Invention was welcome at the Courts of

5.1 Stirling Castle and Palace, approximately from the south, drawn in the seventeenth century by Slezer. Note James IV's four-towered forework, the Great Hall lying behind to the right, and the palace lying to the west (left). (Author's collection)

James IV, his son and his great-grandson. In 1540, a nobleman – a soldier and diplomat who demonstrated an acute appreciation of firearms – came to lose his life allegedly because one of his inventions had misfired.[5] Knock-makers (clock-makers) along with armourers were traditionally those most likely to be inventing; and they were as likely to come from Europe as from Scotland.

None the less, did Damian's early exploit deserve its reputation for absurdity? Anyone looking over the west parapet of Stirling Castle by, say, the Lady's Hole, would realise that someone tumbling down the rock at that point would end up very dead. Moreover, the royal gardens lay at its foot and, although the exact processional route between castle and gardens remains unclear, this was no place for a midden. An early eighteenth-century plan of the town, on the other hand, indicates the nearest midden half a mile away behind the current Smith Art Gallery – well away from the King's Knot. If that was the one in which Damian landed, there is but one conclusion: *the wings worked* (at least to some extent) and Damian had just made a bad landing. That he was not a buffoon is implied by his other task: to investigate gold in the hills and moors by Crawford; and another 'highly skilled alchemist' – Gunther von Lechnichz from Denmark – was appointed in 1525 with approximately the same brief.[6]

The wings worked and there was indeed a Renaissance in Scotland, as recent studies of the culture of the country during the sixteenth century

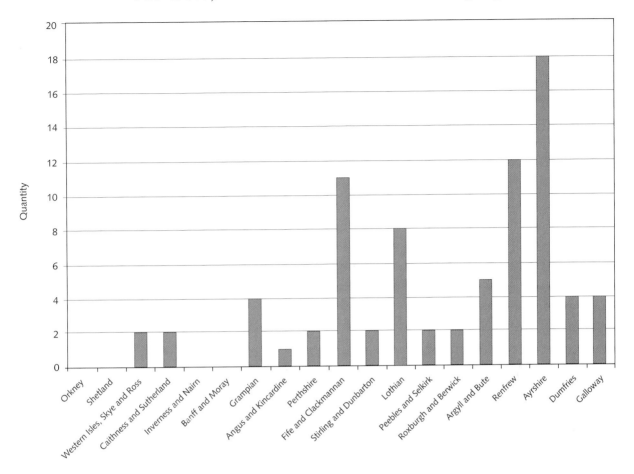

Graph 4 Chateau construction, 1500–42.

have identified.[7] However, music, literature and the fine arts have so far claimed most attention, with considerations of architecture largely restricted to royal buildings. Establishing precise and reliable dates for the construction of country houses during the early years of the century is more difficult because of the absence of records. However, there is some reason to believe that the first decades of the sixteenth century witnessed something of a building boom.[8]

James IV's marriage to Henry VII's daughter implied that some cultural influence from England might have travelled north with her. Yet Scotland's strong ties with Europe were in no way loosened. The Book of Hours the king gave his English wife had been prepared in Bruges, and the Keeper of Linlithgow in his father's time had been the well-travelled Anselme Adorne, who had visited the Pope in Rome and founded the Jerusalem Kirk in Brüges.[9] The towered and crenellated east façade of Linlithgow palace may well have been inspired by the latest fashions from Rome,[10] whereas the courtyard façade of the south wing, as a consequence of Margaret Tudor's arrival, drew on influences from England. The new large-windowed west wing to Holyrood Palace, with its alternating full-height oriel windows and circular heavily glazed towers, resembled English royal palaces, and seemed to presage by twenty to thirty years the designs by Henry VIII for the Palace of Whitehall's river façade which was prepared in the 1540s. Three-storey, largely glazed oriel windows gazing east down over the capital also graced the principal façade of the palace at

5.2 The palace at Edinburgh Castle with a conjectural restoration of its early sixteenth-century oriel windows. Davy's Tower lies to the right. (Author)

Edinburgh Castle: three delicate, semi-octagonal ashlar-glazed projections that commanded the city. Apart from offering splendid views, their primary purpose was display, shimmering in the morning light and providing a vertical rhythm to the palace.

A building of comparable glittering splendour was added to the royal palace at Dunfermline, although a surviving stone carving implies that it might have dated from the following reign. The only record is a Slezer drawing of Dunfermline Abbey, looking from the west. Generally disregarded as a reworking of the west flank of the cloistral range,[11] this two-storeyed building of huge windows (albeit not oriels), framed by buttresses or columns, and punctuated in the centre by what looks like a large well-windowed circular stairtower, was particularly stylish.

Continental influence was apparent in the heraldic entrance or forework facing downhill over the town which James IV added to Stirling Castle. It was appropriately chivalric for a king obsessed with the caparisons of nobility:[12] a four-round-towered centrepiece with tall rectangular towers terminating each end. A round-towered gatehouse of that type was European, and its slender proportions seemed French, calling to mind Carcassone, Fougères, Pierrefonds or Langeais. Yet the way the gateway at the centre is flanked by pedestrian entrances also echoes the form of a Roman triumphal arch.[13] The king's obsession with martial nobility (his death at Flodden in 1513 could be classified as the ultimate chivalric act) was expressed through tournaments – particularly those of 1507 and 1508, the first time that the 'Chevalier Blanc', Antoine d'Arces, Sieur de la Bastie, Knight of the Order of the Golden Fleece[14] (probably Europe's noblest chivalric order) visited the country. De la Bastie was to return in October 1513 as Lieutenant of the French, to help defend the country in its post-Flodden fear of an English invasion, pending the arrival of a new regent.[15]

Following James IV's death at Flodden in autumn 1513, English influence faded for Margaret Tudor, the Queen Dowager, lost her pre-eminence by making an ill-advised marriage to a faction leader – the handsome 'young, witless fool' (in his uncle's words), the Earl of Angus. One never knew, of course, what was happening down on the frontier. Landowners in the Borders and the Merse were those most at risk from periodic English invasions – the ones organised regularly by Sir Thomas Dacre who boasted to Henry VIII how he regarded himself as the 'fiddling stick to keep Scotland in cumber and business' to keep the Scots on edge.[16] Woe betide a Border farmer with his crops ripening, the weather improving and a harvest moon in prospect, for that was when the English preferred to invade. So it can be little surprise that some of the greatest families of the Borders – the Douglases and the Humes in particular – were ambiguous in their loyalties, often seeking escape and asylum in England and, perhaps, picking up ideas when they were there. Little survives one way or another to prove whether they had been influenced by English architecture – save, perhaps, an English-seeming manor house immured within the castle of Hermitage, and Hutton Castle, the extraordinarily English-looking former home of Sir William Burrell.

The regency passed from Margaret Tudor to a French-educated Scot, Jehann Stuart duc d'Albanie (as he signed himself), technically heir to the throne. Although a Stewart, the Regent Albany considered himself a Frenchman. A restless, fiery-tempered man much given to casting his hat in the fire when in a rage, he had made a fine dynastic marriage to his cousin Anne de la Tour d'Auvergne and had become the last Duke of Auvergne by virtue of it. A considerable adornment to the French Court and a prodigious builder, he was appointed regent of Scotland in 1514 and remained in office (if only rarely in Scotland) for the next ten years. He was also widely but improbably rumoured to have struck up a liaison with the dowager Queen Margaret: improbable because Anne was much wealthier than Margaret Tudor (if you believe the latter's complaints to her brother Henry). For that reason alone – never mind Margaret Tudor's temper and Albany's loyalty to France – he was unlikely to quit his wife. Scotland was a responsibility that he assumed between duties as a leader of the French army, ambassador, manager of considerable estates and architectural patron. In 1524, for example, he began the construction of Sainte Chapelle de Vic-le Comte, Puy de Dôme, with a notable programme of Renaissance stained glass.[17] Perhaps he had added those tall oriel windows to Edinburgh Castle in 1516–17;[18] he certainly refortified his castle of Dunbar and garrisoned it with his own people. His taste might be inferred from the troupe of Italian musicians who enlivened his Court.

An efficient soldier, he was capable of moving armies and their baggage train and brass guns wherever need demanded, to enforce order among the somewhat anarchic Scots nobility. His letters imply that he regarded himself not so much as a guardian of the young king, nor even as a contender for the throne, but more as a regent acting on behalf of the king of France. Once the Scots also began to regard him in that light, his days as regent were numbered.

Albany was probably responsible for a heightened French influence entering the country. For, in June 1517, he obtained permission to take a short break in France and was accompanied by heirs of the principal Scots nobility as hostage for their parents' good behaviour.[19] They landed first at Rouen, where Albany concluded the Treaty of Rouen with the French. Thereafter, they passed to the French Court, first at Blois, and thereafter at Amboise, until Albany left the following April to attend the wedding of Lorenzo the Magnificent in Florence.

At that time central France was perhaps one of the most extensive Renaissance building sites in Europe. Josselin was barely twelve years finished; Meillant, Châteaudun, Chenonceau, Blois, Amboise, Azay, St Ouen, Oiron and Romorantin were all under planning or construction; and the Château de Gaillon, the magnificent 1511 palace of Cardinal Georges d'Amboise, Archbishop of Rouen, had only recently been occupied. Both Albany and (later) King James V stayed in Rouen, probably in Gaillon, and it may be no coincidence that the spiralling carved columns of Gaillon are the examples that most resemble those on the façade of the palace at Stirling. Of particular significance for Scotland may have been the custom of François 1er, when at Amboise, to take his guests to meet his pet inventor, the elderly Leonardo da Vinci, in his house at Close Luce barely yards from the walls of the château,[20] for it seems likely that the Scots hostages enjoyed this experience (*see* p. 92).

We can only be sure, at the moment, about the identity of two of the hostages with Albany. One was John, Lord Gordon, heir to the Earl of Huntly, who stayed on in France for several years.[21] The identity of another hostage is revealed by his summons back to Scotland in 1517 to be briefed about what to tell the French king regarding the murder of de la Bastie near Dunbar. Albany had left de la Bastie behind as Warden of the East March, only for him to be decapitated by a consequently disaffected Borderer, Home of Wedderburn.[22] The hostage who had to shuttle diplomatically between Scotland and France was Sir James Hamilton of Finnart (*c.* 1495–1540), the Earl of Arran's eldest (but bastard) son, who was to display an unwonted interest in, and capability for, construction and design which was much remarked upon by his contemporaries.[23]

Born in about 1495, Finnart was great-grandson of a king, and third cousin of King James V. On 20 January 1513, his father, the 1st Earl of Arran, despairing of a legitimate heir, had had him legitimised, made 'heir of tailzie' and knighted 'of Finnart'.[24] Had he not been a bastard, he would have been heir to the throne on his father's death. He was brother-in-law to Lord Somervill, half-brother of the Abbot of Paisley, nephew of the Earl of Hume, cousin to the Earl of Lennox, stepbrother-in-law to the Earls of Argyll and Glencairn, father-in-law to the Earl of Rothes, and

5.3 The axially placed miniature gatehouses Finnart created for the ceremonial southern approach to the Palace of Linlithgow. (Author)

cousin by marriage to both Archbishop James Beaton, and to Cardinal David Beaton. If he was indeed an architect, as shall be seen, he had been born with an unusually fortunate client base.

Finnart's father begat a legitimate child so late in life that when he died at Kinneil in March 1529, his heir, also James, was barely eleven years old.[25] His half-brother, Finnart – 'the bastard of Arran' as he was known – became tutor of Arran (*de facto* acting earl of Arran) until his brother came of age in 1539. He established a personal rapport with the king that was to last for almost all of James V's personal rule, and was lavishly rewarded.[26] The degree of royal affection extended beyond the customary descriptions of 'lovit familiar' or 'familiar servant', for in 1531 the king, considering Finnart to be 'well deserving of regal munificence', permitted him to amend his arms to remove the mark of illegitimacy, and to add the coveted royal escutcheon or double tressure with lilies.[27] It was a signal honour. This close relationship with the king was maintained: Finnart lent him money to play at cards, contributed gold toward the repair of the royal crown[28] and, perhaps most significantly, became embroiled in the king's romantic life.[29] In the late 1530s, he may also have been the judge in a proposed anti-heresy campaign.[30] The last may have proved his undoing. He was accused, in what seems uncannily like a Reformers' ambush, of plotting against the king by firing missiles from a weapon of his own invention from the campanile at Linlithgow, and was summarily executed on 16 August 1540.[31] Contemporary chroniclers were greatly taken aback at his sudden downfall.[32]

It is not easy to distinguish the architecture of the early sixteenth century before James V finally escaped from the effective captivity of the Earl of Angus in 1528[33] and began his personal rule. The probability is that the majority of new houses took the form of a variant of the tower house. The Earls of Lennox had constructed themselves a 'magnificent palace' at Inchinnan in 1506[34] but we know no more. The tower of Saddell, Kintyre, thought to date from when the abbey was suppressed in 1508, appears to be a typical tower house of four striking, tall, harled storeys capped by a parapet and wallwalk and enfolded by a low, walled inner close. But it is longer than customary for a tower house, and its principal floor is split by a cross-wall dividing hall and kitchen. This hitherto rare plan had appeared in the royal hunting seat of Newark, Selkirk, a generation earlier.[35] That it was already customary for the élite to occupy different houses for different purposes is implied by the grant to the Abbot of Melrose of the 'use of the country place of Mauchlin',[36] presumably at times when Dacre's English fiddling stick was rubbing too hard against his abbey down on the frontier.

Considerable effort was being expended upon adding new lodgings to the court of existing seats. Hugh, Lord Somervill's refashioning of Couthally, Lanarkshire began in 1524 with a new main house, followed by some service buildings, a gallery and a study tower (*see* Chapter 9). Some years earlier, his ally Finnart undertook something similar at nearby Cambusnethan, the forfeited seat of Somervill's brother, the recidivist John 'Red Bag' Somervill, which Finnart was granted in 1522. Red Bag had taken the part of the Earl of Angus against the Hamiltons in the dynastic feud between the Hamiltons (Arran) and the Douglases (Angus), particularly the notorious street brawl known as 'Cleanse the Causeway' which took place during Albany's absence in Edinburgh on 20 April 1520. The Earl of Arran, as regent, had summoned a parliament and the Earl of Angus, fearing a forfeiture, sought to prevent it taking place. Arran and his bastard son Finnart had to escape across the Nor' Loch on a collier's pony, leaving some twenty-four dead on the pavement. The nickname 'Cleanse the Causeway' applied by citizens to the affair was one customarily used for sewage disposal.

The 11th Earl of Somervill has left the only description of Finnart's addition to Cambusnethan, later known as 'Hamilton's Lodging', which he thought resembled a barracks too much. It took the form of

> a great building in the form of a court . . . [which] consisted of three quarters, three storeys high, and had in all 20 and 4 rooms . . . I having seen this for myself in the very form it had . . . I have often admired soe excellent a man, and so much admired both for his public and private works, should have contrived so ridiculous a building as this was, having nothing to commend it but a number of rooms, and stairs 12 or 13 foot square, one light and one stinking privy, room for a bedstead in each of the chambers, so that it resembled a hospital, and rather diminished than added either beauty or convenience to the great house.[37]

None the less, Somervill admired Finnart's achievements sufficiently to describe him as 'architector'. So, given the dearth of other records, one way of forming an impression of the country's architectural development during the first period is to follow the architectural career of Finnart.

If his father's had been a Renaissance Court, James V's would be even more so, a profoundly humanist one led by a king who was driven by a cult of chivalry,[38] and required scholarship, wit, musical activity and games of his courtiers. The poet Sir David Lindsay of the Mount, who had been his tutor, lost no opportunity thereafter of instructing the king and courtiers in suitable behaviour.[39] There were frequent jousts and tournaments, particularly to celebrate a royal wedding or birth. In 1531 Lindsay was in the Low Countries to note contemporary chivalric practice of lists and tournaments for the king.[40] James duly ensured the country was properly equipped by sending to Denmark to buy 'cataphract horses as the best kind to use in tournaments'.[41] Finding his realm and buildings plundered, the king restored royal fortunes on the strength of clerical income and aristocratic forfeitures,[42] and was thus able to support a 'cultural renaissance of considerable and distinctive proportions'.[43] He welcomed and encouraged makars (poets), playwrights, historians, philosophers, inventors, composers and musicians, and invested enormously 'in the trappings of contemporary kingship' in Court ceremonial, literature and particularly in architecture[44] as encapsulating and symbolising Scotland's cultural ambitions. In his *History*, the chronicler Robert Lindsay of Pitscottie wrote of the 1530s:

> [The King] also plenished the country with all kinds of craftsmen out of other countries, as, French-men, Spaniards, Dutch men, and

English-men, which were all cunning craftsmen, every man for his own hand. Some were gunners, wrights, carvers, painters, masons, smiths, harness-makers, tapesters [tapestry makers], broadsters [embroiderers], tailors, cunning surgeons, apothecaries, with all other kind of craftsmen that might bring his realm in policy, and his craftsmen apparel his palaces in all manner of operation and necessaries. . . .[45]

James's household was normally 300–350 strong, rather over half that of Henry VIII,[46] its more exotic members including a Keeper of the King's Parrots, the Master of the King's [five French] Minstrels, fourteen trumpeters, tabourers (mostly French), falconers, a Dutch gunmaker, a viol-maker, fiddler, several lutanists, whistlers, songsters, a bard and his wife, dwarf, two fools and a juggler.[47] The king, himself called a 'Prince of Poetry' by Sir David Lindsay, encouraged seven poets at Court besides Lindsay himself.[48] There was lavish regal expenditure on clothes.

Chivalry found permanent realisation in the almost theatrical architecture created by this culturally vivid and inquisitive Court. There was substantial rebuilding of or extension to the royal estate – Holyrood, Stirling and Linlithgow palaces, Blackness, the hunting seats of Falkland and Boghouse of Crawfordjohn, and the castle of Rothesay. Works to Linlithgow and Falkland were particularly pressing with the imminent arrival of a new queen, for Linlithgow was traditionally the queen's jointure and Falkland, as part of the marriage settlement, was to be left to her on James's death.[49] There was also the creation of a lodging from the chapter house of Balmerino Abbey for the dying Queen Madeleine in spring 1537, and a 'new pallice' or New Inns, in St Andrews in 1538.[50] This royal lodging, 'well decored against [Mary of Guise's] coming',[51] and in which she gave birth to Prince James on 22 May 1540, can just be made out in John Geddie's 1588 illustrated bird's-eye map of the town.[52] A large rectangular block, plain but for the principal entrance, it had a decorated gable, crowsteps and rooftop elaboration which Slezer's view of St Andrews 100 years later implies were crenellations rather like at Stirling. Of all these royal works, Finnart was definitely involved in four,[53] and contemporaries and near-contemporaries believed that he had been responsible for most[54] – as might be expected if his cultural function at this Renaissance Court was royal architect or designer. That is certainly what is implied in a charter of 1 January 1540, which empowered him and his men to enter all royal buildings as the need arose. For the charter, directed at the keepers, captains and custodians of royal palaces (senior, and often noble people), was expressed testily, indicating dangerous regal impatience with their failure to comply with a role that Finnart already enjoyed (*see* Appendix 1).

The 1517 Treaty of Rouen had indicated that James V should take a French wife, and in 1534 a serious proposition had emerged in the person of Marie de Vendôme. On 1 February that year, significantly 'at the command of our soverane Lord the kingis grace . . . I, James Hamilton of Finnart, Knight, entered to a new account to the building, mending and reparaling of the Palace of Linlithgow'.[55] It required substantial alterations (as is implied by 'reparaling'): a complete reordering of ceremonial sequence, virtually a new chapel, a realignment of the south façade, completion of the palace's four corner towers, painting of the exterior and provision of gilt finials on the skyline, and the construction of a heraldic entrance from the south. A new apartment for the queen almost certainly lay in the northern wing that collapsed in 1617. The suggestion that the queen's royal apartments lay instead on the floor above the king's in the west wing[56] fails take into account the fact the palace was technically the queen's, in which case her apartment was unlikely to be subordinated upstairs, and that there is no surviving staircase of adequate regal grandeur that reaches the second floor. The north wing, however, enjoys the view out over the loch. One side of an enormous, elaborately worked ceremonial entrance remains immured at the east end of the seventeenth-century rebuilding. Finnart's work also included stained and painted glass for the chapel windows and painted carvings and stonework.[57] His most characteristic touch was the new entry from the Cross through two miniature-châteaux gatehouses rather on the model of Vincennes.

Stirling – the 'fair Snawdoun' apostrophised by Sir David Lindsay – was the cultural seat of Renaissance Scotland and the favoured castle of the Stewart dynasty. Although James IV had added the magnificent forework and the grandiose Great Hall, the regal lodgings were somewhat old-fashioned, and in 1538, work began on what was to be by far the finest royal lodging in the land. The site chosen was the empty south wing of the Upper Square, framed by James IV's Great Hall to the east, the Chapel Royal to the north, and the King's Old Building (royal lodging) to the west. On Whitsunday 15 May 1538 Sir James Hamilton of Finnart 'entered' the works at Stirling replacing Master of Works and Chief Almoner Sir James Nicholson. The castle had been left pretty dilapidated by the Dowager Queen Margaret when she was tempted to part with it for a large sum of money, Methven Castle and a younger husband; and Nicholson had been engaged on substantial repairs ever since.

Creating the palace at Stirling required considerable *a priori* planning, since the steeply sloping site extended down to the forework and was partially occupied by existing buildings. Finnart raised the bottom end of the site by inserting a new service corridor, and on the resulting platform, he placed a seemingly single-storeyed,[58] seemingly orthogonal, quadrangular pavilion of compact regal apartments in a formalised series of king's and queen's apartments arranged around a court

5.4 The plan of the palace in Stirling based on information from the Ministry of Public Buildings and Works. Although the chambers, and the Lion's Den at the centre, are rectangular, the tapering walls indicate the effort needed to regularise existing non-orthogonal shapes into this seemingly simple form. (HS)

called the Lion's Den.[59] The two royal bedchambers abutted in the east wing, and the apartments were tied at the foot by a double-pile gallery in the west wing: an internal gallery (which survives) and a planned open-terraced gallery on the outside, which was possibly never built. The King's Presence and Queen's Outer Chambers are identical in proportion: 1:2:1.5 – in other words, a room twice as long as broad, with an unusually high ceiling (somewhat larger than a double cube) and the Queen's Bedchamber is close to a cube. Of these chambers, possibly the most vivid was the Queen's Outer Chamber, with its two large windows facing westward (the sill on the right one at floor level intended to be a door into the missing terrace or outer gallery). Both the plan of the linked royal apartments, and their position at courtyard level (rather than at the same first-floor level as in the adjacent King's Old Building) represent a sharp break with tradition.

The splendidly lit volumes of the King's and Queen's Apartments are now deprived of their wainscotting, timber panelling and carved ceilings, wall paintings, hangings, the marbling, graining or counter-carving of the great fireplaces, and other details which would have completed their design.[60] No trace survives of the 'antique arms' that once decorated the Queen's Chamber.[61] The ceilings of many of the chambers – the King's and Queen's Presence Chambers at least – were coffered with recessed panels in which were located the Stirling Heads, wooden roundels with carved portraits, a number of which survive.[62] Carved heads emerging from coffered ceilings can be found in the Hall of Heads in the palace of the Wawel in Kraków (royal palace of the kings of Poland), carved by Sebastian Tauerbach some time before 1535. Possibly influenced by one in Diocletian's Palace in Split,[63] the Wawel ceiling has vividly coloured heads surging from the deep dark coffers between its beams. The heads, neither chosen nor placed at random, formed part of a wider decorative programme based upon the Stoic philosophy of encouragement to duty. Interspersed with stars, they represented those mortals who, in Cicero's words, having preserved, aided or enlarged their fatherland, had earned their place among the stars.[64] Stirling's heads may also have conveyed an allegorical message that might have helped to decode the palace's only other surviving decoration – the statues adorning the façade.

The façades of the Palace of Stirling eschew all militaristic and heraldic overtones in favour of a paean to the ancients and to classical allusion. They take the form of a composition of three separate tableaux of cyclopean statues of juxtaposed deities and humans celebrating the virtues, arts and a life of contemplation.[65] On the east and north façades, these figures stand upon a two-stage clasped pedestal; the upper stage generally a baluster carved with anthemion leaf, and the lower a column adorned with rich carvings of wrythen-foliated patterns. Each tableau is composed of alternate projecting and recessed bays, the one containing statuary, the other a window. It is a rhythm similar to that of the contemporary façade of the Palazzo Ducale by Giulio Romano at Mantua, whose columns likewise frame bays with shallow stone arches. The composition is capped by a parapet itself adorned with more statuary sitting on a corbel course of cherubs bearing the physiognomies of corpulent and balding courtiers. The cusped arches which top the recessed bays are reminiscent of those on

Top: *5.5 North façade of the Palace of Stirling. The figures include a Venus and a Stoic.* (RCAHMS)

5.6 A bay on the east façade of the Palace of Stirling. (HS)

the châteaux of Josselin (Brittany), Nancy (a seat of the Guise family), and on the staircase at Châteaudun, where Mary of Guise had lived in mourning for her first husband in the year immediately prior to coming to Scotland.[66] When the glancing light hits the north façade (in the late summer evening) or the east (up to mid-morning), the chiaroscuro effect is remarkable: the recessed cusped bays appear as a dark backdrop to the glinting statues, and the projecting bays as broad giant pilasters.

Some of the statues are known to be modelled upon designs by Hans Burgkmair,[67] but the inspiration for the others remains obscure. The south façade is composed of three young playful figures, standing on single, strongly carved, wrythen columns rising from corbelled heads, surrounding a vigorously carved devil, itself closely scrutinised by a dragon. The tableau may represent the Sun God, invoking his protection for the king.[68] The parapet statues appear to have had a different purpose. Whereas those on the east façade resemble a Renaissance close-harmony ensemble, those on the south are thought to depict soldiers protecting the king's house.[69] Hardly. The figure furthest east bears no military insignia, and his entire shoulder blossoms into a gigantic humanoid sunflower in a most unmilitary manner. His neighbour is carolling to a guitar or lute and the next (in silken pantaloons), normally characterised as a crossbowman winding up his crossbow, could be a master mason with a scribing tool. The principal statue (upon whom all the others have been posited as soldiers) is a man with a long thin face, heavy bearded jaw, a senatorial toga over his shoulder, dressed for Court with a ruff, pronounced codpiece, elaborate carved cuirasses on his thigh, and a broken sword or a cross. This austere old senator is no ordinary soldier, and that long drawn-out jaw is surely characteristic of a Hamilton. That this statue may be of Sir James Hamilton of Finnart himself is supported by comparing its demeanour to that of Finnart's cousin, James V, on the north-east corner (*see* p. 13). They have similar stances but reversed hand positions. If it is, it must be one of the earliest and least modest examples of an architect signing his building.

It was through building – *and paying for* – the Palace of Stirling that Finnart hoped to obtain from his sovereign full legitimisation and an accepted place at Court: a magnate with an uncustomary skill for design, a substantial landholding and, probably, the title of Lord Evandale.[70] So he was unconcerned at his arrest, as Bishop John Lesley reported, on (most likely) 15 July 1540,

> believing assuredly that because he had been so diligent in the King's service, specially in reforming the palaces of Stirling and Linlithgow, and making of new lodgings thereunto, and so tenderly beloved and familiarly treated with the king, that therethrough he had no cause to fear.[71]

Lesley implied that, even by the standards of the time, Stirling's palace remained a source of wonder. But to no avail. On the scaffold on 16 August 1540, Finnart protested in terms very similar to those of Cardinal Wolsey: 'If he had been as good a servant to God as he was to the king, he had not died so shamefully.'[72]

It was the lack of any echo in Scottish country houses of the flamboyance of the façades of Stirling and Falkland that led previous historians (ignoring the imposing 1572 façade to Mar's Wark in Stirling) to conclude that the Renaissance had failed to penetrate Scotland. Yet there was more to the new ideas than surface decoration. There was an inherent proportion, the volumes of the chambers, the development of the three-chamber apartment, the skyline statuary and the perpetual reinvention of the past. With two exceptions, Finnart's non-royal buildings have yet to disclose much evidence of his hand. We know of a town house in Edinburgh; and his Linlithgow one, which he obtained in 1531, had a gallery with unusually large and regular windows like those in the palace at Stirling.[73] There was no doubt, however, about Craignethan. It was probably begun in 1531 on 'part of the lands of Draffane bought by the said James' by favour of the Abbot of Kelso in lieu of the abbot's paying certain taxes direct to the Crown – implying that it was a Crown gift.[74] The 'said castle [of Nauthane] built by the said James'[75] consisted of two wards – the outer containing orchards and service buildings, tall rectangular towers or apple-houses in the corners, and a four-towered inner ward on a site made level by cellars and a transe running along the rear (the same device he was to use so splendidly in Stirling). A free-standing, double-pile lodging stood at the centre – a box within a box, or house within a defensive box. The design implies a strong axial focus from the west through an inner and an outer gateway, rather as Finnart had introduced at Stirling.[76] An axial plan such as this, two courtyards separated by a ditch (the one with the caponier – see Chapter 3), the inner lined by buildings with towers on each corner, in essence greatly resembles Leonardo da Vinci's unfulfilled plan for a palace at Romorantin in the Sologne, upon which he was working in his sketchbook in 1517 which

5.7 Sir James Hamilton of Finnart? Statue on the southern parapet of the Palace of Stirling. (Author)

5.8 Conjectural reconstruction of the plan of Craignethan, based upon the plan drawn by Historic Scotland. (Author)

5.9 Conjectural reconstruction of the western façade of Craignethan. (Author)

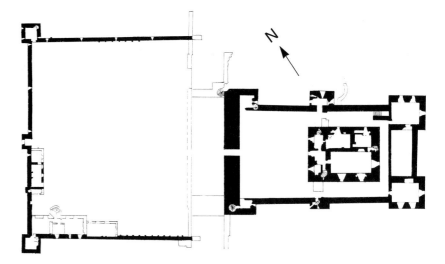

5.8 Conjectural reconstruction of the plan of Craignethan, based upon the plan drawn by Historic Scotland. (Author)

5.9 Conjectural reconstruction of the western façade of Craignethan. (Author)

Finnart may have seen when introduced to Leonardo as a hostage in Amboise that year.

In plan, height or proportion, Craignethan's Lodging represents a complete departure from the tower house. It is far too low, far too cubic and far more sophisticated. The front section is structurally separate from the rear, and has the dual purposes of reception and artillery defence. You enter, uniquely among Scots country houses of that time, into a ground-floor vaulted entrance hall, with another – clearly a service hall – immediately on the left. There is a metaphorical green baize door between. A broad stair on the right leads up to a minstrels' gallery and thereafter to a bedroom floor, whereas a narrower stair at the far end of the service hall leads up to, perhaps, the keeper's chamber and to the artillery platforms. For Craignethan is split by a cross-wall: two storeys of noble chambers to the right and three floors of service chambers to the left.[77] It is a most astonishingly modern house. The brilliantly lit, barrel-vaulted hall, with a continuous stone bench running along its walls, approximately a double-cube in volume,[78] occupies the entire ground floor of the noble side. A room at the far end, reached through the cross-wall, appears to have been Finnart's private chamber, and a tiny, tight stair takes you up to a small mezzanine room inaccessible by any other means. Logically, it was Finnart's charter room or closet.

The parapet of Craignethan comprises five courses of beautifully polished ashlar that used to sport huge statues of Hamilton antelopes,[79] and to accentuate them each of the turrets tapered to a sharp, ashlar point. There are sufficient heraldic beasts for all principal parapets, particularly the two large towers of the east wing. The northern contained a kitchen and chambers, and the southern a chapel. A gallery was possibly intended for the narrow space between (and may never have been entirely finished).[80] It was, after all, well sited for a safe view over the ravine. Since there was also a substantial kitchen within the lodging itself, the one in the east wing must have been to cater for guests and the staff.

Craignethan was a country villa as the Italians might have recognised one: it had guns and gunners, but its staff was predominantly farm servants and foresters under the factor, and there was significant livestock. Here Finnart kept all that was most important to him – his deeds of ownership and his best goods. His standing as a Renaissance patron is implied by the quality and quantity of those goods. His *chapel geir* was fine enough for the king to have it re-engraved for the newly born prince.[81] He had some 20.5 kg of silver, including six large silver cups, and a silver punchbowl, a great screen, a clock, and plentiful linens – all good enough to be carried to Holyrood for the king's pleasure upon Finnart's execution.[82]

What survives today of Kinneil, West Lothian, provides little guide to the palace that played such a prominent part in state life during the sixteenth century; it was already described as a palace by 1561.[83] The north and west wings of the inner court are missing, and the south wing has been sadly shorn and clipped. The principal Hamilton seat in the east of Scotland, here died the 1st Earl, and here came the monarch and Court periodically for banquets or longer visits. It began with a narrow tower at the west end by the ravine, which was extended south to form a three-bay main house in the sixteenth century, when it was given three wide-mouthed gunloops of the type in the Lion's Den in Stirling.[84] The polished ashlar blocks surrounding the seventeenth-century windows on the east façade are of a more russet colour than the grey stone of the remainder, and this implies two dates: perhaps the greyer might be of the vintage of Stirling. The so-called 'palace block' – the truncated, decapitated wing lining the north of the court – is generally presumed to have been built by the Regent Arran in the early 1540s since the Treasurer's Accounts reveal that he was plundering the royal revenues to pay for his extravagances at Kinneil. But whereas much of the internal painting (*see* Chapter 6) may be of Arran's vintage, the unusual double-pile plan resembles Craignethan, Strathaven and the palace at Edinburgh Castle; and the painted vaulted chamber within has the same form as the chapel in Craignethan.

Houses like this had to be ready for a visit by the king on one of his progresses. James and his Court (sometimes a skeleton establishment) made repeated visits to the houses of Dalkeith and Pitlethie, and would stay at Inchinnan, Crawford, Alloa, Dunnottar, Kincardine, Calder, Monimail, Brechin, Ardstinquhar, Blairquhan and Inveraray. He was also thought by the Earl of Somervill to have stayed at Couthally and attended Finnart's wedding at Craignethan in 1536. There was a rhythm to James V's progresses – his annual hunting trips to Glenfinglas and Glenartney, for example – and those with large houses *en route* might well have sought to improve and extend their properties in preparation for a visit.

The country houses most likely to be influenced by developments at Court would be those of the courtiers. Unfortunately the homes of most of the courtiers of James V no longer survive.[85] Of the houses of the Lords Regent who ruled Scotland during James's wedding trip in 1536–7, Eglinton and Kincardine have vanished, and the principal seat of the 5th Lord Maxwell at this time is unclear. He may have been responsible for the fine west wing within Caerlaverock, in which his son was later to insert a magnificent library. Maxwell had a number of duties at this cultured court – being First Gentleman of the Inner Chamber and Principal Carver – and it is unlikely that he remained satisfied with only old-fashioned vertical living in tower houses down on the Borders.

Of the properties of three royal servants who ambushed Finnart, Master Henry Balnaves,[86] Kircaldy of Grange and David Wood of the Crag (*sic*), only Wood's house survives. He held the posts of Master Lardner and Carver to the king, and it was in his principal role as Comptroller that he took part in the coup. His House of Craig rests gently on a most elegiac spot gazing north and downwards over Montrose Basin, far enough down the hill for shelter from the south-westerlies. It was sufficiently elevated to command the prospect. Craig was a manor house, and the structure of its lower storeys implies that it began as a wide tower (now cut down) at the north-eastern corner, extended westwards, and then south and east to form the inner court.[87] (The office of royal comptroller might not have been a bad one to hold if you were bent on building.) Diminutive, stumpy, battlemented towers mark the south-east and south-west corners. The wing joining these two towers is very narrow, and it probably contained a gallery/corridor between guest lodgings in each tower. Mary Queen of Scots stayed in Craig rather than at nearby House of Dun on her progress in 1562, and it was only a relatively small place. Perhaps that was when the heraldic gateway was added to the outer court, with all the appropriate symbolism of round towers and ferocity. It seemed scarcely justified by the few buildings inside. However, given that the royal entourage took tents with them on their progresses[88] (indeed Agnes Beaton of Kelly had two in her cellars),[89] the outer court might have been intended for the pavilions of the travelling royal circus.

Two of a particular group of houses in Ayrshire and neighbourhood which share the same physical characteristics can be linked to courtiers, and one – Dalquharran – can be

5.10 The inner court at Craig, by Montrose, showing the two guest towers of the now missing gallery wing. (Author)

dated to 1538.[90] The other houses – Sorn, Cassilis, Culzean, Brodick,[91] Sanquhar-Hamilton (or Newton) and Thomaston – appeared much lower and broader than the fifteenth-century tower house norm, and showed signs of having been extended by adding a new wing at right angles against the original tower. The old and the new were then tied together by a three-ribbed cord or continuous cornice like a belt, resulting in a horizontally proportioned unity. The particular form of continuous ribbed corbelling appears to be a regional motif.

The king's Purse Bearer and Keeper of the Royal Boxes was Henry Kempt of Thomastown,[92] and the broad and squat house of Thomaston is one of the most unusual. It stood at one corner of its inner close, the entrance to which was beneath a wing of the main house itself. It was a horizontally proportioned lodging, visually barely three storeys, and the surprising number of fireplaces on the principal floor indicates three rooms which may have opened into each other in sequence. Sanquhar-Hamilton was the house of Newton, renamed by Sir William Hamilton of Sanquhar when he took possession. Hamilton was an ally of James Hamilton of Finnart and latterly Depute Master of the Royal Household. The principal records of the house are those contained in Hamilton's lawsuit against Wallace of Craigie for the invasion in 1559 (*see* Chapter 3), and its appearance in the foreground of Slezer's view of Ayr. You can just make out the surrounding yards, gardens and orchards in the drawing; but

5.11 Sorn, Ayrshire, drawn by Francis Grose, late eighteenth century. (Author's collection)

5.12 Thomaston, Ayrshire. Note its horizontal proportions and continuous roll-moulded cornice. (RCAHMS)

5.13 Whitefoorde, later Blairquhan, in the late eighteenth century. (RCAHMS)

from the lawsuit you can form an impression of the luxury within a house not of the first rank.[93] It was well stocked with material imported from Europe: finest silver and gold basins and salt cellars from Paris, quantities of tablecloths and napkins of 'dornick'[94] work, covers and napkins of Breton linen, worsted tablecloths from Flanders, Dutch arras tapestries from the Low Countries, sixty English books, chairs of carved Baltic timber, English pewter water pots, carved Norwegian partitions, and carved and decorated Baltic timber beds. The inventory also reveals that there were five principal chambers in this low house, and that the main house above the hall was divided into two. The verticality of the tower house was being abandoned.

The influence of four-towered Linlithgow and Craignethan is difficult to assess. Enclosures with rectangular corner towers were probably more common in Scotland than is now apparent, and the House of the Binns (West Lothian), Foulis (Ross and Cromarty), Nisbet (Borders) and

Monimail (Fife) may originally have taken this form.[95] Blairquhan, Ayrshire (then known as Whitefoorde) was perhaps the most complete.[96] Built for the Kennedys of Blairquhan, the approximately rectangular inner close had a slender rectangular-turreted tower on three of the corners, and an elaborately decorated laird's lodging, presumed to have been of 1573, occupying the fourth. Other buildings – perhaps offices or guests' quarters – lined the other flanks of the court. It was entered through a particularly imposing and richly carved doorway in the middle of a heraldic frontispiece: a symmetrical six-bay entrance block capped with ornate dormer windows, framed by slender towers.

Equally, the innovation of setting the lodging free-standing within the inner court had only a few known parallels. Bargany, Ayrshire, seat of another branch of the Kennedys, for example, was described in 1696 as a 'hudge, great, lofty tower *in the centre of a quadrangular court* [my italics] that had on each of three corners, fyne well-built towers of freestone, four storey high'.[97] Bargany was abandoned in the late seventeenth century, cannibalised and then destroyed. An attempt at similar geometric regularisation was made in the reorientation of Cathcart Castle, near Glasgow. Cathcart's relatively long but narrow tower house was given a new setting within a rectangular inner close with a round tower on each corner. The symmetry did not carry through into the tower elevation itself, and further exploration is impossible after Glasgow Corporation's fearful demolition of it for being unsafe (a condition in which it had remained stable for at least 150 years). Only recently has excavation revealed that Boghall, low-lying in marshland just south of Biggar and encircled by a handsome drainage ditch, consisted of a tower surrounded by a towered courtyard.[98] Boghall's inner court was D-shaped with gatehouse and round towers flanking the corners.[99] The Flemings, whose house it was, had early formed part of Finnart's bratpack[100] and his influence may have been brought to bear. At some subsequent point – probably the seventeenth century – a new main house was constructed as the laird's lodging to the rear of the court, and the tower demolished.

By the end of the 1530s, therefore, Scottish country houses were moving away from the tall verticality of the fifteenth-century tower house. They had not lost the sense of control and compactness that had characterised the tower, but it was being applied in new ways: in how the house was set within the inner court, and in the use of axis. The verticality of plan, likewise, was being transformed into the horizontally arranged state apartment, albeit restrained within a tight geometric exterior. Had Finnart not died, it is possible that a fashion for ground-floor principal apartments, almost on the English model, might have spread; as also might the inspiration

5.14 Boghall, by Biggar, drawn by Francis Grose, late eighteenth century. Only a desultory tower survives. The tower in the centre of the enclosure had been replaced by the seventeenth-century lodging against the rear wall. (Author's collection)

5.15 Conjectural reconstruction of Avendale, based on Pont and de Cardonnel. (Author)

of four-towered Linlithgow, Craignethan and Whitefoorde, and the towered Mansion House at Greenock (the original lands of Finnart – 'new buildit' in 1541,[101] which passed, after his death, into the hands of the Schaws of Sauchie). The fondness for a house that combined compactness with innovation had begun to result in double-pile lodgings. Left to itself, Scottish country house architecture was moving from one kind of formality to another, the inspiration of which may primarily have been Italian.

However, the influence of the royal building programme was to prove strong, even upon Finnart. He acquired Avendale, Strathaven, as his formal seat in 1533 and is thought to have made substantial alterations to it.[102] The nature of its ruins misled MacGibbon and Ross to conclude that Avendale Castle was simply a rectangular tower with a round one projecting from the corner. The circular, slender, ashlar tower projecting from the corner contained a stair. Yet it may have been, rather, an almost-square double-pile house,[103] which, to reconstruct from Timothy Pont's elevation and Adam de Cardonnel's drawing,[104] may have been a twin-towered composition (rather too incautiously resembling a miniature Holyrood than might have been congenial to a paranoid king very well aware of the Hamilton family's pretensions to the throne). If Craignethan was Finnart's private seat, Avendale was the expression of his power, and it was the title of Lord Evandale which he is thought to have obtained at the point of his execution. More significantly, Avendale represented a radical departure from the geometric regularities of Craignethan, for its round towers and flamboyant skyline not only echo the fore-entries of Stirling, Falkland and the King's Tower at Holyrood, but presage the architectural motifs of the mid-century.

A modish extension was added to Glamis in about 1537. The king had proved particularly skilled at 'conquishing' other people's patrimonies, and once he had hanged Lord Glamis and burnt his wife in 1537, he enjoyed visits to Glamis in 1537, 1539 and 1540. These usually took the form of an excursion from Falkland with a week at Glamis, staying in Dundee each way.[105] The old tower of Glamis would have found it difficult to host the Court for a week, and its rooms were probably old-fashioned. A possibly separate eastern wing was added which, to judge from a thick wall in the middle and several wall curiosities, embraced some earlier structure. The wing provides a sequence of three principal chambers on the same floor, the last being in the round tower itself. If it is of this period, then that circular tower containing a square bedchamber within it – the most private in the apartment – presaged the principal characteristic of houses of the Marian period that followed.

6

Enter the Château: Architecture of the Marian Period, c. 1542–c. 1568

Tout est à la mode de France
Sir John Maitland

Disce meo exemplo formosis posse carvere
Learn by my example to be able to want the beautiful
(carved stone retrieved from Vayne, Angus)[1]

James V died on 14 December 1542, about a week after his daughter Mary was born. Only this 'skittering lass'[2] lay between the devious and indecisive James, Earl of Arran (Finnart's half-brother), and the throne. As heir to the throne, he was duly appointed regent. There was no question that the baby queen should be married to a Cypriot or a Hungarian as had been suggested for her father. She was to have a Frenchman, an Englishman, or even a Scot, and the English and French governments poured money and troops into Scotland to press their suit. The growing English faction favoured marriage between the infant Mary and Henry VIII's young son Edward, whereas the French faction led by Mary of Guise and Cardinal David Beaton (albeit not always in harmony with each other) was determined otherwise. Contemporary sources believed that Mary was bent on a closer French alliance and Beaton upon ensuring that his kinsman Arran would become king. The French proved the most sophisticated at winning friends in Scotland. Although men of great substance like the Earl Marischal supported the English faction, its leadership lacked authority and style: George Douglas of Parkhead and the Earl of Angus appeared colourless, crude and unsophisticated against an alliance of the widowed Mary of Guise and the dangerously glamorous Cardinal Beaton.

Mary of Guise herself, undeniably attractive, succeeded in winning the affection of Scots nobles – even of her enemies[3] – and one of the few records of her speaking (recorded by a mocking John Knox) reveals a

engaging blend of Scots and French, the Frécossais of its day.[4] *Force majeure*, the Scots nobles were even more internationally travelled than before, if only because so many captured at Solway Moss in 1542 had been warded in London for some months. So the particular troubles of the country between 1547 and 1550, and again between 1558 and 1560, could be attributed to the English and the French exacerbating Scotland's internal divisions for their own ends. The blind poet Sir Richard Maitland reflected the national distress:

> England is glad when it is told
> Of Scottis the division
> And for our foolishness they hold
> Our doings in derision
> But would we well consider
> They hound us ay together
> Making their own provision
> For our great skaith and lesion . . .[5]

Culturally, however, there was no contest: Scotland leaned towards France, and the early French Renaissance architecture of the first thirty years of the century cast a spell upon Scotland until the end of the reign of Mary Queen of Scots in 1567. The French influence that had been growing during the reign of James V had been largely restricted to royal buildings, beginning with the king's tower at Holyrood, so seemingly influenced by Vincennes, and the similarly towered reworking of the entrance to Falkland from 1536.[6] In readiness for the king's second marriage, to the widowed Mary of Guise, Scotland produced its most thoroughgoing French design in the courtyard façade of Falkland Palace, completed in about 1539. Because it seemed to have no imitators, the French influence is thought to have waned thereafter.[7] The reverse, rather, is true. The country abandoned the emerging formality and symmetry of the late 1530s country house, exemplified by Craignethan or Cathcart, and embraced instead an architecture of balance and asymmetry, with a concealed rather than an overt proportion, and an enhanced emphasis upon the skyline composition rather than upon the façade below. It was the architecture of early Renaissance France that had crossed the North Sea with Mary of Guise in 1538, rather than the classicising influences of the colony of Amboise and of Serlio, that became dominant in France during the 1540s. This earlier sixteenth-century French romanticism continued to flourish in Scotland for generations after its parent had grown out of it.

Sandwiched as it is between the Courts of James V and his grandson James VI, the culture of the Marian period has tended to be unnecessarily overshadowed by dour retrospection. But the portrayal of the developments of the mid-sixteenth century as grim, reforming, isolationist Scots triumphing over flamboyant continental Europeans cannot be relied upon: indeed the Reformation itself was European. The Court was thoroughly international between 1538 and 1567. Over 100 of Mary's attendants were French and paid from France,[8] including her master of household, secretary, doctors, her ladies-in-waiting, their tailor, and a

Opposite: *6.1 Kelburn, Ayrshire, as drawn by Billings, who has carefully removed all trace of its seventeenth-century extensions.* (Author's collection)

French dwarf called Jane.[9] Her brother, the Duc de Guise, had also kindly supplied her with building craftsmen who may have included Nicholas Roy, who worked on Falkland, and the carver Andrew Mansion, who may have been responsible for the Stirling heads.[10] The Court customarily enjoyed:

> dancing, singing, and playing on instruments, sometimes shooting, sometimes singing and jousting and running of great horse at the lists, with all other knightly games that might satisfy the Queen or do her pleasur.[11]

The continental influence extended beyond entertainment. In 1548 Piero di Strozzi, Prior of Capua, the man charged with blasting Beaton's murderers from St Andrews Castle,[12] was invited back to construct new fortifications of the most advanced European model around Leith.[13] Such far-seeing patronage would hardly have been on the initiative of the Earl of Arran, and demonstrates the influence of Scotland's French queen; an influence that permeated society and transformed its architecture.

Records of house construction during the 1540s are few. Once firmly in power as regent, the Earl of Arran used the Royal Master of Works, John Scrymgeour of the Myres, and at least £2,303 of the royal revenues on his own properties. Doors and windows made in Edinburgh Castle were added to his house on Arran (Brodick),[14] lavish redecoration, stained glass, gilding and painting to his western palace of Hamilton between 1550 and 1552,[15] and major additions to his eastern palace at Kinneil between 1546 and 1553 – when the mural paintings within Kinneil's 'palace' are thought to have been undertaken.[16] Only three rooms were rescued from demolition in 1936, and this was followed by the lucky retrieval from a builder's yard of the coffered oak

6.2 Painted chamber at Kinneil. (HS)

ceiling from one of them. There are at least two superimposed painted surfaces on the walls, probably representing early seventeenth-century painting overlaid upon Arran's vigorous decorative programme. The walls of the room are framed between a confident swirling frieze of youthful figures with arabesque tails enclosing classical profiles within a circular garland, in the manner of the Stirling Heads, and a similar dado band below of scenes from antiquity. The large – almost life-sized – panels between are cartoons of scenes from the Old Testament given form by wayward Ionic columns painted to imply that you are watching the scene through an arcade. These rooms at Kinneil show that the cultural confidence of James V's Court had not died with him.

The other principal house of the 1540s was that built by Beaton for his wife Marion Ogilvy at Melgund in Angus from 1543.[17] Approximately U-plan, this house has a tower at the west end, a palace block in the middle and a projecting wing with a circular tower containing an oratory at the east end. It was once magnificent. A walled garden lay to the east, and a garden stair led up to Marion Ogilvy's chamber. The building is considered to have been completely new-built in 1543, and it has been thought that the anachronistic western tower was designed to imply great lineage. As was suggested in Chapter 2, however, the tower's structure implies that it was part of the earlier manor of North Melgund,[18] and that the spacious square stair and the beautiful main house to the west were added to it. An examination of the masons' marks supports this interpretation.[19] Beaton's addition comprised two very precisely proportioned chambers – the hall and Marion Ogilvy's bedchamber – with small chambers or a gallery facing the inner court on the other side of the cross-wall. A window on the ground floor beneath was once glazed, implying that it faced open air. So this northern façade may once have stood upon open arcades.

The 1540s, however, were dominated by Henry VIII's 'rough wooing' invasion in 1544, and the English invasion of 1547 and partial occupation of south-east Scotland thereafter. For almost three years, the English headquarters was at Haddington, power being exerted in Angus from 'the House of Brughty' (Broughty) and the fort of Bracanrigg (presumably bracken-ridge) on Balgillo Hill, and it appeared to enjoy considerable local support. Battlegrounds remained predominantly between Berwick and Edinburgh. In spring 1550, France and England signed the Treaty of Boulogne, the terms of which embraced Scotland and included the English quitting their Scottish forts. So Scots could look forward to the first lasting peace since 1544 in the frontier lands. That settled, on 8 August, Mary of Guise left Scotland to spend more than a year at the French Court and at her own homes of Longueville, Joinville, Nancy and Châteaudun,[20] accompanied by the Earls of Huntly, Sutherland and Cassilis, the Earl Marischal, Lords Hume, Fleming and Maxwell and many others of the Scots Court. They visited Rouen, Paris, Chartres and Blois. The French secured the support of the Scots by lavish bribes, and the granting of the Order of St Michael to Huntly, Chancellor of Scotland, and the Earls of Arran, Argyll and Angus.[21]

At Mary's childhood home of Joinville, the Scottish visitors found a château with its origins in a *donjon* of the early Middle Ages but which, by the sixteenth century, 'was surrounded by attractive two storey buildings with narrow round towers at almost every angle'.[22] As in so many other French châteaux (like Mary of Guise's seat of widowhood at Châteaudun), the *donjon* symbolised the family's antiquity, and governed the entire plateau. To claim nobility in France, you had to live nobly and belong to an ancient family:

For a family to call itself ancient, its origins had to lie much further back than the memory of the most aged – say three generations. The prestigious families were those who had a Crusader among their ancestry or, even better, a companion of King Clovis.[23]

The way of signalling that architecturally was through the tall, round *donjon*.

The Scots lords were visiting a country in the throes of an architectural revolution. As mid-century approached, French country houses moved from the gay romanticism of the early Loire buildings and reached what the French were later to describe as their 'national style', attributed to the arrival of Sebastiano Serlio in France in 1541.[24] Houses were becoming more controlled, planned with proportion and symmetry vigorously delineated upon the façade by pilasters and other classical elements. Flanking towers – initially circular and then rectangular or square – framed the composition, and the house was normally set upon a terrace or platform, emphasised by a wet or dry moat. The new formalities were propagated through architectural books by Androuet du Cerçeau, Philibert de l'Orme and Serlio himself, whose château of Ancy le Franc was particularly influential.

It seems that Mary proposed to remain in France with her family, and that the French intended a different French regent should replace the ineffective and increasingly distrusted Regent Arran (made Duke of Châtelherault by Henry II of France in February 1549).[25] Since Mary's

Graph 5 Château construction, 1542–68.

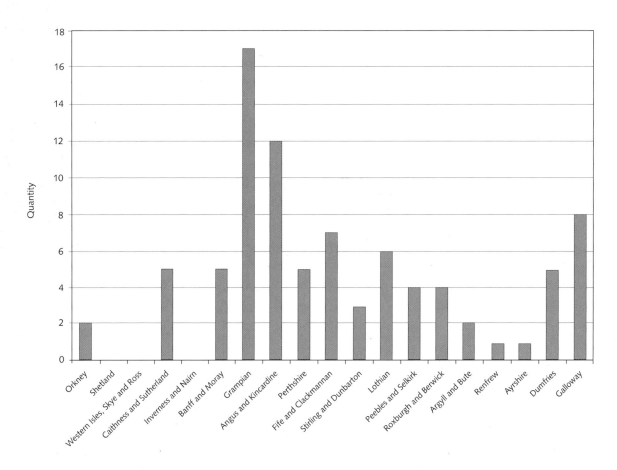

Previous page: 1. *Kilravock, Nairn, seat of the Rose family. The Renaissance wing is entirely distinct from the original tower, but the jardin clos, for which Hugh Rose imported the gardener Thom Daveson and his man in 1536, lies derelict.* (Finnie/RIAS Collection)

Left: 2. *A detail from the 1581 Prestongrange ceiling (see p. 12), now re-erected within Merchiston Tower, Edinburgh.* (Author)

3. *The lower storeys of the ceremonial entrance or* châtelet *to Mar's Wark (the town house of the Regent Earl of Mar), in Stirling. It dates from c. 1570.* (Author)

4. *Craignethan, Clydesdale, the country villa of Sir James Hamilton of Finnart, seen from the west. (For a conjectural reconstruction of Craignethan from this perspective, see p. 92). The outer court is in the foreground, Andrew Hay's seventeenth-century house on the right. The Lodging lies centre of a formerly towered inner court. (Author)*

5. *Looking towards the two-storeyed summer house in the south-east corner of the great garden at Edzell. The rubble on the surrounding walls would have been harled, emphasising the ashlar chequerwork columns and carved cartouches of the Deities and Virtues. (Buxbaum/RIAS Collection)*

6. *Early seventeenth-century plasterwork in the King's Room (or chamber of dais) in the Binns.* (Author)

7. *Plasterwork from 1633 by Thomas White in the King's Room at Winton.* (Author)

8. *The great hall at Glamis as revivified in the 1620s.* (Author)

9. *Carved wainscot now in Arbroath Abbey Abbot's House (once Cardinal Beaton's).* (Author)

10. *Conjectural reconstruction of the Palace of Huntly (without the superlative lettering that lines its two ashlar floors). Note the two-storeyed gazebo on the right and the loggia with a gallery behind.* (Author)

11. *Carnousie, nestling in the folds of Buchan; a neat example of a small, late Marian château – albeit with a rectangular stairtower and public straight stair within.* (RIAS Collection)

12. *George, 5th Lord Seton, Master of Household to Mary Queen of Scots, holding his staff of office. He is the one who declined an earldom, earning Mary's little poem (see note 66, p. 293). (Anon, PGL 309, SNPG)*

13. *Sir Duncan Campbell of Glenorchy: 'Duncan Campbell,/ By my hand,/ The Blackest Laird/ in all the Land' (see p. 138).*
(Anon, PG 2364, SNPG)

Above: 14. *The north (garden) façade of Kellie, Fife, seen through Sir Robert Lorimer's romantic garden. It is almost deliberately informal and picturesque by comparison with the entrance facade (see p.135). The medieval north-west tower is on the right. Note the stair carried on a squinch, and the sunburst aedicule on the 1573 tower to the left.* (Author)

Left: 15. *The diamond-facetted court façade and loggia of the Bothwell wing of Crichton Castle, Midlothian.* (Author)

daughter Mary Queen of Scots was affianced to the heir to the French throne, and likely to become queen of France, Scotland's destiny seemed to be ruled through French regents anyway. However, possibly bearing in mind the last French regency of 1514–24 and Albany's indifferent success in governing the Scots – and the hostility from England that his appointment had caused – Henry II concluded that the most effective regent would be Mary herself. At least she had been crowned by the Scots and had already formed a significant group of supporters. A French outsider imposed upon the Scots could well unite them in favour of England. So Mary of Guise had to return to Scotland, and to emphasise her friendliness to England, she elected to travel through England, meeting and charming Edward VI and his Court on the way.

Bishop Lesley recorded a thriving Scotland after Mary's return:

> The haill realme of Scotland being this maner in quyetnes, everye man addrest him selfe to policie, and to big, plant and pleneise those rowmes quhilkis throch the trublis of the warris, be Inglismen or utheris had been wasted brint, spulyeit or distroyit.[26]

> [The whole realm of Scotland being this manner in quietness, every man addressed himself to policy, and to build, plant and furnish those estates which through the troubles of the wars by Englishmen or others had been wasted, burnt, spoiled or destroyed.]

Beyond the range of English influence, defence was not a primary consideration as the frequent use of the term 'manor house' in official records of the 1550s indicates.[27] The startling assumption that the word 'mansio' was used as a synonym for a fortified residence remains unsupported.[28] Since lack of building contracts and records makes dating difficult during this period, it is a rare advantage to have a reliable datestone – such as the one erected by the Kerrs of Ancrum over their gate: 'Robert Ker and Isobel Home, Founder and compleitar Anno 1558'.[29] Panmure, Angus, which had been badly damaged when defended against the English marauding from Broughty, had been rebuilt before 1560,[30] and the Douglas lairds of Loch Leven had quit their island fastness for their New House on the sunny shores of the mainland.[31] Newhouse lost its purpose and was demolished in 1723, but its quality may be inferred from painted ceiling boards reused in another house in Kinross and the attribution of the glowing crimson wool wall-hangings embroidered in yellow, gold and black (originally thought to have been by Mary Queen of Scots) that once hung below a frieze and above a wainscot in it.[32]

The relentless eastwards expansion of Sir Colin Campbell, thirty-three years laird of Glenorchy, concluded its first phase with the construction of his principal seat of Balloch on the eastern shores of Loch Tay, first recorded in use in November 1559.[33] This turreted, romantic and showy country seat, environed by plantations and formal gardens,[34] surrounded by hills and Loch Tay, does not conform to the geometric simplicity of the tower house. It is fundamentally expressive: a western stairtower projecting from the façade,[35] possibly another tower to the east, and a

6.3 Balloch (later Taymouth) drawn c. 1770 by Moses Griffiths for Thomas Pennant. The original western tower was balanced by another during eighteenth-century alterations by William Adam. (Author's collection)

6.4 William Adam's eighteenth-century plan of Balloch reveals the earlier house, although all the yards have been replaced by the quadrants. (Author's collection)

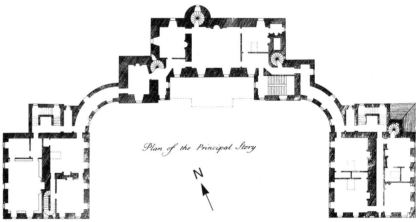

Plan of the Principal Story

round tower projecting to north-east.[36] In some ways, the plan resembled the way that Blair in Atholl had begun to grow out of its original tower.[37] Small turrets clasped each corner. The inventories – and Pont's drawing – imply that the house was surrounded by other structures, including a gallery with a chamber opening from it. This extravagant new house celebrated Sir Colin's marriage to the locally dominant Gowrie family and his establishment in Perthshire. Glenorchy's somewhat partial historian, William Baillie, portrays the family as intelligent, progressive and peaceful agricultural improvers, but there is some evidence that his depiction of their benign demeanor was incomplete. Sir Colin, for example,

was ane great justiciar all his time throch the quhilk he sustenit [through which he sustained] the deidlie feid of the Clangregour ane lang space. And, besydis that he caused executt to the death many notable lymmaris, he beheiddit the laird off McGregour himself at Kandmoir in presens of the Earle of Atholl, the justice clerk and sundrie other nobillmen.[38]

Mary of Guise finally became queen regent in 1554, and began to appoint Frenchmen to both the great and to minor offices of state.[39] In March 1557, the French master mason at Dunbar, Jean Roytel, was appointed 'principal master mason to all Her Highness' Works', and given the same salary of £100 as Master of Works Sir William Makdowall (which might not have been particularly tactful).[40] Although no buildings have been attributed to Roytel, and there are no other recorded payments to him, two later became known as Mary of Guise's palace – one opening off Castle Hill in Edinburgh, and one in Coal Hill, Leith. An elaborately carved aumbry could conceivably have been of the period.[41] Makdowall, however, was working steadily on royal buildings, as indeed he continued to do under Mary Queen of Scots. (Between 1560 and 1566, he was paid over £6,000 for repairs, alterations and extensions to Holyrood, Edinburgh and Dunbar Castles.)[42]

The two most grandiose surviving examples of early Marian architecture lie in the north, and were probably built competitively in time to host Mary of Guise on her justice ayre (circuit) to the north in 1556. She was accompanied by the earls of Huntly and Atholl, and they duly stayed in both Huntly's Palace of Huntly (Strathbogie) and in the Atholl stronghold of Balvenie, Dufftown. Although the lordship of Balvenie had been one of Atholl's earliest titles, it had come to be marooned within the enormous empire of the Huntly Gordons. Despite a bond of manrent between them, rivalry and tension would not have been unexpected.[43]

George, 4th Earl of Huntly, had been appointed Chancellor in the place of the murdered Cardinal Beaton in 1546, and he had been Mary of Guise's principal companion on her trip to France in 1551. That he had grand plans to transform his castle, most delightfully elevated above a meander of the River Deveron secure in the heart of Gordon country, is implied by his seeking parliamentary support for the change of its name from the House of Strathbogie to Huntly Castle. Major work had to wait for peace and his return from France[44] – carved stones dated 1553 imply that it was then under way.[45] The castle had consisted of a motte and a bailey, and in the latter Sir John Gordon had built a massive L-plan tower in the late fourteenth century within an east-facing inner court. Lining the southern edge of the plateau was a three-storeyed rectangular hall block built by the 1st Earl in 1455.[46] This Huntly proceeded to heighten and transform by adding circular towers at the south-west and north-east corners, with a heraldic silhouette at the top. By far the larger was the south-west corner tower – the *tour maîtresse*.[47] In *practical* terms, the new structure was a tower of bedrooms with two staircases – one presumably for the earl and his family's use, and the other for stewards and servants. In *symbolic* terms this great round tower – which became the principal motif in the composition of most of the 'Marian' country houses – was a statement of ancient status, and yet another example of the Scots' preoccupation with reinventing the past for contemporary life. The tall circular *donjon* that the visitors had seen in so many French châteaux had had few parallels in Scotland, for the medieval inheritance of most Scottish country houses took the form of a rectangular tower. None the less, canny Scots were unlikely to invest in a superfluous structure even if they desired its visual nobility, so the fusion of practical and symbolic was achieved by

6.5 The Palace of Huntly, drawn by James Giles, c. 1835. The tour maîtresse *on the left was added in c. 1553 and the superstructure on its right fifty years later. (NTS)*

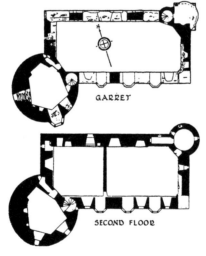

GARRET

THE GRIT CHALMER   THE HALL

THE CHALMER DURRE

THE UTTER CHALMER DURRE

ANE ROUND WITHIN THE GRIT CHALMER

FIRST FLOOR

SECOND FLOOR

GROUND FLOOR

BASEMENT

10 0 10 20 30 FEET

6.6 Plans of the Palace of Huntly, prepared by W. Douglas Simpson. (SAS) placing the bedchambers of the constable, earl and the countess one above the other in the great round tower.

Huntly's six-storeyed circular 'bedroom stack' stands forward from the four-storey and attic main house, and dominates it. With the greatest elaboration, the best carvings and the most ornate dormer windows, it is crowned by a magnificently corbelled parapet supporting a viewing platform all the way round. The entire composition was capped with finials (as one might expect from the example of the royal palaces), one of which remains within the palace in the form of a Gordon heraldic boar. The nearest resemblance to Huntly's tower is to be found in the château of Mortiercrolles, but it may also have been inspired by the drawing of Mehun sur Yvre in the *Très Riches Heures* of the Duc de Berry.

In the diagonally opposite corner lies the entrance or public staircase which balances the composition. It is narrower in proportion than the bedroom tower, probably because it had to be rebuilt after William Schaw excised the north-west corner of the new palace on royal instruction after the Battle of Glenlivet in 1594. He also slighted Huntly's medieval tower by removing internal vaults to make it unusable.[48]

The principal floors of Huntly now contained the sequence of chambers required of a state apartment: antechamber, chamber and bedchamber; and the story of the death of the 5th Earl in 1576 (who suffered apoplexy like his father, but as a result of playing football rather than rebellion) provides an insight into how the chambers were used. They were playing beyond the outer gate when Huntly was struck down. Servants carried him to his bedchamber 'quhilk chalmer was ane round within the grit chalmer of the New warke of Strathbogie'[49] (which chamber was in the round tower reached through the great chamber).[50] After his decease, the earl's 'geir' – wealth and charters – was carried through to his bedchamber for safekeeping, while the corpse was disembowelled and then left in the chamber of dais. Sixteen or twenty of Huntly's entourage and relatives remained in the hall, and his brother was sitting on 'ane form [bench] next to the chalmer door'[51] when he heard 'ane great noise and din in that chamber'. On inspection, it remained empty save for the corpse.[52] The tale illustrates the different degrees of privacy of each of the three chambers comprising the state apartment, and highlights the supernatural element in sixteenth-century Scots history.

That earlier Mary of Guise justice ayre in 1556 had been a success:

And here is to be remembered, that in all this jornay and progres quhair [where] the Quene Regent and her companie did pas, sho was receaved verrey honorablie, and intertenit sumptueouslie in the nobill mennis, prelattis and barrouns housis, so that the Frenche men praised the same verrye meikill [much].[53]

George Gordon, Earl of Huntly, Chancellor, Lieutenant of the North, Sheriff of Inverness, Keeper of Inverness and Inverlochy Castles – the embodiment of the grossly over-mighty subject – welcomed the queen regent into his new palace with a guard of honour of 1,000 men, and then embarked upon splendid entertainment.[54] Allegedly concerned lest her stay might impoverish her host, Mary soon sought to leave, but Huntly responded by showing her his enormous cellars packed with provisions. He explained to her how hunters daily delivered food to his palace from throughout his lands in the Highlands. D'Oysel, Mary of Guise's saturnine adviser, drily observed that here was somebody in need of having his wings clipped.[55]

That clipping was left to her daughter Mary Queen of Scots, and her defeat of the Gordons at the Battle (rather skirmish) of Corrichie in autumn 1562, when the earl died of a seizure coming off the field, and his second son Sir John Gordon was executed soon thereafter.[56] Huntly had made an enormous miscalculation about the tenor of the queen, and the extent of her displeasure at his family's defiance of her in Edinburgh and Inverness. The palace, sumptuously fitted up for the queen's visit,[57] was inventoried after the battle as the result of the family's forfeiture, so we may glimpse what it looked like inside. The walls of the hall were hung with tapestries and gilt leather hangings, and velvet cushions in many colours softened the chairs and forms. Huntly himself sat, presumably in the chamber of dais, beneath a cloth of state of crimson damask fringed with gold and crimson silk. Among the movables taken from Huntly were several large, gorgeous beds – one of violet velvet, another of black figured velvet with pasements of gold and silver, and others finished with silk, velvet and gold-embroidered coverings, eleven tapestries of gilt leather, eight various velvet cushions, forty pieces of tapestry, forty-seven tablecloths ('burd claithes') of varying sumptuousness, twenty dozen serviettes, many dishes, several statues and four gilt chandeliers.[58] The vividness of the interiors is indicated by yellow, crimson, blue, green and violet curtains. Ceilings were curiously painted.

A similar design emerged at Balvenie, said to have been completed by John Stewart, 4th Earl of Atholl, by 1557,[59] but more likely to have been made ready for the Guise visit the previous year. It was certainly visited by Mary Queen of Scots in September 1562.[60] Situated on a bluff above the River Fiddich, and guarding the Cabrach pass to the Braes of Don, a castle at Balvenie was first recorded in 1304. Inheriting a stern, approximately quadrangular castle of enclosure with angle towers projecting from each corner, Atholl built a palace block into the southern portion of the entrance façade dominated by a disproportionately large round tower 28 feet in diameter at the south-eastern corner.[61] The tower is a bedroom stack, with a private staircase in the angle, at the end of a sequence along the east façade of, probably, hall, chamber of dais and bedchamber. As at Huntly, the palace is entered from the courtyard, but there the similarity ends. Two stairs rise from the courtyard at Balvenie, one to the left of the entrance and the other in the heel of the new block. The latter, grander and capped by a square corbelled study, feeds directly into the chamber of dais, and therefore must have been restricted to people of appropriate rank. The other – for ordinary visitors, petitioners, and hangers-on – leads up a wide circular staircase into the far end of the hall, as you might expect. As at Huntly, the ground floor is given over to well-provided chambers rather than to cellars. Balvenie's new palace was more complex than Huntly's in that it is L-plan, extending round the corner with the circular bedroom tower projecting from the heel.[62]

6.7 *Conjectural reconstruction of the Atholl Lodging façade, based on the Billings' drawing. Note the circular bedroom tower, with its private staircase in the angle, and the oriel windows. What look like ferocious gunloops on the ground floor light pleasant chambers inside.* (Author)

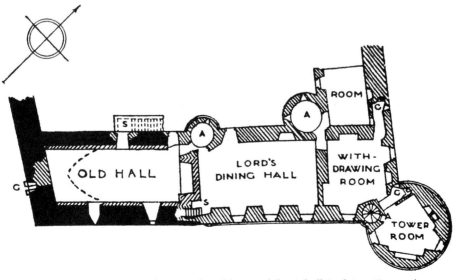

6.8 *Plan of Balvenie, Moray, showing the addition of the Atholl Lodging.* (Drawn by W. Douglas Simpson for the Banffshire Field Club)

If Balvenie's courtyard façade is little more than a large tenement ennobled by its circular staircases, the entrance façade is most carefully contrived. The ground storey is delineated as a plinth by a wide ashlar string-course. The two principal storeys above contain large regularly windowed rooms culminating in the round tower. Windows on the upper floor were delicate bowed oriels. Now, whereas oriel windows were quite the thing in Renaissance Moray and Banffshire,[63] only at Balvenie was there such a magnificent display. The freebooting Atholl motto 'Furth fortuin and fil thi fatris [coffers]' is scrolled across the façade. The palace may have been only part of a wider reconstruction, since a 45 foot long gallery may have been constructed along the north-east side.[64]

Up in Orkney, the esteemed Bishop Robert Reid, a 'man of singular wisdom and experience (who in his time had performed many honourable ambassages, to the credit and benefit of his country)',[65] used the same device to ennoble his palace in Kirkwall. He had added a gigantic round tower capped by a corbelled parapet which contained substantial well-lit bedchambers. On the principal floor, the bedchamber in the tower was reached through the chamber of dais, as normal. Far from being an expression of defensiveness,[66] this stately six-storeyed tower – two storeys in the roofspace and thereby three storeys taller than the house to which it was added – was an expression of power: the tallest and most striking non-ecclesiastical building in the islands. When Reid was Abbot of Kinloss, he had had three of its chapels repainted by Andrew Bairhum and had developed the abbey's reputation for learning and scholarship by expanding its library and inviting the European scholar Giovanni Ferrario to teach there in the 1530s and '40s.[67] Rather than martial, his new Orkney tower was likely to have been sumptuous and filled with his own books.[68]

The nature of Mary of Guise's Court was giving rise to anti-French feeling by 1555, when an Act had to be passed forbidding 'the speaking against the Queen's Grace and sowing evil rumour about the most Christian King of France's subjects sent to this realm for the common weal and suppressing of the old enemies forth of the same'.[69] Sir John Maitland of Lethington found a suitable target in effete French mannerisms:

Thair meit doublet dois thaim rejoice:	[well-fitting doublet]
Thay spread abroad thair buffit hois,	[puffed-out breeches]
Thay taik delyt in nedill wark,	
Thay gloir into thair ruffit sark.	[frilled shirt]
Thair litill bonet or braid hat,	[little bonnet or broad hat]
Sumtym heich and sumtym plat,	[Sometimes high, sometimes flat]
Wattis nocht how on thair heid to stand.	[knows not how on their head to stand]
Thair gluvis perfumit in thair hand	
Helpis meikil thair contenance,	
Et tout est a la mode de France.	[my italics][70]

The queen regent went a degree too far in her increasing dependence upon French advisers. Although fond of Scotland, she appears to have regarded her task as a civilising mission: 'It is no small thing to bring a young nation to a state of perfection and to an unwonted subservience to those who wish to see justice reign.'[71] The Scottish élite felt excluded, and it 'maid thame to conceave sum jolesie aganis the Quenis governement, evin in the beginning'.[72] Nor were the powerful French advisers minded to dissimulate. Sir James Melvill was unimpressed by D'Oysel: 'cholerick, hasty and too passionate. Such are not qualified to rule over remote and form'd countries.'[73] Brawls in the street indicated a popular antagonism against French soldiers. Before the death of Mary Tudor in 1558, Mary of Guise had followed a policy of religious toleration, but afterwards – and in particular following the treaty of Cateau-Cambrésis in 1559[74] – the queen regent became increasingly dependent upon France, and less prepared to tolerate liberty of conscience.[75] The Lords of the Congregation protested to her that their opposition was directed solely at the imperialistic

> Frenche men [who] oppress the Subjects, and that their dear Brethren, members of the Commonwealth, are some of them banished from their own houses, some robbed, some spoiled, some cruelly murdered at the pleasure of inhumane Souldiers, and many live in such fear as if their enemies were in the midst of them.[76]

Once the English invaded in support of the Lords of the Congregation, Scotland, particularly Leith, again became a theatre of war between England and France. Mary died on 11 June 1560, a peace was agreed in July, Leith was surrendered on the 7th, and both French and English left; until, that is, Mary's daughter returned from France as queen on 19 August the following year.

Twenty-seven years later upon the scaffold in Fotheringhay, Mary Queen of Scots would describe herself as 'ane trew Scott and ane trew Frensche and ane trew catholique'[77] – a Scotswoman *and* a Frenchwoman. The sonnets she had scribbled in the margins of her Book of Hours while in prison (for she was also an accomplished poet whose verses earned the commendation of even Ronsard) were in French.[78] Mary arrived in Scotland accompanied by a French staff – including the fool Nicolas la Jardinière (duly dressed in grey by the French tailor Jean Dusow), her tailor Jacques Foulis, tapestry-makers Peir Martyne, Nicola Carbonier and David Lieger,[79] the goldsmith Ginone Loysclener,[80] the parfumer Angelo Marie,[81] three French *femmes de chambre*, and the vivid Sebastien Pagez from Auvergne, one of several French *valets de chambre*, who delighted the queen with his quick wit and music. (She was at Pagez's wedding on the night of her husband Lord Darnley's murder in the Kirk o' Field.)[82] Sebastien was responsible for the masque in the middle of the 'daily Banqueting, Dancing and Triumph' to celebrate the baptism of young James VI, and its apparent mockery of the English ambassadors that came so near to causing an international incident. All Scots knew that Englishmen originally had tails, and the English knew that the Scots knew this of them. So when the satyrs turned their backs to the Englishmen and wagged their tails in their faces, they caused such offence that the ambassadors preferred to sit on the floor behind the table that they might

6.9 Mary Queen of Scots, from a painting in Winton House. (Author's collection)

not have to face it. Sir James Melvill said: 'Mr Hatton said unto me that if it were not in the Queen's presence, he would put a Dagger to the heart of that French knave Bastien who he alledged had done it out of despight.'[83] Even the Christmas fireworks in 1565 appear to have been made by a Frenchman, to judge by his name – Charlis Burdeaulx.[84]

Mary's Court employed a number of musicians: James Drummond and his three trumpeters, hautboy players, four Scottish singers, two French boy singers, Alexander Ure (songster), John Feldie and his children (violars), and three lute players, all adorned in the new royal livery of red and white.[85] Sir William Makdowall was asked to obtain and repair two organs for Holyrood Palace.[86] One of the attractions to Mary of David Riccio – 'Seignior Davie' as he was called – was not just that he was 'a merry fellow and a good musician', but that the queen had established a close harmony quartet among her *valets de chambre* and required a bass voice: 'thus he was drawn into sing sometime with the rest, and afterwards when her French Secretary retired himself to France, this David obtained the said office'.[87] None of which is evident in the first reference to him as 'David Ricio, Italiene, chamber child'.[88] Mary's Court's glamour may be inferred from her own portraits – particularly that in Winton House showing her in a red embroidered dress – and from that of her Master of Household, George, 5th Lord Seton, vividly clad in gold-embroidered scarlet (*see* Plate 12). Since the Church had to issue admonitions against excessive luxury in dress, far from the country turning 'sad brown' after the Reformation, we must assume the contrary. The Treasurer's Accounts imply that money on clothes and tapestry was a principal feature of Court expenditure.

Mary made several progresses into the country, travelling at least twice to Inverness and several times to the Borders. In addition to the exercise of justice and the need to make herself known to her people, these progresses were an important means of building up political support. Their success could be judged by the fact that of the eighty-two lairds or magnates with whom she had stayed, fifty-six supported her after her deposition and the beginning of the civil war.[89] Eighty-two buildings had, therefore, to cope with the arrival of queen and Court. Some, like Tullibardine, were favoured with frequent visits[90] and others – like Balvenie and Craig – only one. More refashioning and some enlargement was indicated.

The houses of the second phase of the Marian monarchy retained the vivid romanticism of the 1550s without that overemphasis upon the bedroom tower as a *donjon* substitute. The bedroom tower was reduced in scale to balance the tower on the opposite angle of the main house (sometimes the main stair, and sometimes a self-contained stack of chambers *adjoining* the principal stair). So the purest expression of the Marian plan – a rectangular main house with circular towers on opposing corners – was the one that resembled French houses such as Montpoupon (Indre et Loire) most closely. The architectural language of asymmetry, round towers and a mythical skyline was not restricted just to the greatest nobility. As in France, it was something to which many aspired. There were at least fifty such houses in Scotland, over three-quarters north of the Forth – most in north-east Scotland. If houses with *rectangular* stairtowers in counterpoint to the circular bedroom tower were added to that number,

Opposite, above: *6.10 Melville, near Lasswade, Midlothian, drawn by Clerk of Eldin, c. 1798. (Author's collection)*

6.11 Earlshall, Fife: a variation on the Marian plan, with its square stairtower. Earlshall evolved over sixty years from the late 1540s . (Author)

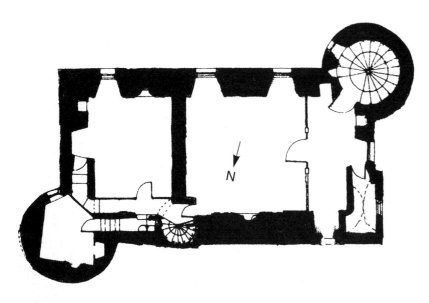

6.12 The plan of the principal floor of Kelburn, Ayrshire. Wall thicknesses imply that this supremely 'Marian' plan cannibalised an earlier house. (Courtesy of Benjamin Tindall Architects)

it would more than double. Although this suggests a widespread architectural movement, the currently accepted dates of the houses' construction extend far beyond the *c.* 30-year period of Marian influence. Craigcrook (Edinburgh), Terpersie (Buchan), Earlshall (Fife), Inverugie (Buchan), Fiddes and Beldornie (Aberdeenshire) are all accepted as having been built before 1562, whereas Kilmartin (Argyll) is thought to date from 1574, Carnousie (Buchan) from 1577, Ballone (Ross) from 1580, Kelburn (Ayrshire) from 1583, and Kilcoy (Ross) a woefully anachronistic 1618.[91]

Circular towers were added to many an inner court as studies (the Glassin Tower in Loch Leven), staircases, guest towers and closet towers. Before he died in 1583 old Glenorchy had added 'the four kirnellis [round towers] of the castle of Ilankeilquhirne [the family's original seat of Kilchurn] and the north chambers thereof', presumably as part of a modernisation.[92] It would be mistaken to interpret them as defensive, providing flanking or enfilade fire along the façade. There is rarely evidence of military intent in such towers. That they contained square- or rhomboid-walled rooms within a circular exterior has been attributed to poor, artisan-based design.[93] Generally, such rooms in a round tower at principal-floor level (although often not in the floor below) may be dated to the mid-sixteenth century. However, their shape is less likely to result from design illiteracy (the same feature appears in many of the greater French Renaissance châteaux) so much as from an attempt to make the room easier to furnish and to decorate with tapestry. The thicker portions of the wall thus created are also sometimes used for stairs, closets or garderobes. Although the tower's form may have been circular for heraldic purposes, there was no need to penalise the users within.

In the house Glenorchy built for his brother Patrick – Edinample in Balquidder – proud expressiveness was the principal feature. Sat on a bluff on the southern shores of Loch Earn, it is now shorn of much of its original character. Much of the spikiness of its heraldic skyline has been cut down, lost or tamed in subsequent rebuildings. The main house (any yards have long been since lost, although the platform is large enough for several) is rectangular, squeezed between two large circular towers diagonally opposite each other. You enter the large-windowed principal floor past a screens passage at the head of the first flight of stairs. Rooms on the floors above would have been restricted to family, household and guests. Edinample was deliberately asymmetrical: it was *balanced*, with a noble composition of towers, turrets and skylines created from the new architectural language.

Two noteworthy examples of the smaller Marian house, in which the second round tower contains chambers rather than the stair, were paradoxically to be found in the hinterland of Reformist Dundee. Wester Powrie is now a massive stump and Claypotts appears approximately as it was refitted in 1588. In 1569, John Strachan of Claypotts had begun construction of a house comprising a rectangular centre with circular towers in the diagonal corners, both of which contain large, well-windowed, flat-walled chambers. Family rooms were in the north-east tower with a small private stair in exactly the same relationship to the private tower as at Balvenie. Those in the south-west tower above the kitchen, reached from the gracious main staircase, were perhaps guest rooms. There is a single well-lit large room at the centre of the house on both the first and second floors; they were originally entered past a screen providing protection against draughts coming up the stairwell. The attic floor, where the public stair ends, is altogether more significant than a mere garret or dormitory.[94] Opening from each end is not a wallwalk but a balcony.[95] This

Top, right: *6.13 West façade of Claypotts, by Dundee.* (Author)
6.14 East façade of Claypotts as it may have originally been conceived in 1569. (Author)

room was once lit by two dormer windows in the form of an aedicule, and the roof was probably lined with timber panelling.[96] The clue to the purpose of this large well-lit chamber with its viewing balconies and large windows lies in the fact the public staircase rises to this room at the top of the house. It must have been a gallery.

Now that it is stripped of its harl and shorn of its principal dormer windows, it is hard to conceive of the original design for Claypotts – worse when you realise that neither round tower may have been completed as originally intended. It is clear from the masonry that the rectangular, flattened, crowstepped rooms do not suit the round towers that they cap. They have been plonked on top with their joints inexpertly sweetened out. The original concept was probably twenty years out of date, too expensive and politically incorrect. A conjectural re-creation of Claypotts, making the assumption that the round towers were originally intended to have been carried up in the manner of the other Marian houses, reveals an emphatic house. Those still wishing to argue a military role for Claypotts and its heraldic gunloops might ponder that the 'wallwalk' did not even command the front entrance.[97]

William Gordon, who built Terpersie in 1561 in a glen not far west of Alford (dated below a narrow window capped with the Gordon boar's head),[98] constructed a miniature Marian house of one principal storey above the cellar floor with a further at roof level. Like nearby Carnousie, the towers are no higher than the main house and appear dumpy in proportion to their circumference. Yet they share a degree of the asymmetrical romanticism of this period of Scottish architecture, without the slightest pretence at heraldic display or martial character.

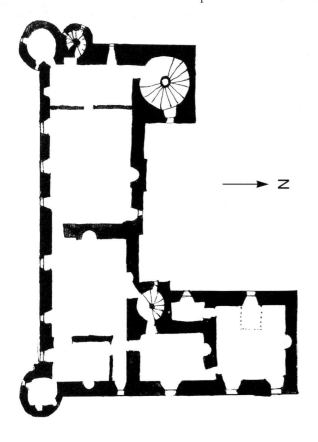

6.15 Probable plan of Kinnaird in the 1550s extracted from a c. 1690 plan of the house by Alexander Edward. Note the twin projecting towers containing circular chambers, the pantry behind the screen with stair presumably down to the wine cellar, and the grandeur of the Glamis-scale entrance stair. (Author)

Curious variants, where *twin*, relatively small round towers appeared on balancing corners of the *corps de logis*[99] possibly took inspiration from buildings like Moncontour in the Loire valley. Kinnaird, Angus, was built by the well-connected Robert Carnegie of Kinnaird, whose son had married the daughter of David Wood of Craig. Carnegie did very well out of Mary of Guise, receiving grant after grant, being awarded joint tack of the Mint in 1549,[100] and acting as ambassador extraordinary to France.[101] In 1555, he undertook substantial alterations to his house.[102] The plans drawn by Alexander Edward for the 5th Earl of Southesk in 1697 imply that Carnegie inherited a tower in the south-western corner of an inner court, and extended eastwards and north-east over the court's entrance pend.[103] Entering up a wide ceremonial staircase to the principal floor, you passed through a screens passage into the hall, the chamber of dais beyond, and bedchamber and closet round the corner, serviced by its own private stair. A tower rose on each corner of the southern façade like – but much more slender than – those at Inverugie and Thirlestane. Although each appears

6.16 *The inner court of Inverugie in ruins, drawn by James Giles, c. 1835.* (NTS)

too small to be a bedchamber, the inventory indicates that in the late seventeenth century these 'rounds' contained a feather bed, bolster and pillow – in the upper floors at least.[104]

By opting for twin-turreted towers framing the main house at Kinnaird, the occupiers appear to have been making a francophile design statement. When the Ogilvies of Airlie, considering their fortress of Airlie to be too remote in its Angus glen, and insufficiently fashionable, purchased Cortachy from a cousin, they likewise used twin towers as the sign of high fashion to proclaim their new house. It was much the same at Dunrobin, where the new courtyard added to the earlier tower was marked by a slender tower at each corner. The noblest example was Inverugie, house of the Earls Marischal – despite the fact that since they were of the Reforming persuasion, one might have assumed they would have rejected French expressionism. But in Renaissance Scotland it was never quite so simple. The Earl Marischal, esteemed to be the richest aristocrat in Scotland after accepting the whole revenues of Deer Abbey, abandoned his huge tower of Ravenscraig on the Ugie for the sunny and fertile haughlands at Inverugie, not far from the estuary where the family was later to found the town of Peterhead. Here he constructed a palace comprising an enormous lodging, with circular bedroom towers at the two corners of its main façade. A small chapel, its ceiling painted in red, black and yellow, was contained within the thickness of the western wall.[105] Inverugie had elaborate inner and outer courtyards, and several walled gardens with statuary.[106]

In 1566, Alexander Ogilvy of the Boyne married Mary, daughter of Mary Beaton, one of the queen's four Maries. He abandoned his old house on its sea-girt rock to construct a new palace not far to the south at Boyne, by Portsoy, and it is reasonable to suppose that his marriage might have been the catalyst. French influence upon country houses as a consequence of marriage may not have been uncommon. George, 4th Lord Seton, and occupier of what was to become the most French château of them all – the Palace of Seton in East Lothian – took as his second wife Mary Pieris, another of Mary of Guise's ladies; and their daughter, Mary Seton, was to be another of the queen's four Maries.[107] (For the palaces of Boyne and Seton, see Chapter 9.)

Mary Queen of Scots was compelled to abdicate in July 1567. On 2 May 1568 she escaped from Loch Leven Castle to Niddrie prior to travelling south to Hamilton and losing the Battle of Langside. The Marian period ended with her exile in England, and the appointment of her half-brother James Stewart, Earl of Moray, as regent. The spitting image of his father James V, both physically and temperamentally, Moray gave himself over to some vengeance. On 11 June 1568, he set out on a punishment tour of the south, with the intention of razing his enemies' seats. Demolition, however, took time and damaged the economy, so he tempered his intention according to how well he was greeted. He invested Boghall (saved); Skirling – 'a notable building' (demolished); Crawfordjohn and Sanquhar (saved); Kenmure (demolished); Kilquonnetie and Dumfries (saved); Hoddam – a strong fort, Annan and Lochmaben (all surrendered); Drumlanrig (retrieved by its owners); Lochwood and Lochhouse (both saved).[108] However, the extent of damage caused when a solid masonry structure is described as ruined or demolished can be regarded with some scepticism. 'The throwing down' and 'destruction' of the castle '. . . are to be understood in the usual limited sense, such expressions being invariably employed to denote only the demolition of the defences of a fortress so as to render the place untenable'.[109] More often than not, it meant destruction of the policies and yards, looting of contents and burning of the roof. It takes great effort to dismantle a five-storey structure with walls 8 feet thick, and it is dangerous. That is one of the reasons why the tower of Pitsligo, doomed to demolition in the early eighteenth century as redundant, survives yet. Much more thorough destruction, as of Hume Castle in 1517, was implied by the use of the ominous phrase 'and the well stopped up'. The partial demolition of houses, and the disrespect for the estate and economy which it implied, made the malevolence of the civil war of the 1570s that much more shocking to contemporaries.

During the Marian period, country house architecture had broken out of its inherited limitations, and by adopting the asymmetrical profile of early Renaissance France, had transformed itself into something wayward and unique for mid-century Europe. But the evident visual relationship between Scottish and French architecture came under increasing pressure as it became obvious that the queen would never return from England. A new dispensation was in power.

7

Early Jacobean Mansions, c. 1568–c. 1600

Gay doings in the boy-king's court of Holyrood, namely running at the ring, jousting and such like pastimes, besides sailing about in boats and galleys in Leith.[1]

If the form of a building can be taken to signify political allegiance, architecture (as Sir Christopher Wren observed) becomes an intensely political act. Perhaps the Marian buildings, with their dominating round towers, implied too close an identification with the previous reign, a risky thing during the difficult years of James VI's minority. Although the characteristic asymmetry and romantic silhouette of mid-sixteenth-century Scottish houses was maintained in essence, it became – as it were – muted and somewhat straightened up, and came to produce some of the country's most distinctive Renaissance buildings. Far from being a fallow period, the years 1570–1600 saw the peak of the building boom.

Nor was there was a sharp break – political, cultural or architectural – with the past, for it is not clear how long it took Scots to accept that the queen was not going to return; perhaps not entirely until the end of the civil war in 1573. To the end of the century, paranoid English spies continued to suspect that a significant proportion of the Scots élite was pro-French, indeed Catholic. From the beginning of James's reign, Burleigh's assiduous *espialls* were amassing and sifting data, gossip and news to brief him with various pen-portraits of the Scots élite, their tendencies, power and following (with details of their seats). George Lord Seton, for example, 'hath been alwayes Frenche in affection, and is in harte a Papiste, thoughe he dare not aduowe it', albeit his power was neither great nor his friends and followers many: 'Of a nature busye and curyous; of more speche than iudgement . . . and a harbourer of Jesuitis, and fugitiues of a countreye, and enemye to a peace [with England, naturally]'.[2]

Burleigh was apprised of fourteen people suspected of receiving pensions from the King of Spain (led by the Earl of Bothwell rather than Huntly), and of how much they were receiving. Indeed, only three of

Graph 6 The boom period of château construction.

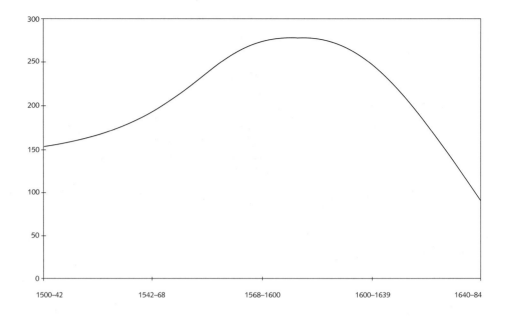

fifteen Scots nobles listed in one report in 1586 tended toward England, one was doubtful and the rest favoured France. The year before, a different spy had listed fourteen noblemen as wanting 'to draw course by France', predictably including Huntly, Lord Claud Hamilton, and the Earls of Errol and Montrose. Most, however, were like the Earl of Bothwell, who was 'nether here nor ther, and so are most of the others that I do not name'.[3] Even as late as 1592, under half of all the Scots earls and lords were reliably Protestant, so Burleigh was informed: ten were young, one doubtful, one suspect, four neutral and thirteen were Catholic.[4] Perhaps too much, therefore, has been made of the inevitable success of the Reformation.

James VI, just over one year old, had been crowned King of Scotland on 29 July 1567, and for the next fourteen years, the country was in the hands of regents, only one of whom, the Earl of Morton, remained in office for long. The last four years of the king's tutelage were dominated by faction, led by favourites who secured the young king's trust. The first, Esmé Stewart, lord of Aubigny in the Sologne, a cousin of James's father, was swiftly promoted to Earl and then Duke of Lennox. His French upbringing rendered him liable to the suspicion of being not only exotic but also Catholic. He secured Morton's execution in 1581 (on grounds of Morton's foreknowledge of Darnley's murder in 1566). A backlash against him took the form of the seizure of the king by the Earl of Gowrie and his supporters when James was out hunting at Ruthven in August 1582. The incident became known as the Raid of Ruthven.[5] The young king's subsequent confinement there seems a not unreasonable date for the construction of its large-windowed, huge-fireplaced long gallery extending to the north-west, complete with a lodging tower at the far end overlooking the steep slope down to the River Almond.[6] Ten months later, James escaped. The successor regime led by the unpopular Captain James Stewart, created Earl of Arran, lasted until November 1585, after which Scotland was under the personal rule of the king. One consequence of the

7.1 Elcho, Perthshire, by
J.C. Nattes, c. 1798. The tower
in the foreground was part of
the now largely vanished inner
court. (Author's collection)

factionalism during the minority was that in the forty years prior to 1608, when bloodfeuds were finally outlawed successfully, feuds and bonds of manrent were at their most frequent.[7]

Educated at length by George Buchanan, one of the finest humanist scholars of his generation (Knox referred to him as 'that singular man' praising his 'erudition and honest behaviour'),[8] the king was unusually learned. James had mastered his classics and, like his mother, was a poet: a poet sufficiently confident to write a book of instruction about how to write poetry – *Essayes of a Prentise in the Diuine Arte of Poesie*;[9] and he encouraged a group of poets (nicknamed the Castalian Band in honour of antiquity) during the early years of his adult reign. He was characterised by an English spy as 'desirous of peace, as appeareth by his disposition and exercises – viz, 1. His great delight in hunting; 2. His private delight in enditing poesies, etc. In one or both of these commonly hee spendeth the day, when hee hath no publique thing to doe.'[10] Like his grandfather, he included an architect, William Schaw, among his close entourage.[11] It was a cultured, inventive Court.

There was little royal building during the minority excepting some reconstruction of the Edinburgh Castle, near-demolished during the civil war.[12] Morton was alleged to have spent most of the available money on

123

his own houses like Dalkeith; and long neglect of royal property might explain the flurry of repairs, reglazing, reslating, cleaning and modernising that took place under Sir William Makdowell once James began to emerge from the shadow of regents in 1579.[13] When Sir Robert Drummond of Carnock surveyed the five palaces of Edinburgh, Falkland, Linlithgow, Holyrood and Stirling in 1583, he found them in a shocking state.[14] The roofs of both Stirling's Great Hall and the west quarter of the palace were about to collapse, and water was pouring into the Chapel Royal.[15] The west wing of Linlithgow was tottering, the walls of Edinburgh Castle remained in ruin, and Holyrood needed to be almost entirely reglazed. Falkland's north gallery was standing roofless and naked, and the south one required urgent work 'or ellis the haill gallerie will decay and fall downe'.[16] Surveying Stirling on 7 May 1583, Drummond made the astonishing proposition that the palace's west wing should be rebuilt as new king's lodgings since it had the best view. It was in such poor condition it would be 'necessary to be taken down to the ground, then to big [build] and build up the same again in the most pleasant manner'. The palace remained the most pleasant part of the castle, but it was the prospect to the west about which he waxed most elegiac:

> It will have the most pleasant sight [view], in special Park and Garden, deer therein, up the rivers of the Teith, Forth, Alloa and Gwddy to Loch Lomond, a sight round about in all parts, and down the river of Forth where there stands many great stone houses, providing there be a fair gallery built on the one side of the foresaid gallery and terrace be buildit and bigit upon the high parts of the foresaid work.[17]

The king's personal interest in architecture was well attested. Whatever help he may have received from William Schaw as architect, he took the large share of the responsibility for the design and construction of the new Chapel Royal in Stirling, erected for the baptism of his son Prince Henry in 1594. It was presumably the king who ensured that the chapel's proportions were those of the biblical Temple of Solomon, and that iconography identifying him as the new Solomon was visible throughout.[18]

James VI had a routine for his progresses, usually to satisfy his obsession with hunting. In August 'his majesty took his ordinary progress of hunting to the west country'[19] by boat to Burntisland, where he sometimes stayed the night (presumably in Rossend), before riding north to spend some weeks at Falkland. Thereafter, he might move on to 'his accustomed hunting in the forrest of Stirling, and then to Inchmerreny, and from thence to Hamilton, according to his custom'.[20] Sometimes, he would pause in Kincardine, the great seat of the Earls of Montrose near Auchterarder. Progresses to the Borders and East Lothian brought him to stay at Dunglass, the Beil and Seton; other favoured spots included Calder House and Hatton (West Lothian), both for hunting; and the palaces of Dalkeith, Dunfermline and Kinneil for banquets with the Douglases, Huntly or the Hamiltons. He would occasionally ride to Lethington (now Lennoxlove) for a consultation with his Chancellor, Maitland, and he seemed to enjoy spending his Christmases with the Erskines at Alloa. It was this routine that provided the Earl of Bothwell with the assurance that the king would be in Falkland in June 1592, ripe for the seizing.[21]

Whether the king was accompanied by a small train, by the entire Court or, as Moysie put it, by 'a sufficient number of his ordinary councellors' who joined him on an ordinary progress lasting from 23 May to 12 August,[22] the country seats had to be ready to cope. James V's Court had consisted of some 300 servants and officials,[23] albeit trimmed down when travelling. Although it is not yet clear how large a train his grandson took with him, an impression can be formed from the many descriptions of the unfolding of the Gowrie conspiracy in summer 1600. On Tuesday 6 August, the king had risen between 6 and 7 a.m. at Falkland to go buck hunting, the weather being 'wonderful pleasant and seasonable'. Even before he could mount his horse, he was approached by Master Alexander Ruthven, the Earl of Gowrie's brother, who whispered a tale of treasure in his ear. Ruthven said that he had imprisoned a disguised base-like fellow in the family's town house in Perth, who had brought 'a great wide pot full of coined gold in great pieces'. By arousing the king's cupidity, the story was devised to entice him to the Gowrie lodging.[24] The king refused to interrupt his hunting, but made ready to leave immediately afterwards. Ruthven attempted to persuade him that companions would not be necessary since he would be returning to Falkland that evening; but a number raced after him even when told that they should not. When James reached the South Inch in Perth, the Earl of Gowrie greeted him with a saddened countenance and a formidable 'three or four score men', whereas the king was accompanied only by fifteen people, largely unarmed because they had been hunting: two of the nobility, three knights and ten gentlemen.

The purpose of Ruthven's haste must have been to separate the king from his entourage, and the reason for his brother the earl's gloom when they met at South Inch was the latter's realisation that Ruthven had not been entirely successful in doing so. They tried again by offering food, for the king ate separately from his nobles. Once James had finished his hastily cooked meal (his entourage, meanwhile, eating in a separate room and unaware of events), Ruthven enticed the king on his own through the gallery, up a turnpike stair, and into a turret (called a study by Calderwood) overlooking Perth's Watergate, there allegedly to meet the man with the pot of gold. In fact the man he met was a probable assassin who was so astounded to discover that the intended victim was the king that it neutralised him. In the meantime, James's companions were advised that he had left suddenly to return to Falkland. Leaving their meal to follow him, they were booting up in the court – some already through the gate into the street – when they heard the king shout for help from the turret window. By the time they reached the head of the stairs, they found that the king had wrestled Ruthven to the floor (proving the value of including wrestling in the learning programme of a Renaissance prince). Ruthven and the Earl of Gowrie were swiftly dispatched.[25]

The hospitality implications of this odd tale are several. While the king might enjoy conversation with his hosts at dinner, he ate alone. Others of rank ate in a separate room. Moreover, since the household was unprepared and the king and his entourage had had to wait irritably for

7.2 and 7.3 The Gowrie Lodging, Perth, drawn by Charles Tarrant in the 1740s when it was being used as a barracks. The king may have eaten in 'D' and his entourage in '15'. By the 1740s the turnpike stair on the courtyard side at the bottom of D, and the study turrets on the floor above '10' had been removed. (NLS)

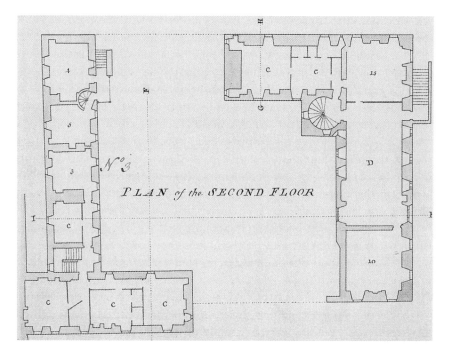

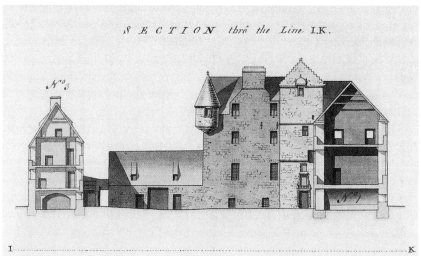

even a welcome drink, and over an hour for food, the conspirators had obviously not intended to feed him. But in the event they had had no option if they were to separate the king from his unexpected companions.

That all lay in the future. During the early years of James's minority, there was localised annihilation – worst during the civil wars of 1568–73 as supporters of the newly crowned infant king (the King's Men) sought to reduce supporters of the queen languishing in English prisons (the Queen's Men). The elderly Châtelherault represented the queen's party among the westland lords (as Huntly did in the north), but since he could never win free of the suspicion of wishing to revive his family's own claims to the throne,[26] he became the principal target. The author of the *Diurnal of Occurrents*, making monthly lists of properties demolished in the capital, also recorded the beginning of the first harrying of Clydesdale on 16 May 1570:[27] '. . . the said lordis, with the Inglis army, come fra Glasgow to the toun of Hamiltoun, and thair thay herijt, wasted and demolished all the landis and houssis of the frindis and partakeris of my lord duke [of Châtelherault] in sic sort and maner as the lyk in this realm hes nocht bene harde befoir'.[28] The *Diurnal*'s author compiled a list of Clydesdale's destroyed 'castellis, palices, houssis and places'.[29] The following week, the gallant army turned its attention to the Hamilton territories in West Lothian, burning Pardovan, Binning (The Binns or Binny?), Kincavill, the Peel of Livingston, my lord duke's lodging in Linlithgow[30] with other gentlemen's houses.

The queen's men were equally assiduous in the north: in 1571 'wes Adame of Gordoun, brother to the said Erle of Huntlie, dantounand [daunting] the north pairtis of this realm, in taking of houssis and puneishing of thair personis that wald not acknowledge nawayis the auctoritie of the quene'.[31] It was in this campaign that his men burnt the House of Corgarff, with Lady Forbes, children and household – twenty-seven in all – inside, which inspired the ballad *Edom o'Gordon*. The Regent Morton retaliated by invading Fife and destroying the Houses of Grange and Hallyards, both belonging to Sir William Kirkcaldy of Grange, the captain defending Edinburgh Castle for the queen. However, between sixteen and twenty-six years later, when Timothy Pont was

Graph 7 Château construction, 1568–1600.

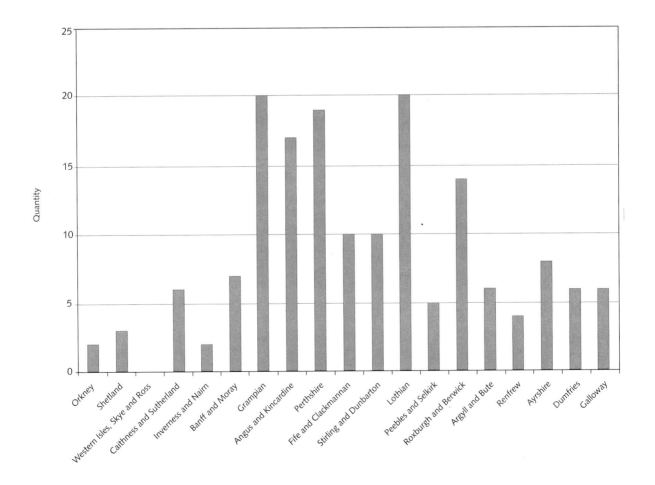

7.4 Drochil. The ashlar stonework with holes for window grilles or yetts, on the left, indicates the three huge windows that once lit each storey of Drochil's central hall. (RCAHMS)

drawing building elevations for assimilation onto his maps,[32] Clydesdale and Linlithgowshire had become as thickly spotted with noble country houses as parts of the Loire valley (among them Roploch, Hamilton Palace and Pardovan), which implies prodigious and rapid reconstruction.

In 1578, the grasping Regent Morton (Scotstarvet accused him of 'gross avarice and extortion')[33] constructed for himself the great house of Drochil in the Borders hills not far from Peebles.[34] The fact that it was used for dispensing justice in the 1580s implies that it was completed by then and had a more important role than a hunting seat.[35] Almost square in plan, with large circular towers in opposite corners, at least one of which corbelled out to square in its topmost storeys (much as Claypotts became after 1588), Drochil has a double-pile plan: that is, two parallel sequences of spacious, well-lit chambers on either side of a corridor; hall and, presumably, chamber of dais on the south; and three well-provided

7.5 *The grasping Regent Earl of Morton (d. 1581). Behind his shoulder is a vignette of the towered and domed Tantallon.* (Attributed to Arnold Bronkhorst. PG 1857. SNPG)

private rooms on the north. There was a timber balcony opening from the central private chamber, implying it was Morton's chamber of dais, and, probably, a viewing platform or gallery at very top of the main house. Details at the head of the round tower imply that its corbelled rectangular superstructure might have risen to two storeys – as did Blair's. The double-pile proved advantageous since by 1649 half had been unroofed, whereas the remainder was still occupied (as also happened at Castle Lachlan in the eighteenth century). Drochil's plan has been compared to that of Chenonceau, but the parallels are slender.[36] During his regency Morton was painted, probably by Arnold Bronkhorst, and perched behind his shoulder was Tantallon with a skyline of cupolas and domes. It is not entirely fanciful to suppose that Drochil was intended to stand out as a similar gesture of architectural magnificence in this fairly bleak upland location.

Of Morton's principal seat of Dalkeith, only the ghost of a tower to the north-west and Renaissance wings lining the remainder of the peninsula can be discerned embedded within James Smith's magnificent palace for the Dukes of Buccleugh.[37] Morton's seaside villa was Aberdour, Fife. In place of the taut geometry of Drochil, a rectangular lodging was casually attached to the south-east of the old tower by a wide staircase with substantial corridors on both ground and principal floors. It is almost as though the new Aberdour Lodging were Drochil sliced in half. The earl's chamber of dais was probably the well-appointed, if small, room opening from the gallery, with its subsidiary chamber and its garderobe. When seeking greater privacy, Morton could retreat along the corridor to the rear chamber, which not only had its own garderobe and subsidiary chamber above the garden stair, but a smaller rectangular stairtower which led both up to the dormer-windowed top storey, and down to the terraced gardens and doocot which he created on the slopes to the south. Once a principal feature of the place, the terraces are being reinstated by Historic Scotland.[38]

The long gallery and lodging extending eastwards at Aberdour are normally attributed to 1632 – the date on a finely elaborate dormer window – but they appear so similar to the now vanished gallery at Huntingtower, that a start date during the Morton period seems not inappropriate. It has lost much of its original splendour: its roof has been lowered, and the large dormer windows that once gazed out to sea and the aedicules that faced into the inner court are now truncated and deprived of their dormer-heads.[39] Elaborate carvings imply the former substance of the place. In contrast to Drochil, however, Aberdour is not so much relaxed as ill-planned, lacking in overall conception.

A wonderfully abrupt 'main house' that exemplifies the change from the Marian period was completed by the Hendersons of Fordell in 1582. Fordell sports towers on the opposing north-west and south-eastern corners of the main house – but they are rectangular and slender, rather than circular and flamboyant. One contains the public staircase, and the other a narrower, family staircase; and neither has chambers until the third floor, once the public stair has ended and a private corbelled stairtower has taken over. Each principal floor contains only two chambers, the eastern ones presumably being private, joined to each other by the private stair. The hall chimney-stack – that signal of hospitality – commands the entrance on the north. Despite its relatively small size, a sophisticated designer was at work at Fordell. The upper storeys of the north-west stairtower, capped by a battlemented viewing platform, are superimposed like a thin layer upon the surface of the main house.[40] Earlier, while central Scotland was in civil war, Bishop John Carswell was constructing an imposing seat of powerful rectangularity at Carnasserie, above Kilmartin, with the full support of the Earl of Argyll. He added a tall main house and entrance tower to an existing tower, and had them tied into one composition by string-courses and elaborate detail. The entrance tower projected to the north, in balance with the tower, thus presaging the U-plan of the next generation.[41]

So the most obvious architectural change was the transformation of circular corner towers into square or rectangular ones, echoed by the occasional substitution of circular turrets by rectangular ones nicknamed 'pricks'.[42] But the principal difference with the previous generation was other than stylistic. For the stair and bedchamber towers of the Marian period 'main house' grew in importance, becoming larger and squarer. The entrance tower developed into a tower of chambers, almost certainly for guests, projecting its turreted gable toward the main entry, whereas the bedroom

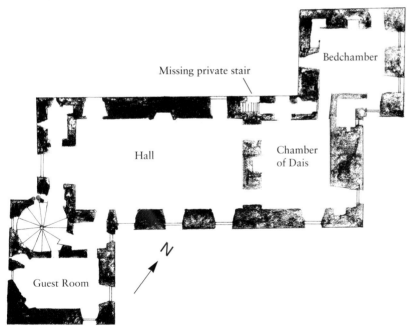

7.6 Menzies, Perthshire – the epitome of the larger early Jacobean mansion. (RCAHMS)

7.7 Plan of Menzies. (Author's collection)

Bedchamber

Missing private stair

Hall

Chamber of Dais

Guest Room

N

stack in the opposing corner began to mutate into something rather like a laird's wing. One architectural consequence was that the predominantly vertical ethos of the previous generation ceded to a horizontal one.

Menzies (originally Weem), lying in the flatlands of Dull to the east of Loch Tay, may have begun as a small fifteenth-century square tower at the eastern end of the current main house, with a smaller separate tower to the south-west, joined by the inner court.[43] It was burnt, re-edified and, according to the 'Chronical of Fortingall', burnt again in September 1502 by Nigel Stewart of Gart.[44] It was evidently repaired and reoccupied in the following decades, but in 1572 Menzies secured the powerful alliance of the Earl of Atholl when he married the latter's daughter Barbara Stewart and, as recorded on the façade, set about re-edifying the house between 1572 and 1577 (presumably with the dowry). He added a square tower to the rear (north-east) of the old tower, set back slightly so that it did not block one of the existing kitchen windows; and probably completed the western end of the main house so that the towers were all joined in a unity.[45] Menzies was probably the earliest of this type of house and, from its extraordinary resemblance to Hatton (*see* pp. 67 and 134), it seems to have been influential. Ironically, what now appears as pure form was the consequence of practical adaptation of inherited structures.

The ceremonial staircase in the entrance tower at Menzies, rather narrower than in the other houses of this type, leads unusually up to all floors of the house. Although there was a second stair corbelled from the rear of the main house, exactly at the junction between the old tower and the sixteenth-century extension, Menzies is significantly under-staired by comparison with its peers. The main stair debouched through a small antechamber and probably a screens passage into the hall – the first room

7.8 The north and west façades of Elcho facing the Tay, drawn by Billings. The control of the entrance façade is replaced by sheer expressionism. (Author's collection)

of the three-chamber state apartment. The hall is divided from what may have been a chamber of dais by the substantial wall of the original tower. A large well-lit bedchamber with its own closet lies in the north-east tower beyond. On each floor, the principal chamber has three large south-facing windows, with a broad fireplace against the north wall. The dowry must have been good, for Menzies was unusually well appointed. Comparable refashioning work was also being undertaken at Blair by Menzies' father-in-law the Earl of Atholl, whose principal seat at the time was Dunkeld.[46] The latter's altogether nobler ancient inheritance of towers was transformed into a more imposing but not dissimilar country seat.

Elcho, on the sunny south side of the Tay looking north to the Carse of Gowrie and the Sidlaws, took its present form some time in the late sixteenth century, although the Fife-based Wemyss family had owned the lands for some time. It was their foothold in Perthshire, nicely close by boat to Perth itself. Most people would have journeyed to Elcho by river and arrived at Elcho's own dock (now a rose garden), walked westwards around the edge of the house and its yards and entered the inner close from the south. Elcho is Janus-faced. To the Tay, it presents a sheer five-storeyed harled wall rising from a bluff, rippling with circular stairtowers swelling out from the main house, each capped with a diminutive, crowstepped study. The entrance, facing uphill, is rigid and rational and appears lower. The spacious stair-and-guest tower on the left is almost certainly a reconditioned relic of an earlier building.[47] Cellars and kitchens connected by the transverse-vaulted service corridor occupy the ground floor. The wide, shallow, ceremonial staircase curves up only to the principal floor: two principal rooms – hall and chamber of dais (which may also have acted as principal bedchamber). The small round chamber to the rear was probably a closet. The chambers on the principal floor of Elcho are large, well volumed, well lit by south-facing windows, and were adorned with a luxurious plaster frieze when John, Lord Wemyss was made an earl in 1633. The clue to the functioning of the house lies in its plethora of staircases. On the assumption that one does not build staircases without a purpose, why should a middle-sized house like Elcho require four of them – half of which fail to interconnect at the top? They must reflect a change in the household organisation. All staircases are narrow above the first floor, presumably to be used only by members of the family, the household or by invited guests.

When Lawrence, 4th Lord Oliphant reached fifty-one (a reasonable age for that time), he began the construction of Hatton, by Newtyle, on the sunny slopes of the Sidlaws facing north across Strathmore. Burleigh's spies were quietly impressed by Oliphant: 'not of great revenue . . . but good landes and profitable; few gentlemen of his surname and so of small power; yet a house very loyall to the state of Scotland, accompted no orators in their words, nor yet fooles in their deedes'.[48] His principal seat was Dupplin, in Strathearn, so it is unclear what led him to build in Angus and Fife, save perhaps that his daughter had married the laird of nearby Glenbervie. Albeit facing north (for the view), Hatton strongly resembles Menzies in its enjoyably neat plan. The ground floor has cellars and kitchen (further cellar or possibly larder beyond).[49] The principal floor of the main house is divided into two rooms – the hall (almost exactly in the

7.9 Hatton from the north. The circular stair to the left may once have been where the circular tower on the right is now, displaced by the construction of the rather grander scale-and-platt stair. (Author)

proportion of 1:2) and the chamber of dais, with a secondary staircase contained within the northern angle exactly in line with the partition between. Off the chamber of dais opens a metal-lined mural chamber which could have been a safe or muniments room. A further chamber – presumably the principal bedchamber – lies in the wing.

The smart scale-and-platt stair contained within the projecting entrance wing, however, is typical of the early seventeenth century. There were two building contracts for Hatton, the delay between the two possibly caused by the Master of Oliphant's sojourn in exile,[50] which might explain odd levels and blocked windows. Equally Hatton's original main stair may well have been a circular *escalier d'honneur* rising from bottom to top which was moved to the north-eastern angle when fashion began to favour a guest wing and a scale-and-platt stair in 1618,[51] by which time Oliphant's son, the 5th Lord, despite a well-endowed marriage to the 1st Lord Madderty's daughter, had wasted his enormous dowry and substantial inheritance, and Hatton was in other hands.[52]

The House of Kellie by Arncroach in Fife was another Oliphant seat, and sports the insignia of an improving marriage: namely to Margaret Hay, daughter of the Earl of Errol, in 1573. Constructed on an idyllic flat plateau at the foot of the Lomond Hills gazing south over the Forth to the Bass Rock, Kellie was not in the slightest defensible. Compared to its peers – abandoned, ruined, gutted or destroyed – Kellie is remarkably fortunate in having survived with much interior decoration and most of its atmosphere intact. During the later eighteenth century, it had been used as part of a farm, and was largely unscathed if somewhat dilapidated when James Lorimer, Professor of Scots Law at Edinbugh University, took a repairing lease of it in 1878. An inscription above the door records how

the building was rescued from owls and crows. Lorimer's younger son Robert, Scotland's finest Arts and Crafts architect, was responsible for the garden and the idiosyncratic garden house.

Kellie's origins lie in the thick-walled north-western fifteenth-century tower extended by a courtyard wall to another tower of similar dimension.[53] A third tower, added at a slight angle to the east, has a blocked arched doorway in its south wall that implies access, possibly by a wallwalk, to what may have been a fourth in the front courtyard.[54] Medieval Kellie might, therefore, have resembled a manor house like Mugdock, Stirlingshire, with slender rectangular corner towers enclosing a courtyard. The eastern tower was elaborately reworked, kitchen and stair added, for Oliphant and his wife in 1573 to make it a self-contained living unit. The upper storeys of Kellie's east tower are typical of a late sixteenth-century miniature tower house, with turrets, closets and stairtowers perched on corbels sitting upon a squinch. The aedicular window with a sunburst facing east over the garden is a common detail in French châteaux, particularly in Brittany.

At some point, probably in the mid-sixteenth century, the space between the two western towers was filled by the insertion of a low building, supported on a vault running longwise,[55] which may have been a hall. In 1603–6, however, the spendthrift 5th Lord Oliphant refashioned and extended it, adding the upper, dormer storey and fine turrets and dormer windows to the towers.[56] The house now had the state apartment sequence of principal chamber (originally hall but now drawing-room), smaller room (probably chamber of dais and now dining-room), and third chamber (the laird's bedroom). The importance of each is signified by its excellent and expensive plasterwork. Kellie's

7.11 Maclellan's Lodging, Kirkcudbright, built by Sir Thomas Maclellan of Bombie in 1577 on the site of an earlier castle. The view is from the south-east. The near-side tower rises up to a viewing platform. This was an extraordinarily fashionable and large house. (Author)

similarity to Elcho also extends to the contrast between the controlled entrance façade, with its well-spaced and large windows, and the maverick north façade with its irregular windows, stairtowers and rooflines – save that Kellie's northward-projecting towers are rectangular rather than circular.

In 1613, when Kellie became the seat of Viscount Fenton, later Earl of Kellie, the house was reworked again, probably to reach its current state. For the new earl had money: as Sir Thomas Erskine of Gogar, he had accompanied James VI to Perth on the day of the Gowrie conspiracy and had done very well thereafter. The plaster within the state rooms is largely seventeenth century, and some can be dated to 1617 since the same moulds were used for refitting the palace at Edinburgh Castle for James VI's return that year.[57] Other contemporary details include the square ashlar chimney-stacks set on the angle which rise from both the centre of the west gable and from the north-west tower.[58] Signs of that evolution remain on the ground floor and up among the bedchambers, with their wonderful coved ceilings and plasterwork above. The Earl's Room (above the hall) is several steps higher than the Vine Room (above the dining-room), indicating that they may not have been built at the same time. The absence of any connection with the eastern tower at this level emphasises the extent to which the latter was self-contained and probably for the family. The north-west tower was, by contrast, fully absorbed and partially cannibalised by the new main house. The substantial upper chambers of the south-west tower (each with its own closet) are reached by a wide, well-lit ashlar turnpike stair in the angle, and their lavish appointment implies that this was the guest tower.

Not all such houses were in the east central Lowlands. In 1585, Sir John Maxwell, 12th Baron of Pollock and his wife Margaret Cunningham, daughter of the laird of Caprington,[59] built their villa of the Haggs on gentle south-facing slopes some 2 miles south-west of Glasgow. Its current shape (and function as a City of Glasgow museum) is the consequence of late nineteenth-century rescue from ruin. The construction proved difficult since Pollock had to seek financial help from his father to complete the internal plasterwork, 'otherwais I had never enterprysit sic ane work'.[60] What earns Haggs a place in this group, given that it lacks the second, private tower to the rear, is not just the sweeping circular stair leading to the first floor, nor even the corbelled viewing platform capping the narrower, private stair five storeys up, but the secondary staircase, corbelled out from the *piano nobile* at the junction between the hall and the chamber of dais, like Hatton. The inner room was the private laird's room and this staircase, larger than the smaller one rising in the guest gable, is the family staircase.

In its details, Haggs is very much a building of the westlands. Surrounding the door and its inscription is ornate cable or rope moulding, tied in the middle by another rope which, acting like a horizontal string-course, circumnavigates the building at the foot of the *piano nobile*, anchoring the corbelled stairtower on its way. Such exuberant carving was a western phenomenon, appearing on Newark, Port Glasgow, Whitefoorde, Cowhill and Kenmure, but is at its most distinctive when embracing Haggs' two-storeyed dormer window.[61] The lower window pokes its head through the chequerboard cornice which is forced sufficiently upward to embrace an attic window above. Ornate carving resembling diapered pillars occupies the space between, and little carvings of mannikins once decorated the flat skewputts.[62]

A house similar to Hatton was erected at Finlarig by the west end of Loch Tay by Sir Duncan Campbell of Glenorchy, Black Duncan of the Cowl, not long after he inherited in 1583.[63] A chapel had existed on the site since before 1523 but there is no evidence of a house until Black Duncan 'biggit the castell of Finlarg, pitt and office howse thairoff, repairit also the chapell thereof, and decored the same with pavement and paintrie, for the bigging and warkmanship he gaiff ten thowsant pundis'.[64] Sir Duncan Campbell was a man of stern ambition, considerable taste and a fondness for books. A portrait of him, resplendent in black velvet, with pearls and caressing an ornate sword hilt, shows him to be not untypical of a sixteenth-century European aristocrat. Indeed, in April 1602 'he passed to the courts of England and France, and thereafter thought good to take a view of Flanders, and of the wars of the town of Ostend, finally returning through England'.[65] Upwardly mobile, he forged new alliances by marrying first the daughter of the Earl of Atholl, and second the daughter of Lord Sinclair, while one of his sisters married the Earl of Menteith and the other Campbell of Ardkinglas. His daughters likewise did duty: Margaret was married to the laird of Weem (at Castle Menzies, thus protecting the eastern approaches), Anna to the laird of Inchmartin, and Jean to Campbell of Cawdor. Dowries and bridal gear cost the father the princely sum of 96,000 merks.

Duncan was greatly given to building. He spent 18,000 merks on erecting the tower of Achallader, presumably as a hunting seat, north by Rannoch Moor; the House of Lochdochart – a fishing pavilion, perhaps, on an island; a four-storeyed great house in Benderloch in 1601; and completed nearby Barcaldine in 1609. The year before, he had spent 10,000 merks on stopping the Tay from 'destroying the place and yards of Balloch'. In 1613, he rebuilt the hall at Kilchurn and three years later commissioned John Drummond of Drummondernoch to build a three-storeyed building at Kilchurn between the great tower and the kitchen with a chapel on the top floor. He also appears to have been a considerable agricultural improver, lending his son Robert 2,000 merks to build a salt pan in Lorne, making parks at Balloch, Finlarig, Glenloquhay and Kilchurn 'and caused sow acorns and seed of fir therein, and plantit in the samen young fir and birk'.[66] He stocked the island of Inchesaile with fallow deer and rabbits once he had obtained a rent-free tack for nineteen years from his cousin the

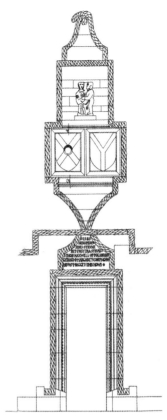

7.12 Detail of the decoration surrounding the entrance of Haggs, by Glasgow. (Drawn for the National Art Survey/Author's collection)

Earl of Argyll, and he was particularly proud of his horse stud. In 1597, he obtained a 'meikle gray cursor' from the king with which to cover his mares.

The Glenorchy Campbells' campaign of attrition and conquest of the lands of the McGregors of Glenstrae was undertaken in the most contemporary way – through friends at Court, legal writs, and by endless bonds of manrent, some of which compelled hunting the McGregors to the death.[67] One victim was Duncan Laudosach McGregor who was duly beheaded with his sons on 16 June 1552. Duncan Laideus' *Testament* was a lament for the beauties of the 'garden of pleasance' of Glenalmond:

> Fair weill Stratherne, maist cumlie for to knaw
> Plenisit with plesand policie preclair
> Of touris and townis standand fair in raw
> Gar thy wyffis, gif thow do na mair,
> Sing my *dirige* aftir *user Sarum*
> For oftymes I gart thame alarum.

> [Farewell Stratherne, most comely for to know
> Filled with pleasant and bright estates
> Towers and towns standing fair in a row
> Get thy womenfolk, if thou do no more
> To sing my *Dirige* after the use of Sarum
> For often I caused them alarum.]

The more successful Glenorchy became, the more traditional the McGregors were in their retaliation, and it was no difficult matter to persuade the establishment in Edinburgh who had the just cause. In 1590, James had written to Black Duncan seeking venison for his forthcoming wedding feast, and Glenorchy had dispatched Drummond of Drummondernoch accordingly. Intercepted by the McGregors, Drummond was decapitated. The McGregors invaded Glenorchy's land again in about 1610, killing forty great mares and the 'fair cursour' sent from London by Prince Henry. It was not a subtle way of persuading the Court of their claims.

There was nothing primitive about Black Duncan Campbell nor about his hospitality; nor, probably, about his houses, nor the seat of his family. Finlarig's steward was responsible for holding fifteen silver spoons, cups with silver bowls, and a quantity of other silverware in his pantry. The cushions were sewn with the arms of Black Duncan and his wife.[68] Indeed, as a marginal manuscript note reveals –

> Duncan Campbell by my hand
> The blackest laird in all the land[69] –

he relished his reputation and had a good sense of humour. The form of his new house of Finlarig was not at all unlike Castle Menzies (then the House of Weem), which was being erected under his watchful eye just to the east of Balloch. It comprised a main house, entered through the customary rectangular entrance tower on the left, with a scale-and-platt stair leading to the single principal room or hall on the floor – double the width to length (36 × 18 feet). The probable tower to the north would have contained a further chamber with, presumably, its own stair. Through the *Black Book of Taymouth* we know something about Duncan's ambitions for Finlarig. It was not free-standing, since Duncan was forever adding substantial structures to the court – a two-storeyed building with four fair chambers on the west side, then a two-storeyed building with two larger chambers on the north side, and then a park. This implies that Finlarig may have been primarily the family house, with guest quarters and offices in the remainder. All that remains is a fragmentary ruin and a water tank or cistern, smaller than that at Dunnottar but accorded by legend a second use as a McGregor beheading pit.[70]

Finlarig was more modern and more private than Balloch. The restriction of public activity to a single chamber on the first floor compares curiously to Balloch with its chamber of dais, ceremonial portraits and gallery in the formal informality of the earlier generation. There is no evidence that Finlarig had a gallery. The Campbells of Glenorchy entertained more grandly and more frequently in Balloch, which was the principal seat. Yet guests also visited Finlarig from time to time. On 28 June 1590, the laird entertained the Earls of Bothwell and Menteith, Lord Inchaffray and 'sundy other strangers' for a week, and they drank gallons of the best home-brewed ale, wine imported from Dundee, and ate old cheese, new cheese, spices like saffron, ginger and pepper (also imported through Dundee), bacon, six wedders, old Loch Tay salmon, freshly caught salmon from Loch Dochart and Inverawe, fresh beef, hard fish and skate.[71]

The relationship between the two houses is evident from the furnishings: Balloch had thirty-two feather beds whereas Finlarig had only nine; Balloch had four arras tapestries, but Finlarig only one; there were sixteen chandeliers in Balloch but only six in Finlarig. Finlarig (and Balloch) had substantial storage in 'My Lady's garderobe', and the household garderobe in which to store their enormous quantities of stuff. There was a kitchen, pantry, larder, wine cellar, brewhouse, woman house (laundry because it contains cauldrons?) and also the 'ladies' gallery'.[72]

Erected possibly from scratch, the house of John Gordon of Glenbuchat and his wife Helen Carnegie, daughter of Sir Robert Carnegie of Kinnaird, arose in 1590 on an inclement hilltop amid the braes of Don, cannily re-using stones from nearby ruinous Kildrummy Castle.[73]

7.13 Glenbuchat, Aberdeenshire, drawn by Billings. (Author's collection)

Glenbuchat is similar to but smaller than Menzies. The public stair to the *piano nobile* does not wholly occupy the rectangular western tower, leaving some inconvenient residual space, the purpose of which is unclear. It is almost as though the masons got the dimensions wrong, or the stair was bought prefabricated from elsewhere and did not fit. The principal floor (now split by a cross-wall) originally comprised a principal chamber with a private room in the far tower, with its own staircase projecting in the angle. That stair, and its twin rising in the angle behind the entrance tower, are carried on squinches. In this part of Aberdeenshire, they must have appeared rather flash. Remains of only four third-storey turrets survive, but whereas two are circular, two are large and rectangular – the pricks referred to by Lowther, carried upon an elaborate double-corbel course.

Without doubt, the most extraordinary feature of Glenbuchat is indicated by the long strips of ashlar at roof level above the main entrance. They cannot have been part of a cornice, since they descend rather than being horizontal. Instead, they have been hollowed into a channel to form a gutter to carry water from the roofs. In his reconstruction,[74] Douglas Simpson recognised this and proposed a downpipe, without questioning why Glenbuchat had not put the downpipe in the corner rather than carrying it over the entrance with the risk that it might splash. He appears to have noticed neither the hole in the wall of the adjacent chamber, nor the twin drainage holes cut through the corbels of the chamber's circular turret.[75] Glenbuchat's guests had a third-floor bathroom.

These houses all share the common features of the sweeping, often circular stair leading to the *piano nobile*, concealed within a rectangular wing. Given the expressiveness of mid-century architecture, and the wild informality of the other façades, this concealment must have something to do with a growing formality of the entrance façade. These self-contained, compact houses, largely lacking in heraldic overtones and noble accoutrements, were planned with maximum economy of space and of structure. Some components of the first-rank country seat are lacking: no gallery, rarely a chapel (Kellie has a chamber later dedicated to a chapel), nor even a rooftop viewing platform. Orientation, view, shelter and cultivation outside, and comfort within. They are remarkably plain and well proportioned, with elaboration left, for the most part, to a skyline of dormer windows and turrets. That there is no obvious differentiation between the harled plinth and an elaborate superstructure indicates that they predate seventeenth-century expressionism. They eschew unnecessary height. The imagery of a businesslike, agriculturally improving late sixteenth-century Scotland was a sober one. Houses should not be unreasonably tall, and although echoes of a romantic past were permissible in the occasional turret or stairtower, they were best kept out of sight to the rear.

By the end of the sixteenth century, however, the separation between laird and family from the main body of the house, and from guests in the farthest away tower, was more or less complete. Although it may have been inevitable that the multi-functional medieval great hall would be replaced by several single-function chambers, the change could also be taken to reflect a growing formality in Scottish life at odds with its traditions.

8

Early Jacobean Tall Small Houses, c. 1570–c. 1600

*All the gentlemens houses are strong castles, they being so
treacherous to one another that they are forc'd to defend
themselves in strongholds; they are commonly built . . . with
many towers and strong iron grates before their windows.*

Thomas Tucker, 1679[1]

The majority of 'gentlemens houses' of Scotland were neither the seats of
the greater magnates, nor castles. But they were sufficiently martial in
aspect to deceive splenetic English gentlemen travellers like Tucker. Many
lairds of lesser standing, predominantly in the Lowlands and particularly
in the south-west, had inherited or otherwise acquired ('conquished') a
small tower, or a property requiring a new house, and had proceeded to
build. The new small house divided into two broad categories – those that
developed vertically, which Tucker mistook for castles, and those that
hugged the ground, which he appears not to have noticed. Most opted for
height; a stalk, as it were, upon which the developing Scottish
architectural details of corbelled staircases and studies, turrets and 'many
towers' clustered like Brussels sprouts. The concentration of such detail in
a small house produced a much more romantic – almost raffish – air when
compared to their larger brethren like Hatton or Menzies. They are
entirely recognisable as belonging to the period between 1570 and 1600,
and were possibly built in greater numbers than any other type of country
house during the Scottish Renaissance.

Their ground-hugging, horizontally proportioned counterparts were the
Scottish equivalent of the small English manor house. Sometimes only two
and a half storeys high, they were designed for convenience rather than
appearance, and maintained and extended the suite of apartments on the
same floor. Usually delightful, these houses were often L-plan, with a stair
in the angle, or T-plan with a projecting stairtower. When a grander family
built such an unpretentious house, it was usually for the heir during his
pre-inheritance period, or perhaps for a dower house. Where the buildings
constituted the principal home, their owners were largely those who did

not have to bear a huge pedigree. Houses like Newton of Doune, Old Leckie and Fountainhall were built for minor scions of a family, or for successful merchants and professionals.

A particular group of houses in the hinterland of Dundee – Invergowrie, Wester Powrie, Pitkerro, Murroes, Blackness, and probably Logie and Gagie as well – were unusually low and plainly rectangular, adorned only by a stairtower, cylinder-like bedroom tower, occasional turret and crowsteps. There was normally just a single apartment of two or three chambers sandwiched between kitchen and cellars below and dormer-windowed attic rooms above. Invergowrie, a minor tower of the Grays (until occupied by the Clayhills family – merchants and Dundee councillors), was extended northwards in the sixteenth century, and again in the seventeenth and eighteenth. Blackness, a similar house a mile nearer Dundee, was the seat of the Wedderburns, Dundee councillors and Baltic traders. So perhaps these houses may be categorised as merchants' villas.

The focus of this chapter, however, is upon those who decided to enhance the *verticality* of their house in the teeth of domestic logic. Why erect a tall house – sometimes an *unconscionably* tall house – when height was not required for defence? Probably because the owners considered height as a way of signalling status and lineage in a society preoccupied with history, genealogy and precedence. Perhaps, also, they were determined that their seat should be visible above the tops of the increasingly protected trees;[2] or even that this was the form of house required by their status or their pocket. However, if they were going to build tall *and* embrace the new ideas, they had to rework the plan, and the Renaissance equivalent of the medieval tower emerged as the new compact

8.2 Fountainhall, East Lothian, in the 1920s, a substantial country house entirely lacking in martial pretension. It was photographed by the National Art Survey. (Author's collection)

Opposite: 8.1 Greenknowe, Berwickshire, a delightful, small hunting lodge for the Setons of Touch. (RCAHMS)

8.3 Balbegno, Kincardineshire. The new wing added in 1569 rises above the truncated original tower out of sight to the left. (Author)

house. It was not just a matter of building an abbreviated version of Menzies, shorn of its second tower and shorter by a bay. The sequence of chambers required appropriate adjustment – as was demonstrated in the House of Partick.[3]

The tall small house of the 1580s shared only height with the tower house. It had much thinner walls, and a new aesthetic of stairs, corbelled stairs, turrets and subsidiary chambers. The cheapest way to start for maximum effect was to extend an existing tower by building a new stairtower against it, as the Brown family did at Carsluith, near Creetown, in 1568. That is also what Andrew Wood, hereditary Thane of Fettercairn, did to Balbegno just south of Fettercairn, dated 1569 on its elegantly carved parapet. Set in a typically indefensible location part-way down a shallow brae with a stunning view south-east over the Mearns, Balbegno now looks like a squat L-plan tower; but the wing, containing two chambers per floor and a spacious stair, is not tied into the tower as it would have been had it all been built at the same time. Its glorious red ashlar parapet, embellished with carved portraits of Wood and his wife, could not be continued round to embrace the original tower, since it is at a higher level. The house is shot throughout with many other curiosities.

What may have happened is that Wood had inherited a smallish, three-storeyed and attic rectangular tower which he transmogrified in pursuit of some chivalric objective. He first secured eight good new apartments with a stair by attaching the five-storeyed wing. He then lowered the original tower, sliced off its roof, parapet and crenellations, and rendered it visually subordinate. Lines in the plasterwork, blocked doorways, widened windows and truncated fireplaces imply that at some time Wood or his architect removed the upper floors in the tower to insert a mock-medieval groin-vaulted hall (at 30 × 19 feet disproportionately large for that size of house)[4] on the first floor. This extraordinary room is wholly imperceptible from the exterior. Fifteen of its sixteen vaulted compartments are painted with the slightly faded swirls, swaggers and mythical beasts of the escutcheons of those Scottish earls who caused the involuntary removal of the Earl of Morton as regent on 31 December 1580 and formed the Privy Council of James VI thereafter, including those of James Stewart, the

upstart Earl of Arran and prime mover in the enterprise.[5] The sixteenth compartment is thought to have contained the arms of the Earl of Gowrie, which were painted out when the earl was forfeited in 1584, allegedly for having held the king hostage in the 'Raid of Ruthven' three years earlier. Wood could easily afford the reduction in living space required for his new room of state given the chambers provided in his new wing.

The resemblance between Balbegno's groin-vaulted hall and that of Towie Barclay in Buchan naturally leads to the supposed designer of Towie, the shadowy Alexander Con (or Conn) of Auchry, assumed to have been practising in Aberdeenshire in the late sixteenth century.[6] Other buildings attributed to him, dated from carvings and armorial panels, are Craig (1559), Delgaty (1570), Towie (1593), and Gight (attributed to 1560–70). They are all L-plan, broad, stumpy (save Delgaty) and lacking in any of the flamboyance of the preceding Marian period in which surrounding Aberdeenshire had been so immersed. Craig resembles a fort. Rooms and stairs lie within the thickness of the walls in the ancient

8.4 Balbegno, the groin-vaulted ceiling of the hall painted with the arms of the administration that overthrew the Earl of Morton in 1581. (RCAHMS)

8.5 The vaulted hall of Towie Barclay, Aberdeen, drawn by Billings. (Author's collection)

fashion. They all share a particular feature of the plan: that the entrance, rather than giving directly onto an adjacent staircase, leads instead into a corridor running through the vaults to the far side of the ground floor. The stair debouches into the hall upstairs from within the wall. This distinctive plan was also shared by at least Fedderate, Lesmoir and Culquhonny.

Unfortunately, there was certainly no Alexander Con available in the 1590s and it is unlikely that there would have been one still alive and working as a mason in the late 1560s.[7] There were two Alexander Cons – one born *c.* 1480 and the other *c.* 1510. The latter, the first to style himself 'of Auchry' (thereby landowner) in 1553, would have been unusually long-lived for the time if he were still practising as a mason in the 1560s or later. If the buildings were indeed attributable to Con of Auchry, perhaps he was developing a variation of the tower house with its curiously sophisticated spatial experience when tower houses were still evolving in the first decades of the century, as had been the case in Ayrshire. If that was so, perhaps his buildings were all later reworked when they were also dated – and one reason for such reworking might have been the Counter-Reformation in north-east Scotland between the 1570s and 1590s. These houses, with their anachronistic groin-vaults and elaborate interiors containing carvings and decoration that would have been recognisable to any visitor as being strongly Catholic,[8] concealed within the blandest of old-fashioned façades. So just as Balbegno's vaulted hall may have been inserted in an earlier building, the 'Arma Christi' and other Catholic insignia were inserted into those houses long after Alexander Con of Auchry was dead if they formed part of Counter-Reformation propaganda. The identity of the architect who carried out the work is implied at Edzell. The ground floor of the summer house in Edzell Castle[9] is groin-vaulted, and still on display are the remnants of its oak panelling with Catholic motifs. The ornate gunloop beneath its southern window is the trademark of Thomas Leiper (*see* Chapter 9).

That somebody was reworking these buildings in the later sixteenth century is supported by datestones. Towie, whose chunky exterior conceals the splendour of a groin-vaulted roof over its hall (an oratory at one end where one might have expected a gallery), not only has a datestone of 1593, but a particular swastika mason's mark. That same mason's mark was discovered during the demolition of the Errol Lodging (the town house of the Earls of Errol) in Turriff – whose dormer window head was dated 1590.[10] It was the Earls of Errol and Huntly that led the Catholic forces to face the army of the Crown in 1594 at the inconclusive Battle of Glenlivet. In the later sixteenth century, Catholicism did well in north-east Scotland under such powerful protection: nothing quite as overt

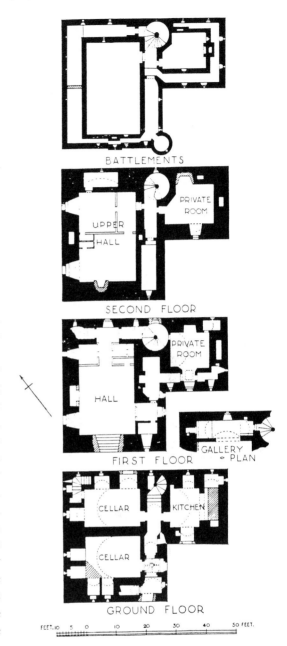

8.6 Plan of Craig, Aberdeenshire, showing the typical arrangement of houses possibly associated with Con of Auchry, its ground floor corridor leading to a stair at the rear. (SAS)

as the virtual Catholic proclamation Huntly had engraved upon his main entrance at Huntly in 1602, but distinctive none the less. Native caution at laird level probably indicated that such enthusiasms were best kept indoors.

That so many early Jacobean landowners preferred to build more vertiginous houses – sheer height in proportion to mass – indicates a particular architectural agenda, however. In 1600, Sir John Charteris rebuilt a narrow rectangular tower, only *c.* 31 × 28 feet, in the corner of the inner close of his ancient seat of Amisfield in Nithsdale, containing a single chamber each on the *piano nobile* and on the floor above.[11] In that it contains his arms and those of his wife – Agnes Maxwell, daughter of the 4th Lord Herries – it might have been paying respect to the architectural preferences of Charteris' father-in-law. The latter had repaired the nearby ancestral seat of Hoddom after its 'throwing down' by the Earl of Sussex in 1568 and, about the same time as the work was carried out at Amisfield, was adding a two-storeyed superstructure on top of Hoddom's tower. A closer association between Amisfield and Hoddom than mere marriage is implied by the same craftsman undertaking

8.7 Elevation of Amisfield, Dumfriesshire, prepared for the National Art Survey, which was begun in the 1880s. (Author's collection)

Right: *8.8 Section through Amisfield, prepared for the National Art Survey.* (Author's collection)

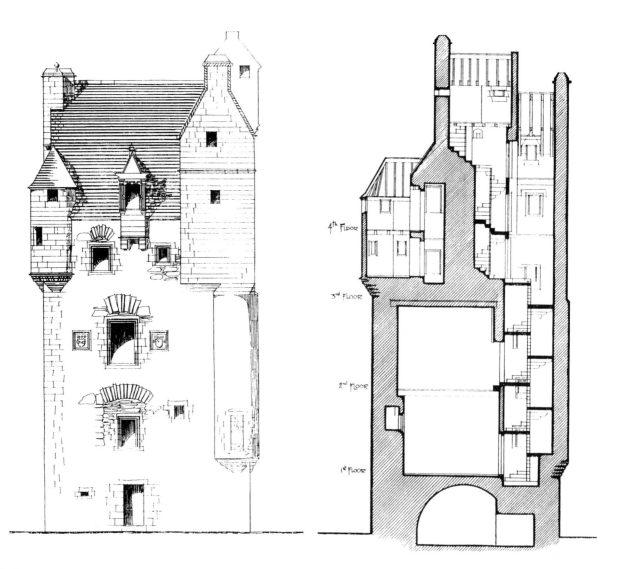

similarly carved and painted doors for the two houses in 1600 and 1601 respectively.[12] The way the corners of the superstructure at Hoddom swell and curve, and are capped as though they are two-storeyed turrets resembles the way Amisfield's two-storeyed ashlar turret fades into the flat wall plane.

A preoccupation with Amisfield's shot-holes, watchmen's viewing points and machicolations has overshadowed the oddity of erecting such a tall, narrow building so late, and obscures its architectural achievement. Three, formerly harled, lower floors (the walls becoming thinner with each later rebuild)[13] act as a plinth for the superstructure. The plinth is elaborated only by the entrance, the armorial panels, and the corbelling and gentle curves of the staircase swelling out of one corner.[14] The upper three floors, however, burst out in a wonderful confection of polished red ashlar two- and three-storeyed corbelled turrets, roll mouldings enriched with nail-head decoration, oriel and dormer windows. Ceilings of several rooms were stuccoed and painted with ornaments 'of the most grotesque kind'.[15]

The corbelled oriel window, projecting above the main entrance from the attics above the fourth storey, has a pedimented dormer-head distinctive for its flattened ends which project like wings. When viewed close up, it can be seen to be sitting within a cornice of miniature corbels, with a ropework moulding (a more slender version of that framing the gable and chimney of the south-east tower) outlining its pediment. The window itself is framed by twin columns with a fretwork moulding above.[16] It clearly has symbolic significance. So has the swelling staircase tower; for the staircase itself is contained *entirely within* the wall

8.9 The 'heraldic' window guarding Amisfield's façade, prepared for the National Art Survey. (Author's collection)

8.10 Amisfield drawn by Clerk of Eldin in the later eighteenth century, showing its relationship to the inner court and the early seventeenth-century house. (Author's collection)

thickness, without any need for the masonry to bulge outwards. Moreover, this masonry goitre is not even to the same diameter curve as the staircase it encloses. The designer wished to express the staircase, even though there was no functional necessity for it.[17]

Scottish Renaissance houses like Amisfield defy both classification and logic. Once the veil of 'military necessity' is removed, why should Charteris, with the wealth and taste to commission such a flamboyant piece, have opted for a house so much tighter and narrower than the norm? Why decorate so lavishly and proudly a house which his peers would have regarded as providing but primitive accommodation? Perhaps he did not. Perhaps another building within the inner court was the main house at Amisfield – for the tower appears to have no kitchen. Even if a now-vanished courtyard building had produced food for carrying into the tower, it would have been perverse for the seat of somebody who had just married into one of the most powerful Border dynasties.[18] That Charteris chose to refashion the upper storeys of an existing tower rather than build anew leaves the strong impression that this was not the principal residence; and the lavishness of its decoration implies that he was not short of funds. So the 'main house' or mansion might, instead, have been the nearby building that was refitted with rows of aedicular windows in 1631.[19] The tower must, rather, have played a different role within Amisfield's inner court – a decorated summer house, a guest tower, or perhaps a dower house (albeit not much use for the elderly), which could also double as a lookout if needs be.

The location of towers even narrower and more slender than Amisfield confirms a purpose other than that of the principal country seat. Gylen, for example, clasping its crag on the very southern tip of Kerrera looking across to Mull and south to the Garvellachs, to Jura and to Colonsay, was a seigneurial beacon. Originally called Dun Donachy according to Pont, Gylen was probably built by Dougall MacDougall, fifteenth of that name, perhaps when he inserted a marriage datestone of 1582 – which suits the architecture neatly.[20] The seat of the clan was the larger but much less fashionable Dunollie, situated on a rock guarding the entrance into Oban Bay. It then probably consisted of the original Gaelic curtain-wall castle with added tower house. Tiny Gylen – the main house *c.* 21 feet square and the stairtower about half that – is a remarkable work of high ingenuity. Using the varying levels of the cliff to maximum effect, each façade is designed to look as though it is of a different height: the entrance elevation appears three-storeyed; the east (courtyard entrance) elevation four-storeyed; the south five-storeyed; and the western elevation facing the sea six-storeyed.

The massing of the building is intended to accentuate this effect with a harled plinth of varying height (according to your viewpoint) focusing upon a superstructure of corbelled turrets, stairs, dormer windows, chimneys, crowsteps stepping up to a delightful cabinet at the apex.[21] The intricate carving of cable moulding and miniature corbels at the base or the turret and around the principal dormer window is of the westland school (*see* Chapter 7) and included carved figures (like Dunderave and Tolquhon), an angel skewputt, three faces and a written exhortation to MacDougall's son neither to sin nor to worry about what other people

8.11, 8.12, 8.13 *The sea, entrance and court façades of Gylen, Isle of Kerrera, drawn in the 1950s for proposed reconstruction by Leslie Graham MacDougall. Note how each façade gives a different impression of height, and how the magnificent corbel course identifies the tallest one.* (Courtesy of Morag MacDougall Morley)

said.[22] To underpin the impression of verticality – and indeed to emphasise the layering of the design – a shallow projecting corbel course steps up from the rock across the west façade, adding not a jot to the space inside. It must have been intended to stress MacDougall's nobility to those passing or arriving by sea.

You enter the court through a pend beneath the *piano nobile*, and up quite a wide stair to the three storeys above. The brilliantly lit principal chamber on the fourth floor has a window facing in each direction and a slender, two-windowed turret in the north-west corner. One of the windows is a beautifully corbelled oriel overhanging the main entrance, like Amisfield.[23] A tight stair corbelled from the sea façade led further up to the corbelled cabinet or study at the very top. There seems to be no provision for a kitchen, as there was none in Amisfield.[24] So it is not unreasonable to suspect that Gylen was a summer house or a fishing lodge of the MacDougalls of Lorne. Tall, narrow Keiss (Caithness), erected at approximately the same time by a cadet of the Sinclair family clutching a crag overlooking the North Sea is much the same with similar filigree decoration.

Such vertical pavilions provided lovely, well-lit (if small) chambers, well placed for the view. All used architectural modelling devices to exaggerate height, deployed or reinterpreted Scottish Renaissance detail, and made an explicit show of wealth and sophistication in their carving. Arguably, they were all pleasure houses for families whose principal lodging was elsewhere. However, the curiously narrow, four-storeyed tower at Pittullie, in delectable flat lands by Fraserburgh overlooking the Moray Firth, similar in concept, was very different in execution. Constructed as the focal point of his courtyard villa by Alexander Fraser, younger of Philorth, after his marriage to Margaret Abernethy of Saltoun in 1595, the tower rises from a large inner court on axis with its entrance. Reached by a stair corbelled from its north wall, the 'laird's room' on the third storey[25] was a large chamber lit not only by two curious, ashlar rectangular oriel windows set on the corner but also a square window set on the diagonal facing the entrance.[26] The stairtower carried on upstairs, probably to a viewing platform with stunning views over the Moray Firth. The curiously domestic appearance of Pittullie might be accounted for by the fact that it was built for the heir to be occupied only until his father died. The necessity to emphasise lineage architecturally could be restricted to the principal family seat of Cairnbulg.

Hunting lodges came into a comparable category of compact, purpose-designed small house. Sir George Home of Wedderburn, for example, 'was so much given to diversion that he built a hunting-house, which he called Handaxewood, in the hills of Lammermuir, in which he might divert himself in the night-time'.[27] Royal hunting lodges were the most elaborate – Falkland, after all, was one. There was another, now vanished, at Boghouse of Crawfordjohn designed and built by Hamilton of Finnart. Gaunt towers in inhospitable locations were as likely, therefore, to have been hunting lodges as evidence of some remote laird's penury. Forter, which became the Airlies' hunting seat up Glen Isla, had been purchased from the Abbot of Coupar in 1560 on condition that the family kept the house well planted 'with birks, erchis, osaris, and sowchis' and behaved respectably.[28] In most respects it differed little from the L-plan house of the later sixteenth century. Tall Invermark, at the head of Glen Esk, with its roof raised to cruciform in the sixteenth century, and Birse. Just over the head of the glen to the north were likewise tall, remote and probably hunting lodges.

Blairfindy, built in 1586 in the Braes of Glenlivet, was the northern hunting seat of the Earls of Huntly, and whereas it has at least a substantial kitchen, the only cellar appears to have been for wine.[29] What provision Huntly made for his guests, servants, huntsmen – never mind horses and falcons – is unclear. Perhaps they were under canvas. A corbelled oriel window rises over Blairfindy's doorway (similar to those in Gylen and Amisfield). The traditional interpretation is defensive – the window seat could lift up so that the corbels could be used as machicolations through which to bombard unwelcome visitors below. However, many such oriels have closed corbels which could not possibly have been used like that, which implies that such windows had a heraldic rather than military purpose. In any case, Huntly was the most powerful magnate in Scotland with sufficient might to take on the Crown several times during the sixteenth century. He was never going to be surprised in Blairfindy in his own heartland. Furthermore, the aristocratic tendency when an army approached was to avoid being trapped in houses. When threatened by James V in 1528, the Earl of Angus was 'unwilling to shut himself up within the Wals of any strength, having ever in his mouth this maxime (which he had received from his Predecessours) That it was better to hear the Lark sing, than the Mouse cheep'.[30]

Building upwards *by choice* remained the option adopted for houses even where their courts and yards could have provided space for new lodgings. Situated on a bluff on the west bank of the Annan, and formerly standing in one corner of now-vanished yards, the House of Spedlins was refashioned in 1605 by Sir Alexander Jardine of Applegarth, one of the knights entrusted by James VI with enforcing good order upon the newly pacified Borderlands. Retaining only the bottom two storeys of his tower, Jardine added two and a half new storeys above, with walls two and a half times thinner. The upper two storeys are double-pile around a central corridor servicing four modern, well-lit, approximately square chambers, each with its own closet. The heavily ornate fireplace in the hall closely resembles that in Newark, Port Glasgow.[31] Double-pile superstructures were perhaps more common than is appreciated to judge by twin-gabled houses in eighteenth-century engravings. Stonebyres, Lanarkshire,[32] just one example, had a double-gabled superstructure some six storeys from the ground, with a fantastic skyline of dormer windows, almost on the scale of Huntly (*see* Chapter 11). All this is very curious, for it implies that some proprietors were caught on the cusp of desiring fashionable and convenient chambers on the one hand, and wishing to demonstrate their respect for their ancestors and lineage on the other. The two were not always compatible.

The Seton family's foothold in West Lothian – Niddrie Seton – was likewise upgraded in the sixteenth and seventeenth centuries, a process that may have been begun during the 1540s by George, Lord Seton, possibly because his Palace of Seton (*see* Chapter 9) had been burnt by the

8.14 Stonebyres, Lanarkshire, c. 1790, by Reid and Scott. (Author's collection)

English, and their continued presence at Haddington between 1547 and 1550 made its reoccupation hazardous.[33] Seton embellished the inner court that surrounded his majestic tower with, possibly, a hall lining its west wing, and added small round towers to each corner: indeed, had not the north-west corner been inhibited by the nature of its outcrop, Niddrie's plan would have resembled that of Cathcart. None the less, some time later, the family decided to extend their tower by two further storeys upwards rather than develop further buildings at the lower levels. Rising flush with the parapet, like Hoddom, the new extension was adorned by twin ogee-curved dormer windows tied together by a continuous roll-mould. It is suggested that the dormers are of French inspiration and may be dated to the 1540s or '50s.[34] It is not credible, however, to believe that this vertical extension was the consequence of a fear of violence.[35] With relatively minor change to the existing structures on site, Niddrie had been refashioned for the mid-sixteenth century and was fit to receive royal visits, including Mary Queen of Scots on her escape from Loch Leven.[36]

Preston Tower, Prestonpans, having first been fitted with a timber balcony or gallery at *piano nobile* level, was then extended upwards by the Hamiltons of Preston in 1626 with the construction of a delicate pavilion just two years before Sir John Hamilton and his wife Kathryn Sympson began work on Hamilton House barely 100 yards away. The pavilion perched on top of the tower was the last word in fashion: a cubic, sky-high gazebo providing a single, gracious room per floor, beautifully lit by ornately pedimented windows with superlative views north over the Forth. The roof, which appears to have been a flat viewing platform reached up a narrow flight ending in a cupola, is gracefully edged with a wavy parapet in fond memory of the rise and fall of crenellations.[37] This was a gazebo, pure and simple. Living was done in the ground-hugging Hamilton House.

The late sixteenth-century compact house is well represented by Greenknowe (Borders), once surrounded by gardens and avenues.[38] Its efficient, well-lit, conveniently interconnected chambers are romantically expressed on the exterior with the minimum of means.[39] Built by the Setons of Touch, Stirlingshire, who recorded a marriage with the Edmonstones in 1581,[40] it was a secondary house for the family. Its datestone is again misleading since two different types and colours of masonry, and records indicate an earlier building.[41] The main house, 25 × 33 feet, comprises a hall occupying the entire first floor and two rooms on each of the upper floors, similar to Partick (*see* Chapter 4).[42] The square tower encloses a wide circular public stair up to the first floor, thereafter rooms above, the staircase (unusually rectangular) corbelled from the angle. A great chimney guards the entrance, and the house's personality is expressed by the wayward string-course that clasps the corbelled stairtower and streaks across the east gable.

Baltersan, just above the Abbeymill Burn, beside Crossraguel Abbey, in Carrick, Ayrshire, is not just slightly grander, but also much more thoroughly researched.[43] It was an old site, for here Egidia Blair, Lady Row, had her mansion house in which she died in 1530. Her legacies to John Whytefurd and David Hynd underline the emphasis placed upon improving agriculture in this fertile part of Ayrshire, since she made them conditional upon the money 'being laid out upon the land'.[44] In 1575,

John Kennedy of Pennyglen and his wife Margaret Cathcart took possession of Baltersan, with its mansion, orchards and meadow,[45] and on 1 March 1584 began what was later described as a 'stately Fyne house, with gardens, Orchards parks and woods about it'.[46] Kennedy, stepson of the Earl of Cassilis, erected his house when much of that part of Ayrshire was a construction site and most of his kinship were building: his cousin Kennedy of Bargany, his kin Kennedy of Blairquhan, and his brother-in-law John Cathcart of Carletoun, who was about to rebuild Killochan two years later. The Kennedy of Culzean, who had built 'ane proper house with brave yards',[47] was painted at full length in 1592 probably by Adrian van Son. The portrait shows an astute, confident-looking 43-year-old peering out from rich clothing, a slashed richly buttoned doublet and an embroidered hat.

Baltersan was a mansion of middling rank, unusually well built and finished to a high degree with elaborate carving. The proportions of the hall were close to a double cube – 36 × 19 × 15 feet, and the rooms in the stairtower were 19 feet square. The entrance lay up the wide public stair which leads to both first and second storeys. The uncommonly well-lit five-windowed hall was partitioned by a screen from the main stair and from the tight stair down to the wine cellar. A narrow, private staircase in the south-west corner continued up to the roof. A secret chamber may have been concealed in the volume between the head of the wine cellar

8.15 Baltersan, Ayrshire, conjectural restoration by James Brown, showing how it might have been tightly surrounded by its yards. (James Brown)

155

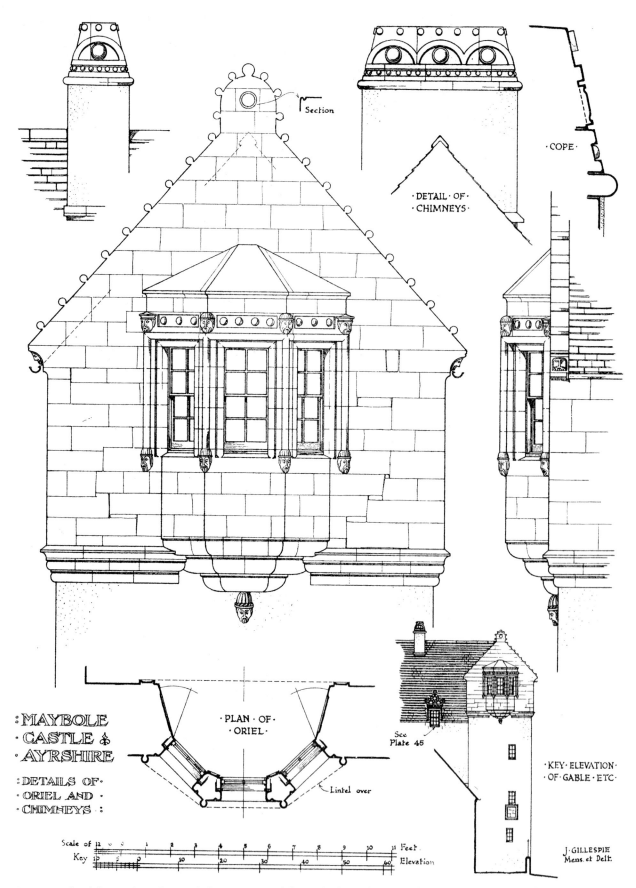

Section

·COPE·

·DETAIL·OF·
·CHIMNEYS·

·MAYBOLE·
·CASTLE &·
·AYRSHIRE·

:DETAILS·OF·
·ORIEL·AND·
·CHIMNEYS·:

·PLAN·OF·
·ORIEL·

Lintel over

See
Plate 45

·KEY·ELEVATION·
·OF·GABLE·ETC·

Scale of 12 6 0   1   2   3   4   5   6   7   8   9   10   11 Feet
Key   10   5   0   10   20   30   40   50   60   Elevation

J·GILLESPIE
Mens. et Delt.

8.16 Details of the oriel window and chimney caps of the Earl of Cassilis' town house in Maybole, Ayrshire.
(Author's collection)

156

stair and the ceiling of the hall, for there is no evidence that this tiny stair carried on up to the second floor. The resulting residual space remained unfinished: no plaster on the walls, and only a single tiny, and almost imperceptible, window very close to its floor. In the absence of a more plausible explanation, this may indeed have been a secret chamber, perhaps with access by removable ladder. It would have been a neat place for the muniments.

So much for the plinth. Once the public stair ends, and the private stair, corbelled from the re-entrant, takes over, two small, well-appointed and well-lit chambers occupy the stairtower. The top one – at fifth-storey level – is delineated by a continuous corbel course above which it swells out. It was likely a study – but a study provided with a petite oriel window facing the view. The top floor of the main house is elaborated by two thin-walled circular turrets opening from opposite corners, one for each chamber. The one to the west has a hole at its base. It is too small for a machicolation[48] (anything dribbling through this tiny hole would have slithered down the face of the wall and missed its intended target) and is entirely in the wrong location (as is the oriel window) to provide protection to the entrance to the house. The hole must, therefore, be for drainage; and perhaps there was once a roof structure and gutters arranged to collect rainwater like at Glenbuchat.

Baltersan's finishes were expensive: good dormer windows, fine corbelling, some smart, incised carvings around large rectangular aumbries, sliding shutters and spacious, well-finished window embrasures. The overall architectural effect was achieved through its efflorescent silhouette of turrets, study, turreted stairtower and crowstepped gables. Nothing inessential. The entrance, as in so many other similar Scots houses, was guarded by the tall chimney-stack. Baltersan was far from unique.[49] It represented the fashionable house for a rising man of good pedigree. Its height implied status and provided excellent views; and the rooftop study was just the place from which to observe the yards and plantations around the foot of the house.

Of all such tall houses, perhaps the town house of the Earls of Cassilis in Maybole might be the one with which to conclude. The favoured plan of a nobleman's town house in Renaissance Scotland was generally a U-shaped *hôtel* (*see* Chapter 10), or perhaps the simpler, plain *corps de logis* like the town house of the Hays of Delgatie in Turriff. To build tall in a town was aberrant; yet at one end of the High Street of Maybole the Earls of Cassilis built a vertical town house and, at the other, the Kennedys of Blairquhan did likewise. The Cassilis house has one principal and two other floors above cellar and kitchen, and has the most ornate details for a house of its period in Ayrshire. The principal façade is composed of a large chimney sandwiched between ornate dormer windows, carved as though they were three superimposed earl's coronets. (Similarly treated windows were recorded by Alexander Edward on the north gallery at Falkland in the late seventeenth century.)[50] The tapering top of the chimney heads themselves are similarly carved. The stairtower, as usual, is carried a storey higher than the main block, and terminates in a study or 'prospect room'.[51] This room is defined by a corbel course, like Baltersan's, but there is a qualitative difference. Instead of the gables being crowstepped, there are straight-edged skews elaborated by repeated scrolls or volutes; and its western façade is ashlar. At the centre is a semi-hexagonal ashlar oriel window adorned with carved heads. The nearest parallel is that on the Palace of Huntly.

A group of houses sharing these characteristics would not be wholly surprising if dynastic patterns could explain it. However, buildings resembling Baltersan occur beyond that part of Ayrshire, so another possibility which might explain the group is that they shared a designer. The laird of nearby Robertland, David Cuninghame, became Master of the King's Works after the death of William Schaw (*see* Chapter 10) and may have been an architect. He may have visited his father, exiled for the murder of the Earl of Eglinton, in Denmark. Once Master of Works, he followed the Court to London, was knighted in 1604, and between 1604 and 1606 was Surveyor to the Works in England. Thus far, no architectural work in Scotland has been attributed to him. But the likeness between the unusual dormer windows of the Cassilis house at Maybole and the royal palace of Falkland is significant. An investigation of a group of sophisticated, smaller houses of the right period, some close to his home, might be a useful place to begin looking.

9

The Scottish Renaissance Palace

For, I heard say, this noble earl [of Atholl] gart make a curious palace to the king, to his mother and to the ambassador [of the Pope]; where they were so honourably eased and lodged, as thought they had been in England, France, Italy, or Spain . . . a fair palace of green timber, wound with green birks . . . which was fashioned in four quarters, and in every quarter, and nuik [corner] thereof, a great round, as it had been a block-house, which was lofted and gested the space of three-house height; . . . there were two great rounds on ilk [each] side of the gate. . . . And also this palace within was hung with fine tapestries and arrases of silk, and lighted with fine glass windows in all the airths . . . and the halls and chambers were prepared with costly bedding. . . . The Ambassador of the Pope seeing this great banquet and triumph . . . thought it a great marvel, that such a thing could be in Scotland, considering that it was named the Arse of the World, *by other countries.*

Robert Lindsay of Pitscottie describing the building prepared for James V's Atholl hunting trip in 1531.[1]

The focus of this chapter is the 'place' or 'palace' – the courtyard country house that was either created as a homogeneous whole or displayed an identifiable design agenda. Deriving from the Latin *palatium* implying courtyard, the term 'palace' has sometimes been taken instead to signify a building of particular size, nobility or importance in a confusion with royal palaces and their overtones of majesty. Misunderstanding this has led to entirely unnecessary embarrassment, requiring apologies for a modest house like Culross Palace which, by virtue of being called palace, appears to have had ambitions above its station.[2] In Scottish Renaissance terminology, Culross was indeed a palace, but only in the sense of taking the form of a courtyard house. The word 'place' or 'palace' (they appear to have been interchangeable)[3] was 'descriptive of a particular class of building and had no reference to the rank of its occupant',[4] and contemporary use implies that the class of building in question was a

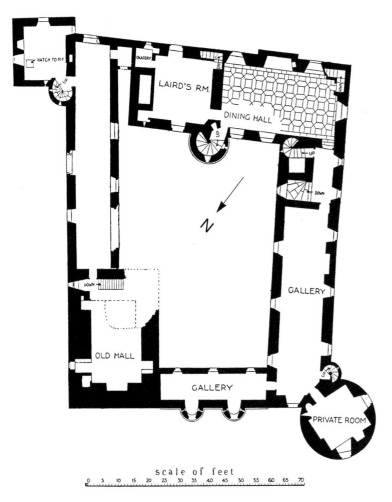

9.1 Plan of the palace of Tolquhon, Aberdeenshire, drawn by W. Douglas Simpson in 1938: the principal lodging lies to the rear of the inner court and the entrance is framed between the old tower (left) and the guest tower (right). (SAS)

substantial courtyard. Moreover, although the term indicated no rank, it did imply substance and at least moderate magnificence.

'Palace' referred to the inner close or court – the *cour d'honneur* – of a larger establishment. Service buildings, stores and stables lay beyond. By comparison with the striking individuality of the châteaux of the Marian period, or the substantial, self-contained houses of the Early Jacobean, each part of the palace subsumed some of its personality into the whole. Although the laird's lodging was usually the principal structure, and almost always contained state rooms on its principal floor, it remained domestic in character: the nobility of the palace lay in the *ensemble*.

The enthusiasm to create and embellish courtyards was well abroad by the early sixteenth century. After taking Janet Maitland (of Lethington) as his second wife in 1516, Hugh Lord Somervill went to live in 'the tour of Carnwath toun'. His brother, Lord John, head of the family but insane, occupied the much more imposing and extensive family seat of Couthally, surrounded by loch and marshland. Embarrassed by 'the barenesse of the tower of Carnwath, haveing noe planting, yea, not soe much then as a kaill-yard',[5] Hugh could barely wait for John's death so as to inherit Couthally and modernise it. But his crazy brother's continued occupation and his own searing feud over lands with his cousin John Red Bag Somervill of Cambusnethan[6] prevented the move for the next seven years. Finally able to take over Couthally in 1524, he found it in a state of decay. There was an outer close of office-houses and an inner close, and his brother had lodged just in the L-plan tower house in one corner of the latter. The four-storeyed round and square towers at the corners appear to have been largely unused, given that guests had to be lodged in nearby Carnwath Tower.

Somervill, probably assisted by his close friend, ally and former brother-in-law James Hamilton of Finnart, added what they considered changing fashion would require – and created a palace. The first building was an enormous four-storeyed, nine-bay rectangular main house, 24 feet deep and 108 feet long, lining the north side between the great tower and the round tower.[7] A spacious turnpike stair projected from the centre of its courtyard façade. The principal room on the first floor was a 60 feet long great hall, with a square chamber at each end. The 'chamber upon the west of the hall had the benefite of a large studie from the round [round tower] upon the south west corner'. Each of the upper storeys contained nine rooms. In 1528 'a long building conforme of a gallery, standing upon seven vaults' was added along the eastern side of the inner court, matched by a similar-sized building on the west side. Although it is not clear where guests would be lodged, the old towers might have been reconditioned to take them. There is no mention of a chapel. Couthally presents in microcosm what was to occur quite frequently throughout the sixteenth century in the larger country seats. Existing structures would be retained, partly for reasons of economy, partly for filial piety, and partly because lodgings would be required during building works; and to them would be added new lodgings with state apartments, a gallery and office buildings. Somervill's narrative implies that each phase of construction followed a predetermined master plan.

Once it was complete perhaps Couthally resembled the place of Duntreath, Stirlingshire, seat of the Edmonstones of Duntreath in an idyllic valley near Strathblane, just north of Glasgow.[8] Duntreath probably reached its most complete form in the 1570s under Sir James Edmonstone, 6th of Duntreath, who added a curiously ornate set of his arms above the gatehouse. Its inner court was made up of a tower, the diminutive but powerful gatehouse, a chapel, a gallery along its western flank, and a lodging block lining the north. After nineteenth-century overblown extensions and embellishments, and twentieth-century excisions, most has now vanished. Given the need for country houses to provide hospitality for possibly large numbers of visitors, as suggested in Chapter 4, it is odd that the descriptions of Duntreath do not identify the guest tower or lodging.

Guests at the palaces were probably accommodated in self-contained towers or wings, as implied by the inquest into the dreadful fire on 8 October 1630 at the House of Frendraught in Buchan. Probably started deliberately, the fire killed Viscount Melgum, heir to the Marquess of Huntly, Gordon of Rothiemay and four of a retinue. But it was not the whole of Frendraught that was burnt: indeed, Crichton of Frendraught, his wife and servants were not only unhurt, but watched the spectacle. Father Gilbert Blakhall, who knew the district well while acting as priest and chamberlain to Melgum's widow, Lady Aboyne, a few years later, noted that Frendraught had 'lodged the nobleman and his followers in a toure separated a little from the bodye of the castell',[9] at least three storeys tall with a vaulted ground floor and its own staircase.[10] Not a particularly flammable structure. The guests were killed by smoke, they thought, passing through a hole in the vaulted ceiling of the ground-floor cellar, and the fire possibly began in some chests that should not have been there. One cause of the fatalities was that the guests could not escape through the large windows of the guest tower since they were sealed with iron yetts, as was customary. The suspicion that the fire was deliberate was reflected in the initial arrest of Frendraught's master of household, steward, cook and gardener. The failure to pursue the criminals thereafter was viewed gloomily by Catholics as proof that the objective behind the fire was less Rothiemay (on account of his feud with Frendraught) and more the removal of Melgum as the potential Catholic leader. There were even rumours of the complicity of the Bishop of Aberdeen. The mystery was never solved, and Frendraught moved on to greater things. Almost certainly, the corner tower at Tolquhon was a similar guest tower (*see* p. 172).

Greater magnates had usually inherited castles or palaces that were already largely complete by the early sixteenth century, so that any modernising had to take the form of inserting a fashionable house into an existing court. Just as the trend for the early Marian great houses had been set by earls at Huntly and Balvenie, so likewise was it set by earls when it came to the matter of embellishing an existing palace. The earls of Bothwell, Gowrie, Argyll, and Nithsdale all inserted a Renaissance wing into the courtyards of old castles.

Bothwell recast the western flank of Crichton Castle with extraordinary bravura after his return from Italy in 1581. He was an ambiguous figure who had to leave Scotland in 1595 in disgrace after his third fruitless attempt to detach James VI from Chancellor Thirlestane by kidnap, but the quality and the innovation of the work which he had carried out at Crichton indicates he had no thought that his actions would lead to exile and death in penury. While he undoubtedly carried out improvements elsewhere within Crichton, and may have added the chapel,[11] his focus was upon the western wing – the one facing the principal route from Edinburgh, the village and the collegiate kirk. At the hinge between the south and west wings, he placed a three-storeyed straight staircase, with a loggia to the court and large windows illuminating the platforms facing the west, in the manner of the best Renaissance staircases of Europe – a resemblance emphasised by its stone-panelled carved ceilings and ornately carved entrances.

On each floor, the new wing comprised a principal chamber facing the court and a private chamber sitting in a square ashlar tower (itself framed by slender rectangular towers – stair in one, closet in the other), which had been added behind Crichton's old tower. An antechamber to the state apartment was not necessary since that public function was provided by the hall across the courtyard. The west wing of Crichton was deepened to accommodate wider chambers, the extra width carried upon an arcaded loggia sitting upon very idiosyncratic fluted columns decorated with armorial shields. The wall above is wholly subsumed beneath a pattern of diamond-shaped stone projections in red ashlar. Although the inspiration for Crichton's *diamante* façade might have come from late fifteenth-century Palazzo dei Diamante in Ferrara, decorative treatments like this were widespread throughout Europe for unusually high status buildings.[12]

The splendours of the courtyard tend to overshadow what Bothwell must have intended as a heraldic emblazon facing visitors from the west. Below a grossly over-elaborate string-course, the new wing was heavily plain in its harled geometry, like the remainder of the castle. Above the string-course, however, enormous chamber and stair windows were framed by the square ashlar turret to the north and a smaller, octagonal tower which projected from the corbel course at the south-west corner. The silhouette above was one of square and octagonal towers, old thick towers and modern slender towers, chimneys, gables, string-courses, turrets and finials; a flamboyant fantasy probably more resembling

9.2 The 1580s facetted façade in the courtyard of Crichton Castle, Midlothian, drawn by Billings. Note the coffered ceiling above the staircase to the left. Crichton Collegiate Church may be discerned in the distance through the middle window. (Author's collection)

9.3 Conjectural reconstruction of the west façade of Crichton Castle. So much is ruined that the silhouette is speculative. (Author)

contemporary buildings in north-west Spain than anything elsewhere in Europe. Crichton presented an achievement of compressed quality, and the way the new work threaded very fashionable ideas in, around and between two medieval towers was an ingenious piece of design,[13] which required someone not only well acquainted with current European ideas but also equipped with architectural inventiveness. Its presumed date is within the period of William Schaw's appointment as Court architect to James VI,[14] and the design might be his.

Largely ruinous additions to the eastern wing of Castle Campbell display comparable ingenuity in introducing contemporary architectural ideas into an ancient setting, exploiting much that was already on the site. Campbell, high on a plateau overlooking Dollar Glen, was originally called 'The Glume' until the Earl of Argyll purchased it as his lowland seat and petitioned the king to change its name.[15] The tower lies in the north-eastern corner of the inner close; and additional living accommodation was probably first provided by a

9.4 Conjectural reconstruction of the 1590s ashlar courtyard façade of the east wing of Castle Campbell. The original tower lies to the left, and the palatial south wing is to the right. (Author)

block extending south[16] and then by a spreading hall and chamber block overlooking the gardens along the south wall. The staircases at each end were joined by a gallery overlooking the court. Although not normally one of the stopping places in royal progresses, Castle Campbell had played host to Mary Queen of Scots and her Court between 9 and 12 January 1563 when the 5th Earl of Argyll's sister married James Stewart, Lord Doune.[17]

The parallel with Crichton, however, lies in alterations made some time in the early 1590s to the short eastern wing between the tall tower and the southern apartment (likewise within the professional lifespan of William Schaw). It consisted of a polished ashlar screen constructed a short way forward of existing buildings. Unlike Crichton, the inherited chambers behind – with their unusual groin vaults – were apparently untouched. New staircases were added to each angle, the spacious northern one rising fully six storeys to the parapet of the tower, the southern barely more than half that. There are few clues to the upper storeys that lay between save the fenestration of small, paired rectangular windows, and each floor framed between string-courses. Entrance at courtyard level was through a finely detailed two-bay loggia. The narrowness of the chambers in the new work implies a corridor, although they fail to connect as corridors should. 'The little gallery in the head of the new work' and the 'Low Gallery in the new work'[18] mentioned in a 1595 inventory of the castle probably indicate their real purpose.

The state apartment lay along the south and east wings: it comprised the kitchen (at the west end of the hall), the hall, My Lord's Outer Chamber, My Lord's Inner Chamber, and My Lord's Inner Cabinet. The 1595 document was only a partial inventory, or maybe an inventory of permanent furnishings that did not move when the household moved, for whereas it waxes enthusiastic about napery, tapestries, leather chairs, quantities of tables and Campbell's forty-seven beds, there is no mention of paintings, books, guns nor ornaments. Remains of stained glass discovered 100 years ago were probably of heraldic glass from the principal chambers.[19]

When the Earl of Nithsdale came to upgrade his splendid shield-shaped, fourteenth-century Maxwell castle of Caerlaverock in 1636, however, there was no room for him to place a similar fashionable screen in front of his old-fashioned buildings, since the medieval triangular court was too narrow. The first Renaissance alterations to Caerlaverock had been broad, well-lit chambers along the west wing reached via a wide staircase. They were plain by comparison with Nithsdale's rebuilding of the wing opposite to celebrate his elevation to the peerage, and the probably contemporary work on the south wing. Our knowledge of the building derives from an inventory made after the earl capitulated to the Covenanters in October 1640 on the instructions of the king. Only including details of 'such things as were left in the house of Caerlaverock at my lord's departure', implying that much had already gone,[20] it hints at opulent living – not least the five noble beds (two of silk, each with three coverings, each bed valued at £110 sterling), ten lesser beds and seventy beds for servants, the forty carpets, damask bedchamber, two great chairs and nine stools of silver cloth, two dozen red velvet chairs and stools, five expensive sets of wall hangings, sixty turkey work chairs and stools, a library with books worth £200, several clocks, portraits, seventy stand of napery and forty pairs of sheets worth £704 sterling, curtains and curtain-rods, four barrels of sack and three hogsheads of French wine. However, most of the items are baldly stated and practical – guns, iron spades, trunks, fire shovels, chamber pots and five pots for easement.[21]

The now-missing southern wing, with its classical ground-floor screen wall and entrance, may well be the 'Long Hall' mentioned in the inventory. The adjacent, wide, straight *escalier d'honneur* leads up to now-vanished chambers, perhaps to the 'New Hall' – but not into the Nithsdale apartments other than accidentally. If that were so, it represented a formal separation between the public (and perhaps guest) parts of the house, and the owner's private apartments. The glory of the Nithsdale apartments lay in their glossy façade of large blocks of polished red ashlar, rather than in the relatively small chambers behind. Ornately carved, overscaled pediments boasting Maxwell armorial achievements and iconography top each window.

Each floor of the Nithsdale apartments appears to have been a self-contained suite of two chambers with a closet, each room with one large

9.5 Façade of the Nithsdale Lodging, Caerlaverock Castle, Dumfriesshire, drawn by Billings. The Lodging had its own turnpike staircase to the left (smaller window), leading, on each floor, into an outer chamber and a principal chamber. (Author's collection)

window facing the country and another facing the court, and an overscaled Renaissance fireplace (of similar character to the one in Spedlins) squeezed across the corner. They lack the public room or antechamber of the palace plan, such functions presumably being provided in the south block, although there were, somewhere, both a dining-room and a drawing-room. My Lord Maxwell's apartment consisted of his chamber and an outer chamber containing a bed, and thereafter the turnpike stair.[22] His room, 'all hanged with tapestry', contained a damask bed overlaid with gold lace, chairs and stools of damask, two chests, a wardrobe, a carpet, a clock and a water pot – and, since the place had just been under siege, twenty-eight muskets and bandoliers, and two claymores.[23]

Unlike these grander castles, or Atholl's timber hunting palace, most 'places' *emerged and evolved* rather than being conceived *a priori*. The first step was sometimes to add a wholly new tower at some distance.[24] Whereas the construction of two completely separate tower houses at Laurieston, Edinburgh,[25] is usually attributed to the burning of the first tower in Hertford's raid in 1544 and the decision to build a totally new tower a short way away rather than repair or extend the old, the impulse was probably fashion. Once the old tower, smallish, thick-walled and rectangular with subsidiary chambers and stairs compressed within its walls, proved unappealing in the 1570s, the Laws added a new T-plan one at the other end of the inner close two storeys taller, more slender, thinner-walled and larger-windowed, replete with dainty turrets and a corbelled staircase.

Sir James Colville set about improving the house of Easter Wemyss (now called Macduff's Castle, overlooking the Forth near Wemyss, Fife) once he had exchanged his house at Ochiltree in Ayrshire for it,[26] by adding a further tower with large, regularly ordered windows. He joined the new tower to the old one by a gallery running above the main entrance. A similar evolution may explain Huntingtower, or the Place of Ruthven, by Perth, seat of the Ruthven Earls of Gowrie where two separate but close towers framed the entrance to the inner court. They were joined into a single building in the eighteenth century.[27] Kenmure, on its haunting eminence overlooking Loch Ken, which was refitted after being 'cast to the ground' by the regent in 1568,[28] took the form of new lodgings built between two slender towers at opposite ends of its inner court.[29]

Normally, the principal sixteenth-century addition to the inner court of a palace would be the 'main house' or laird's lodging, containing two rather than three state chambers *en suite* on the principal floor, usually as the rear wing. Their design appears to have been intended at least to complement the old tower and sometimes to dominate it. Provided with the most fashionable attributes – a great stair, a private stair from the hall to the wine cellar, another up to the family apartments, the largest windows, the most elaborately decorated fireplaces, and the finest carving – this lodging or main house was the focus of the palace. Several of the 'castles' that survive today in Scotland – Farnell (Angus) and Drumminor (Aberdeenshire), for example – were probably built as the main house of a place or palace whose surroundings have vanished.

There might also be a chapel, gatehouse, range of offices, guest accommodation and a gallery. Chapels were rarely placed within the inner close, and those that were – such as at Duntreath, Dunnottar and Stobhall – were unusual. More commonly, chapels were located outside the inner close and possibly beyond any of the surrounding yards. Most that survive lie significantly detached from the house in the same relationship as Crichton's.[30]

The gatehouse or porter's lodge was partly practical – it managed the entry – and partly to impress visitors. There is little evidence of martial requirement save the very occasional guard-house. The shambolic porter in *Macbeth*, staggering down from his eyrie above the entrance, is probably close to contemporary reality. At its simplest, the gateway would be a large opening in a screen wall, capped by a platform – rather as may still be seen at Muchalls and Mains, Dundee. The homely two-storeyed house at Hills Tower, Dumfriesshire – a large arched entrance below, porter's lodging above – is less usual, although the elaborate relic at Harthill, Aberdeenshire, may have been similar.

Houses of greater ambition signified their entrance by adopting a variation on the French *châtelet* (or miniature château) for it. Perhaps the inspiration had been provided by Finnart's two single-storeyed *châtelets* controlling the entrance to the Palace of Linlithgow.[31] Nor could you discount the influence of the beetling foreworks to Stirling and Falkland, and the similarly rhythmic and powerful King's Lodging at Holyrood. They all hinted at the military inheritance of Caerlaverock and Kildrummy, or inspiration from Langeais, Chaumont and Pierrefonds. Such expressions of grandeur, however, completely eluded the genial John Mure: when refashioning his ancient seat of Rowallan, in 1562 he added a *châtelet* to his tight courtyard house on its eminence. Its ashlar towers were diminutive, their pantomime scale now exaggerated by outsize classical windows. Its design entirely domestic, his new gatehouse was too small to beetle. In place of moats and drawbridges, entrance to the palace was up a long flight of steps. Mure delighted in 'policy of building and planting' and was proud of his orchards and gardens,[32] and his formidable gatehouse was almost a sarcastic commentary upon militarism.

9.6 Power without ferocity. John Mure wholly transformed his ancestral seat of Rowallan with an imposing but peaceable new entrance. (RCAHMS)

Drum-towered entrances, adopted to proclaim ancient lineage, were built at the palaces of Seton, of Dudhope (seat of the Scrymgeours in Dundee), and of Boyne, seat of the Ogilvies of Boyne. The forework of Seton (as it was called) was built probably in emulation of royal construction, by Jane Hepburn, widow of George, 3rd Lord Seton, after his death at Flodden,[33] but it was badly damaged during the 1647–8 English occupation of Haddington, when 'the Englishmen . . . came and ley at Seton, burnt and destroyed the castle their . . .' and rebuilt thereafter.[34] Twin drum-towers were added to the Sinclairs' principal seat of Thurso, and the Frasers' House of Philorth – though they, like at Fyvie, did not flank the main entrance. Some *châtelets* were joined at the top to form a triumphal arch like that at Touch, Stirlingshire, or Saltcoats, Gullane, built by the Lethingtons of Saltcoats in 1593.[35]

An entire wing of the palace was customarily occupied by a gallery. Originally indoor exercise rooms, galleries had been built in royal palaces by the late fifteenth century,[36] and Somervill's inclusion of a gallery in his refitting of Couthally in 1524 indicates that the broader aristocracy aspired to them pretty early. In addition to being an indoor exercise room, they were also used as corridors to link one part of the palace to another – for example, the 'gallery of communication' that John Macky observed joining Queen Anna's new belvedere in Dunfermline with the royal apartments.[37] By the later sixteenth century, it became one of the places to display part of the family collection of portraits. Witness the Earl of Gowrie in 1584, lamenting to Hume of Godscroft the politics that would lead eventually to his downfall, his too-slow escape to Dundee, his arrest boarding a ship there and his subsequent execution:

> Looking very pitifully upon his gallerie, where wee were walking at that time, which he had but newly built and decorated with pictures, he brake out into these words, having first fetched a deep sigh – 'Cousin,' says he, 'is there no remedie? *Impius haec tam culta novalia miles habebit! Barbarus has segetes!*'[38]

The gallery in Crathes – a 'skied' gallery at the top of the house virtually in the roofspace – was also used for the exercise of justice. Once the medieval hall had been converted into a dining- or drawing-room for the family, the gallery came to be the largest public room in the palace; indeed, Dunnottar's also doubled as the palace's entrance hall. Customarily the thinnest rooms, one tall storey high above cellars and kitchens, galleries were usually lit by tall windows that penetrated the roof line in a series of majestic dormer windows. Some had a small stairtower at one end to allow direct entry without the need to pass through the main lodging first (for example, Dunnottar and probably Fraser), and others had a small lodging at the far end (Aberdour and Ruthven). They usually occupied the wing with the view – over a glen, river, ravine or out to sea. Consequently, the wing of a palace for which no evidence survives, such as the west wing of Boyne, is likely to have been the gallery if it faces over a river valley. The long block of the Bishop's Palace facing the river at Dunblane, for example, was probably the gallery, as a hitherto unnoticed oak corbel embedded in the wall, which may have supported a timber balcony, might testify.[39]

Galleries were overt signs of sophistication. Dunnottar's, thought to probably have been built in time for the young king's visit in May 1580,[40] presents a rank of tall chimney-stacks like masonry guardsmen, corbelled from the ground floor and alternating with tall dormer windows. The gallery was 'curiously ceiled with Oak and after a very rich form, excellently lighted', and featured a carved Roman stone from the Antonine Wall in pride of place.[41] The chimneys heated a row of chambers below which, according to a 1699 inventory, were rooms for the use of clerks and servants (but were no longer in use by then anyway).[42] The galleries at Pinkie[43] and the palace of Birsay are similarly identified by a long rank of tall chimney-stacks – far more chimney-stacks, indeed, than there seem to be fireplaces, implying that they had a symbolic function. Moreover, they almost certainly had ornamental caps like those you may see in Egeskov, Denmark, Hampton Court or on the houses in Venice. The 1682 drawing of Hamilton Palace by Isaac Miller[44] confirms their use in Scotland. The up-and-down rhythm of crenellations had been important for country house silhouettes when martial symbolism had been required, and the rising and falling silhouette of alternating chimneys and dormer windows provided a similar rhythm. It is as though this device symbolises the transformation of swords into ploughshares, just as James VI was to require the melting down of iron yetts into ploughshares.

The Place or Palace of Pitsligo, part-way down a gentle slope facing north over the Moray Firth, just above the harbour at Rosehearty, was

9.7 Conjectural reconstruction of Pitsligo, Buchan: model by Simon Montgomery. The palace block lies on the left, the round bedroom tower is in the foreground, and the gallery extends to the right. (RIAS)

once the home of the celebrated Quietist Jacobite John, 4th Lord Pitsligo. It exemplifies the gradual evolution of a palace for a substantial local magnate.[45] A massive tower, erected by Sir William Forbes in 1423 on the southern, uphill edge of the site was probably extended eastwards in the early sixteenth century with new chambers and a more fashionable staircase. Possibly at the same time a wing was constructed across the western entrance façade, which most likely contained a chapel or oratory judging by a holy water stoup or aumbry at first-floor level. A three-storeyed laird's lodging in the form of a Marian palace block was then added to the north-east corner, perhaps in mid-century. It has the customary two well-lit rectangular chambers opening into a bedchamber within the round projecting bedroom tower, a private mural staircase leading to a comparable apartment upstairs. The middle chamber, which lies immediately above the warmth of the kitchen, was in all likelihood the chamber of dais. The palace was completed by the addition of a long, narrow gallery and chamber along the north wall, facing over the walled garden and out to sea. The gallery was probably built by the 1st Lord Pitsligo (who had married the Earl Marischal's daughter) when the rectangular staircase tower was added in the angle between it and the palace – in 1603, if the datestone with the royal arms may be trusted. Although now badly mutilated and lacking its top two storeys and the pediment originally above the entrance, the Pitsligo stairtower is of high quality – a worthy cousin to that built the following year in nearby Fyvie.[46] Its upper-storey chambers and the viewing platform on its roof were reached by a turnpike stair apparently rising from a squinch.[47] The main entrance from the walled pleasance is so ruined that save for an achievement of stacked armorial panels above the pend, little of its original grandeur can be imagined. Since there was little left to indicate the broader quality of Pitsligo but for a carved blue-stone dormer window head set into a wall of a warehouse in Rosehearty, a conjectural model of the palace was built in 1990.[48] It revealed how all the grandeur and ambition of Pitsligo was probably focused upon that stairtower and the palace block behind it.

In contrast to the evolution of Pitsligo, William Forbes of Tolquhon deliberately set about refashioning his house all of a piece between 1584 and 1589, and recorded the fact on the façade. What survives now is his inner close, some walls of the outer close and a desultory fruit tree. Although Forbes' own inscription states that the house he inherited consisted of only the tower, judging from oddities and curious angles he also reused the walls and some buildings of his father's inner court. Forbes was a man of substance, proud of his library[49] and, to judge by his tomb in Tarves churchyard, he was a cultivated patron. When he set about building his new palace, he selected the best local architect, Thomas Leiper, whom he permitted to sign his building on one of the corbels. His new palace consisted of a narrow gallery running east from the old tower to a far lodging tower with bakery and prison below and substantial chambers above – perhaps for the keeper (*see* p. 160). The east wing was almost entirely taken up by the laird's proud new four-storeyed main house – effectively T-plan since the family's private staircase protrudes into the courtyard deliberately on axis with the entrance. A gallery then ran

9.9 Conjectural reconstruction of the entrance façade of Tolquhon, old tower on the left, guest tower on the right. (Author)

9.8 Tolquhon châtelet, *drawn by Billings.* (Author's collection)

along the south wall leading to what appears to have been a guest tower of the kind that may have existed in Frendraught. The entrance front on the west side, probably built last, was a symmetrical miniature *châtelet* comprising an entrance between two diminutive two-storeyed circular towers with a long chamber in the floor above the entrance.[50] The design was completed by small statues – presumably of Forbes and his wife – on the façade, and Leiper's trademark of ornate and highly fanciful triple gunloops, the central one being diamond-shaped.[51]

Leiper's distinctive handiwork emerges not only in the strong expressionist forms – each building having its own character derived from its purpose – but in its strong modelling and profile. The apartments in the laird's house are well planned and immensely well lit: the hall with a patterned stone floor and private chamber on the *piano nobile*, and two chambers per floor above. The second floor was probably the domain of his wife, and the floor above that for family and household servants. His library may well have been contained in the square corbelled projection at the head of the private stair – a 'cabinet for your books', as Kerr wrote to Ancrum.[52] Forbes referred to his establishment as 'his house [the laird's lodging at the rear], tower [inherited tower] and place [the courtyard] of Tolquhon' and happily listed 'my halls, galleries, chambers, wardrobe, kitchens, cellars, larders, pantries . . .' in his inventory: multiples of everything save the wardrobe.[53]

We know only too little about the houses of the Keith Earls Marischal, allegedly the richest nobles in Scotland. In view of their wealth and status as the Marshals of Scotland, their houses were likely to have been

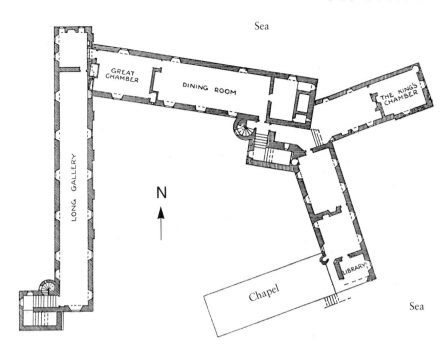

9.10 First-floor plan of the palace at Dunnottar, Kincardineshire, drawn by W. Douglas Simpson. (SAS)

magnificent. Inverugie's main house was a swaggering laird's lodging of the Marian period (*see* p. 119).[54] It was surrounded by several courts and walled gardens with statuary.

The earl's southerly house was Dunnottar, by Stonehaven – 'rather a village of dwellings than one dwelling. It is a Palace and a fort . . .'.[55] The palace appears to have been built on the flat lands to the north-east of the peninsula *c.* 1580, bounded by cliffs on two sides, and incorporated the medieval chapel as its south wing. Although now in ruins or partially reconstructed in an unconvincingly flat manner, the palace was of a magnificence appropriate to the Marshal of Scotland:

> Mars bellows round upon its walls in Thunder,
> It's marvellous above, more in the Cells that's under.
> It scorns the sea, and doth triumph upon it;
> It mocks the Land, and stands a distance from it:
> Who doubts the same, come see, for I do cease
> Only it's fitter for War than Peace.[56]

The first phase extended north from the chapel, along the cliff, with a pendicle reaching to the very edge of the cliff over the North Sea.[57] It comprised a family wing and a library, with the earl's private wing in the pendicle (later known as the King's Chamber after Charles I's visit on 8 July 1650).[58] The next construction was probably the long gallery along the west flank overlooking the bowling green; it was freestanding at first, rather than accessible through the chamber of dais, hence the gracious staircase at its southern end.[59] The north wing, which completed the court, most likely contained the great hall (later called dining-room) with its two large oak tables, and great chamber (perhaps chamber of dais) beyond,[60] with a broad straight staircase at the hinge. The sides of the inner court

9.11 Conjectural reconstruction of Dunnottar's palace courtyard. (Author)

were paved and a large cistern was placed near the centre. The north wing was extended thereafter over the sea gate, so that the Earl Marischal could reach his gallery without having to go out of doors.[61]

The palace at Dunnottar had a short life. The family decamped to nearby Fetteresso once the countess (a Lowlander Hume) found the ululating of the seals around Dunnottar rock insupportable.[62] The Earls Marischal embellished the early sixteenth-century manor at Fetteresso, beautifully environed with gardens and parks, serially extending it into a small courtyard mansion – to judge by datestones – quite frequently in the later seventeenth century. Through an inventory of pictures prepared for the forced sale by the York Buildings Company in 1722 following the family's forfeiture and the Earl Marischal's exile in Europe, you may glimpse something of its standing.[63] Fifty-one portraits of kings, queens, Cardinal Richelieu and Scots aristocrats were being sold, but sixty-one others – the better and larger ones – were being retained. Twenty-one had hung in the King's Room and twenty-eight in the drawing-room, but only two in the dining-room.[64] For all its painted, white, and green-stamped rooms, its King's Room and lettermeat hall (lower hall), Fetteresso lacked a gallery.

In 1597, Sir Patrick Maxwell began with a small tower and chunky entrance gatehouse on opposite sides of an inner court on the very rim of the Clyde beside what is now Port Glasgow, and concluded with the great house of Newark. Between the tower and the gatehouse, along the seafront, he added a virtually U-plan laird's lodging of most expensive detail. A strict symmetry informed the façade facing the river. The gables of the wings, with their turrets and elaborate aedicules, were set back to emphasise the projection and nobility of the main house. Its façade was designed about a circular staircase corbelled from the first floor. The stair rises into a turret at the centre, echoed by more at each corner, and is flanked by tall, slender chimneys framed by dormer windows on each side. Were Newark's harling restored, the brilliance of its design would become apparent. Restitution of its harling would also benefit the courtyard façade by highlighting the array of splendid tall aedicular windows with their broken pediments modelled on the Porta Pia in Rome[65] and the heraldic achievement above the principal doorway.

It is an odd paradox that the most splendid of all Scots Renaissance palaces, and the most frequented by its monarchs, was not the seat of one of the primary earls.[66] The triangular[67] Palace of Seton, East Lothian, was the home instead of the Lords Seton, later Earls of Winton, favourites of the Stewart dynasty.[68] Built on a peninsula bounded by a deep glen to the north-west, a minor burn to the east (the collegiate church lying just beyond it), and a wonderful view of the Forth to the north, Seton survived just long enough to be visited by John Macky and sketched by Robert Adam's great friend John Clerk of Eldin. Here skulked James V the day his cousin James Hamilton of Finnart was tried and executed; here came Mary of Guise and her daughter for whom George, 5th Lord Seton, was Master of the Household; here stayed both James VI and Charles I. Seton's gorgeous uniform as Master of Household of red laced with gold was, apparently, matched by his furniture which was of 'crimson velvet laced with gold'.[69] It was probably to celebrate Charles's visit that the palace was painted by Kierincx.[70]

Although in its final, seemingly triangular form, entered through a twin-towered *châtelet*, Seton resembled Chaumont-sur-Loire, it had evolved through several phases, starting with three ancient towers – the Great Tower (which collapsed in 1561), Jacob's Tower and the Wallace Tower. In the 1550s, the south-east wing was built and the forework rebuilt ('more sumptuous' than previously), by the father-in-law to the 4th Lord Seton – Sir William Hamilton of Sanquhar.[71] The poet Sir Richard Maitland thought it a 'pretty house', its projecting circular stairtower clasped by two oriel windows, and Macky found within 'a very noble apartment of a Hall, a Drawing-Room, a handsome Parlour, Bedchamber, Dressing Room and Closet'.[72] He dated the work to Mary Queen of Scots' time:

For on the Ceiling of the great Hall are plaistered the Arms of Scotland, with the Arms of France of the one hand, and those of Francis the Second, then Dauphin, with his Consort Queen Mary, in

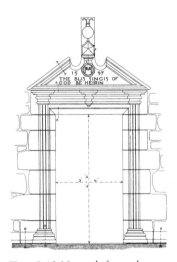

Top: *9.12 Newark from the Clyde, harling and ornamental chimney cappings conjecturally restored. Note the careful symmetry facing this principal water highway.* (Author)

9.13 Newark entrance from the National Art Survey. (Author's collection)

one Escutcheon, on the other; the Arms of Hamilton, Duke of Châteauherault, with several other Noblemen's Arms and Supporters, with the French Order of St Michael around them.[73]

If the ceiling did indeed date to the queen's reign (for the heraldry indicates a date in the mid-1550s), it implies that elaborate plaster ceilings were in use in Scotland long before the English influence of the early seventeenth century. That wing ended with the twin-towered *châtelet* on its south-east corner.

To the west of the châtelet stretched a two-storeyed wing, fashionable square chimneys set on edge, hinged upon the circular tower in which James VI stayed on his way down to London in 1603 and then continuing north. These wings had the windows, dormer windows, strapwork decoration and pediments of the early seventeenth-century Court style, and Viscount Kingston's date of 1630 seems entirely likely.[74] It resembled work still to be seen at Winton and associated with designers like James Murray of Kilbaberton, Sir Anthony Alexander, William Wallace and William Ayton.[75] Perhaps one of the two large galleries filled with pictures and observed by Macky ran along this façade, although by the time of his visit most of the paintings had been sold by the Commissioners of Inquiry or stolen by servants. On the second storey of the older, plainer northern wing, which has been attributed to William Schaw,[76] Macky found the apartments of state – 'very spacious; three great Rooms, at least forty Foot high'. Palatial in every sense, Seton was well organised to receive royalty.

Dudhope, more physically prominent on its bluff overlooking Dundee but less prominent historically, was likewise extended from a tower, had a similar drum-towered forework and long south-facing main house, flanked at each end by round towers. Almost nothing survives of its

Renaissance interior – nor indeed of Lord Charles Hatton's sumptuous remodelling in the late seventeenth century.[77] The roof has been flattened, thus removing the dormer windows evident in the Slezer drawing, so that the building is more of a restored plinth than the majestic seat it may once have been.

The Palace of Boyne, by Portsoy, has the distinction of being built on a new site. Although generally attributed to Sir George Ogilvy of Dunlugas who bought the estate from his cousin Sir Alexander Ogilvy of Boyne in 1575,[78] this seems wholly improbable both from the dating of its architecture and from the marriage of Alexander Ogilvy to a fashionable lady of Court, Mary Bethune (Beaton), in 1566.[79] It is more likely that Alexander built this impressive new palace for her. He selected a low sheltered spot on the south-east side of the Boyne Water not far from Portsoy, commanded from all sides (as Grose noted)[80] and thereby indefensible. Here arose a carefully quadrilateral house, round towers in each corner, and an entrance through a round-towered *châtelet*. The inner court had kitchens and service rooms against the north wing, perhaps a gallery along the vanished west wing, public rooms along the entrance façade, and the main house lining the south, framed between two

9.15 Conjectural reconstruction from the south-east of Boyne, by Portsoy, based upon drawings by Grose, Daniell, and MacGibbon and Ross. Most of the entrance front has now collapsed. The walls to the right contained sunken herb gardens. (Author)

substantial corner towers. The great stair lay just inside the entrance in the angle between the entrance and southern wings. The south-west tower, at the far end of the wing, had a corbelled balcony like that at Huntly, implying that it was the principal bedroom stack. There is little record of Boyne's state or of its furnishings when it was complete; only notes about its decoration, avenues, rows of aged trees and orchards that yet abounded with various fruits in 1791:

> Within [the walls] exhibit the mouldering memorials of many historical paintings. In the largest tower, where the apartments seem to have been assigned to devotion and philosophy, the paintings have been preserved by a peculiar fortune. It appears from some dates that about a hundred years ago, a new coat of plaister had been laid over the whole, probably when the zeal of reformation led them to obliterate every relic of the Catholic institutions; but now that coat of plaister is dropping off, and discloses saints and prelates pourtrayed on the walls, and in departments between them, many parts of the History of the New Testament designed. Figures also in devotional attitudes, with emphatic scrolls in Saxon characters, 'Sursum corda', 'sic itur ad astra' etc. . . . . One female figure, in particular, appears intent on the celestial sphere, in deep meditation; while an Apollo, pointing to the heavens, seems to teach its application. . . .[81]

9.16 The palace of Birsay, Orkney, already roofless by the late seventeenth century. (RCAHMS)

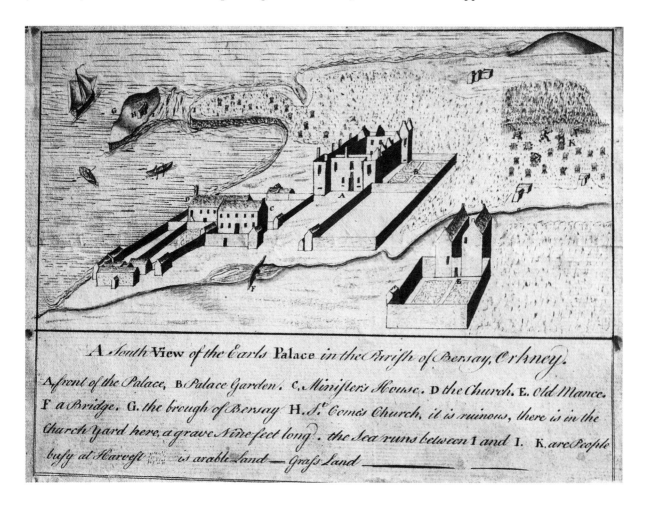

A South View of the Earls Palace in the Parish of Bersay, Orkney.

A front of the Palace, B Palace Garden. C Minister's House. D the Church. E. Old Mance. F a Bridge. G. the brough of Bersay H. S.ᵗ Comis Church, it is ruinous, there is in the Church Yard here, a grave Nine feet long. the Sea runs between I and I. K. are People busy at Harvest . . . is arable Land — Grass Land

The formal planning of Boyne was refined and tightened some twenty-five years later when Sir John Seton of Barnes began (but never completed) a similarly opulent palace on a new site near Longniddry, East Lothian, not long after his return from duty as Master of Household of Philip II of Spain in about 1590 (note: the curiosity of a Scots Master of Household to the King of Spain during the Spanish Armada). What had been circular at Boyne had become rectangular at Barnes, and there was greater rigour, symmetry of plan and consonance between courtyard and entrance façades. The majority of the accommodation had moved to the entrance wing.

Birsay, Orkney, had been the original seat of the Bishop of Orkney before his translation to Kirkwall, and the Earl's Palace was begun there as a retreat from Kirkwall by the grasping Earl Robert Stewart some time before 1574.[82] Flanked on two of its quarters by the shore, the palace was an imposing structure for this remote, flat spot. A seventeenth-century axonometric drawing of it shows conically roofed, rectangular towers at each corner (*see* p. 54),[83] a gallery running along the front façade above the entrance (as at Tolquhon), and another (identified by its array of tall chimney-stacks) along the west wing overlooking the ocean. Judging by the elaborate dormer windows (now all gone) the earl's lodgings themselves lined the north flank as you might expect. The chapel lay outside the enclosure, and around the other inland quarters were the walled yards or garden enclosures – the plant yard, the kail yard, the herb yard and the flower yard. The principal entrance ran alongside the bowling green, and bow butts lined the eastern wall of the herb and flower garden.[84]

It appears, therefore, that towards the end of the sixteenth century, the Marian round-towered palaces were giving way to the return of the rectangular-towered formalisms of the Early Renaissance. Hamilton Palace, located on the flat Clyde haughlands and originally at the centre of the town of Hamilton, was forever victim to attacks and destruction by powder by the Earl of Morton in the first harrying of Clydesdale in view of its association with the over-powerful Hamiltons.[85] It proved, however,

9.17 *Entrance elevation of Hamilton Palace taken from a drawing by Isaac Miller prepared in the 1670s. Note particularly, the flanking rectangular towers, the viewing platforms, the ornamental cappings to the chimneys, and their alternating rhythm with dormer windows.* (RCAHMS)

9.18 *South façade of the palace of Fyvie.* (Author)

9.19 *The superstructure of Fyvie's centrepiece, drawn by Billings.* (Author's collection)

remarkably resilient, and in 1595 Lord Claud Hamilton was completing a large U-plan palace whose show-façade was flanked by four-storeyed rectangular towers topped by viewing platforms, with a lower entrance wing of a gallery lined by ornately capped heraldic chimney-stacks. It is impossible to gauge how much of this palace dated back to the time of Finnart's occupation – or indeed that of Châtelherault. James VI chaffed Lord Claud for being 'more occupied with building rather than hawking' (a heinous matter in James's eyes) and used that as the excuse not to return Hamilton's hunting dogs to him meantime. He would be far too busy to need them.[86] An eighteenth-century painting shows that the palace was harled with stone dressings.[87] The public rooms lay in the central wing, and the two wings to the rear, with projecting rectangular stairtowers like Craignethan, may have contained family and guest lodgings separately.[88]

The outstanding surviving palace must be Fyvie, Buchan, obtained for 65,000 merks in July 1596 from the bankrupt Meldrums of Fyvie by their distant kinsman Alexander Seton, Lord Urquhart, brother of the 6th Lord Seton.[89] He took his new title – Lord Fyvie – from his new acquisition, and his architectural programme was to celebrate it as the seat of his power and influence. He may also have asked his architect friend William Schaw[90] to advise in its conception, as Renaissance patrons were wont to do,[91] and it is probable, from the detail, that the mason/architects Bel were involved. The castle/palace that Seton purchased was approximately quadrangular: lodgings lining the west wing, indeterminate – but probably entrance – buildings to the east, a chapel to the north,[92] and two rectangular towers, not in alignment with each other, joined by a much thicker and earlier curtain wall facing south. The south façade received most attention. It was metamorphosed into a giant, seemingly symmetrical composition of a central drum-towered *châtelet* squeezing a deep red-purple ashlar centrepiece and doorway (perhaps echoing his brother's at Seton) with flanking rectangular towers, unified by harled plinth and romantic superstructure. A triumphal arch soared above, capped by a pediment flanked by dormer windows and turrets, fusing classical and Scots motifs. The swelling detail of the central dormer windows bears a strong resemblance to those drawn by Clerk of Eldin in the supposed Schaw block at Seton.[93] The flanking towers are likewise elaborated above the string-course with a formal composition of dormer window flanked by two exotic turrets.

Yet it was all for show. The south façade does not seem to have been the entrance façade, as it was not in Huntly, even if once it had been in medieval times. That red ashlar doorway led only to minor corridors and stairs: neither into the court behind, nor to the great staircase. It was an unusually impressive garden façade. Even odder is how that staircase, Scotland's outstanding *escalier d'honneur* added in about 1604, is imperceptible from the court. This masterpiece of ashlar, a broad, sweeping, shallow stair with its carvings, delicate vaulting and plasterwork, is hidden within the western wing, with no indication of its presence whatsoever on the façade. They do things differently in France. In Blois, such a stair is celebrated; in Fyvie, its glories are concealed. The chambers served by the stair now appear much less imposing than the staircase itself, and it is difficult to assess their nobility now that they are

9.20 Fyvie's Great Stair, drawn by Billings. (Author's collection)

clothed in pleasant eighteenth-century interiors with wonderful Raeburns. They have great charm but little grandeur, and the other rooms that continue insouciantly behind the gatehouse, rather as though it were not there, convey the impression that the south façade of Fyvie was organised outside in: the symmetry of the façade has taken precedence over the organisation of the chambers within.

Having greater freedom to build than the great magnates, and more resources than the lesser lairds, the Forbes of Tolquhon, Ogilvies of Boyne, Scrymgeours of Dudhope, Setons of Fyvie and Forbes of Pitsligo created impressive courtyard houses or palaces within which they lived lives of a certain spacious elegance. Such walled yards and orchards as remain act as a reminder of this. But the thrust of Scottish architectural development was inexorably moving towards more compact forms.

10
Later Jacobean Court Architecture, c. 1590–c. 1640

To the Right Reverende Noble Lord, Alexander Seton, Lord Urquhart and Fyvie. . . . Among the rare Maecenases of this Land, your name is with the highest rank vnder his Maiestie to be mentioned.
Robert Pont's dedication of his *Newe Treatise of the right reckoning of Yeares and Ages of the World* in 1599[1]

A happy home is preferable to a large house; often toil and sorrow dwell in palaces, peace and happiness in cottages.
Inscribed in the ceiling of the gallery at Pinkie House

It was perhaps with undue modesty that Chancellor Alexander Seton, Earl of Dunfermline, implied that his house of Pinkie was but a mere cottage; but he certainly perceived it as a *villa suburbana* according to Serlio's definition, to which to retire from the stress of his office and the pressures of the capital. It was wealthy without being ostentatious (on the exterior at least), it was heraldic without needing dynastic or martial overtones, and it was comfortably fitted out without being too formal. As such, it represented the changing aspirations of those clever people who were officials in James VI's Court or part of its extensive network – the people the king astutely preferred to higher nobility for the offices of state, being 'such as he might convict and were hangable'.[2]

The new men – many of them scions of ancient families – derived their influence from the Court and from the increasing prosperity of the country.[3] Many would continue to do well even after the Court went south. Their rise, however, was viewed with anxiety by the ancient aristocracy who began to feel marginalised and isolated in their country demesnes, and whose disquiet was exacerbated by the substantial changes that were occurring among their own circle. The burden of the acerbic Sir John Scot of Scotstarvet's book *The Staggering State of Scots Statesmen*[4] was the decline and fall of Scotland's ancient families through

riotous living, debauchery, the burden of debt, quarrels and the splitting of estates between heirs, forfeiture, war and bankruptcy.[5] This was exemplified by the failure of the Meldrums of Fyvie to cope with their wadsets[6] resulting, as was shown in the last chapter, in the sale of their lands to Alexander Seton.

Seton (1555–1622), who was to enjoy influence with the king and queen that the great aristocrats of the past believed was rightly theirs, was hardly nouveau.[7] Younger brother of the Earl of Winton, he had been granted the priory and lands of Pluscarden as a *godbairne gift* (godchild present) from Mary Queen of Scots before his dispatch to Rome for schooling.

> He was held in great esteem . . . for his learning, being a great humanist in prose and poecie, Greek and Latin; well versed in the mathematicks, and had great skill in architecture and herauldrie.[8]

In other words, he had acquired the knowledge and grace expected of a Renaissance patron. When only twenty-one he was admitted an Extraordinary Lord of Session as Lord Pluscardine, becoming an ordinary Lord of Session two years later as Lord Urquhart, and President of the Court of Session in 1593. Robert Pont's dedication of his book to Seton (quoted at the head of this chapter) not only identifies Seton as the

10.2 The courtyard at Pinkie, East Lothian, villa suburbana *of Chancellor Seton, by William Leitch. Note the two rectangular 'pricks' flanking the balcony on the left overlooking the Forth estuary.* (RCAHMS)

Opposite: *10.1 Argyll's Lodging, Stirling, principal elevation to the inner court, from the National Art Survey.* (Author's collection)

10.3 Pinkie from the garden, pictured in the nineteenth century when it was still harled. It had lost its dormer windows and ornamental chimney cappings. (RCAHMS)

principal patron in the land but suggests that he exercised an extensive network of influence. Acknowledging Seton's kindness to him 'since my first acquaintance', Pont sought to be admitted 'among the clientele of your friendship', certain that Seton would be interested in his mathematical concepts. Eighteen years later, John Napier's dedication to Seton of what became called 'Napier's Bones', likewise addressed him as a Maecenas.[9]

Seton's particular interest in architecture – whether practised by himself or in conjunction with 'his true-hearted friend' William Schaw, royal Master of Works – is evidenced in Lord Somervill's invitation to him to provide the 'contryvance' or design for a new house at the Drum, since he regarded Seton as 'one of the greatest builders in that age'.[10] In autumn 1604, he was appointed Chancellor in place of the Earl of Montrose and, on the following 14 February, Queen Anna:

> seeing it has pleased his Majesty to grant to him [Seton] the dignity of an Earl . . . [gave] her full consent to his taking the title of the earldom of Dunfermline, although the lordship of Dunfermline is her own proper Lordship, given to her by his Majesty in morning gift.[11]

Having obtained Dunfermline Abbey's lands of Pinkie, by Musselburgh, he completed the first phase of reshaping the building there into a villa between 1607 and 1613. Above the door is the conventionally *faux-modeste* apology in Latin: 'The Lord Alexander Seton built this house, not according to his wishes, but to the manner of his fortunes and site'.[12] He never completed it.[13] Pinkie now consists of the east and south wings of an inner court, at the centre of which is the finest surviving early seventeenth-century fountain in Scotland, whose Doric columns support an etiolated imperial crown. The eastern wing embraces an earlier tall house of the Greenknowe model, whose projecting wing contains the main stair up to the first floor; the customary subsidiary stair corbelled from the angle leads up to a viewing platform framed by slender tourelles similar to those at Bog and Hoddom. Seton adorned this east range with a three-storeyed bay window against the south gable, and a balcony framed by two rectangular closets[14] on the north overlooking the sea.[15] The bay window is the only one of this form to survive in Scotland.[16] It is thought to demonstrate English influence, but English architects would not have been flattered by the idea. The Pinkie bay window does not stand proudly forward like an enormous glazed box in the approved English manner. Rather it emerges as an extension of the gable, its side and roof melting back into the wall plane as though the delightful rooftop oriel windows of Maybole and Huntly had been extended down to the ground. The otherwise immensely plain exterior of the house has deceived: 'the external appearance . . . appears to lack the artistry of the mainstream Court Style, a fact difficult to explain'.[17] In fact, Pinkie was a noble conception, Stoic in its austerity, but magnificent in realisation. Best appreciated from the garden, this nine-bay horizontally proportioned sheer box, defined by the parallel ashlar string-courses which would have stood out against the harling, acted as the plinth for seven tall chimney-stacks. Likewise once harled and probably ornamentally capped, they alternated with dormer windows rising above the roofline to convey suitably understated power.[18]

There was not the slightest hint of defensiveness about Pinkie, as Seton recorded in the garden wall:

D.O.M. For his own pleasure, and that of his noble descendants and all men of cultivation and urbanity, Alexander Seton, who above all loves every kind of culture and urbanity, has planted, raised and decorated a country house, gardens and suburban buildings. There is nothing here to do with warfare; not even a ditch or rampart to repel enemies, but in order to welcome guests with kindness and treat them with benevolence, a fountain of pure water, a grove, pools and other things that may add to the pleasures of the place. He has brought everything together that might afford decent pleasures of heart and mind. But he declares that whoever shall destroy this by theft, sword or fire, or behaves in a hostile manner, is a man devoid of generosity and urbanity, indeed of all culture, and is an enemy to the human race.[19]

10.4 *Pinkie's draw-well, drawn by Joseph Weekes in 1902. Its Latin inscription boasts, eliptically, of the chill and purity of its water.* (Author's collection)

A Scot would have found this denunciation of war resonant, since the disastrous 1547 Battle of Pinkie, which the Scots lost so needlessly and so badly to the English, took place within sight of the house's windows.

The principal floor was the second one and it contained the King's Room, two others and the long gallery. The chambers have the typical elaborate plaster ceilings of early seventeenth-century Scotland. Thin-ribbed designs in the customary geometrical formations enclose heraldic motifs – crowns, coronets, fleurs-de-lys, crescents, roses and people – in the less important chambers; a more regal thick-ribbed ceiling of three ribs converging and tied together with knops adorns the King's Room. The vividly painted coved gallery ceiling – 85 feet long, 19 feet wide – is the glory of the house. The frame of the design is that of a painted *trompe l'oeil* groined vaulted ceiling with a principal cupola at the centre – rather like a classical version of the Ely Cathedral lantern – and a smaller one at each end. The cupola appears to have been influenced by Vredeman de Vries' recently published book on perspective.[20] The ceiling is divided into seventeen bays, eleven containing emblems or themes from sometimes only relatively new books – such as the *Emblamata Horatiana* by Otto Vaenius, first published in 1607, and de Batilly and Boissard's *Emblamata* of 1596. The remainder is held to be original to Pinkie. There is nothing casual about the paintings on the Pinkie ceiling. They were intended to convey the Stoic philosophy that had emerged repeatedly in Scotland during the sixteenth century, whether in the ceiling of heads in the Palace of Stirling or in the person of George Buchanan, the greatest humanist in sixteenth-century Scotland and tutor to James VI. The gallery ceiling was probably modelled upon the painted gallery in Athens in which the philosopher Zeno taught ethics through historical and moral paintings. Pinkie preached and presumably – to Seton at least – exemplified the qualities of the simple rural life advocated by Horace in contrast to a weariness with the world at Court.

The antecedents of other architectural patrons of that era were no grander than Seton's. Edward Bruce, Master of the Rolls in London, became Lord Kinloss and created Culross Abbey House; Thomas Dalyell, rebuilder of the Binns, had been his deputy; the 'very learned but choleric' Sir Thomas Hamilton, builder of the U-plan villa of Tyninghame, East Lothian, was king's advocate, Clerk Register and Secretary; and his father, Lord Priestfield, may have built Priestfield (now Prestonfield House, Edinburgh) about the same time.[21] This extensive network of new men included Sir William Alexander, a minor Clackmannanshire laird who became Earl of Stirling and conjunct Secretary of State with Sir Archibald Acheson. As a young man, Alexander had travelled through France and Italy with 'his lord-superior the Earl of Argyll', where he became fluent in the languages, and was 'respected for his poesy and his edition of the Four Tragedies and Doomsday'.[22] His second son Anthony became an architect and designed for Alexander the romantically towered U-plan *hôtel* now called Argyll's Lodging, Stirling. At exactly the same time Alexander's fellow Secretary, Acheson, was having built the more compact, more austere, but equally lovely U-plan *hôtel* facing Baxter's Close in Edinburgh. Of the two, Acheson's was much more in tune with the new practicality.

The group of eight professionals (hence Octavians) chaired by Seton, appointed first in 1593 to organise Queen Anna's finances and – following their success – the Crown's finances thereafter, was perceived as a threat by the old landed families.[23] Several had been educated abroad, too many were Catholic, and they seemed to enjoy the type of access to the king and queen previously the preserve of the nobility. Public pressure led to the disbandment of the group in 1597, but the Court – particularly Queen

Anna's Court – remained full of such people, and early seventeenth-century Scotland was sufficiently fluid a society to absorb, promote and reward them. Those rewards were often reflected in stone.

Such people were at the front of a modernising state whose king was keen to encourage experiment and invention. Landowners were proceeding with improvement. The Earl Marischal founded a new town at Peterhead in 1593, Sir Alexander Fraser established one at Fraserburgh, and each created a university. In 1592, the Earl of Crawford planned a formally laid-out new town at Edzell,[24] in 1609 the Earl of Argyll founded Campbeltown – 'a burgh to be inhabited by Lowlanders' in Kintyre,[25] the Earl of Nithsdale began the town of Langholm in 1629 ('each house of stone and lime, two house height, a street of 30 feet between'),[26] and some time in the seventeenth century, the Strathmores founded their new town of Glamis.[27] The country was becoming proficient in manufacturing many of its own building materials and in importing others: a patent was granted for a glassworks in 1610, and in 1612 Sir George Hay, later Lord Kinnoull, took over the glassworks and an ironworks at West Wemyss.[28]

How did these new courtiers think? Always practically – as evidenced by the extensive letter from Sir Robert Kerr, a gentleman of the King's Chamber in London, to his son, the Earl of Lothian in December 1632.[29] Aware that the earl intended to undertake refashioning his house of Ancrum, Kerr poured out advice and suggestions – which he expected to be followed 'if I paye for it'. Kerr's general principles were these:

> You must make all things of beauty, ornament and use, not only for yourself but other folk; and I love to see a house not 'straitted' or 'minsed' but to have enough of room in a large and noble manner; nor is it all to be done at once, but piece and piece.[30]

The laigh hall should be replaced by a gallery since it overlooked the garden and faced the sun – 'which in Scotland is a main consideration'. On the other side of the court, the gallery should be balanced by:

> the principal fire rooms of my house, with a low hall, and the accesses in the fashion of this country [presumably England] or France; and that to be kept sweet for the entertaining my friends at solemn times, a whole body of a lodging with back stairs, and easy lodgings to lodge a great man.

The quality of the outer court and main approach reflected upon the owner:

> you must have special regard to them, to make them fair and easy and noble and pleasing as the ground will afford, for you must not contract them nowe, but rather extend them to a form *suitable to your quality* [my italics].

Kerr recommended gardens, yards, arbours, and many long walks planted with plane trees, and the planting of 'a fair orchard of the best fruits you can get in the abbeys about you' and a cherry garden. Never plant a fruit tree, he wrote, where it will not grow well: 'It is lost labour to plant them where the north winds come.' The policies should be enclosed with high walls so that 'it would compare then with an English park'.

As for the old tower, its dark chambers could be made larger by removing partitions to make a single chamber out of several, and lighter by widening the window embrasures on the inside, taking them down to floor level. The stone slabs on the floor should be removed since they were 'ungracious' on the timber beams beneath, and stairs should be limed. The bedroom floor above could keep its partition so that a servant could lodge behind it 'with your trash'. The little room at the head of the stairs would make a fine cabinet for his books and papers.

The tower, however, should be left 'as strong as you can for the world may change again'. That phrase has been taken to refer to the lawlessness and backward behaviour presumed to be endemic in Scotland. Its context, however, far more implies an uncertainty about the stability of the Union of the Crowns, and that Ancrum might once again find itself upon a national frontier. Kerr then warned against devaluing the tower by removing its battlement (*see* Chapter 3).[31] Nothing remains of Ancrum from which one could judge just how much of the advice was followed.

The origins of Jacobean Court architecture lay some decades earlier, perhaps in 1589 when the king, having sufficient faith in the stability of his country and its institutions, decided to take ship to collect his new wife Anna from Denmark. In his immediate entourage, he took the architect William Schaw, who, at the instance of Sir James Melvill, had been one of those directed to greet and entertain the first Danish embassy three years earlier.[32] It was an indication of the already high reputation that Schaw had gained at Court within four years of being appointed as King's Master of Works.[33] During his trip, the king travelled to meet Tycho Brahe at his laboratory of Uranienborg on the island of Ven, which profoundly impressed him.[34] The king stayed in both the splendid courtyard castle/palace of Kronborg at Elsinore (where King James's apartments are still shown) and in the even larger establishment at Fredericksborg. Anna was sister of Christian IV, who was to become one of the great clients of architecture in Danish history.[35]

The extent of the Danish influence in Scotland is difficult to assess. Schaw had been dispatched back from the Kronborg on 19 February 1590 both to brief the Privy Council and to ensure that Holyrood was made ready for the queen's arrival. The king wrote to Robert Bruce, Minister of Edinburgh, that he trusted Schaw would be successful

> in getting als manie good craftsmen as may be had for ending out the half-perfytted Abbey, that lies in such a dead thraw as did the hoastie of *Hoc est enim cor* betwixt the Spagnell priest's hands.[36]

> [in getting as many good craftsmen as may be had for ending out the half-perfected Abbey, that lies in such a dread twist as the cough of *Hoc est enim cor* between the Spanish priest's hands.]

But although sufficient money for the work was made available,[37] progress on the abbey church was so slow that Queen Anna had to spend five days in Leith before she could progress up to it to be crowned.[38] It does not seem to have prejudiced her against Schaw who became her close confidant and chamberlain; and to judge by the statement on his tomb that he 'won the warm affection of every good man who knew him',[39] Schaw was also engaging company. In his other role as Master of Ceremonies he was responsible for the coronation, and for the queen's entry into Edinburgh on 19 May 1590 with its set-piece tableaux, orations and extraordinary devices.

> The steeple of St Giles was festooned with streamers and its interior bestrewn with flowers; there were not one but two tableaux with artificial globes, and large sums were spent on tapestries, paintings and other decorations, many of them depicting classical and mythological scenes.[40]

He was, therefore, also probably accountable for the three days of festivities celebrating Prince Henry's birth in 1594 which included two tournaments, a formal banquet, and elaborate inventions and machinery,[41] and also for the much less flamboyant ceremonies that greeted the baptism of further royal bairns – as well as the design of their cradles.[42] So the breadth of knowledge expected of him included building design, furnishing, invention, heraldry, symbolism, and the classics.

In 1596, Seton was given charge of Dunfermline Palace with the responsibility to keep all its edifices in good order 'lest, by negligence, or the injuries of time, it should happen that any of them might fall'. The queen had more than adequate funds to pay for what became necessary. Schaw remodelled the upper parts of the façade of the wing overlooking Pittencreiff Glen, and facing the town to the north constructed what became called 'Queen Anna's belvedere' or 'the Queen's House' – 'a delicately and princely mansion' in which Charles I was to be born.[43] An inscription stated:

> This gateway and its temple-like superstructure collapsed and was destroyed by age and the injuries of time; it was reconstructed from the foundations in this more ample form and resumed [in occupation] by Anna, Queen, most illustrious daughter of Frederick, King of the Danes the Year of Grace 1600.[44]

It was the tallest building of the horizontally proportioned palace: an approximately cruciform house rising above the entrance into the palace courtyard, an oriel window facing into the town possibly signifying a gallery running along its north front, and joined to the palace buildings at the rear by a long gallery.[45] Schaw may also have assisted the king (or vice versa) in the design for the new chapel required for the baptism of Prince Henry in Stirling Castle during 1594.

On Schaw's death in 1602, extraordinary encomiums were paid him. Queen Anna instructed that a monument to him be set up in Dunfermline Abbey 'to the memory of a most admirable and most upright man',[46] and a separate panel, implying that Schaw had endured recurring ill health, was dedicated to him by Alexander Seton who probably designed the monument itself. After recounting how Schaw had travelled through France and many other kingdoms to improve his mind, the monument states that 'accomplished in every liberal art, he excelled in architecture'. All this implies that he was much better known and admired as an architect than the few buildings ascribed to him today would indicate. As was seen in the last chapter, there are some significant designs of the appropriate period for which no designer has been identified. Moreover, back in 1586 (three years after Schaw's appointment) the king had been informed of the 'great decay and ruin of his castles, palaces and houses, and of the scarcity of munitions and plenishings of the same', and had been persuaded (by who else but Schaw?) that their repair was 'soo great and necessary a work'.[47] He therefore determined to divert the income from vacant prelacies for that purpose – and given that Holyrood was deemed half finished by the time the king was in the Kronberg, building work had evidently been under way.

If Schaw's hand was indeed behind the James VI chapel at Stirling, it showed him to be conversant with European pattern books,[48] but given the knowledge within Scotland at the time – and the growing interest in emblematics deriving from European sources – that familiarity may have been unexceptional. The *façade d'honneur* at Fyvie demonstrated both a capability to design in a way that merged European formality with Scottish architectural motifs and great architectural ingenuity in its transformation of the existing structures. The double-layered superstructure of the new Seton Tower, for example, may even have been a reference to Seton's two lordships of Urquhart and Fyvie.

In his capacity as royal Master of Works, Schaw also claimed the position of General Warden of Masons in Scotland, in which role he drew up the first set of Statutes for codifying the rules of masoncraft in December 1598.[49] Appropriately for a modernising kingdom, these statutes would not seem particularly out of place for a twenty-first-century professional organisation. They addressed the quality of service by codifying rules for entry, training, apprenticeship, inspection and control. Even more modern was their underlying ethos of extending central control to a heterogeneous and locally based industry.

On his death in 1602, Schaw was succeeded as Master of their Majesties' Works first by Cunninghame of Robertland and then by Sir James Murray of Kilbaberton in 1607. Murray became 'architectus noster'[50] and thus James VI's Scottish Court architect,[51] and was knighted by Charles I in the Palace of Seton on 14 July 1633. From the accounts, it is evident that Murray was acting as architect rather than tradesman, not only from the disparity in the relevant salaries,[52] but in respect of employing, directing the work of, and promoting operatives. One such was Master Mason William Wallace[53] who appears first in 1617 as a carver in stone, but was claiming credit for the 'extraordinary service in the Frame [presumably design]' of George Heriot's Hospital by 1629,[54] which implies that he judged that he had attained architect status. Murray, however, was of a different kidney, being closely associated with Hay and his glassworks, friend of the enormously wealthy banker Sir William Dick of Braid (who maintained an agent in London and a branch in Paris), and a friend, even, of powerful Chancellor Seton.[55]

The only record of Murray preparing plans as architect was when he was paid 'for drawing of the modell of the workes of the Parliament and counsel hous'[56] – the design of the Parliament House of Scotland – on 1 February 1633. He had earlier been responsible for the rebuilding of the palace at Edinburgh Castle for James VI's return in 1617, for the rebuilding of the north wing of Linlithgow palace after it had collapsed the same year, and further refashioning of Holyrood Abbey. Given their current condition, the magnificence of this work can be underestimated. The ashlar-faced courtyard façade of Linlithgow's north wing is composed around the octagonal staircase at the centre, the finely carved pediments above each window, and the fine array of square ashlar chimneys rising from the cross-wall on the skyline. Doors and the chimneys were marbled, and the entire courtyard façade was overlaid with oil colours and gilded.[57] The contrast with the similar wing in Denmark's royal palace of Kolding must have been striking, for, lacking Scotland's fine stone, Denmark had to make do with plastered brickwork and stone was restricted to a few significant details.

Murray may also have been the architect of a number of villas and houses associated with members of the Scottish Court – particularly those sharing the new villa plan, if one judges by a number of consistent motifs and architectural devices. Yet since the origins for most of the features of the new villas lay largely within the Scottish architecture of the previous century, such houses may represent another evolution of Scotland's strong and vigorous architecture to include some northern European overtones, rather than an italianisation.[58] 'A conscious historicism [was] at work' in seventeenth-century Scotland as much as during the two previous centuries, particularly in the refitting of Edinburgh Castle in 1617.[59]

In 1612, Sir James and his wife Martha obtained the lands of Baberton (or Kilbaberton), now on the western outskirts of Edinburgh, and ten years later were completing a good, if diminutive, example of the Jacobean villa. The fundamental difference between the villa and the houses of the earlier generation was the relocation of the private wing from the rear to the entrance façade, producing a much more formal and controlled design. Since they now governed the approach and the entrance, the gables of the two projecting wings received particular emphasis. In Baberton, both have pedimented and pilastered windows on each principal floor, and both are crowned by an ashlar chimney-stack rising above a flat ashlar skew. The skews finish in ornately carved triangular finials sitting upon columns. The walls below are edged with buckle-quoins – corner-stones carved in relief in the shape of a strapwork buckle.[60] The carved elements of the windows, string-course, finials and chimney would have stood out proudly from the harling.

In addition to its principal staircase rising to the first floor in the west wing, two further circular, private staircases led to Baberton's upper floors.[61] On the principal floor, the main house is divided into main chamber or hall and private room (chamber of dais), with the principal bedchamber and its own closet in the wing behind. The chambers above the entrance stair wing might have been guest rooms, and those in the far wing for the family. Crucially, every chamber in the house could be reached from a staircase without needing to pass through another.

10.5 Conjectural reconstruction of Baberton, by Edinburgh, Sir James Murray's own suburban villa. Note how the buckle-quoins emphasise its verticality. (Author)

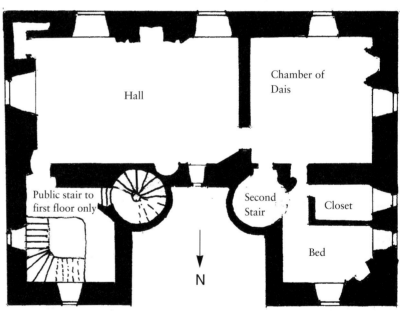

10.6 Plan of Baberton, after MacGibbon and Ross. (Author's collection)

However, although Baberton might to some extent be explained as a regularisation of the Menzies plan, it is not symmetrical[62] and the drawing by MacGibbon and Ross, which implies that it is, misleads. The wings are of slightly uneven width and the windows are at different levels. Perhaps the need to believe that Scots were at last building symmetrically is yet another manifestation of the idea that the only acceptable Renaissance tenets were those of order and proportion emanating from France or Italy. Throughout the seventeenth century, Scots would build what appeared to be in symmetry, but what was only

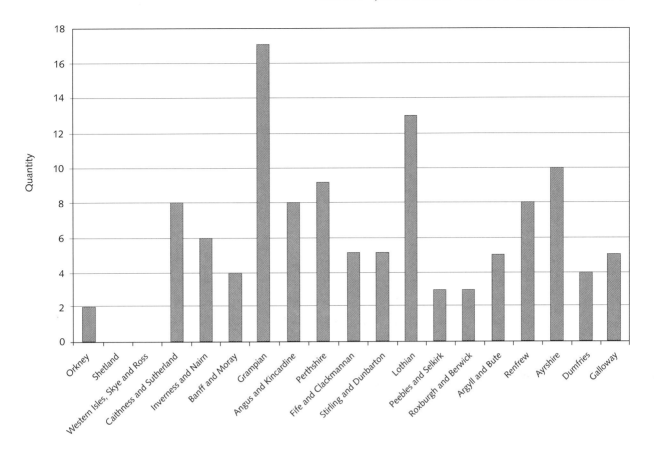

Graph 8 Château construction, 1600–39.

in *apparent* symmetry. It was, instead, *in balance*. That this was the intended result, and not just another manifestation of provincial design illiteracy, may be gauged from the effect at Sir William Bruce's first house at Balcaskie (*see* p. 252). Scottish architects were simply not adopting the patterns being developed in England or Europe. They were taking an idiosyncratically national line and *things were not what they seemed*.

At least twenty buildings, located with only a few rare exceptions in east central Scotland, appear to form part of this school, and all seem to be villas rather than great country seats. To some degree at least, they represent a generic Court style, which began with Schaw or Murray and was later developed by Sir Anthony Alexander. The architecture was one of smooth harled horizontality, punctuated by elaborate dressed-stone windows, square chimney-stacks set on edge, dormer windows, finials and strapwork details.

An extravagantly flamboyant version was built close to Edinburgh for a cadet branch of the Napiers, the Napiers of Wrichtishousis in Bruntsfield.[63] Entered through a north-facing court, the Wrichtishousis comprised two taller wings dominating a lower gallery between, like a diminutive Caledonian response to Hatfield House. Both wings appear to have had their own entrances and stairs, whereas the ceremonial entrance at the centre led solely upstairs into the gallery, which in turn gave access to both wings. The entrance pavilion itself was designed like a miniature *châtelet*, capped by an array of tiny turrets very like those perched on the apex of the great barbican of Lûbeck. The east wing seems to have been for the family, with the public rooms in the western one. The Wrichtishousis' stairtowers, in their accustomed place in the angles, were chamfered for their first two storeys (similar to nearby Gogar). A turnpike stair corbelled from the larger western tower (possibly edged with buckle-quoins) led to rooms above and, eventually, up to a richly scrolled, parapeted viewing platform at the top.

In the house's four principal gables, the Wrichtishousis entered the lands of fantasy. Ornately carved pedimented heads, allegedly containing Roman heads in profile rather like the new Bourse in Copenhagen, were contained within the pediments of the aedicular windows on the two principal floors. Above, at the centre of each gable there was a vesica (oval or round window) flanked on each side by a finial at the wall-head. The apex was composed of the crowstepped gable framed by twin chimney-stacks.

How the Wrichtishousis was organised is implied by the manner in which the Earl of Haddington extended the old tower of the Lauders of the Bass at Tyninghame after he bought it in 1628. Haddington added two parallel wings to his tower: the eastern contained the Great Hall, with its oak and fir tables, whereas the western had just a hall with several (implicitly smaller) tables and a clock. The chamber of dais opened off the latter. The distinction between the two wings becomes clear on the floor above. The bedchambers above the Great Hall on the east are plain,

10.7 Conjectural reconstruction of the Napier villa of Wrichtishousis that used to adorn Bruntsfield Links, Edinburgh. The view is from the north: family wing probably to the left; public and guest wing to the right. It was demolished in 1800. (Author)

whereas those on the upper storeys of the west are more lavishly furnished with a marble table, mirrors, chests – and one had a cabinet. So the west wing must have been the family wing, and the east wing the public and guest wing. So what had happened to the original tower lining the north?[64] It was cut down to fit; cellars, kitchen and transe were modified to provide access into the new wings, and two lavishly appointed bedchambers were created in its second storey. The tower's principal floor became the Lettermeit (*sic*) Hall, adorned with an oak table, two fir tables, six benches and a surprising number of guns:[65] an eating hall for those of lesser status.

When the favoured U-plan had to be created from existing structures, it required more substantial reordering. Thomas Dalyell, who had married the bastard daughter of his boss, Lord Kinloss, bought the lands of the Binns and Manerstoun in 1613,[66] when he was either an indweller in Edinburgh or acting as Deputy Keeper of the Rolls in Bruce's household in London. From time to time he had also been acting as the London agent for the immensely wealthy Sir William Dick of Braid, and trading in butter.[67] He was to be father-in-law to the poet William Drummond of Hawthornden. At the time, the Binns probably consisted of a principal tower to the south-east (above the current kitchen) and two smaller corner towers to the north-east and north-west, the latter two joined by a lodging block sitting on cellars with a service corridor – perhaps not unlike Craig. These he metamorphosed into a villa – a place in which to contemplate nature, and enjoy 'blisful ease' in the countryside. The plan[68] indicates that he lowered all the towers to a constant height of two and a half storeys above ground, and fashioned a U-plan villa facing southwards to Binnie Hill. The house was homogenised by its constant roofline – emphasised by highly charged dormer window heads, and aedicular windows in the gables. Dalyell then cut out the ground-floor cellars at the centre of the north wing to install a 'laigh hall' commemorated by its fine 1622 fireplace. Columns carried the weight formerly borne by the vaults. The principal stair may have been a straight internal flight where the eighteenth-century stair now is, rather like that at nearby Duntarvie; if so, it was to be the first of its type. Subsidiary private stairs project to the north (unlike Baberton or Wrichtishousis), probably because they were there already.

The Binns also heralds the emergence of the laigh hall. 'Laich' means 'low', and therefore 'laigh hall' meant lower hall, a reception room on the ground floor. The result was to increase the formality of movement upstairs to the principal chambers, since some of those who had once met the laird in the hall or in the chamber of dais might not now approach any closer than the laigh hall. There was a coincident growth in 'business rooms' or rooms (like that shown on an early Glamis plan) where the laird would meet tenants. 'Laigh', however, also carried a slighter greater symbolic meaning. When referring to the buildings of the inner or outer courts, the 'laigh biggings' did not always mean physically low since they could reach to three storeys tall. The term also implied subordinate or subsidiary, and that may well also have been one of the meanings of the new ground-level hall. Since, with the exception of Craignethan and Stirling, the public rooms of the grander Scottish houses had remained determinedly upon the first floor, the establishment of a principal reception room downstairs was of significant symbolic moment.

Although the horizontality, the homogenisation of different periods of building, and the laigh hall at the Binns were new, the house remained wholeheartedly Scots in plan and detail. Even more than the courtiers and officials who had remained behind in Edinburgh, Dalyell represented the successful mercantile Scot on the make in London, a man whom one might have expected to import fashionable architectural ideas from the south of England as a way of demonstrating both wealth and London sophistication. That did not happen.

Dalyell's employer Lord Kinloss completed the extraordinary Culross Abbey House, Fife, in 1608. In utter contrast to his industrialist brother's comfortable and unpretentious palace down by the shore, this gracious, horizontally proportioned and masterfully controlled ashlar-faced mansion, sits high on a bluff gazing south over the upper Firth of Forth. It was an extension of the 1590s commendator's house that lay behind.[69] The attenuated two-storeyed house was built of large blocks of polished grey imported stone, flanked by taller ogee-domed towers in the manner of the Low Countries. Except for the ordered ranks of twelve pedimented and framed windows lining the principal floor, the façade is powerfully austere, lacking the projecting centrepiece customary in compositions of this nature on the continent. The house being double-pile, an enormous gallery with a superlative view occupied the south front at first-floor level.

10.8 Culross Abbey House today, following a severe Procrustean post-war truncation. (Author)

Slezer's drawing of Culross Abbey House in the later seventeenth century depicts it as the centre of terraced gardens, orchards and wildernesses, strongly resembling the 1550 Villa d'Este at Tivoli, underlining its role as a villa rather than a statement of ancient lineage. The designer is unknown, but James Murray had been appointed Principal Master of all the king's works the previous year, so it may have been his work. An apparently similar house that attracted widespread comment was the great mansion of 'hewen work' built before 1607 by Sir George Home of Spott, Earl of Dunbar within the castle ruins of Berwick upon Tweed. 'A stately, sumptuous and well seated house', thought Brereton, with a fair long gallery with 'the daintiest prospect to the sea, to the town, to the land and the river, with a viewing platform above it' whose timber mantelpiece, all of a piece, was near 5 yards long.[70] The surveyor George Chaworth commended its 'exceeding heyght, and yet magnificent turrets above that heyght, a goodly front, and a brave prospect open to the meanest aned most distant roome, and that uniforme proportion everye waye generally, as wold stodye a good architector to describe'.[71] The description implies a similarity with Culross. Upon Dunbar's death in 1611, the house was swiftly demolished by Sir James Douglas, some of its ashlar blocks transported to London for reuse, stone being a rare and prized material for a private house in the capital, and the balance to a new wing at Cowdenknowes.[72]

A similarly motivated effort to refashion Auchterhouse, just north of Dundee, was made by the Earl of Buchan in 1633. Buchan extended the main house westwards with a laigh hall, but compared to the slightly subfusc nature of the other laigh halls, Auchterhouse's is no subordinate space. It is a tall, well-lit chamber with a magnificent columned and carved overmantel, and an elaborate plaster ceiling heavily patterned in alternating squares, circles and lozenges, each containing figures or devices, highlighted by three ranks of encrusted, low hanging plaster bosses. The plasterwork indicates that this was the most important chamber and not a laigh hall at all. Perversely – appropriate for the scatty Buchans – the withdrawing chamber was upstairs on the other side of the staircase. On a more domestic scale, the Little family modified their sixteenth-century house at Liberton, near Edinburgh, by cutting out the cellars from the east wing to create a gracious, very well-lit ground-floor hall – entered, uniquely, through the gable and via a new antechamber to the south.[73] The remodelling required the alteration of all floors above.

The heavily elaborate plasterwork that characterised the state rooms of early seventeenth-century Scots houses like Auchterhouse may have been imported from England. But although the plasterwork of the 1606 palace of Bromley by Bow, east London, was indeed to prove significant,[74] plaster decoration seems to have been used in Scotland much earlier,[75] and painted decoration with contemporary motifs continued to appear in buildings of high fashion until the later seventeenth century.[76] So the two forms of decoration coexisted. The introduction of heavy ornamental plasterwork fundamentally altered the character of rooms. By deepening the ceiling, it made the chambers appear smaller and more compact; and by concealing the beams and vaults above, it conveyed a more unified appearance. The horizontal emphasis was accentuated by a fondness for deep, ornate friezes.

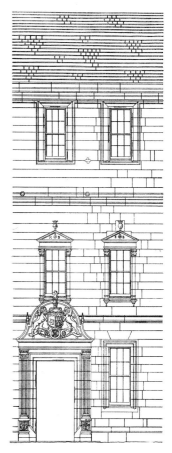

10.9 Culross Abbey House, north façade and doorway, drawn by T. Aikman Swan in the early twentieth century. (from Details of Scottish Domestic Architecture*)*

Section.

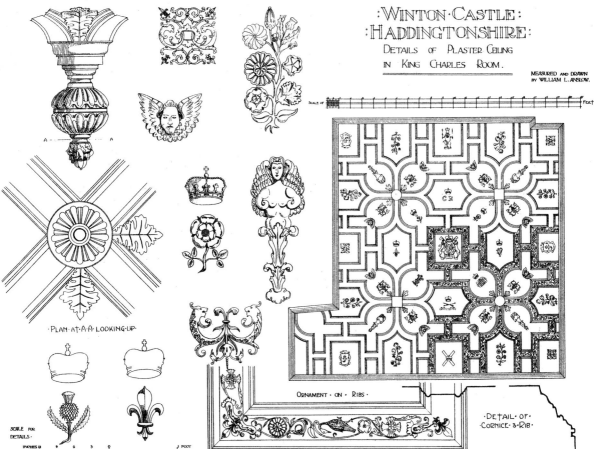

:WINTON·CASTLE:
:HADDINGTONSHIRE:
DETAILS OF PLASTER CEILING
IN KING CHARLES ROOM.

MEASURED AND DRAWN
BY WILLIAM L. ANSLOW.

SCALE OF FEET.

A——A

·PLAN·AT·A·A·LOOKING·UP·

SCALE FOR
DETAILS·
INCHES

FOOT

·ORNAMENT·ON·RIBS·

·DETAIL·OF·
·CORNICE·&·RIB·

Top: *10.10 Plaster ceiling from Pinkie House drawn by R. Watson for* EAA Sketchbook, *1883–6. 10.11 Plaster Ceiling from King Charles's room at Winton, drawn by William Anslow (from* Details of Scottish Domestic Architecture).

Plaster ceilings had an emblematic role comparable to painted ones, although their variations were rather more subtle. The surface was divided into compartments by projecting ribs, between which appeared heraldic motifs, mottos, dates, flowers, emblems and figures from classical myth (such as Hector, who appears in ceilings at Thirlestane, Balcarres, Muchalls, Craigievar, Glamis and Bromley). Sheets of engravings were issued of the Seven Virtues, Four Seasons, and Nine Worthies and of profiles of Roman emperors in roundels.[77] The ribs would be either wide and ornate, covering the ceiling in a strapwork pattern which dominated its surface, or thin and pointed which, being less dominant, placed greater emphasis upon the figures and emblems. The heavier ribs may have been reserved for the private or withdrawing room – formerly chamber of dais – as in Winton, the Binns and the King's Room in Pinkie.

Decorative moulds for parts of the ceiling – figures, cornice and ribs – would travel from house to house; and an imperfection in one of them allows that same mould to be tracked. The mould for the common cherub or putto used for the Kellie ceiling, for example, had a slight dunt in its left forehead which should allow its peregrinations to be tracked. A fragment of frieze found during repairs to the palace at Edinburgh Castle was from the same mould used in Muchalls.[78] Some of the moulds used by Murray on refitting the palace of Edinburgh Castle had to be collected from Kellie in 1617.[79] Kellie was then owned by Sir Thomas Erskine of Gogar, Viscount Fenton and future Earl of Kellie, who may well have brought fashionable moulds back from London, which was why they were so greatly desired.

The way plasterwork was introduced can sometimes illuminate a building's history. The great rooms on the *piano nobile* of the Binns, fitted out for a royal visit in 1617, have most elaborate plasterwork, whose geometric patterns give proportion to the room by using the windows as the principal point of reference. Reharling, however, revealed that the windows had been moved slightly east. So the plasterwork not only provides proof of a pre-1617 building, but is evidence that the building fabric had to be expensively modified to accommodate an *a priori* plasterwork design. It therefore seems contradictory that the ceiling bosses are so low that you would hit your head on any chandelier hanging from them. James VI may have been short-statured, but it would have been inept to build on the assumption that everybody else was. However, the window embrasures are also much closer to the floor than normal – which reveals what must have happened. When five years later, Dalyell created his laigh hall from the earlier cellars, he must have raised the floor level with the consequences seen upstairs.

Not all plasterers were equally proficient, and not all buildings were equally accommodating to the geometries implicit in the new decoration. The heavy cornice, dating from *c.* 1640, which outlines the Blue Room at Brodie, for example, is done in a way that precludes a symmetrical design in this smallish vaulted chamber. Instead of working around the manifest idiosyncrasies of the chamber, the plasterers must have begun in one corner with an *a priori* design that turned out not to fit. Some of the motifs lying between the wide plaster ribs vary so substantially that they are likely to have been drawn freehand by local craftsmen.[80] Much better

10.12 Interior of the Blue Room at Brodie, Morayshire. The plasterer must have had a preconceived design that did not fit. (NTS)

fit was achieved, for example, by John, 2nd Earl of Kinghorn in the Great Hall at Glamis in 1620, or by William Forbes at Craigievar in 1626.

The Earl of Winton completed the wholesale refashioning of the old tower of Winton, near Haddington, high on a bluff overlooking the River Tyne, in 1628. It was transformed into an approximate U-plan villa of outrageously pretty flamboyance. Not only was there lavish glasswork, but Winton had also imported 9,000 Caithness slates to roof it.[81] Its similarity in date and form to Baberton implies Murray as architect. The south façade rears up as a punctured wall unadorned but for dormer windows, as though it were an extension of the steep terrace on which it was built. By contrast, the north front was broken up in form and height, its picturesqueness a demonstration of the contemporary belief that house and countryside should be in harmony.[82] Approximately U-plan, the main house between the two towers was originally set upon stone arcades.[83] Two staircases for such a compact house confirm the departure from the enfilade of one chamber leading to the next, for they provide separate access to each of the two state chambers, as well as to those in the wings. The main chamber, now drawing-room, its status underscored by its ornate columned fireplace, has the proportion of $2 \times 1 \times \frac{2}{3}$ to emphasise its horizontality. Winton's plasterwork, executed by John White, is exceptional, but only five years later, some had to be redone for a royal visit. On the 1633 ceiling of the King Charles Room (what would have earlier been the chamber of dais) heavy plaster ribs frame the Honours of Scotland, Prince of Wales feathers, a Tudor portcullis, the initials CR for the king, and the motto *Nobis Haec Invicta Miservnt CVI Proavi* (One hundred and six kings have left this to us unconquered) beneath an imperial crown and a crossed sword and cannon firing a fleur-de-lys.

Winton's polished grey ashlar is unusually fine: its windows carved by William Wallace (presumably under Murray's direction), its spacious octagonal, ogee-domed, ashlar tower containing the principal staircase, and its slender stair in the corner of the other wing leading to an ornately balustraded viewing platform. Three tall chimneys rising from the central

*10.13 North-east façades of
Winton House, East Lothian.
Billings has eliminated the early
nineteenth-century buildings
with which John Paterson
obscured the original entrance
façade and its loggia.* (Author's
collection)

10.14 Winton today. (Author)

10.15 Pitreavie, Fife, seen in the late nineteenth century from the north before it was baronially extended. (RCAHMS)

wall-head face the approach, the outer ones wrythen, the central one carved with foliage. They set a new standard in non-martial aristocratic display. The similarity between Winton's chimneys and those formerly on the Murray-designed palace at Edinburgh Castle appears to confirm his association with Winton.[84] Winton was a compact house, offering nothing comparable by way of accommodation to Seton, only a few miles away. Its concept implies that this was the Wintons' *villa suburbana*.

For lesser men, however, limited to but one country and one town house, villas represented their principal rural dwellings and were, therefore, rather more than just a retreat. Witness the sober villa of Pitreavie, near Dunfermline, built for the Wardlaw family in about 1614.[85] Sir Henry Wardlaw had succeeded William Schaw as Chamberlain to Queen Anne, and may have shared some of Schaw's architectural interests; but Pitreavie is not dated, and the armorial panel above the door is that of his son, implying a date in the 1630s. When Sir Anthony Alexander, returned from his travels abroad 'by his learning and travellis abroad, haveing acquired skill in architectorie'[86] to join Murray as Master of Works, he married Wardlaw's daughter Elizabeth in 1633 and was knighted in 1635. Perhaps it was Alexander who refashioned the existing house into a pure U-plan.[87] The public staircase in the wing only rises to the first floor, and circulation thereafter is by two circular staircases, one in each angle rising through the height of the building providing independent access to each chamber.

Decorative plasterwork was of an ordered, geometrical kind, and walls were panelled with tapestry.[88] Pitreavie's three-storeyed southern façade was decorated only by a swept Dutch gable chimney-stack. There were no crowsteps at Pitreavie: it was an architecture of pure mass.

Alexander's romantic and rather French additions to the *hôtel* known as the Argyll Lodging at Stirling seem, therefore, slightly regressive by comparison. This U-plan nobleman's lodging (altered in the late seventeenth century after its purchase by the Earl of Argyll who had many of the earlier carvings cloured off and replaced with his own monograms)[89] was extended by Alexander from an L-plan house and conformed to the villa in its homogeneous roofline, staircases in the angles, and its fine classical screen to the street. In expression, however, it rejected the new Stoicism: both client and architect (father and son) had spent time in France. The circular corner stairtowers are wide and taken up into turrets, and the strapwork scrolls above windows and door have a flamboyance utterly eschewed at Pitreavie.

Essays in Court-style architecture sometimes required draconian action if created from existing houses. The small tower and adjacent house of Monkton, just south of Edinburgh, for example, was obtained by Sir Alexander Hay, Clerk Register, from his uncle Hay of Yester.[90] Hay (or maybe even Murray in view of its buckle-quoins) regularised its windows, added chimneys and a new stairtower, built a grandiose entrance gateway to the inner court and added a gallery along the west side. The latter has two extraordinarily wide mullioned and pedimented dormer windows in the manner of Steenwinckel's Rosenberg Palace in Copenhagen.

Echoes of Court architecture could be heard on islands far from the Home Counties. A 'palace of the Yards' – as distinct from Robert Reid's 'castle of Kirkwall'[91] – had been Robert Stewart's residence in the capital of Orkney, and between 1601 and 1607 Stewart's son, Earl Patrick, constructed a U-plan villa on its north side.[92] Earl Patrick was not a man to cross (indeed there was an implication in his subsequent trial that forced labour was used to build his villa). He

never went from his castle to the kirk, nor abroad otherwise, without the convoy of fifty musketeers and other gentlemen of convoy and guard. And siclike, before dinner and supper, there were three trumpeters that soundit till the meat of the first service was set at table.[93]

Patrick's villa was on a sufficiently regal scale to be known as the Earl's Palace, and was constructed of exemplary quality red sandstone ashlar.

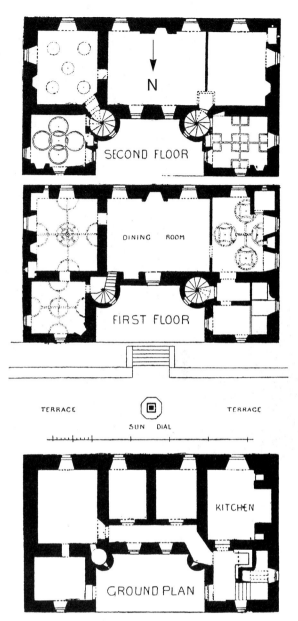

10.16 Plan of Pitreavie from MacGibbon and Ross. (Author's collection)

10.17 Conjectural reconstruction by Historic Scotland of the entire Kirkwall palace. In the foreground is Bishop Robert Reid's tour maîtresse (see p. 112); the earl's palace occupies the top corner. (HS)

The great chambers lie at the centre, staircase and guest chamber to the right and a three-storeyed private wing for the earl to the left. The hall is proclaimed by its enormous swelling bay and oriel windows and triplet of tall slender round-headed windows on the gable, and the chamber of dais by its ornate oriel facing west and enormous bay window facing east. The earl's 'tower' with its private stair and two-storeyed corner turrets tied together at their midriff by an ornate string-course, dominates this powerful and claustrophobic composition. Although its plan was modern, the expression of the earl's palace was that of an earlier generation – as indeed was the behaviour of its builder: Earl Patrick was executed for oppression and rebellion in 1618.

Castle Stewart, 6 miles east of Inverness, was built or rather refashioned into a U-plan house by the Earl of Moray in about 1625. It differs from the lowland model in that the twin staircases are concealed in the outside angles to the rear, rather than playing an architectural role on the façade. Turrets decorate the east wing, a viewing platform caps the west, and the façade between is lined by dormer windows. Two-storeyed rectangular oriel windows are corbelled from the two rear corners, on the angle like those at Pittullie (and those that used to be at Cluny). In the badlands to the south, John Grant of Freuchie had similarly been altering his ancient seat of Freuchie or Ballachastle. Behind the kneecaps of the Laird of Grant's piper William Cumming in Richard Waitt's celebrated portrait,[94] you can just make out the substantial U-plan mansion sitting at the back of a platform, with an elaborate dormer-windowed skyline and two projecting crowstepped wings adorned with turrets embracing the inner court. The painting duly celebrates Grant's successful application in 1694 to have the 'castle and manor place of Freuchie' retitled Castle Grant.[95]

Extensions to Drum, Aberdeenshire (*see* Plate 18), took the villa form rather than the spectacularly vertical reformatting of ancient buildings that was the regional preference (*see* next chapter), despite the fact that Alexander Irvine, 9th Laird of Drum, known as 'Little Breeks', probably used the same architect, Ian Bel,[96] as had been employed at the neighbouring houses. The fourteenth-century tower of the Irvines of Drum had been extended to the south, probably in the sixteenth century, and the southern wing was wholly reformatted between 1615 and 1621[97] into an approximately symmetrical U-plan house containing the principal rooms above a ground floor of cellars, kitchens and a well-lit service corridor. The flanking wings are more like closet towers than wings – and only

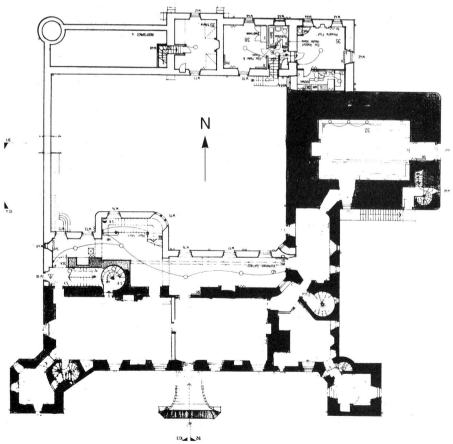

Scale 1:100

10.18 Principal floor plan of Drum, Aberdeenshire. (NTS)

10.19 *Conjectural reconstruction of Careston, Angus. The roofs appear to be largely of later date. The left, western tower was almost certainly capped by a viewing platform reached by a stair in the rear angle, rather like the contemporary Castle Stewart. The later arcade between the wings may replicate an original – as existed, for example, at Winton.* (Author)

large enough to contain business rooms or tiny bedrooms. The principal stair to the west leads up past a business room to the hall, private room and then bedroom with closet. The original seventeenth-century entrance and stair were – at least up to the first floor – extraordinarily similar to those at Craigston for which there is even stronger evidence of Ian Bel's hand.[98] There is something determinedly relaxed and less showy about Drum when compared to Bel's vertical châteaux. Perhaps Little Breeks, a scholar and benefactor of Marischal College, was building according to different values.

The 'wild, prodigal and tyrannical'[99] Sir Harry Lindsay of Kinfauns, formerly Master of Household to Queen Anna and afterwards Earl of Crawford, refashioned Careston, not far from his principal seat of Finavon, Angus, into a villa: a

neat and most delicat house, well built, brave lights [windows], and of a most excellent contrivance, without debait the best gentlemen's seat in the shyre; extraordinaire much planting, delicate yards and gardens with stone walls, ane excellent avenue with ane range of ash trees on every side, ane excellent arbour. For length and breadth, none in the country like it.[100]

This tall, compressed U-plan villa still contains an unusually rich interior. Its imposing scale-and-platt staircase, with much carved stonework, ends in a wide lobby at the head, with twin panelled doors surmounted by a carved overmantel. At the principal floor, the stair opens into a tall groin-vaulted antechamber to the hall, and reveals the first of a number of outstanding fireplaces and overmantels in exquisitely carved stonework (by contrast to the more frequent plaster) described by Alexander Warden:

> All the principal rooms and the old staircase were particularly rich in sculptured and other decoration . . . of armorial bearings, allegorical representations, and curious grotesque ornaments. . . . The Dining and Drawing Rooms, the grand staircase and about half a dozen bedrooms are decorated with the sculptures and heraldic bearings. . . . On the right and left of the fireplace are male and female satyrs. A well executed sculpture of the Royal Arms of Scotland, around which are banners, shields, and other military trophies, and two nude human figures riding on llamas, adorns the mantlepiece in the drawing room. Nude figures of a man and women, about life size, with cornucopiae in their hands, festooned in a tasteful manner, and united by a Pan's head decorate each side of the fireplace.[101]

It is unlikely to be coincidental that so many of these new villas were built by courtiers or officials close to the queen, and a study of the iconography of the plasterwork and carving might reveal a consistent body of thought and allegory.

The controlled U-plan villa did not really survive inflation to palatial scale. Scone Palace, created from the abbey buildings by Sir David Murray of Gospertie, Comptroller (later Lord and Viscount Scone) after the forfeiture of the Earl of Gowrie in 1600, was called a palace presumably as a result of its courtyard form.[102] The state chambers included a lobby, dining-room, king's chamber (and cabinet within same), the long gallery and the Duke's Chamber (or apartment) comprising three separate rooms.[103] Murray eschewed the towered entrances of the other palaces in favour of an overblown version of the E-plan villa. Its three gables were crowstepped, with prominent pedimented windows and armorial cartouches. But Scone's scale was too broad for that architectural device, lacking even the heraldic chimney-stacks of Wrichtishousis. It fell from favour: 'in all respects inelegant and unworthy of notice', according to Thomas Garnett in 1800. The ceiling of its disproportionately narrow long gallery, 160 feet long and only 18 feet wide, stretching along the east front, was

> arched and covered in painting. On one side is represented the hunting of a stag, in all its different stages; and on the other, the diversion of hawking, and hunting of the wild boar. James VI appears in every scene, attended by the nobles of his Court, many of the portraits of which were drawn from life. The spaces between the different scenes are filled up with family arms, fruit, flowers and other ornaments. These paintings appear to have had considerable merit, but are now much defaced.[104]

In the early seventeenth century Sir John Maxwell of Cowhill, Dumfriesshire, planned a two-storeyed and basement E-plan mansion of extraordinary elaboration, its courtyard façade entirely of ashlar.[105] A chamfered ashlar stairtower at the centre was corbelled out to square for a viewing platform at the top. Windows on the *piano nobile* were outlined by a rich cable-moulded string-course like that at Haggs or Kenmure. Only one side of the house ever appears to have been completed. Less ambitious landowners just wishing to update a tower with minimum disruption might roof over their battlements to form a gallery, as happened at Comlongan, but customarily would replace the battlement with a balcony or viewing platform framed between gazebos at each end like Pinkie's, as was the case in Cassilis (Ayrshire), Kilbryde (Stirlingshire) and even Neidpath (Peebleshire). Slender, rectangular stairtowers were occasionally grafted onto an existing building on each side of its main entrance as, *inter alia*, in Nisbet (Borders) and Dalquharran (Ayrshire).

Since few of the new villas had corridors on the principal floors, the main change in early seventeenth-century house planning was to provide independent access to all principal chambers by the creation of additional staircases. Smaller houses were likewise amended. The L-plan house was tightened so that the single staircase was placed where it could lead directly into the centre of the large (usually south-facing) main house, avoiding the former enfilade, as was the case in Peffermill. Peffermill (possibly the model for Sir Walter Scott's Dumbiedykes in *Heart of Midlothian*) was built in 1636 for Edward Edgar in a sheltered spot beneath Arthur's Seat (*see* p. 34). Harled, dormer-windowed, with sundials similar to those on George Heriot's Hospital, Peffermill exemplified the single-staircase lowland house, its design lifted by the wide, circular, string-coursed staircase in the angle, with its lovely strapwork entrance. Walls were painted within.[106] However, the T-plan house – a straightforward affair of a main house with a rectangular staircase projecting halfway along – was becoming more fashionable. Houses of this form – Old Leckie, Pilmuir and Grangepans, for example – tended to be couthy and domestic in appearance. So the sophisticated refashioning of the house of Luffness, Aberlady, probably by the Earl of Haddington

10.20 Conjectural reconstruction of the T-plan villa of Luffness. (Author)

soon after he bought it in 1634, stands out by virtue of its ranks of high-fashion square ashlar chimney-stacks set on the angle soaring into the skyline from their ashlar plinth. It may also have been Haddington who transformed Cowdenknowes, Borders, after he purchased it the following year, by adding a self-contained U-plan villa similar to, but more sophisticated than, that of Drum. Completely separate from the old tower,[107] the new house was flanked by square, projecting towers, and entered through and up the western one.

The early U-plan villa, framed by ornate gables, gradually gave way to a new U-plan villa framed by rectangular – and sometimes flat-topped – towers, like Duntarvie, near Winchburgh. Long a ruin, it was probably built in the 1620s by Francis Durhame of Duntarvie in competition with his fellow heritors.[108] Its north-eastern aspect was sandwiched between two rectangular towers each capped by a balustraded viewing platform, symmetrically heralded by a chimney-stack and reached by corbelled secondary stairs in the angles. Duntarvie's innovation, however, was the straight flight of stairs at the centre of the three-storeyed main house, from a lobby between hall and drawing-room on the principal floor down to the garden. Thus the house plan evolved. Lobbies between the drawing- and dining-rooms became popular,[109] halls and corridors emerged, and the communality of the sixteenth century ceded to the formality of the seventeenth.

Despite the overt rejection of martial imagery in favour of villa clothing (to which the owner could retire to contemplate nature and his plantations), notions of nationalism were never wholly absent. They were implicit from the array on the skyline and explicit on much of the

10.21 The north-east façade of Duntarvie, West Lothian, drawn c. *1870 by W.F. Lyon. The large window at the centre lit the straight staircase. (RCAHMS)*

10.22 *The withdrawing-room of Carnock, Stirlingshire (since demolished), as it was probably refitted in the early seventeenth century, drawn by David MacGibbon.* (Author's collection)

decoration within. Elaborate plasterwork boasted the royal coat of arms, plaster overmantels, carved fireplaces, and an infinite quantity of cartouches and plaster figurines of thistles, roses, fleurs-de-lys, in addition to the families' own heraldic devices, and endless reworkings of classical morality tales. It was largely the same in houses where the decoration was painted and the walls wainscotted, panelled or even hung. Rooms in which monarchs had stayed on progresses (and there were many) remained named, suitably, the King's or the Queen's Room, with appropriate decoration. More significant, perhaps, was that motto: *Nobis Haec Invicta Miservnt CVI Proavi*. It was a bittersweet celebration: pride that the Scottish king had become King of Britain, but a permanent reminder of Scotland's hard-won independence – a far longer independence (if you believed the myth of the Scottish royal lineage extending back to Fergus I) than England had had. The key word in the motto is 'invicta' – unconquered. The more that Scotland felt remote from decision-making, the more it would emphasise its own identity and hard-won freedoms.

11
Later Jacobean
Nationalism,
c. 1590–c. 1640

Bogagieth, the Marquess of Huntly's palace, all built with stone facing the ocean; whose fair front (set prejudice aside) worthily deserves an English man's applause for her lofty and majestick towers and turrets, that storm the air; . . . It struck me with admiration, to gaze on so gawdy and regular a frontispiece, more especially when to consider it is in the nook of a nation.[1]

If the Loire valley in the early sixteenth century could be called a regionally scaled building site, so could north-east Scotland in the early seventeenth. It is almost as though no property of substance was left untouched between 1590 and 1640 in a wave of almost competitive rebuilding, modernising or extending – sufficient to provide an excellent market for architects, masons, painters and plasterers. The new architecture of the north-east – with its influence trickling south to Angus and west to Inverness – was very particular, and perhaps the easiest way to characterise it would be nationalist. For the country magnates shared in the heightened nationalist sentiment, but instead of restricting it timidly to plasterwork and carving as the Lowlanders had, they applied it to an entire building programme which, contrary to the tendency towards horizontal plans and proportions of the previous century, expressed itself in height.

The modernising of Scotland had accentuated rather than loosened its ties with the past. By deciding to improve rather than abandon Caerlaverock, Castle Campbell, Dirleton or Crichton, the greater lowland magnates – Maxwell, Argyll, Gowrie and Bothwell – were emphasising their status as nobles through the medium of their ancient fortresses. Scions of noble families churned out histories – sometimes minor relatives like David Hume of Godscroft with his *History of the House of Douglas*, and sometimes the aristocrats themselves, Sir Robert Gordon on the House of Sutherland, Viscount Kingston on the House of Seton, Lord Somervill on his own family, or Sir William Mure on the House of Rowallan. Magnates once created and shaped history rather than wrote about it: which implies that the myth-making had something to do with a feeling of being sidelined in the new politics of Great Britain. If they felt remote from Edinburgh, how much more were they remote from London. Perhaps it was a reaction against a sense of being patronised by the larger country that had swallowed up their king. The celebration of Scottishness by transforming architectural devices of Scottish history rather than those of the classical past had begun well before 1603 and the king's move south; it appears to have accelerated and become more extravagant thereafter.

Generally regarded as the fiefdom of the Earls of Huntly, their kin and their dependants, north-east Scotland also embraced the Earls Marischal, the House of Forbes, and dependencies of, *inter alia*, the Earls of Atholl, Mar and Moray – not to mention the 'broken men' of the Grants, MacGregors, and Mackintoshes, hanging out in the fastnesses of Glen A'an and very flexible about their loyalties given the right inducements.[2] The largest footprint was Huntly's, whose power extended from his original base in Strathbogie to his fine new house within the castle at Inverness,[3] a palace at Rosemarkie and a castle at Ruthven in Badenoch. The fact that Huntly was reported to the King of France in 1586 as harbouring two or three Jesuits in his house appeared to confirm the assessment of the spy who informed Burleigh that Huntly was 'in religion doubted and in affection French'.[4]

Huntly was fiercely proud of his lineage and enjoyed privileged access to the king. When, on 21 July 1588, he married his cousin Henrietta, the French-educated sister of James's favourite the Duke of Lennox (she had been brought up in the Stewart fiefdom of Aubigny), the king extended himself to compose a masque to be performed before the wedding joust which demonstrated a regal knowledge of contemporary European Mannerist aesthetics.[5] The wedding was accompanied by 'a great triumph, mirth and pastime',[6] as the elegant Melvill put it, or 'great balling, fireworks and other triumphs' according to the more prosaic David Moyses.[7] Yet Huntly was to try the regal patience with a putative rebellion only the following year, with his continuing obvious and unconcealed Catholicism, his negotiations with Philip II about the possibility of a Counter-Reformation in Scotland[8] and his half-hearted rebellion in 1594 which led to the Battle of Glenlivet. Yet he and his wife remained favourites with the king. Fulminate as the entire kirk did,[9] Huntly remained protected.

It has been suggested that Huntly was too great a magnate to topple: but James's mother had not found it so in 1562 when she chastised the earl's grandfather fatally at the Battle of Corrichie. Perhaps the threat of a widespread Catholic revolt was less significant than the Protestants proclaimed, or the earl was more of an asset to the Scottish Court than the frantic Bothwell. Due admonitions and exhortations were issued and Huntly, in his turn, played his part by undergoing brief exile after Glenlivet and making repeated 'conversions' and penitences on his return to placate both the kirk and the English queen. Yet in 1602, he had carved the overtly Catholic insignia above the entrance to his *escalier d'honneur* at Huntly; and when he died in Dundee on 13 June 1636, he was still Catholic.[10] Huntly, like Bothwell, was acting out an aristocratic role that was becoming anachronistic in modernising Scotland, as the failure of his

11.1 Bog o' Gight, by Fochabers (later Gordon Castle) drawn from the south-west by Slezer in c. 1680 (but mistitled by him as Inveraray Castle). (Author's collection)

son to raise his kinship and dependants in the north-east in support of the king in 1640 was to emphasise.

It was said of the Huntly Gordons that they built two houses in a bog, the Bog of Plewlands, by the Loch of Spynie, and the Bog o' Gight in the Forest of Enzie, by Fochabers. Plewlands became Gordonstoun, and Gight (or Windy Bog as it was also called) became Gordon Castle. According to his admirer John Spalding, Commissary Clerk of Aberdeen, Huntly was 'fully set to building and planting of all curious devices'[11] and in his youth had been a 'prodigal spender'. In his early twenties, perhaps in anticipation of his marriage, Huntly began to extend the plain tower at the Bog, as Bog o' Gight came to be known.[12] By 1586, it had become his principal seat,[13] and Slezer's drawing shows it in the 1680s to have been a resplendent affair rearing above the flat lands of the Spey estuary. Daniel Defoe visited a few decades later:

> A noble, large and ancient seat; as a castle, much is not to be said of it, for old fortifications are of a small import as the world goes now: but as a dwelling or a palace for a nobleman, it is a very noble, spacious and royal building; 'tis only too large, and appears rather as a great town than as a house.[14]

Huntly most likely began by adding a tower to the north-west.[15] He then built a five-storeyed entrance tower of almost square chambers to the south-east, balanced by a lower smaller rectangular tower, probably containing closets or cabinets, to the south-west. Both were topped by balustraded viewing platforms.[16] The principal living accommodation was increased by doubling the house northwards to make it double-pile,

11.2 Elevation of Bog in 1766 by W. Anderson prior to the building's recasting by John Baxter. Note how its arcades have been filled in.
(Reproduced by permission of Keeper of the Records of Scotland)

providing two wide scale-and-platt stairs (one capped with a striking pyramid roof) and a ground-level hall. Slezer depicts what appears to be a gallery extending north-west overlooking another walled garden. The whole was surrounded by walled gardens, orchards and yards adorned with statues, which gave the house some privacy from the adjacent town of Fochabers. The Bog's unique feature was the sophisticated arcaded loggias opening from the principal chambers on the first floor, and the balconies on the floor above. High-level loggias, otherwise unknown in Scotland, were quite the thing in contemporary Spain, where the climate demanded shaded open-air walks.[17] Huntly's known connections with Spain at the time imply that his inspiration may have come from there. That those same arcades had been filled in by mid-eighteenth century[18] might be taken as a comment on the climatic differences between central Spain and the Windy Bog. In mid-sized lettering above strapwork, the east gable boasted of its builder, the inscription beginning on the southern corner 'George Gordovn, Marquess . . .'. With most curiously ornate pediments and cartouches initialled GG/HS, it implied that embellishments were still under way in 1599.[19]

If Huntly already preferred to live in Bog rather than at Strathbogie,[20] the king's instructions to William Schaw to slight the latter after the Battle of Glenlivet appear less draconian than has been thought. All Schaw did was to remove the floors and vaults of the medieval tower to the north of the inner court,[21] take down the east-facing outer gatehouse, and damage the superstructure and a small portion of the north-east corner of the palace where the stair now is.[22] It has been suggested that the king's appreciation of the architectural qualities of the palace (for James himself had stayed with his court at Huntly after the affair of the Brig o' Dee in 1589) caused him to limit the destruction.[23]

The new work, which repaired the damage and transformed Huntly into the architectural showpiece of the north, was complete by 1602, the year Schaw died. Although the basis of Huntly's palace block remained the same,[24] the new work was a clever architectural device interlocked with the old. The retained portion – the harled lower storeys and the tower of the Marian building at the west – was clasped by the ashlar new work above it and framed by a smaller, but just as prominent, rectangular ashlar turret or gazebo at the east end (*see* Plate 10). Corbelled from the eastern gable, this substantial two-storeyed gazebo contained brilliantly lit, almost curtain-walled, chambers. The principal staircase was rebuilt wider and corbelled out to square at the top for a cabinet or study. The three-room sequence of state chambers was transformed in the upper floors by the creation of a thin red sandstone ashlar curtain-wall punctuated by three delicate and two-storeyed oriel windows,[25] ornately carved with fleurs-de-lys and lettering.

16. *The street façade of Argyll's Lodging in Stirling: a U-plan* hôtel, *most of the design being attributable to the architect Sir Anthony Alexander for his father during the 1630s.* (Author)

17. *Pitcullo, Fife, without its east wing, as restored during the later twentieth century, after centuries of dereliction. This modest laird's house eventually ended up as a U-plan villa.* (Author)

18. *The garden façade of Drum, Aberdeenshire, a scholar's relaxed, virtually U-plan villa in counterpoint to the contemporary baronialism burgeoning all around.* (Author)

19. *The roofscape of Winton, Midlothian, from the western viewing platform. Note the extravagant aedicule window, the dormer window and the varyingly wrythen chimney-stacks.* (Author)

20. *The Queen's Room, Crathes.* (NTS)

21. *Improving scenes (note the headless figure) and inducements to culture: Nine Muses and Seven Virtues in the Muses' Room in Crathes.* (NTS).

22. *A skyline of studies: the west vista from Glamis. Note the carving on the apex, much borrowed by Glasgow style architects in the 1890s.* (Author)

23. *The House of Bog, Bog o' Gight, later Gordon Castle, Moray. Conjectural reconstruction after Slezer (see p. 215). Note the viewing platforms, galleries and balconies.* (Author)

24. *The House of Bog drawn in 1768, probably by A. Roumieu, prior to its transformation by John Baxter. The Renaissance policies and walled gardens have already given way to baroque vistas, canals, and wildernesses; and these in turn were soon to be superseded.* (NAS RHP2379/6. Reproduced with the permission of the Keeper of the Records of Scotland)

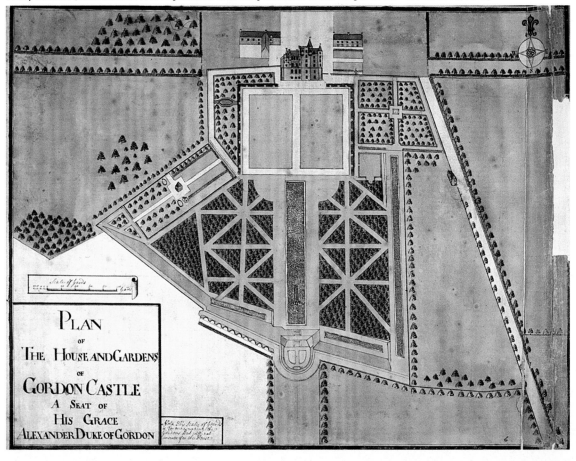

25. *Midmar, Aberdeenshire, painted in the early nineteenth century by James Giles. (NTS)*

26. *Castle Fraser from the north-east, painted in the early nineteenth century by James Giles. (NTS)*

27. Innes, by Elgin, from the south. (Author)

28. Methven Castle, Perthshire – 'My love's bonny strong house' as Agnes Keith would refer to it, possibly designed with deliberate reference to castellated nobility by James Smith. (Author)

Overleaf: 29. Thirlestane's western façade after its mid-nineteenth-century upper superstructural facelift by David Bryce. (Author)

This polished russet superstructure provided the palace with its climax: the horizontality emphasised by banding and string-courses, and the verticality by the tower/turret at each end, and by the oriels between. Since the kitchen chimney-stack could not be moved, it was colonised as part of the design, and they made rather a good fist of it. When complete, this superstructure was a flamboyant celebration of Huntly's elevation to Marquess in 1599 and read: 'GEORGE GORDOVN FIRST MARQUESS OF HVNTLIE' and, beneath, 'HENRIETTE STEWART MARQUISSE OF HVNTLIE'.

Whereas the reformatting at Crichton, Caerlaverock and Campbell had been inward-looking, Huntly's new work added little to the quality of the court save the doorway with its armorial panel. His magnificent display faced neither entrance nor court, but south over the terrace, and a loggia added to the east faced pleasance and country. Enhancing the 'private' experience of the inner court had become subservient to proclaiming status, power and culture to a wider world.

Huntly's Catholicism may not have been furtive (his uncle James was the Jesuit superior in Scotland, after all)[26] but his proclamation of it was restricted to the relative privacy of the courtyard. Above the entrance, a huge heraldic table was erected and exuberantly carved in red sandstone. It comprises Huntly's arms, the royal arms and (before their defacement in 1651) the *Arma Christi*, and the head of Christ surrounded by a sunburst, surmounted by a statue of St Michael the Archangel.[27]

The richly carved red sandstone fireplace in the principal chamber, adorned with the arms of the king, Huntly and his wife, is framed by caryatids, and carries obelisks capped by a crescent and a fleur-de-lys.[28] There are only residual traces of the ornamented plaster friezes. The quality of the interior finishes – particularly the painting – is implied by the fact that in 1617 John Anderson was summoned from Huntly to Edinburgh to decorate James VI's birthplace in Edinburgh Castle, the hall, and the Council House in Holyrood. It is an indication both of Anderson's

11.3 Huntly drawn by Major General John Brown in the late eighteenth century. This is the only known record of the missing eastern pavilion of the superstructure. (MS 8026, f. 28v. NLS)

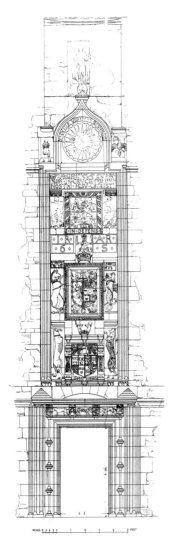

11.4 The heraldic entrance to the palace of Huntly, drawn by F. W. Troup for the EAA Sketchbook, *1883–6.*

quality and the Marquess of Huntly's standards that he should have employed a figure of such high standing.[29] In 1776, some apartments were

> still preserv'd pretty entire. They are painted with a variety of subjects, in small divisions: a few lines of poetry underneath each describe the subject of the piece. In these, the virtues, vices, trades and pursuits of mankind are characterised by emblematical figures, which though not the most elegant, are expressive. In the chamber, which was appointed for a chapel, or place of worship, the parables and other sacred subjects are represented in the same style. The whole opens to one a field of various reflection and entertainment, well enough adapted to amuse a leisure hour.[30]

The survival of the plaster cornice is somewhat at odds with the painted ceiling, since it represented a different architectural language. Perhaps earlier painted ceilings had been plastered over in Huntly's rebuild, but that plaster had collapsed by the late eighteenth century revealing earlier decoration beneath.

Huntly was a furious builder – town houses in Edinburgh and Elgin, New House on the Dee, Aboyne, Ruthven in Badenoch twice rebuilt, and Bog of Plewlands extended with dumpy wings.[31] Save for the high quality of the stonework and finishes, there appears to be little design consistency between these building adventures. Huntly was, as Gilbert Blakhall recorded, a hands-on sort of person:

> For he was so much taken up with his newe buildings, from four hours in the morning until eight at night, standing by his masons, urging their diligences, and directing and judging their worke, that he had scarce tyme to eate or sleep, much less to wreat [write].[32]

Among these craftsmen was the master mason of Strathbogie during the late 1630s, George Thomson,[33] and the English master mason Ralph Rawlinson, whom Huntly employed on his house at Rosemarkie, and who, likewise with Anderson, was summoned south to the king's works in 1617.

Huntly's houses offer an introduction to north-eastern Jacobean nationalism between about 1585 and 1640 (and longer in the west, if Glengarry were to be included). The earlier phase appears to be associated with the masons/architects Thomas Leiper and George Bel (or Bell), and the later one with David Bel and IB – John or Ian Bel. Thomas Leiper proudly signed his initials on a skew in the laird's lodging of Tolquhon, and if we can interpret his design approach from that palace, then his direction appears to have been the separate and romantic expression of each part of the house with the token formality of a self-contained, symmetrical gatehouse focused axially on the stairtower of the laird's lodging behind. Each part of Tolquhon is given its own vigorous character (*see* Chapter 9). To Leiper may also be attributed the addition of the Michael Tower to the north-west of Castle Fraser in 1576, complete with the *Arma Christi* iconography and a small room called an oratory; the great round tower possibly in the 1580s;[34] and finally the extension westwards of the old tower, perhaps in the 1590s. Given Leiper's penchant for expressionism, it seems possible that the Michael Tower had a distinctive skyline to counterpoint its parent. Taking his ornate gunloop design for Tolquhon as a signature, he might also have been responsible for a number of other houses in the locality.[35] James Leiper, possibly Thomas's son, was later involved in the paving of the hall at Castle Fraser and the construction of the courtyard, but, having taken Andrew Fraser's money, he failed to do the work and, as a consequence, was put to the horn (outlawed) in 1623.[36] Nothing more has been discovered to prove whether or not there was a Leiper contracting dynasty.

The expressively romantic variety of building forms that Thomas Leiper provided at Tolquhon points up the significance of the work of Ian Bel. Of Bel père (if that is what he was), very little reliable information exists – solely George's gravestone in Midmar kirkyard inscribed *George Bel, Meason, 1575*. He is thought to have been responsible for the lower storeys of Ballogie between 1565 and 1575,[37] which would fit very well a house with the round bedroom tower of the Marian period (although not the spacious, later, staircase). Of David Bel(l) there is evidence only of a repayment bond that he organised. Its significance is that it not only ties him to both Leslie of Pitcaple and Cheyne of Pitfichie in 1607, but implies that he was their equal.[38] The initials of his putative relative Ian – IB – appear only on Castle Fraser's great armorial in 1617, and upon its round tower the following year. None the less, there were at least seventeen houses in north-east Scotland built or altered between 1596 and 1629 which imply either the Bels' hand or, at the very least, the same school of design.[39]

For example, the new scale-and-platt staircases installed in Balbithan, Drum, Midmar and Craigston all provided a porter's room beneath the stair's rising: a neat and obvious thing to do but not to be found, by comparison, in Kellie, Elcho or Hatton. Consistent decorative details – corbelling in the form of a label or chequer course, large ashlar rectangular oriels with finialled gables, two-storeyed turrets or studies (their upper rooms lit by oval oculi)[40] all reinterpreted or reworked ancient devices. These buildings also exemplify the desire to *heighten* the houses as far into the clouds as possible. Although bedrooms, studies, cabinets, wardrobes, storage, nurseries and servants' rooms were contained in the new heights, there were also public rooms – and almost always at least two staircases, one for the family and the other for visitors and guests. The latter led to 'skied' (i.e. high-level) galleries, and viewing platforms above. Perhaps Craigievar's unique provision of two viewing platforms can be explained as one for the guests and the other for the family, slightly too far apart to share the same champagne bottle. It was the obverse of what was happening in the Lowlands.

That building high was a design decision, rather than simply making the best of a warlike and threatening environment in which the only safe way to build was upwards, becomes obvious from considering other houses in the region. Nothing inhibited the lairds of Tolquhon, Drum, Pitsligo, Edzell or Muchalls from enjoying the expansive horizontal living patterns of the rest of Scotland. Indeed, Aberdeenshire hosts some of the finest Marian houses, and Huntly's outward-facing loggia implies his response to

doubts about security. So, that they decided to revert to a tall compact form – a form, indeed, that took considerable ingenuity if the three-roomed sequence were to be maintained within the constrictions of a tower (generally it took the form of a helix) – must have reflected a particular priority. Those galleries in the roof space were not put there for defence like sweet grapes put beyond the reach of the fox. They expressed pride: for they were probably the gathering space before going further up to enjoy the prospect from some of the highest man-made viewpoints in the land.

Most of these north-eastern designs were superstructures grafted upon much thicker-walled earlier houses, and the change in their structure may often be traced in their upper storeys. The Bels' architectural approach appears to have been to transform the upper storeys into a single romantic composition with consistent details. Their houses encompass an enormous range of ambition, from great seat to relatively humble dwelling. Indeed, since their characteristic chequer – or 'label' – decoration appears in its most

11.5 The details of Ian Bel's design exemplified in Billings' drawing of part of the superstructure of Castle Fraser, Aberdeenshire. Note the cannon as waterspouts, corbels in imitation machicolations, and oculi windows that look like gunloops. Note also how Billings and his engraver manage to put sunlight on the north façade of Fraser, and draw carefully detailed stonework where there is, in fact, harled rubble. (Author's collection)

elaborate form in the extraordinary corbelled stairtower added to Allardice, near Inverbervie in Angus (*c.* 1600), their influence may have spread southwards too. John Allardice had married Beatrix, a daughter of the Earl Marischal, who might have brought Aberdonian fashions south with her. Perhaps similar details that appear on nearby Fiddes, or on the circular and square corbelled turrets of the House of Kellie, indicate that she persuaded the architect to sojourn in the Mearns for a while.[41]

The reshaping of Crathes is thought to date from 1596 as the result of a datestone bearing the names of Alexander Burnett of Leys and Katherine Gordon of Lesmoir (although one of the painted ceilings is dated three years later).[42] The house falls just short of square in plan. The stair winds up to the tall, vaulted hall that occupies the entire west side of the *piano nobile*. Residual plasterwork neatly painted with grey, red and green strapwork survives in the window embrasure. The 'wing' contains, probably, the chamber of dais (now drawing-room). Upper floors hold a variety of chambers and bedchambers.

Crathes has 'the most extensive programme [of painted decoration] to have survived in any building in Scotland',[43] and some of its chambers –

11.6 Crathes, showing the clambering corbel-course and the finialled rectangular oriel on the right. The viewing platform at roof level and the circular stairtower below masterfully mask an otherwise plain skyline of twin gables. (RCAHMS)

the Nine Worthies' Room and the Muses' Room – now take their names from what is painted on the ceiling. The space between the joists in the Nine Worthies' Room is painted with vivid patterns of blue and ochre flowers and arabesques, and alternating Worthies – Hector of Troy, Alexander the Great, Joshua, King David, Charlemagne, King Arthur, Judas Maccabaeus, Godofried, and Julius Caesar. The Worthies were exemplars in the Renaissance sense of providing examples of noble behaviour worthy of consideration. The soffits or underside of the joists are painted with doggerel rhetoric on ancient themes:

> King Arthur crownit was Emperiour and wan
> Gryt bounds in France and all the lands of Spain
> The knichts of the round table he ordained
> Whais praise sall sound unto ye warldes end.[44]

The Green Lady's Room is painted with full-length figures, but the texts are generally improving apophthegms taken from the Geneva Bible rendered into Scots ('Wine wemen taken insatiablie/Has brocht gryt kings to miserie'), and in the Muses' Room, the Nine Muses and seven Cardinal

11.7 Crathes' rectangular oriel or study drawn for EAA Sketchbook, 1883–6. (Drawn by J. Scott Lawson for *Details of Scottish Domestic Architecture* (Edinburgh, 1921))

Virtues are decorated about with scrollwork and grotesque devices with suitable poetic accompaniment. Burnett could have expected both family and guests to be aware of the significance, mythology and symbolism of the figures.

The extent of Crathes' painted work has been attributed to the nature of the client himself. Sir Alexander Burnett was one of six high-achieving brothers, one of whom practised medicine in England, another philosophy in Basle, and a third became a priest. Perhaps so, but it might also be attributable to an accident of survival. Few Scottish Renaissance buildings were without painted decoration. Some of the Crathes ceilings were rediscovered beneath plasterwork only during restoration in 1876. There is a high probability that other painted ceilings survive in other buildings beneath a later cloak of plaster. A fine, oak-ceilinged long gallery (perhaps on the model of Dunnottar's) is at the top of the house. But instead of lying north–south above the hall, as one might expect, the structure has switched at this level so that the gallery runs east–west; and that seems to be where Bel made his mark.

This impression is confirmed on the façade. The division between the plain, harled, round-cornered plinth of the lower storeys and the vivid superstructure above is marked by a wonderfully elaborate corbel course with Bel details. It descends on the south façade to embrace some more heraldry and the base of a (presumably new) semicircular stair, which rises right to a viewing platform between the twin gables of the roof. It adds not a jot to the space within. It is instead part wall-patterning, and part delineation between old and new Crathes. (Its flat matt cement harling reduces rather than enhances the contrast between the wall surface and the carved stone, underlining the qualitative difference between modern cement-based and the older lime-based harls. The latter glow in the Scottish light.) A corbelled, elaborately pedimented dormer window, similar to that at Amisfield, projects high above the main entrance. There are three rectangular corbelled oriel windows, gazebos or cabinets at parapet level, with delicate, plain skewed gables enhanced by finials. They are also characteristic of Midmar and Glamis, and were probably intended for Craigston.

Midmar, formerly the House of Ballogie, had been damaged in October 1594 in the chastisement of Alexander Gordon, fourth laird, for being present at the Battle of Glenlivet.[45] As at Huntly, so also at Midmar. During its slighting by the Earl Marischal, the essence of the house was left little damaged, but the superstructure was removed and the staircase tower destroyed. It is a compact house of three volumes joined at the angle: stair, main chamber, and the circular bedchamber. Midmar's rebuilt spacious and well-lit scale-and-platt staircase provides the formal route up to the bright, almost square hall, with the rhomboid bedroom in the round tower behind with its private stair as normal. It is difficult to discern how much of the interior fitting is original. Probably very little. Yet the door in the Great Chamber, attributed to the late seventeenth century,[46] is most curiously panelled in a manner reminiscent of the label corbelling of the rectangular turrets outside, and similar to early seventeenth-century work elsewhere, like Rowallan. Two floors above, shallowly projecting rectangular oriels probably housed closets or cabinets, and on the floor above again, a rooftop gallery had dormer windows similar to Claypotts.

11.8 Midmar, Aberdeenshire, from the entrance court. Note the turrets or studies and the rectangular oriel. (RCAHMS)

Once the stair is taken out into the corbelled turnpike in the angle, the upper storeys of the entrance tower contain good chambers with a glorious, almost square room at the top with two windowed turrets in each corner. That these rooms cannot be reached from the rest of the house implies that they might have been the guest lodgings.

If Midmar's interior planning has charm, its external expression is glorious. Stair, main house and tower are orchestrated. The entrance tower is the herald – circular turrets on three of its corners and the stair turret on the fourth: its height is emphasised by a slender swelling in the middle running up two storeys. The main house is defined by the flat rectangular oriels whose elaborate corbelling runs off and extends over the wall plane. The majestic round tower dominates, its crenellated viewing platform reached by an ogee-roofed staircase (like Bog) almost certainly part of the reworking. Above the second floor, a delicate squinch – beginning on a corbel but fading into the harl on the other side – joins the two curved surfaces of the private turnpike and the round tower, allowing for a flat plane above. It has no internal function whatsoever. It exists for the whimsical pleasure of being viewed.[47]

Cluny, designed by Bel in 1604,[48] is now invisible beneath a granite 'mushroom tenement like a cotton factory'[49] designed between 1836 and 1840 by John Smith, but it once was similar. Its pure Marian form of round towers on the angles was subsequently transformed with an even taller superstructure of rectangular turrets poking out from angles, circular towers corbelled out to square, and the entire fantastic composition crowned by a parapeted viewing platform reached by a slender corbelled

11.9 Cluny, Aberdeenshire (now transmogrified), after a sketch by James Skene of Rubislaw in MacGibbon and Ross. (Author)

stair. Skene considered that 'the work appears suspended by magnetical, if not by magical influence'.[50] His sketches made Cluny resemble baby Neuschwanstein.

In 1604, John Urquhart began rebuilding the House of Craigston in Buchan: 'THIS VARK FOVNDIT YE FOVRTINE OF MARCH ANE THOVSAND SEX HOVNDER FOVR ZEIRIS AND ENDIT YE 8 OF DECEMBR 1607'.[51] A connection with Bel is implied by the carving of a heart on either side of the keystone which, since it also appears on Fraser, may have been his signature.[52] Craigston is unique among north-eastern houses in that the extent of its rebuilding comes close to making it a completely new house. Turning its back upon the romantic asymmetry of all the others, this four-square building with two projecting wings is the most obviously modern of this group of houses. This clever house has been interpreted as a piece of pseudo-medieval fantasy fitting for the Urquharts, inspired by medieval precedents like Borthwick, Midlothian. To see it as aberrational and Gothic, as it has been described, is to read too much into the Urquhart family and, in particular, the glorious Sir Thomas Urquhart, magnificent translator of and improver upon Rabelais, author of *The Jewel*, and family historian who traced the Urquhart lineage not just back to the *arriviste* King Fergus, but back to Adam himself.[53] Craigston *is indeed* aberrational, but not for anachronism. It is the contemporary lowland U-plan villa, like Pitreavie, overhung by Jacobean nationalism. All elements take the eye up to the balustraded viewing platform at the top, presaging the manner of the later seventeenth century – as in Dunkeld House, Hatton, Queensberry House and Moncreiffe.

Two unequal but balanced gabled wings frame the entrance, joined four storeys above by a triumphal arch, with painted ribs beneath. Corbels provide support for unrealised corner rectangular oriels at each of the four quarters (the walls within thinned, ready for action), and the gallery runs between, above the arch. It is heralded by several layers of corbelling and gargoyle water spouts, and a tableau of large vigorously three-dimensional grotesque figures and faces framed by squat columns, one of whom, in a smart seventeenth-century hat blowing his own trumpet, might have been Urquhart himself, celebrating. A sign of Craigston's modernity was its plan to collect water from the flat roof, and direct it down lead-lined channels to a stone drain and, presumably a cistern – similar to what had been attempted ten years earlier in Glenbuchat.

A straight public stair leads to the large principal chamber or hall that occupies the entire first floor of the main house, a chamber in each wing. Because the 'U' is so compressed, there is room for only one of the customary twin staircases in the internal angles; so the public stair to guest

rooms and gallery rises in the angle, whereas the private one lies against the north wall. Although slightly less efficient than the lowland U-plan model like Baberton, the effect is the same – separate access to almost every chamber. Craigston's proportions are handsome, and its rooms well lit. The vigour of its surviving woodwork – carved wooden panels of the Virtues, the Worthies, Evangelists and classical figures (probably copied from pattern books) – makes one regret what has been lost.

Some time before 1617 the first Lord Fraser asked Ian Bel to complete the rebuilding of Castle Fraser (then called Muchall). To judge from the plans,[54] he took the front wall of the old tower down to second-floor level and rebuilt the upper storeys. Whereas the original roof rose behind, presumably, a parapet, Bel extended the roof over the former parapet space, right out beyond the corbelling. He gave Fraser a new unity through its vivid superstructure (now miserably dissipated by the ill-advised de-harling of part of it in the 1950s). The Michael Tower (as in the entrance tower of Midmar) has corbelled turrets clinging to each angle – elaborate, two-storeyed structures, the upper windows being oculi. The main house is likewise turreted, but in all other respects plain save the great armorial – once gilt and painted – facing north over the court. The climax is the round tower topped by an expansive, balustraded viewing platform reached up a corbelled stair with a charming ogee-domed caphouse lit by a clerestory taking the form of an arcade of windows. The internal benefits to the house of the reordering appear to have been fairly slight: the two rebuilt upper storeys have ranks of four large windows, and the fourth floor – with its five three-windowed turrets – must have seemed

Top: *11.10 Craigston, near Turriff – an extraordinary marriage between the lowland villa and north-eastern nationalism. Square oriels were intended for each corner.* (M. Finnie/RIAS Collection)

11.11 Blowing his own trumpet: a joyful creature from Craigston's parapet. (RCAHMS)

11.12 Castle Fraser from the east. The long, possibly gallery, wing was begun in the 1630s by James Leiper. The view was drawn by Billings. (Author's collection)

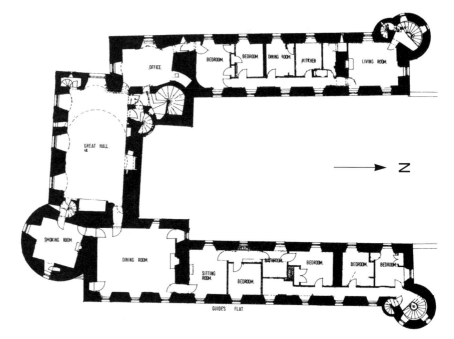

11.13 Castle Fraser, first floor plan (McCombie and Mennie/NTS)

particularly bright. Bel must have enjoyed adding the staircase up to the viewing platform on a different line from the existing stair, for where the two circular mural stairs meet on the fourth floor there is a wonderfully complex junction. Fraser had a skied gallery (until its conversion to a library in the nineteenth century) and perhaps a lower one added when the elegant wings (once lined with arcades) to the inner court were built in the 1630s. The north section of the eastern wing might have been a gallery, conveniently accessible from the dining-room, and provided with a stair from the ground at the far end, like Dunnottar's. It has the customary form of tall windows extending up into dormer windows.

Fraser demonstrates a designer making a coherent composition from disparate materials. What it lacks of the control of Craigston, it makes up in majesty. But perhaps the most spectacular achievement of this designer, or of this school of design, is Craigievar. It was bought by Willie Forbes, younger son of Forbes of nearby Corse, in 1610. He had made his fortune in the Baltic trade – hence his nickname 'Danzig Willie' – married the daughter of Edinburgh's Lord Provost, and returned determined (as siblings are) to eclipse his elder brother and the family seat. By 1625–6 his new house was sufficiently well advanced for the plasterers to be in. The enormously thick walls of its lower floors represent the structure of the earlier house;[55] and the gallery three floors further up, on a different orientation to the hall below, represents the structure of the new one. With the exception of a stair corbelled out from one corner (like Amisfield), the lower three storeys are plain and pink-harled. The transition is signalled by an elaborate cornice that slices across at fourth-floor level, less wayward than Crathes' but embracing, like it, the corbelling of all the turrets. On the south elevation at least, the corbelling is a decorative echo of machicolation. The superstructure is composed of slender, two-storeyed turrets, crowstepped gables, half gables in an echo of the rectangular turrets, and a climax of two separate granite-balustraded viewing platforms, each with its ogee-capped stairtower – one of which overlooks the main entrance. From these slender, perversely separated viewing platforms, the prospect over the hills of Aberdeenshire – never mind over the yards, plantations and Chinese garden at the foot of the house – was unmatched.

A gracious scale-and-platt stair leads up to the hall, above which the stairs are relegated to slender turnpikes which protrude from the wall surface to minimise interference with the tight space within.[56] Visitors enter through a screens passage into the soaring double-height groin-vaulted hall. It is wholly commanded by the disproportionately large fireplace on the west wall which is surmounted by an outsize rendering of the royal arms framed by grotesque Ionic columns expressed as naked nymphs on plinths. The foci of the richly plastered ceiling are the

11.14 Castle Fraser from the north, drawn by Billings. (Author's collection)

pendants, perhaps once designed to support chandeliers, the central one composed of four volutes. The ceiling is patterned with a strapwork of thick ribs enclosing decorative motifs and roundels containing the profiles of Roman emperors, possibly in a plaster echo of the Stirling heads. Some of the moulds had been used previously within the much more slender-ribbed Great Hall ceiling of Glamis in 1621, and in Muchalls in 1624.[57] The oak panels of the screen are framed by fluted Corinthian columns joined by cusped arcades in a timber echo of the façade of the palace at Stirling. The table in the Great Hall may be original. Decorative plasterwork survives in several other rooms, usually with the thinner ribs that characterise lesser rooms – but sometimes with a geometric pattern that recalls the chequer corbels, and the door in Midmar.

The upper storeys of the house become progressively lighter, with thinner walls and more frequent windows. They have the customary two staircases. At gallery level, the north staircase has a complicated crossover between one flight going down and the other up to the roof. However, on plan, the shapes – particularly of the turrets – are, at this level, perverse and inconsistent. There are thirteen turrets on the fourth and fifth floors, only one of which is even approximately semicircular – *from the inside*. From the outside, they look perfect: all of which implies that in this case at least, Ian Bel was designing outside in rather than just expressing internal function.

11.15 Craigievar from the north. Note the distinction between the plain plinth and the elaborate superstructure above the corbel course; and the twin cupolas of its viewing platforms. (RCAHMS)

11.16 Plan of the gallery floor at Craigievar. The staircases facing each other across the gallery both lead up to viewing platforms. Note, also, how uncircular the turrets are inside. The principal chamber shifts on this floor from east–west to north–south orientation, perhaps indicating the new work of Ian Bel. (McCombie and Mennie/NTS)

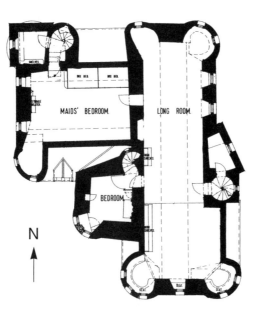

Craigievar has long been accepted as one of Scotland's most distinctive contributions to European architecture. To justify this accolade, it has been desperately scanned for signs of the classicising tendencies of England and Europe. The east elevation, for example, with the viewing platform rising at the centre has been adduced as showing a movement towards symmetry. Quite the opposite. The viewing tower is itself unbalanced and it is set at an angle to the wall; moreover,

11.17 *The hall at Craigievar, drawn by Billings. Note the original table, timber screen and wainscot.* (Author's collection)

11.18 *Plasterwork roundel in Craigievar's Hall showing one of the most frequent Renaissance 'exemplars of nobility' – Alexander the Great. Drawn by J. Scott Lawson for* EAA *Sketchbook, 1883-6.* (RIAS Library)

11.19 *The plastered and panelled Blue Room on the fourth floor of Craigievar gives a rare glimpse of what Renaissance bedchambers may have been like.* (RCAHMS)

the roofs on either side do not match. *Symmetry was never intended.* What Bel sought was *poise* and balance. The essence of such buildings was a striving for nobility and majesty through height and silhouette.

There were a few comparable buildings outside Aberdeenshire. 'The house, from the height of it, the greatness of its mass, the many towers atop, and the spread of its wings, has really a very singular and striking appearance like nothing I ever saw.' Thus wrote the poet Thomas Gray to a friend following a visit to Glamis in 1765.[58] To celebrate the elevation of the lords Glamis to the earldom of Kinghorn, the house had been

11.20 Glamis, Angus, from the approach road. Note how it sits in a hollow. (Author)

11.21 A turret or study at Glamis. (Author)

refashioned between 1606 and 1620.⁵⁹ Much more of the original L-plan tower was retained in the final design than in the Aberdeenshire examples, possibly as the result of the decision by the Glamis family to provide new accommodation in lower wings. The eastern wing, which ends in the 'round' (tower), was quite possibly built in about 1537 when the house became royal property after the forfeiture of Lord Glamis in 1536. It was much visited thereafter by James V for hunting.⁶⁰ Although Kinghorn's grandson Patrick, Earl of Strathmore later claimed to have constructed the western wing himself (admitting that he had to destroy buildings of the inner close to do so),⁶¹ Pont's drawing appears to indicate not just the eastern wing but also balancing buildings to the west. Moreover, the tall house at the centre is already crowned with a heraldic superstructure and what looks like a cupola.

The strategic move was to build the swelling red ashlar four-storeyed *escalier d'honneur* in the angle. It surges up to a crenellated viewing platform and flagpole emplacement, reached by an ogee-domed stairtower. Its polished red ashlar must have appeared all the more extravagant when set against harling on the rubble walls (*see* p. 40). The old roof and parapet were then replaced by an altogether more exotic confection. What Kinghorn did at Glamis was probably what his grandson tells us he did at his other Glamis seat of Castle Huntly, 15 miles away, in 1637. Finding it was vaulted in the top and flagged over with only 'ane old scurvie battlement, he put on an inteer new roofe upon the Castle and Jamm [wing]'.[62] Evidence of work at Glamis similar to Craigievar lies in the slender corbel course which lines the north façade (plain by comparison with Bel's corbel courses), and a distinctly thinner wall above, indicating a rebuild (as in Castle Fraser). There are five regular windows and five dormers above. A two-storeyed, shallowly projecting square oriel arises from the north-east corner (again distinctly old-fashioned by comparison with Bel's since its gable is crowstepped and not finialled). At the centre of the entrance façade, where Amisfield has its corbelled oriel window and Winton its trio of chimney-stacks, Glamis has a proud turret, perhaps the earl's cabinet, supported on columns and surmounting a window framed by fluted columns. A slender two-storeyed ashlar turret is corbelled from each corner visible facing the entrance court, its upper window an oculus like those of Fraser and Lickleyhead. The wonderfully bright rooms within – some with shelving – are entirely consistent with being a cabinet or study.

An oriel window bellies out at the head of the stairtower (as at Huntly and Maybole), and some chimneys are circular (as at Invergowrie). So much appears clearly to be of the early seventeenth century. The strapwork parapets that crown the south and west gables of the rooftop viewing platform and their corbelled, domed gazebos are probably also of this period, although Patrick, Earl of Strathmore added the exotic thistle-capped iron cresting and other details in 1689.[63]

The door is pretty idiosyncratic. Flanked by fluted columns and headed by a richly carved armorial, it is capped by a circular niche containing a bust of Kinghorn himself in a curious attack of three-dimensionality. Whereas Huntly grouped his heraldic panels above the door, Kinghorn inserted a long horizontal frieze along south and east walls composed of six armorials framed between string courses. The introduction of the staircase necessitated considerable reorganisation within. The sweeping staircase with its shallow treads and hollow newel was, by its very scale, difficult to coordinate with existing floor levels;[64] and since it is on a level neither with the under hall, nor indeed with the ground floor but only with the Great Hall, the latter must have been taken as datum.[65] The principal stair was on a level with the principal chamber, and all others

11.22 The great hall at Glamis drawn by Billings, showing its transformation by plasterwork. (Author's collection)

11.23 The south front of Innes House, Moray, dominated by its new stairtower, drawn by Billings. (Author's collection)

would have to make shift. The stair walls were plastered and lined out to resemble masonry, but these 'false stone markings' were removed in 1890 to expose the ashlar beneath.[66]

The Great Hall was reworked in 1621. It consists of a single vast barrel vault running from end to end, with an enormous fireplace against the south wall, decorated with strapwork, and surmounted by an armorial panel flanked by pairs of columns with naked half-caryatids (really herms) carrying the frieze above.[67] The plaster ceiling, which springs from a frieze and a cornice, has thin-ribbed compartments, giving much more space to the devices between, many unique to Glamis. There are elaborate chandelier pendants as in Craigievar.[68] The chamber in Glamis' south jamb has the thick-ribbed plasterwork associated with a chamber of dais.

Paying little heed to the murmurings of war, or to its preliminary skirmish at the Trot of Turriff on 13 May 1639, the laird of Innes decided that the 'place' of Innes in the flat lands of the Lossie estuary near Elgin was too old-fashioned.[69] Heretofore it had been assumed that Innes was a new house of 1644, built to a platt devised by William Aytoun of Edinburgh, since among the records of the construction[70] is the payment of the reasonable sum of £26 13s 4d for 'drawing the form of the house on paper'. That he selected Aytoun – the 'Maister Maissoun at Heriott his work' – indicates the laird was ambitious and presumably well acquainted with lowland fashion, for Aytoun was the sole survivor of the group of people (Alexander Seton, Sir James Murray, Sir Anthony Alexander and William Wallace) upon whom early seventeenth-century lowland Scotland had depended for its Court architecture. However, Pont's map indicated a substantial house at Innes, which figures in Spalding's *History* long before 1639. It was at Innes that John Urquhart of Craigston, grandson of Craigston's builder, died in 1634.[71] In 1998, an investigation was undertaken to study whether Innes was indeed new-built from 1639 or incorporated an earlier building.[72] The results were surprising. A medieval house probably remains within the fabric of Innes; as does a sixteenth-century palace-block, with typical service corridor.

So what made Innes decide to upgrade his house at such a tremulous period in the seventeenth century? He was well aware of the new architecture of Craigston through his son-in-law. The late starting date might be attributed to the fact that he had been faced unexpectedly with the responsibility for settling many of his son-in-law's and grandson's debts.[73] However, once equipped with Aytoun's design for regularising the various parts of the place of Innes, he proceeded in a manner similar to Kinghorn at Glamis: namely the construction of an entrance and staircase tower, the reordering of the house around it, and a new superstructure. The key was the rectangular, almost square, staircase added in the angle.[74] Wide, well-lit short flights of steps with platforms rising up three storeys required sometimes inconvenient access to be cut (into the Drawing Room, for example) or the blocking of earlier windows. In its two topmost storeys, the staircase withdraws into a corbelled turnpike, allowing chambers on the top two floors of the tower. At the top, there is a fine balustraded viewing platform with incomparable views north to the Moray Firth and south to Ben Rinnes. The turnpike stair is capped by a turreted, fish-scale slated roof, rather than the ogee form of Aberdeenshire, and the strapwork-patterned balcony is finished on each corner by a layered finial like a torch.

Aytoun's platt, however, may also have required a complete re-façade. Each floor is delineated by an ashlar string-course standing proud of the harl at a slightly higher level than the window so that it has to dip down to embrace the windows: again, a curious paradox of vertically interrupted horizontality. The windows have been regularised to suit the design and, in some cases, new ones were opened.[75] Each window is capped by a slightly overscaled and detached pediment (as though aedicular columns had been planned but never executed), semicircular on all floors save the first, where they are triangular and capped by a star.

Whatever may have been the varying roof structures of Innes, they were homogenised to the same height (the structure implies that the west wing may have been lowered and the right wing raised). The roof was flattened and broadened to extend over the tower's parapet to end in a slim cornice.[76] Flattened gables provide a plinth for triplets of fashionable square chimneys set on edge. (Such chimneys, common in the Lowlands, may also be found at Drumminor and Leslie.) Like Baberton, Innes' gables end in finials which, in the west wing, take the form of curious mythological figures or griffins within a half-pediment. Only the heavy plaster frieze in the drawing-room survives of the original interior decoration.

The desire for height as an expression of nobility also permeated the Highlands. The Macdonells of Glengarry rebuilt Invergarry in the seventeenth century and although it was referred to as a 'new house' in the 1670 contract to complete it between Lord Macdonell and the mason Robert Nicholson,[77] there is much that implies Invergarry was significantly older, but was being reworked. The form of the house – an L-plan with a round tower projecting from its heel – is similar to the MacNaughtan seat of Dunderave on the shores of Loch Fyne. Invergarry was similarly tall, although on a more commanding site and, as the contract makes clear, rose from a surrounding close.[78] Yet some aspects of its appearance were distinctly passé for the later seventeenth century, provincial compared to the splendours within.[79] For Invergarry's refitting, probably begun during

11.24 Invergarry, reconstructed after a drawing by Brigadier Petit. (Author)

11.25 Plan of Invergarry after that by Brigadier Petit (see also p. 32). This plan of the principal floor of Invergarry shows an enormous, well-lit, columned chamber – a descendant of the feasting hall, perhaps – occupying the entire main house, with a small turnpike down, probably to kitchen and wine cellar, and a larger turnpike up, presumably a private stair to the principal private apartments. The north wing contained a regal staircase up to the first-floor with chambers above. In the angle is the straight, tight but probably private stair up to other chambers perhaps including guest chambers and a 'skied' gallery. (NLS)

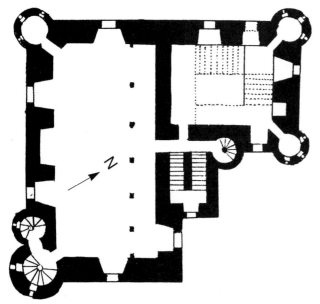

the interregnum, had created an impressive interior. The main house was aligned parallel with the loch with a jamb extending west. That jamb contained a spacious *escalier d'honneur* up to the principal floor, and good chambers on the floors above – the stair being taken out into a square tower of its own like a smaller-scale version of Innes. The *piano nobile* was entirely occupied by a vast, well-lit columned hall. By comparison, its skyline of underscaled turrets, unrelieved roof ridges and of the circular tower corbelled out to a square study that Brigadier Petit drew in 1703 was anachronistic.

Invergarry makes a fitting conclusion to this group of unusually tall and proud houses, with their ferocious skylines, rooftop viewing platforms, high-level galleries and compressed room plans. It was distinctly martial in ethos and not in the slightest martial in fact. Whereas the forms of the superstructure were mostly ancient motifs put to decorative new use, the emphasis upon unconscionable height is best explained as a statement of national identity: modern living being compressed within a nationalist surcoat.

12
War and Peace, 1641–84

Now about this time [January 1639] . . . there came out of Germany, from the wars, home to Scotland, a gentleman of base birth, born in Balveny, who had served long and fortunately in the German wars and called to his name Felt Marischal Lesly, his excellency. . . . He caused send to Germany, France, Holland, Denmark and other countries, for the most expert and valiant captains, lieutenants and other offices, who came in great haste upon hope of bloody war, thinking, as they were all Scots soldiers that came, to make up their fortunes upon the ruin of our kingdom.

John Spalding, *History of the Troubles*[1]

Scotland was unaccustomed to professional warfare being waged at home (*see* Chapter 3). Even by the standards of the English harrying of the Borders and East Lothian between 1544 and 1550, the Troubles that tormented the country after 1639 were regarded as peculiarly vicious. But Scotland had exported soldiers to fight in Europe for centuries, and it was now about to taste some of its own medicine. The wars began slowly and in a reasonably gentlemanly manner, for it was some time before the layers of decency and honour were stripped away. During that period, soldiers were uncertain about how far they could go. The priest Gilbert Blakhall, acting as chamberlain at Aboyne, saw the approach of between forty and fifty Cameronians on their way back from eastern Aberdeenshire, and went down to the inner court as they were 'readie to come into the house'. The porter bade them to go to the outer gate to make their demands. They complied 'lyk simple fooles when they might have been maisters of the house'. In the meantime, Blakhall had sent out to the fields for support, and once 100 men had gathered, he outfaced the Cameronians and offered only food.[2] It was the second time that he had had to take such action, and both episodes ended peaceably.

It had been in the nature of things that soldiers might get killed, but property was normally accorded respect. No longer. Both John Spalding and Patrick Gordon of Ruthven[3] recorded the destruction of Renaissance Aberdeenshire and Banff, and Spalding lamented the fate, for example, of Lord Banff's arcaded palace beside Banff (predecessor to Duff House):

the soldiers fell quickly too to cutting and hewing down the pleasant planting and fruitful young trees, bravely growing within the laird of Banff's orchards and gardens (pitiful to see!) and made up huts to themselves to lie at night and defend them frae storms of rain; they violently brake up the gates of his stately house of Banff and went through the haill houses, rooms, and chambers belonging thereto; broke up the victual girnels . . . for their food, and spoilzied his ground . . .[4]

It may be that Covenanting zeal had something to do with the new savagery. Armed with a fanaticism apparently justified by the Scriptures, they were bent on the 'utter rooting out in all hostile manner' of all who opposed them.[5] Ruthlessness became commonplace. Argyll, the master of the veiled threat, wrote to Sir John Ogilvy of Inverquharity that he had been informed that the latter was concealing Lord Ogilvy in his house. 'Onlie I will give you this warneing that if ye press to conceall my lord Ogilvy in your house at this time, it will be moir to your preiudice than ye ar awar off, and so I hope ye wil be wyse.'[6] Now Argyll had already shown his quality at the nearby Ogilvy seats of Airlie and Forter. Airlie had been fortified for the king, but had surrendered to Montrose who installed his own garrison, and informed his ally, Argyll, that 'he need not be at pains to draw his people thither, seeing the house was already gained'.[7] However, the latter's soldiers

> syne spoiled all within both houses, and such as could not be carried they masterfully brake down and destroyed. Thereafter they fell to his ground, plundered, robbed, and took away from himself, his men, tenants, and servants, their haill goods and gear, corns and cattle, whatsomever that they could get, and left nothing but bare bounds of sic as they could carry away with them, and what could not be destroyed, they despitefully burnt up by fire.[8]

Argyll's malevolence must have been motivated partly by a desire for plunder and partly by the settling of old scores. So Inverquharity could well comprehend what his threat implied. Spalding's outrage emphasises how alien he considered such behaviour. It might be acceptable on the continent, but the returning soldiers had no right to bring the habits of the Thirty Years War back with them. They had. In July 1640, Major Munro, with some 800 men, cut a swathe through 'horse, nolt, sheep and kine' as they swept from Kintore (past Harthill which they 'spoiled pitifully') down into Strathbogie:

> The first thing they entered to do was hewing down the pleasant planting about Strathboggie, to be huts for the soldiers to sleep in, on the night. . . . Then they fell to meddle with the meal girnels, whereof there was store within that place, took in the office-houses, began shortly to bake, brew and made ready good cheer.[9]

When they left, they burnt their huts, took away what they could carry, destroyed any bestial they could not, leaving Strathbogie 'almost manless, moneyless, horseless and armless so pitifully was the same borne down and subdued'.

It was no better four years later. The Covenanting General Baillie marched into Atholl in May 1645, 'and burn[t] and destroy[ed] that pleasant country. This is not the first fire the Covenanters raised in Scotland.' Spalding's distinction between those like Montrose, who took fire and sword now legitimately on behalf of the king, and the illegitimate actions taken by the Covenanters must have appeared somewhat esoteric to the victims.[10] Moreover, Montrose proved as adept at taking minor and personal revenge as Argyll – for he harried Arbuthnott, sacked Findowrie and invaded Brechin to ruin its laird's town house for entirely personal reasons. His ally Alasdair MacColla (or General Sir Alexander MacDonald) earned the fearsome Gaelic nickname 'the destroyer of houses'.[11] Perhaps it was to be expected that Campbell houses might fall prey to MacColla – particularly Inveraray in December 1644 after his victory over Argyll at Inverlochy (albeit all Glenorchy's houses were spared) – but Montrose took his vengeance north to Nairn and to Moray, to plunder, burn and spoil Ballindalloch, Grange Hill, Brodie, Culbin and Redhall. After his subsequent victory over General Hurry at the Battle of Auldearn in May 1645, Montrose directed that the estates of those on Hurry's side – for example, Campbell of Cawdor, Innes of Innes, the Earl of Moray – should be laid waste, and that a good number of houses in Elgin should be destroyed.[12] To judge from the survival of the new-formatted Innes, instructions were not always followed.

Hurry himself, although a soldier of fortune and of uncertain temper, was moderate in his treatment of the places through which he passed – he 'raised no fire nor did any wrong to the stately palaces of Strathboggie and the Bog'[13] – which tends to imply that only where the armies were led by the Scottish magnates did personal animosity figure larger than military need. In revenge for Montrose's sacking of Castle Campbell in Dollar, the Earl of Argyll ordered General Baillie to destroy the House of Menstrie belonging to Sir William Alexander (Argyll's former travelling companion around Europe) and the house of Airthrie, threatening even Alloa itself.[14] Application of the rules of engagement – requiring orderly surrender and withdrawal from a house and its subsequent protection, as was achieved in Caerlaverock – became increasingly rare. General Middleton's progress through Strathearn targeted Montrose's principal property – his great seat of Kincardine – and, later, the sacking of his 'statelie house of Mugdock' by Strathblane.

Spalding watched miserably as the great houses and improved estates went to wrack. In March 1645, Montrose decided to take revenge upon the Earl Marischal:

> They fired the pleasant park of Fetteresso: some trees burnt, other trees being green could not burn; but the hart, the hind, the deer, and the roe, skirled at the sight of fire, but they were all tane and slain. The horses, mares, oxen and ky, were all likewyse killed and the haill barronies of Dunnottar and Fetteresso utterly spoilzied, plundered and undone.[15]

Yet the rage of war varied from locality to locality, for the Earl of Traquair felt able to undertake some rebuilding. His house appears to

12.1 Traquair, Peeblesshire. It was reworked in 1642 when the tower to the east (right) was probably reduced in height. James Smith's 1695 scheme to replicate it on the west never materialised. (RCAHMS)

have grown with a large tower to the east and a small one to the west; a fine mid-sixteenth-century palace block lay between.[16] It seems likely that in 1642 he reduced the height of the original tower to lower than the sixteenth-century western wing, capping it with new turrets and dormers (rather similar, in effect, to what Wood had done at Balbegno in about 1570).[17] The nobility of the ensemble thus transferred from old tower to modern house. The Covenanter James Wallace added a fashionable stairtower with viewing platform and broken pediments to his House of Auchans, Ayrshire, in 1644, and the modest house of Ecclesiamagirdle, Perthshire, was built in 1648. Ostentatious construction remained rare, and once Oliver Cromwell entered the country in July 1650, the cycle of destruction began again. Seton was made 'into a common inn, his rich furniture and stuff plundered, and all the enormities that could be offered by Jews or Turks to Christians, he suffered daily'.[18] After the Restoration, Sir Alexander Irvine of Drum was only one of many who sought relief from taxation on the grounds that destruction of property had been so great he could not afford to pay. Irvine lamented that he had 'been twice fined £4,000 sterling, four times garrisoned and at length totally plundered, and his wife and children turned out of doors'.[19]

Although the towns began to thrive again after 1652, and Glasgow rebuilt itself after its disastrous fire in June that year, with streets most splendidly lined by ashlar arcades, the same could not be said for the nobility. In 1655, the Principal of Glasgow University Robert Baillie lamented: 'Very many of the Noblemen and gentlemen, what with imprisonments, banishments, forfaulters, fynes, as yet continueing without any releasement, and private debts from their former troubles, are wracked or going to wrack.' 'Our noble families are almost gone', he wrote three years later. Lennox had little left unsold; Hamilton's estate – saving Arran and Hamilton itself – likewise; Argyll was as drowned in debt as in public hatred; the Gordons were gone; the Douglases little better; Eglinton and Glencairn were on the brink of breaking; 'many of our chief families states are cracking'.[20] He recorded in his journal: 'For our State, all is exceeding quiet; A great armie, in a multitude of garrisons, bydes above our head, and deep povertie keeps all estates exceedingly at under; the taxes of all sorts are so great, the trade so little, that it's marvell if extreame scarcity of money end not, ere long, in some mischief.'[21]

Yet the less prominent and less vulnerable lairds were already about rebuilding and replanting to recover their income. Three years after his marriage in 1654, Thomas Stewart set about modernising the family seat of Coltness in Lanarkshire. He found his inherited and very old-fashioned pile mansion 'straightening' (i.e. too constricting): just a narrow tower

12.2 Auchans, Ayrshire, its new stairtower added in 1644, drawn by Billings. (Author's collection)

built by Hamilton of Uddestoun (Uddingston?), one room per floor reached by a turnpike stair with a small study or cabinet on top. He decided to build a new four-storeyed house alongside with 'six fire rooms [rooms with chimneys] with closets'. The three-roomed state apartment in the new house of Coltness began with a 'low parlour' at ground level (performing a function similar to that of a laigh hall or antechamber), and the dining-room on the principal floor leading into the principal bedroom and closet. There were two further bedchambers with closets above, and two 'roof rooms' at the top. It was thus slightly old-fashioned in lacking the old chamber of dais as a withdrawing-room. The original tower was transformed into storage.[22] A woman house on the ground floor with nursery above was added later. The bakehouse, brewhouse, garner room and men servants' bedchamber lay on the north side of the inner court. There was an outer court with stables, and a third with well, byre, barn, sheep house, hen house and dunghill – in other words what was later to become the 'Mains' or Home Farm.

Stewart was very particular about improving his gardens. He terraced them down from the south façade according to baroque fashion: a square parterre or flower garden, flanked by cherry and nut gardens, then walnut and chestnut trees, and finally a strawberry bank. There was a fishpond for pike and perch, a terrace set against a south-facing wall to ripen and improve the finer fruits, a good orchard and kitchen garden with broad

Graph 9 Châteaux construction, 1640–84. Predictably, any analysis based solely upon castellated houses shows a great falling off during this period. This graph therefore conceals the enormous quantity of country house building in Scotland in the later seventeenth century.

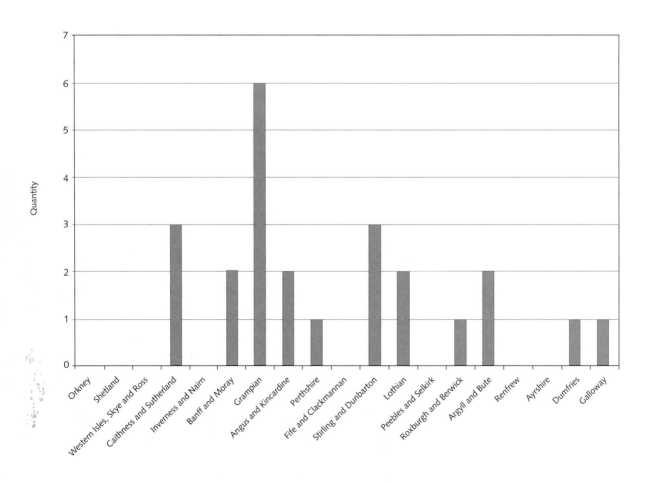

grass walks. In the later seventeenth century, some gardens were to become as important as the house or, in the case of the diminutive house of Barncluith on the banks of the Avon in Clydesdale, more so. Barncluith was completely outshone by its topiary terraces:

> A very Romantick garden . . . which consists of Seven hanging Terras-Walks down to a River Side, with a wild wood full of birds on the opposite side of the River: in some of the Walks are Banquetting Houses, with Walks and Grottoes, and all of them filled with large Evergreens, in the Shapes of Beasts and Birds.[23]

Slezer's drawing of Hatton, Midlothian, shows how terraces with their ornamental ponds, their fountains, their fruit espaliers, their orchards, wildernesses and banqueting houses, might be arranged.

12.3 Barncluith, Lanarkshire: south-east elevation of the baroque gardens terraced down the steep slopes of the River Avon. (Cadzow is barely a mile upstream). (RCAHMS)

12.4 Hatton, West Lothian, with its gardens, in the late seventeenth century, seat of the unpopular Charles Maitland, Lord Hatton, brother of Lauderdale, and owner of Dudhope, Dundee. The view was drawn by Slezer. (Author's collection)

Writing from the perspective of the early eighteenth century, Stewart of Coltness's memorialist and descendant, Sir Archibald Stewart, condemned his forebear's approach to architecture as

wholly irregular as to the outside appearance, and both house and policy were more contrived for convenience and hospitality, than for beauty of regular proportion; and so was the humour of these times, that if there was a lodging, warmness and plenty within doors, a regular front or uniform front were little thought of.[24]

His criticism highlights the change that occurred in the sixty years after the Restoration. The informal evolution of a house for convenience and hospitality that had largely characterised Scottish architecture over the previous 150 years was to be replaced by a house design with a regular plan and uniform façade. That Thomas had adapted and extended rather than beginning from scratch was a world away from the tightly planned, compact, formal houses of the age of William Adam.

For the most part, the architecture of the early post-Restoration period approach evolved from design traditions established before the Troubles, and the starting point remained this: what attitude should be taken to the inherited house? It was a matter of degree. Some lairds undertook refashioning works within an existing skeleton, environing it with new terraces and fountains. Some added a new structure to the inner court but otherwise left the ensemble largely as it was. Others opted for an entirely new house but on the old site. A minority decided to start from the beginning on a new site. That so many of the Strathearn gentry opted for the last two categories can be taken as a reflection upon their fate during the Troubles and their wealth after the Restoration.[25] Many families

12.5 Castle Lyon (now Huntly) drawn by Slezer. The superstructure is very similar to Glamis' north front. Note the walled bowling green, croquet player, terraces, topiary, walks and pavilions added by Strathmore. The inner close, with its entrance, lies to the top right. (RCAHMS)

upgraded their existing seats to bring them into line with the preference for an approximate symmetry – in the course of which height was usually sacrificed to length and breadth. Yet height was still regarded as a signal of nobility, as may be inferred from the Duke of Lauderdale's firm instruction to Sir William Bruce to add another storey to the corner closet towers of Brunstane (clearly against Bruce's architectural judgement), for Lauderdale could not live with it otherwise.[26] The six–seven storeys of the earlier seventeenth-century house, however, were rarely taller than the four (corner towers) and three (main house) of its counterpart forty years later.

Attitudes to the tower varied. Haddington had cut down the one at Tyninghame and used its former great hall as a lettermeit hall.[27] The old tower of Craigbarnet remained in use and well furnished even after Sir Mungo Stirling of Glorat added a spacious modern block with a new kitchen, laigh hall, hall and chambers above to the inner court in 1662.[28] Similar treatment was impossible at the tower of Huntly, by Longforgan, perhaps because it was perched on a rocky outcrop overlooking the Carse

12.6 *Interior of Castle Lyon in the late nineteenth century.* (From A. H. Millar, The Historical Castles and Mansions of Scotland, *Paisley, 1890)*

of Gowrie. The 1st Earl of Strathmore had inherited it as the family's summer residence,[29] but it was 'a place of no consideratioun, fit for nothing else but as a place of refuge in the time of trouble, wherein a man might make himself a prisoner'.[30] Anyway, since the countess disliked moving back and forth to the family's principal seat at Glamis because of the damage to the furniture, the family decided to remain in Huntly (which they duly renamed Castle Lyon) for the first ten years of their married life. Although Strathmore's father had begun work to its roof and the outer court (Slezer's drawing shows the superstructure greatly resembled that of Glamis), the tower itself was chilled, dank, dark and inefficient, 'with scarce a spare room furnished to lodge a stranger in'. Anyone sitting in the hall could not avoid witnessing servants slopping out the bedchambers above since the only route upstairs crossed it.[31]

Strathmore's programme was to create more fashionable chambers, greater convenience and access, guest accommodation and greater privacy. He cut into the rock so as to extend the plinth upon which the house sat, and in the new space he put a nursery. He then cut out the tower's two upper vaults to create space for additional floors, added two back stairs, and created seven closets within the thickness of the walls. He thinned the walls of the drawing- and dining-rooms, cut and enlarged windows, and panelled the interiors. Once he had finished, his old furniture no longer matched the new house, so he sent the old stuff to Glamis – 'a place not easie to be filled'. Castle Lyon was then kitted out as smart as could be, 'so that at this day [1684], it stands compleitly furnished and verry fashionable'.[32] So what counted as 'verry fashionable'? Perhaps the Black Marble Room, with its purple silk hangings with yellow trim, or the Suede Room, or the clocks, Japan screens and armchairs, or the square folding oak tables, Russia leather chairs and ten upholstered chairs, tartan plaids and chequer board in the Lower Hall, or the fifty-nine paintings that adorned its walls.[33]

Strathmore levelled land to the east for a bowling green and a little garden with statues. He built two summer houses – the Low one with a marble table, and the High Summer House with cane chairs, flowered silk curtains and damask hangings.[34] In its essentials – the creation of privacy, the cutting out of the vaults, the thinning of walls and the construction of new stairs – the draconian work at Huntly was not untypical of what was happening elsewhere in Scotland. Similar work, probably in the 1670s, took place in the principal wing of the palace of Kinneil: its vaults likewise cut out, also given a new flat roof and viewing platform, and similarly provided with new stairtowers.

Not all old towers were savaged in quite so Procrustean a manner. Proud Finavon on the banks of the South Esk, for example, remained in full use. Seat of the Earls of Crawford, and originally sited for its proximity to the royal forest of Plater,[35] it had been the tallest house depicted by Pont. A 1712 inventory reveals how this ancient giant had continually been refashioned within. Its sixteen main chambers, all richly furnished, were mostly colour-coded: the gold-coloured room had gold-coloured bed-hangings, seven gold-coloured chairs and gold-coloured wall hangings. There were red, yellow and two green rooms, and the laird's chamber was clearly the blue one. The 'Fine Room', by contrast, was a lady's, to judge from its contents of dressing glass and dressing box, patch boxes, brushes, a japanned box, cabinet, table, glass and stand – hung with arras. High and low dining-rooms each had twelve chairs (upper ones cane, lower ones of Russia leather), but the lower one was better appointed with tables and had more pictures on the wall. That there was a painted room with green hangings implies a painted ceiling, perhaps installed during the peak of the painted ceiling fashion by the 11th Earl who made some additions in 1593.[36] Continuing modernisation of Finavon in the later seventeenth century is implied by its gilt and japanned mirrors, olive-wood cabinet and a clock, and by the fact that the high dining-room was hung with gilded leather 'beautifully embossed with . . . representations of Ceres, Pan and other deities'.[37] Walls clad in embossed leather were largely of later seventeenth-century date.

Whereas some families with the wealth to rebuild were still investing in their ancient towers, probably more typical were the Forbeses of Pitsligo who had abandoned theirs, initially to servants and storage, thereafter beginning a half-hearted attempt to demolish it which resulted only in the removal of its battlements and attic.[38] The tower of Monkton, near

Edinburgh (an altogether smaller establishment) was reduced to the height of the remainder of the house. The four principal building periods of Monkton – likely to have been fifteenth, sixteenth, early and late seventeenth centuries – were homogenised beneath a constant roof pitch and probably harled over, so that the joints so visible today were invisible. About this time began the fashion of raising the levels of the garden around such houses to provide a direct entry into the principal floor. The former entrance floor – with its vaulted cellars and kitchens – would be relegated to a basement.[39] Thus did the below-ground basement of cellars and kitchen appear in Scottish architecture.

What was implied by modernisation varied from landowner to landowner. In the case of the House of Ravelston, sheltered in the south-east flank of Corstorphine Hill, by Edinburgh, which Sir John Foulis began to modernise in 1679–80, it was just a matter of internal redecoration and refurnishing, and substantial work to the policies. Not much now remains of it: just a stairtower, some walls, exemplary parkland and an avenue of trees, a fountain, fireplaces, gateway, stable yard and an alleged ghost. There are very few illustrations of it before its destruction by fire, but Sir Walter Scott indicated that it, along with the (also missing) House of Dean, were the inspirations for his detailed descriptions of the House of Tully-Veolan in *Waverley*. Scott wrote:

> There is no particular mansion described under the name of Tully-Veolan: but the peculiarities of the description occur in various Scottish seats. The House of Warrender . . . and that of Old Ravelston have both contributed several hints to the description in

12.7 House of Dean, Edinburgh, drawn by Paul Sandby, c. 1760. (D 2653. NGS)

the text. The House of Dean, near Edinburgh, has also some points of resemblance.[40]

Scott wrote that the garden, in particular, was modelled upon Ravelston's. Dean and Ravelston were U-plan villas of presumably early seventeenth-century date, and Tully-Veolan was described likewise. It is truly ironic that Scott regarded them as 'baronial' – a term that would probably have repelled their builders. Ravelston was a middling U-plan villa built by Foulis' father George in 1622–4:[41] never a great seat, but one of considerable charm and quiet substance. Its relatively recent construction implied that the work in 1678–9 was modernisation rather than structural change.

There is no contract for the work at Ravelston, but in February 1680 Foulis had a meeting with a wright, and workmen were on site by May. Given that Foulis himself appears to have been responsible for buying most of the materials and having them delivered, this has the appearance of being a separate trades contract.[42] Patrick Chambers, wright, may have been in overall charge, but other wrights included the expensive James Bain and William Rodger. Bain was not only His Majesty's Wright, working on Holyrood and Panmure, but a substantial timber contractor obtaining, shipping and supplying timber from northern forests such as Balnagown, thus turning a laird's asset into a cash crop.[43] Judging by his cost, this appears to have been his role at Ravelston. The mason (probably master mason, for others appear to have been on site) was James Potter, and extensive glasswork is implied by payments to the glazier Thomas Houlatestone. Work inside the house included dressing six chimneys with new lintels and pavement, and much timberwork – perhaps new or repaired floors or even wainscotting. Henry Fraser marbled the chimneys,[44] painted the walls below their hangings, 'whyt[ed]' roofs and kitchen corridor,[45] and decorated the hall in 'sad colour'. That everything was to be 'conform to agreement' suggests a contract and possibly a design. Interior quality is implied by the purchase of substantial furniture, yellow silk for the bed, and a chiselled pot of silver which cost £60 on its own.

Foulis was a keen improver: new park walls, a hen house, yards, beehives, new painted gates, new doors with new locks. The land was to be fertilised with lime sea shells. Rorie the gardener was dispatched to Robert Currie in Cramond to buy seventeen plane and ash trees for the doocot green; and out again to Muirhouse, Cramond and Dalry for twenty cherry grafts, four pear grafts, and grafts for apple, plum and apricot. From the gardener in the Surgeon's Yard in town, he obtained grafts for the rarer black pippin, pear dangerous, two honey pears, a bon critean (bon chrétien?), a swaneg (?) and a bona magna plum. On a national scale, this was nothing particularly remarkable. But if Foulis were typical of people in the rest of the country, it becomes clear why Sir Robert Sibbald established the Botanic Garden and why being in the building industry provided a good living.[46]

There was much building going on thereabouts to judge by the activities of Foulis' circle. A brisk, middling sort of gentleman, he had friends of like ilk with whom he spent much time dining, and his largesse extended to drinksilver for the masons also working at Newliston and Barnton at the same time. His recreation included fishing at Cramond, taking his family to the races at Leith, hunting, much golfing (12 shillings on golf balls at one time) and frequently staying in his town house in Edinburgh so that he could go to the *Comedie*. The household comprised a chaplain, eight indoor servants, the gardener Robert Rorie and his men, and a shepherd; and Foulis' self-esteem is indicated by his commissioning a portrait of himself by David Scougall.

Patrick, Earl of Strathmore, noted in 1684 in the *Glamis Book of Record*: 'Generally improvements here have been more since the time of the King's happie restoratione then has been in a hundred years before, and every one almost att the instance or example of some leader has done more or less.' So what of this architectural culture of the post-Restoration country seat? With true retrospective objectivity, and a deep-seated belief in the power of classicism to civilise even the most recidivist of people, most historians have found it difficult to consider seventeenth-century Scottish architecture in terms other than a stumbling and late move towards classicism, and the subsequent overwhelming of Scottish architectural traditions.[47] Partly, that has been the consequence of an indifferent perception of those earlier traditions, and how they had evolved over the previous 150 years. Naturally, if you regard the Renaissance in Scotland solely in terms of variations of tower house or (even worse) 'keep', later seventeenth-century country seats must appear revolutionary. But they were not. They were entirely within Scottish architectural tradition. So far as can be told from contemporary documents, the principal architectural preoccupation in Scotland was not the introduction of classicism. It was, instead, what attitude to take to the past. Was it to be filial piety, transformation or rejection? Ruminating from exile in the 1720s, the Earl of Mar implied that although his family had kept up Alloa Tower because they had been insufficiently wealthy 'to undertake the building of a new house all at once', there was a deeper consideration:

there is something in the old Tower, espetially if made conform to the new designe, wch is *venerable for its antiquity* [my italics] and makes not a bad apearance, and would make one regrait the being oblig'd to pull it down, wch must be done were there a new house to be built . . .[48]

Total rejection of the past was extremely rare. The tone was set by the Duke of Lauderdale in the conversion of Holyrood into a palace fit for a regent and with architecture by Sir William Bruce. Instead of discarding the old palace, burnt and rebuilt as it had been by the Usurpers, their plan was, in essence, to retain the Royal Lodging on the north-west corner, to complete James V's original concept of a balancing tower to the south-west corner, and then to create a regal-scaled and classically detailed *hôtel* in the courtyard: a fusion of old, new and classical with Scottish.[49] Will Bruce (as he was known)[50] had earlier begun to refit the duke's seat of Thirlestane, Lauder, in which this delight in the juxtaposition of old and new, Scottish and continental – the Scottish architectural anti-syzygy – was already manifest. James VI's Chancellor Maitland had constructed an enormous linear four-storeyed seat in part of the English fort built during the 1547 occupation at Lauder (some immured towers of which peek out from the undergrowth downhill to the south) set on an eminence above

12.8 *The architecture of accrual and inheritance – Old Penicuick House, Midlothian, by John Clerk of Eldin, mid-eighteenth century. The composite old Scots mansion is of at least three building periods, bristling with early seventeenth-century viewing platforms and secondary staircases, but balanced by a later wing.* (Author's collection)

the Leader Water. It provided a state apartment on each floor extending, uniquely, to *five* chambers in enfilade rather than the customary three. Both east and west gables were framed by giant 'rounds' or circular towers (possibly joined at the top as a triumphal arch). Its north and south flanks rippled with shallowly projecting round towers which, when they were still harled, must have resembled those of Loches.[51]

Lauderdale was insistent upon an adequate 'front at the entry', and Bruce designed an entry from the west, between the two great towers which he framed with four-storeyed tall-roofed pavilions, joined by a raised balustraded platform between. A lower, outer court, similarly defined by (smaller) pavilions, was intended. Lauderdale then conceived of adding comparable pavilions to the eastern frontage, for balance and for effect from the garden, and asked Bruce to develop the idea,[52] but although they were drawn by Slezer, they were never built. Bruce transformed the skyline with a pediment joining the two towers above the entrance, and lined the upper storeys of the main house with balconies of the form originally intended for the unbuilt pavilions.[53] Two apartments were inserted in the old house (the third and top floors being left as they had been in the Chancellor's time). The entry floor apartments were private: vestibule, antechamber, dining-room, withdrawing-rooms, a closet each for Lauderdale and his formidable wife the Countess of Dysart, and a bedroom each in the two rounds at the east end. The north-west tower was hollowed out to take the ceremonial staircase, most gorgeously caparisoned with plasterwork, leading up to the state apartment. The

12.9 Proposed Thirlestane entrance façade drawn by Slezer, c. 1680. (Author's collection)

12.10 Thirlestane garden (south) façade drawn by Slezer, c. 1680. The eastern pavilions (on the right) were never built. Note the similarity in massing to Panmure. (Author's collection)

249

apartment's almost square, jewel-like antechamber is one of the most perfect seventeenth-century chambers to survive in Scotland. The state apartment unfolds in enfilade thereafter – the Great Dining Room, Withdrawing Room, Bedchamber with dressing-room and closet. The proposed pavilion at the far end was to have contained a library opening from the bedchamber. Thirlestane's seemingly old-fashioned pattern when compared to the double-pile houses being constructed elsewhere in Scotland may best be explained by the conjunction of filial piety, and Lauderdale's assumption of regal state.

Lauderdale's desire to celebrate this creation of his ancestor could be said to parallel that of the Earl of Mar who, some forty years later, planned to have painted the words 'sic dominus coluit monumenta parentum' ('Thus did the Lord make the monuments of our parents fruitful') painted below the parapet of his tower at Alloa.[54] Similar sentiment imbued the Earl of Strathmore who, at almost exactly the same time that Lauderdale was transforming Thirlestane, finally turned his attention away from Castle Lyon to the family seat of Glamis 'in the year of God 1670'. 'We came here as new beginners, where we past the winter and lodged ourselves all in that storry of the old house which is at the top of the great staircase' (for it was the only one still glazed). The house was typically decrepit after military occupation by its English garrison, but was otherwise pretty modern after all the work by his father and grandfather.

Strathmore's intent was to create a setting worthy of his splendid house. Glamis was low-lying and surrounded by drainage ditches that might, at one time, have served as a defensive moat. It had gated outer and inner courts. The latter consisted of a collapsing east wing, and a ruined hall with chamber of dais, stables and offices (some turned into stables and smiddies by the English) on the west. The latter were all rotten and had to go. First, he drew out a plan:

> I did upon my first resolutione of the change which I have made here, make a skame and draught of my whole project, for unless men soe do, they will infallibly fall into some mistake – do that which they will repent themselves after, and be obleidged to pull their work down again. Therefore necessarie it is for a man to designe all at once (chalk is not sheers [cheese?]) . . . I confess I am to blame that designing so great a matter . . . I did not call such as in this age were known and repute to be the best judges and contrivers. . . . Being resolved to perform what I have done with little money, and by degrees, and more to please and divert myself than out of any ostentation . . . [I] never judged anything of my owne small endeavours to make so much noise as to call for or invit to either of my houses the Public Architecturs.[55]

Strathmore was protesting too much. He had seen what they did in Paris, and devised for Glamis a baroque vision of ceremonial gateways, grand vistas, a balustraded inner court framed by balanced wings, gardens, parterres, statues and the most elaborate sundials – well worthy of any 'Public Architectur'. It was a work of carefully crafted design, and the intention was balance: 'Tho it be ane old house and consequently was the

more difficult to reduce the place to any uniformity yet I did covet extremely to order my building.' (His implication that architects were necessary only where ostentation was required is an intriguing comment on the changing status of the profession – and Glamis was neither modest nor insignificant.)

The eastern wing, on the verge of collapse, was re-roofed, tied to the tower by a new straight stair, and its round tower raised in height. The grilles were removed from the windows, and a new floor was created in the roof space for the younger children and the better favoured women servants. The ruinous buildings on the west were replaced by a western wing (almost certainly incorporating some earlier structure) mimicking the eastern one. The apogee of the design was Strathmore's grandfather's great stairtower in the angle (a device earlier used by the Earl of Mar at Braemar in 1628). By adopting his forefathers' language of gables and towers[56] Strathmore chose to persist with the national architecture rather than follow the accelerating trends for larger, lower and squarer houses. That said, his new western pavilion was largely flat-roofed and acted as a viewing platform in the fashionable manner 'which is of great convenience and use to us who live for the time in this side of the house'.[57]

The way in which Scottish architecture was evolving was more apparent in new-build, or where sufficient of an extension occurred as to make virtually a new house. In April 1666 the Earl of Panmure determined upon

12.11 The design of an outrageous romantic. The proposed eastern façade of Glamis after the drawing by Slezer, showing the new western wing (not quite completed as drawn), harling restored and skyline perspective altered. The earl lived in the west wing and the children in the east.
(Author)

251

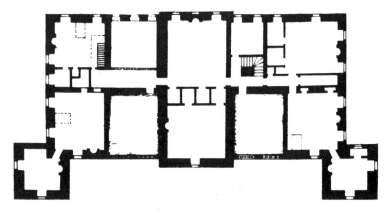

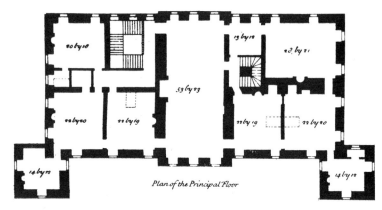

Plan of the Principal Floor

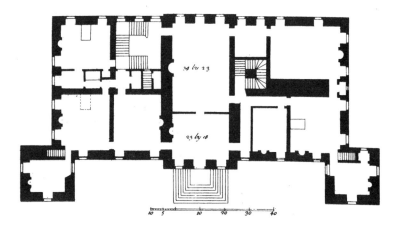

Plan of the First Floor of Panmure House.

12.12 *Plan of Panmure, taken from* Vitruvius Scoticus. *William Adam was planning the publication of a volume of drawings like* Vitruvius Scoticus *from 1726 and material was prepared from the following year onwards. It was not published until 1812, however.*

a new house, probably incorporating the mansion of Bowshen in which he was then living, and contracted with John Milne, Master Mason to the Crown, to have it built. Although Milne appears to have been both designer and main contractor for the structure,[58] Sir William Bruce certainly designed the chief entry into the court from the west in 1672. Moreover, the design of Panmure displays so great a resemblance to Bruce's contemporary transformation of his own house at Balcaskie as to indicate Bruce's design hand in the former as well. To an existing thick-walled L-plan house on the east, the earl added a balancing structure to the west, regularised it and framed the conception by square five-storeyed, ogee-roofed closet towers projecting beyond the corners. The spreading eleven-bay horizontally proportioned house was firmly symmetrical, organised around the three-bay centre, flanked and framed like a coronet by taller chimney-stacks. Although Panmure's entrance was up a flight of steps above the kitchen/basement level, the principal floor still lay on the floor above. The saloon, which occupied the entire centre front to back, separated the two wings of the house which, to judge by the staircases, were the family wing to the right, and guests' to the left. The entrance façade, enormous chimneys, corner towers and half gables were a new formalisation of the inherited Scottish architectural tradition. At the third storey, the roof was pulled back to each side in order to provide a viewing platform on either side of the centre. This array of chimneys and gables echoed the martial skyline of the older châteaux, even though everything of which it was composed had an overtly peaceable purpose.

Bruce's own more or less contemporary house of Balcaskie, Fife, *c.* 1668, was remarkably similar. Likewise eleven bays long and extended from an L-plan house, the addition of a main house and balancing eastern wing produced a northern elevation of gables and chimney-stacks in approximate symmetry and perfect balance. Unlike Panmure, its corner towers are lower

than the main house, and there was no formal array of chimney-stacks around a centre. None the less, a vertical house became horizontal.[59] Balcaskie's plan evolved from the Jacobean villa whose two wings framed the hall or gallery between them – with the significant difference that the centre had grown and the towers had diminished in importance. The main house became double-pile – that is two three-roomed apartments disposed lengthwise on each side of a spine or cross-wall.

Bruce reworked and terraced the walled gardens to the south, and organised the ensemble so that the vista was directed upon the Bass Rock lying towards the southern shore of the River Forth. He also transformed the inner court to a much more formal forecourt: the laundry and coach-

12.14 Entrance elevation and quadrants of Sir William Bruce's first house at Balcaskie, Fife. (RCAHMS)

*12.15 Caroline Park,
Edinburgh, photographed for
the National Art Survey.*
(Author's collection)

house were removed into small two-storeyed pavilions in the forecourt tied back to the house by a curving quadrant screen wall with niches and urns and capped by ball finials.

An even plainer double-pile house with closet towers was Gallery, Angus, begun for Sir John Falconer of Balmakelly in 1677. In plan and elevation – particularly the great chamber extending the length of the building (equivalent to the gallery in Culross Abbey House) – Gallery was a descendant of Culross built seventy years afterwards.[60] The main house had become the dominant feature of the design, taller than its closet towers. By contrast, the unusually effulgent roofs on the towers of Caroline Park, Edinburgh, were once again the focus of the design, as they remained in Black Barony, near Peebles, after Sir Alexander Murray, the Royal Master of Works, had reworked it about 1700. He doubled an L-plan house into a new symmetry, but restored the closet towers to their former dominance.[61]

Towards the end of the century, few constructed *châteaux*. Most were building in the emerging style of the compact three-bay Scots mansion, short cross-walls containing the fireplaces, with public apartments on both ground and first floor. The remainder – in the words of several of Sir Robert Sibbald's correspondents preserved in Macfarlane's *Collections* – were building houses 'after the English modell' or 'of the modern fashion'.[62] Indeed, the replies he received from country gentlemen and ministers provide a glimpse into their changing perceptions. The double-towered *châtelet* at Thurso was allowed 'very fine tho' antique', whereas the courtyard house of Strichen was deemed 'old fashion'd'.[63] What was being implied by these descriptions? The 'English manner' may well refer to a house with reception rooms on the ground floor rather than up on the *piano nobile*. That Strichen's courtyard was considered old-fashioned implied that houses around a court were being superseded by compact mansions with quadrants and a ceremonial entry along an axis. Lesser structures of the inner and outer courts were regularised out of sight, as they had been at Glamis.

Yet barely more than half of the houses redrawn for William Adam's *Vitruvius Scoticus* had the compact villa plan. A significant minority, buildings like Callie, Preston Hall, Cammo and Elphinstone, retained the long, rectangular double-pile plan with a spine wall of Culross Abbey House and Balcaskie. Almost as many showed clear evidence of being U-plan houses, the centre filled in with a classical frontispiece. It is in homage to that inheritance, perhaps, that William Adam's plan for the House of Dun takes so similar a form. Many of the designs in his volume have a regularised façade, adorned with a classical or baroque frontispiece below an emphatic Scottish silhouette of gables and chimney-stacks.

None the less, there remained a residual demand for an even more flamboyant grandeur that could not be met just by closet towers and chimney-stacks. A *château* was the deliberate choice of Patrick Smyth of Braco, overseer of the Duke of Atholl's new palace at Dunkeld, for his new seat in Methven, in which he employed many of the same craftsmen. Throughout the project, Smyth always referred to Methven as a 'castle' even though his retention of this large and venerable seat of Queen Margaret Tudor and the Dukes of Lennox was limited to a fat cross-wall.[64] His wife Agnes Keith of Keith Hall, who oversaw the work while Patrick was busy elsewhere, generally referred to it as 'my love's bonny

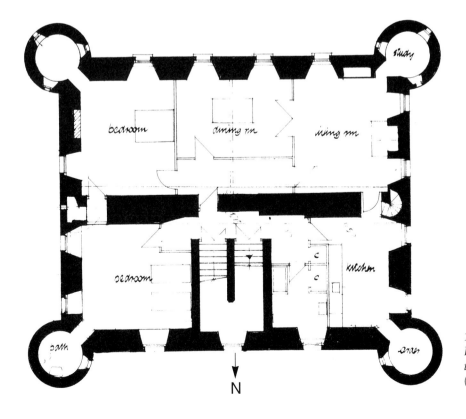

12.16 Plan of Methven, Perthshire as adapted for twentieth-century living. (Courtesy of Ken Murdoch)

12.17 *Methven in the late eighteenth century, drawn by Reid and Scott.* (Author's collection)

strong house', even though it was but a new-built villa. Since James Smith had the draught in 1678, he appears to have been the designer.[65] Methven presents a conundrum: a compact new building that rejected almost all of the earlier fabric but none the less aped ancient form through circular towers on each corner. In plan and proportion, it resembles Craigston: a closed U-plan with a long main house to the rear and two wings projecting closely to the north, between which Smyth or Smith inserted the staircase that rises within the envelope from bottom to top. What had happened to the great stair up only to the principal floor? Methven's stair was either very old-fashioned or the harbinger of the new. Then, to each corner of this plain-harled near-cube, they added a slender closet tower – a *circular* tower rising full height and given an ogee-shaped roof. Even more curious, given what Bruce was doing at Balcaskie and Thirlestane, and Strathmore at Glamis in abandoning the inner court for a forecourt and grandiose vista, they re-created at Methven a formal high-walled inner court. The only concession to external visual modernity was an abbreviated viewing platform above the staircase, squeezed by gables on both sides. Yet it was modern, in the way the Prestonfield House, Edinburgh, also thought to be by Smith, was modern. For, save its round towers, Methven is a powerfully plain rectangle. Here, perhaps, was the *château* for a new age.

Nor was it the last. Up in Cromarty, the House of Tarbat appears, likewise to have been *Methvenised*. The unusually fine Jacobean U-plan villa, octagonal stairs in both angles and square chimneys like Innes atop was cursed by curiously inappropriate round towers added to its principal corners which negated the precision of the earlier.[66] It cannot have been a coincidence that Patrick Smyth was also 'Servant of Cromartie'. In the 1680s, James Fraser of Tyrie began to build a 40 foot square house near Fraserburgh, which contemporaries considered 'built fancifully after a foreign model'.[67] It was: 'invironed with fyne gardens well planted and walled with Rounds on every corner, half rounds on each side, of fore and

256

back entries, on the east and west . . . and standing in the low Parlour has a small visee to each airth'.[68] Tyrie was distinctly odd. Its top floor consisted of a single 40 foot square room – like a 'skied' gallery – with views in each direction. A round tower on each corner, however, and half-round tower along each wall (presumably flanking the entries) were the components of the *château* that survived until revivalism became respectable.

In a book about mock-military country seats, it has not been germane to examine the formal symmetrical classical house exemplified in Bruce's second house at Kinross. Save for an echo of the earlier seventeenth-century villas in the way the roofs of its pavilions more resemble flattened wings than end pavilions, Kinross is of a different architectural persuasion. Nor is it appropriate to consider James Smith's imposing classical houses and villas, or his work on Dalkeith and Hamilton Palaces as his only important designs. Both Bruce and Smith were adept at designing in two languages at the same time – and even when they were designing in the grand manner, their Scottish accent made itself heard. Smith was probably responsible for the great house for the Duke of Queensberry at Drumlanrig in the wilderness of upland Dumfriesshire at the same time as he was involved with Methven. ('The surprise of seeing so fine a building in so coarse a country adds to its Beauty', thought Macky.[69]) A large, uneven courtyard palace that had grown from the fifteenth century, Drumlanrig was regularised into a resplendently harled courtyard palace,[70] a tall square tower at each corner, an entrance façade in polished red

12.18 Entrance façade of Drumlanrig, reproduced as plate 38 in Vitruvius Britannicus *which was published in London between 1715 and 1725.* (RCAHMS)

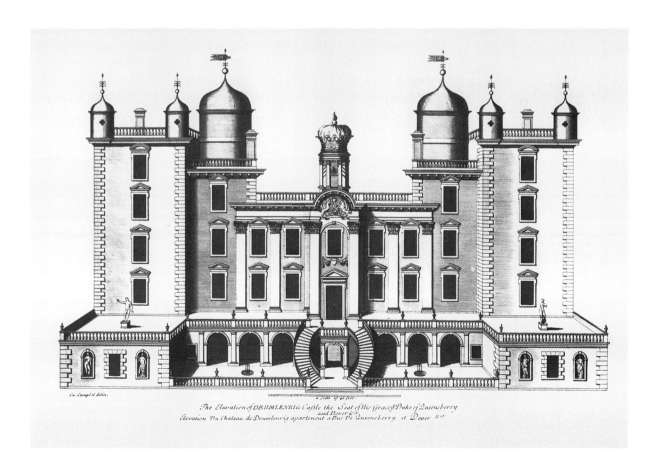

The Elevation of DRUMLENRIG Castle the Seat of His Grace ye Duke of Queensberry and Dover &c.
Elevation Du Chateau de Drumlenrig apartenent a Duc De Queensberry et Dover &c.

ashlar, and a fantastic skyline of ogee-capped stairtowers and chimney-stacks.[71] A gallery runs from end to end above the entrance. There were many echoes of motifs from earlier works of architecture: the entrance façade, capped by a ducal coronet above a baroque centrepiece – Holyrood; the raised balustraded entrance platform – Thirlestane; and the stepping down from the corner towers to a balustraded viewing platform above the entrance – Panmure (save that Drumlanrig's roofs and gables are flat); the four-towered composition echoes – the Scots Renaissance palaces of the days of James V, and Craignethan and Linlithgow; the gallery over the entrance – Craigston and Hamilton. From this ancient inheritance Smith created a contemporary palace that visitors allowed to be noble.

Continuity in Scottish architecture, so much the key to how it had developed during the Renaissance, remained extremely powerful long afterwards. When, in 1695, Smith was asked to prepare plans for Traquair, he designed a romantic regularisation within the tradition described above. He proposed to match the lower, decapitated (albeit turreted) tower projecting to the south with a replica to the north, the two tied together by a screen wall. It was never built.[72] Given this historical perspective, however, a Scottish source appears more credible as the inspiration behind later romantic piles like Inveraray or Douglas Castles (each with, it should be noted, a round on each corner) than English medieval prototypes like Bodiam Castle. After all, Roger Morris's original plan for Inveraray Castle was virtually Methven doubled in width.[73]

The influence of both Bruce and Smith remained strong for at least another fifty years – and particularly upon William Adam. Adam's later alterations to Balloch, where he balanced an existing tower with another and joined the two by a balustrade, was clearly influenced by Bruce's approach at Balcaskie and Thirlestane. Even more striking is the influence of Drumlanrig upon Adam's Duff House in the 1740s. The court has been compressed into a top-lit stairwell and the cupola with earl's coronet replaced by a pediment, but Duff, with its taller, rectangular corner towers clasping a lower double-pile block between is evidentially within the Scots tradition, emphasised by *a skied gallery* running north–south at the west end of the attics. Curiously, Smith's Melville House and Adam's Duff House, both defined by rectangular corner towers, are both called *houses*. Inveraray and Douglas Castles were both characterised by circular corner towers, and both were called *castles*. For revivalists, the distinction between house and castle was determined by the geometry of the corner towers.

On the face of it, the swift decline of the château in the late seventeenth century offers proof that these houses were defensive and were abandoned as no longer necessary. Reality was more subtle than that. The architectural traditions of the château never died. They lived on, semi-assimilated and somewhat mutated, through the designs of William Adam and his son Robert. *That* was the continuing tradition of Scottish architecture. But it lasted, long enough to be dusted off by the Romantics in the later eighteenth century. Thereafter, misunderstood and misinterpreted, it was eventually reinvented for entirely different purposes.

Epilogue
The Castle of Dreams

But pray take care to giving up too much of yr time to such a bewitching thing, as perhaps I did to my archetectur and designing. Amusements, tho necessary, to recreat and unbend our spirits and minds from more serious things . . . ought never to make us neglect our affairs or what we may be more usefully emploied about.

The Earl of Mar to his son, March 1726[1]

The quaint old Scotch gate pillars with the spire resting on 3 or 4 stone bullets . . . tell of a time when Scot[land] was much more friendly with france than with England, and so our castles much more resembled the French Château than the manor of our neighbour country [sic].[2]

Charles Rennie Mackintosh

What lies in a name? The early focus of this book upon the title 'castle' was less concerned with what people called their mock-military country house (particularly given the tendency for Scots aristocrats to rename their seats castles at the slightest opportunity) than with the assumptions about Scotland's ignorance of Renaissance culture which were based upon it. As in the rest of Europe, country houses provided reasonable passive defence in case of extremity since 'no palace wanted to be vulnerable to enemies of the regime'.[3] But the appearance of Scottish country houses appeared to imply a very much more dangerous culture. The houses looked uncouth if not recidivist when compared to the joyously glazed confections of their contemporaries in England with whom they were now bracketed within the same culture. The notion of the 'château revé' or the castle of dreams sat uneasily alongside the sensible large-windowed southern manor houses. The concept of the appearance of a house being 'an imposing mask'[4] might make more sense on the continent. What was not understood was that Scottish château had the *garb* of martial nobility but not its *substance*. Perhaps the real nobility of Renaissance Scotland lay in the fact that castle-like fortifications on the continental model were so little necessary.

So once Scotland and England were joined in the same culture, explanations were sought for the dissonance between Scottish and the English Renaissance country seats; and from early on, the favoured one used to justify the 'castle-wise' appearance of the Scottish houses was the exaggerated portrayal of noble feuding. The implication was that such behaviour was much worse in Scotland than elsewhere. As memories of Scottish accomplishments faded, so also did the understanding of the metaphorical *mock-military* nature of these houses. Imitation battlements and gunloops became proof of a warlike country. They suited the Scottish self-image of a nation of soldiers quite well, and provided a picturesque background to the country's later eighteenth-century role as the home of romantic if primitive warriors. So by the time that historians, annalists and compilers of historic information selected their documents in the nineteenth century, they were predisposed towards portraying the country as uncultured by comparison with those on the continent. It did not occur to them that the case might be otherwise: namely the assimilation of two different cultures into a single country had led to the reinterpretation of the weaker in terms of the stronger.

For the last thirty years, studies of Scottish Renaissance poetry, music and other aspects of culture have unravelled the myth that Scotland had stood aside, untouched, as the Renaissance passed by. But perceptions of its Renaissance architecture and built culture had lagged far behind until very recently.[5] Witness our preoccupation with battlements, bretasches, yetts and gunloops – and the entire subculture that still hungrily feeds upon them. Moreover, the emphatically *Scottish* nature of its architecture, so different from the norms of France and Italy, was interpreted as implying a culture deriving from an inward-looking isolationism. So it comes as a surprise to realise that, in warlike terms at least, a Scot – so long as he remained in Scotland – was more likely to live a long and untroubled life than a citizen in a high Renaissance Italian city state. It is a further surprise to appreciate the extent to which Scots were embedded in the developing European cultures, and maintained a high reputation within them. The Scots noble who had not been abroad for some education – or perhaps warfare – had to be apologised for.

This book, therefore, has only marginally examined the matter of 'castles'. It has, rather, examined buildings *now called castles* in terms of the culture of the country seat with its emblazoned skyline, its yards, orchards, gardens, surroundings and estate, in comparison to those in England and Europe. From their construction, plan, opulent and comfortable furnishings, idyllic and improving settings and landscape, a way of life may be inferred very different from that portrayed by Robert Chambers and his fellow historians; and also from the imaginative re-creations of country houses by Arts and Crafts architects like Sir Rowand Anderson, Sir Robert Lorimer and their successors. However picturesque their 'restorations' might have been, and however faithful to the Arts and Crafts philosophy of 'truth to materials' (another death-knell for harling), they were fundamentally unscholarly. They 'restored' what they saw solely on the basis of intuition and sensibility.

Since architecture is inescapably entwined with the culture and society of its time, it was an objective of this book to examine whether the reigns of monarchs might provide suitable time-frames for a study of the Scottish country seat. It has largely proved to be so. Scottish Renaissance architecture evolved chronologically, generally in the line of one reign to the next. Common to all periods was the country's basic technology: vaulted structures of load-bearing masonry, harled geometrically to provide a plinth for the elaborate superstructure varying according to the degree of the occupier.

There was considerable country house and villa construction in all decades between *c.* 1500 and *c.* 1680, and in most parts of Scotland – exceptions being the Highlands and Galloway. The early Renaissance period remains architecturally the least coherent. Non-royal houses mostly took the form of a changing tower – lowered and broadened, several chambers per floor in place of a single one, surrounded by improving yards and seeking symmetry and axis. French-inspired royal construction heralded the Marian period of the mid-sixteenth century, and its continuous construction provides a corrective to the belief that, ravaged by civil war, Scotland was a cultural desert between the death of James V and the majority of his grandson in 1585. The country was building, developing, and improving its agriculture; it was furnishing its houses in great style from several European and Baltic countries. Some of Scotland's most strikingly flamboyant great houses, particularly in Aberdeenshire, date from this period. Their romantic appearance tended to conceal that they were now horizontally proportioned to reflect the three-chamber state apartment.

More country seats were built or extended in the early Jacobean period – *c.* 1568 to *c.* 1600 – than during any other period covered in this volume. Their architecture, less curvaceous, sterner and more obviously Scots, seized the opportunity provided by yet a further change in living patterns – namely the growing separation between family and guest accommodation – to create greater visual complexity with a family wing, guest lodgings, and the proliferation of cabinets and closets. Privacy had become a determinant of architectural form.

Although the architecture of the later Jacobean period, taken to extend up to the Troubles in 1640, refined that of the previous generation, the architectural expression of Court and country parted company. Those close to the Court adopted the low, horizontally extended U-plan villa, the Scottish *villa suburbana*, where family occupied one wing in privacy, opposite another wing containing public chambers and guests. The emphasis upon skyline was now focused upon the gables of the wings, upon aedicules, finials, quoins and chimneys. In the country, particularly in the north-east, the push was ever upwards, even at the expense of utility – long after conditions of defence might have required it, so great was the desire to emphasise lineage and nationality through height and skyline. There is such consistency in the unusable gunloops, chimney-stacks, corbel courses, dormer windows, turrets – and in the silhouettes where all such preoccupations came together – as to imply an architectural vocabulary of as yet undecoded messages, understandable by their peers, if not yet by us. This was a national architecture, paradoxically becoming even more vehemently national once king and Court had left for England, once the smaller partner in this new union began to fear for its identity. Unconquered since King Fergus reigned in 330 BC, the poets proclaimed:

Scotland come never yet in servitude
Since Fergus first but ever has been free;
And has always been bruiked be a blood,
And king of kings descended gree by gree.[6]   [by degree]

Unconquered, echoed the buildings. Their grandeur implied that the élite had no intention of allowing themselves to be conquered now.

Although the savagery of the Troubles must have caused many to question the value of such rhetoric, there was no rejection of the country's traditions in the late seventeenth century. Scots had not yet become embarrassed about how their architectural culture differed from those of England or France. But power was moving to London and away from many old families by the end of the century. What value an architecture of power and lineage when such concepts were weakening for all but the greatest in the land? The tight symmetrical houses of James Smith are redolent less of the civilising power of classicism than of the fading of this preoccupation with reinventing history. The exhortation of Mar to his son that he should 'recall to your mind the great and noble things you see in history that our ancestors the brave Scots have done in their days for the ffreedome and preservation of our country'[7] was fine rhetoric, but out of keeping with the time. All it earned Mar was exile and penury (even though he anticipated ducal treatment on arrival in heaven by way of recompense). The world had moved on.

Yet there was far more continuity than dislocation, both during the Renaissance, and after it. The formalism that was emerging in the 1530s at Craignethan, for example, although overwhelmed by the Francophiliac romanticism of the mid-century Marian period, reappeared again at the end of it in, for example, Hamilton Palace, Birsay and Barnes. It then re-emerged eighty years later at Drumlanrig, again seventy years later at Duff House and then indeed, 100 years further on in William Playfair's hands at Donaldson's Hospital in Edinburgh. Thus did the sixteenth-century architectural battle of styles resurface during the nineteenth century – and history repeated itself. For once again, the formal axial design had to cede to the asymmetrical Marian romanticism of the baronial period: David Bryce's designs for houses like Ballikinrain, the Glen or Castlemilk proved far more popular. That true romantic eclectic, James Gillespie Graham, used both. He was formal in his resplendent, rectangular, towered Jacobean house of Murthly, and informally baronial in Brodick and Ayton, and concluded that the baronial of the latter allowed him much more freedom of expression as designer:

> On carefully considering the ancient Scottish style of architecture, I felt much impressed with its very great capabilities, both of picturesque and commanding external effect, and of easy adaptation for all the conveniences of modern life.[8]

When that otherwise astute observer and interpreter of Scottish historic architecture, Charles Rennie Mackintosh, came to hymn the national architecture of his country, he drew a sharp distinction between the romantic asymmetry of 'baronial' and the formalism of symmetry, and dismissed the latter as degraded, evidence of the corrupting influence of England.[9] Mackintosh was a victim of his own time, as much as MacGibbon and Ross upon whose books he drew so heavily.[10] Scottish Renaissance architecture was, to him, limited to the tower house – principally because he was hugely attracted to its architectural freedom and to its uninhibited method of piling material upon material. Indeed, it seems clear from his papers, that he perceived these houses to be the work of architects:

> The next quality I will mention is the extraordinary facility of our style in decorating constructing [*sic*], and in converting structural and useful features into elements of beauty. . . . The treatment of windows supplies an endless treasury of architectural loveliness. . . . And generally whatever feature, whether homely or otherwise, which construction or utility demanded, was at once enlisted, and that with right goodwill and heartiness, among the essential elements of the design.[11]

Conversely, it was that same lack of inhibition that persuaded most architectural historians (rather than architects) that such buildings were 'instinctive and arbitrary', purely the work of inspired artisans;[12] and the latter view proved more influential.[13]

The architecture of the Scottish Renaissance was not merely the work of inspired artisans. It was created by people who were regarded as architects by their contemporaries, and of whom high cultural achievement was

The Hill House, Helensburgh. Charles Rennie Mackintosh's masterpiece. (Author)

expected (*see* Appendix 1). Their duties resembled those required of an architect today, in respect of being responsible to others for design, contract and inspection on site.[14] Since the contracts (the specifications, rather) were insufficient for the construction of a building, architectural drawings would also have been required. Some designers were gentlemen of substance – Finnart, for example, Schaw, Conn of Auchry, Drummond of Carnock, Strathmore and Sir William Bruce; whereas others attained that status by rising from within the building industry – the Mylnes, Bels, Leipers, Murray and perhaps James Smith.

Being accepted by their peers or their clients as architects was one thing; but if they were architects in the sense of their equivalents elsewhere in Europe,[15] what explanation was there for their almost wilful rejection of the developing classical, Mannerist and baroque architectures of the continent? How could one gauge the quality of Scots designs in the light of the independence that the Scots showed from mainstream European architectural evolution? This book has not taken the route of scouring buildings for slight traces of classical influence, principally because most of the houses claimed to be symmetrical in that desperate search turn out to be far from symmetrical. Moreover, it was not the 'just-missed' symmetry of heavy-handed provincial architectural amateurs. Those houses were *fundamentally asymmetrical* and equally fundamentally *in visual balance*. They include two designed by two acknowledged architects building for themselves – Kilbaberton by and for Sir James Murray, and Balcaskie by and for Sir William Bruce. If ever they were going to get it right, it would be for themselves. So – after the 1530s at least – symmetry cannot have been the objective.

Left to itself, axis, symmetry and a broader classical language might well have come to direct Scottish architecture as it did elsewhere – to judge by Craignethan and some of its contemporaries, or by the control demonstrated in the palace at Stirling. This evolution was disrupted during the Marian period. The romantic asymmetry that then entered the national architecture – and still beat strong a century later – was essentially old-fashioned never mind how contemporary the plan of the state apartment which it clothed. Thereafter, the principal architectural objectives of the Scottish Renaissance country seat or *château* remained the expression of status and lineage, and the development of a contemporary national architecture founded in true Renaissance manner upon past models, ideals and details. Architecture was one of the principal ways in which the nobility contributed to the national cultural obsession with the reinterpretation and reinvention of history. Yet it was but an 'imposing mask' – for display only. Behind it, their plans were wholly unsentimental in their rejection of the communal life of the Middle Ages. Privacy and the separation of guests from family (and, indeed, the separation of the higher household from the lower household characterised by the emergence of the lettermeat hall)[16] were keenly embraced; and it was these changes that principally governed how the Scottish château changed its form. The preoccupation with the past was largely restricted to decoration and external expression.

So to what extent did Scotland seek to create a national architectural style in the mid-sixteenth century as has been suggested was an overt intention in France?[17] The changes to Scottish architecture over the 200 years were so substantial that it is far from clear which period could be taken to represent any national style. The evolution of its early Renaissance architecture was rudely interrupted, and the succeeding sparkling Marian period was too thoroughly French. The later Jacobean architects split between Court and country. So if there were, indeed, a national architecture, it would be found in the somewhat unromantic early Jacobean period – which happens to have been the most prolific. Architects like Mackintosh found it easy to identify the Scottish national style: anything before the early seventeenth century and the introduction of English-induced symmetry. They lumped the previous 150 years together as though they formed a homogeneous whole, as have so many since then. Yet when Smyth was building Methven in 1678, with its tight, symmetrical U-plan, he could justifiably claim to have built within a Scottish national style, for the house which he constructed would not really have been at home in any other country.

Scottish national architecture probably followed only a few simple precepts: functional modernity; adventurous but not innovative engineering; honouring the past by reusing the past; and communicating rank and status. The Victorians nicknamed the Earl of Huntly's house in Edinburgh the 'Speaking House' on account of its many mottos. The Scottish *château* was also a speaking house – a true 'architecture parlante' – to all those who understood its language. But Scots became strangers to their historic culture after the Union. The apparently warlike mien of their country seats was regarded as uncouth, and its lack of classical virtues an embarrassment. Its language became foreign.

This book has traced the Scottish château from 1500 to 1680; and, from a legacy of ruins, faint echoes and scanty documents, has attempted to retrieve and make sense of a largely vanished architectural culture. Fortunately, two contemporary voices articulate the country seat as they saw it – representing hospitality, lineage and ancient values, safely distant from the corruptions of the city. Writing in 1578, Bishop John Lesley observed that:

> The noblemen had rather dwell in the fields, where not only are palaces but castles of strength and towers, which each has according to his substance; here I say they had rather dwell than in the towns. . . . With glad will and freely they use to lodge kin, friend and acquaintance – yea and strangers that turn into them.[18]

When Sir Richard Maitland, much travelled judge and father to Mary Queen of Scots' Secretary William and also to James VI's Chancellor, retired to his beloved House of Lethington in East Lothian in the 1550s, he invoked Virgil in his apostrophe to his house and his ancestors. As he sang (at length) to each part of his house, to its setting and to its view, he embraced in microcosm the subjects of this book. He hymned its walls, its construction, its height, its battlements reaching to the heaven (it is well understood that Maitland had become blind, for Lethington is far from the tallest of such houses – squat, even), its orchards, knots, alleys, its butts and its calm silence after dusk:

Lethington (now Lennoxlove), East Lothian. (RCAHMS)

O Lethington
Which standis fair on Tyne,
Whose worthy praises and renown
Transcendis my ingyne.   [imagination]
Thou meritis Homer or Virgill
Thy worship to advance
And put thy name digne and noble,   [dignified]
In due rememberance . . .
Thy groundis deep and toppis high
Uprising in the air,
Thy vaultis pleasant are to see,
They are so great and fair . . .
Thou hast a thousand pleasures more
That my tongue cannot tell.[19]

Appendix 1
Design and Construction

All things anent the finishing of the masonwork cannot be set down in writ.

> Contract, George Hutcheson and William Miller 1611

The only way not to be cheated is to have no work.

> Patrick, 1st Earl of Strathmore in 1686
> on the building industry

Some fabric of almost 1,000 country seats built in Scotland between 1500 and 1680 has survived, and records imply that the number would be multiplied several times if one were to include those that have since been destroyed or altered beyond recognition. If the known programmes of extension and alteration were taken into account, that figure would rise commensurately. It is an enormous quantity of building for a small country of low population. This appendix focuses particularly on architecture, design and contracting and how they might have interrelated.

There is a general presumption that Scotland remained an architect-free zone until the late seventeenth century – a presumption that synchronises beautifully with the revision *downward* of Scotland's Renaissance culture. Given that there were no architectural academies in Scotland, and that no drawings survive from before the later seventeenth century, there has emerged the belief that the architectural profession only began with Sir William Bruce, followed by James Smith. Most of the country's earlier Renaissance architecture was described as *vernacular*, or one shaped by masons working to ideas imported by their patrons.[1] Most Scottish châteaux are described as such. Vernacular, by definition, implies rather more than just being built within native traditions. It characterises buildings constructed *without intellectual input*: created within tradition and with traditional materials and only slowly reactive to cultural movement or technological change. So a virtual inverted snobbery emerged in the twentieth-century insistence on describing a skilled designer as a mason, even when his seventeenth-century clients called him architect:[2] witness the perverse desire to disallow Tobias Bauchop, who designed Logie Church in 1684, the title architect[3] which his clients for the

Steeple at Dumfries Town House ascribed to him.[4] His ashlar-faced town house in Alloa was one of the most sophisticated small town house compositions of later seventeenth-century Scotland, and he must have enjoyed the patronage of the Earl of Mar. Although John Mylne had been entrusted with the plan of Panmure, and Robert, his nephew, was not only the undertaker of Holyrood under Bruce, but also architect-developer of two squares of mansion flats – Edinburgh's Mylne's Court and Mylne's Square – both men are still classed as masons, building operatives,[5] implying that they had, perhaps, got above themselves by claiming the title on their gravestone. Qualitatively, their designs far outshine some of the sublunary products of nineteenth-century provincial architects, for whom attribution of the title architect appears to present no difficulty.

The distinctiveness of Scots houses of the earlier periods was ascribed to ignorance of architectural movements on the continent.[6] Such assumptions – strange in view of Scotland's cultural and trading links, and widespread knowledge of contemporary poetry, music, literature and of emblematics – are based on lack of understanding of the rationale underlying Scottish architecture. It is evident from the books on emblematics from England or Holland that speedily reached those painting Scottish interiors,[7] or from the contemporary engravings of Hans Burgkmair used by those carving the Palace of Stirling in 1538–40 that access to the culture of the continent presented little problem.

Whether or not there are any architectural plans surviving undiscovered within libraries, architectural plans there most certainly were. Murray was paid for one for the Parliament House, as was Wallace for Heriot's and Aytoun for Innes; and Lauderdale was forever exchanging designs for Brunstane and Thirlestane with Bruce and annotating upon them. Again and again surviving building contracts refer to a 'draught'. Even Strathmore waxed vehement on the need for a plan. Moreover, some surviving contracts have been used to demonstrate how architects (even if they had existed) would have been bypassed by a contract directly between client and mason, thus perpetuating the old ways. However, a close reading of some of those building contracts implies otherwise. Despite their great detail, it would usually have been impossible to build the house from those contracts without any visual accompaniment. They resembled, rather, the detailed specifications that later architects wrote on their drawings.

One of the very few Scottish non-royal library catalogues that survive for the period, that of Adam Bothwell, Bishop of Orkney (he who conducted the disastrous marriage of Mary Queen of Scots to the Earl of Bothwell in Holyrood in 1567, was then deposed for doing so, re-appointed and then charged with simony),[8] contains the appropriate treatises. Catalogued after his death in 1592, the library was that of an educated, learned and sophisticated humanist, and contained, besides many religious tracts in Latin, French and Italian, the works of Rabelais, the great deeds of Pantagruel, Macchiavelli, and countless literary and poetic works, several books on architecture, including Serlio's third volume, and four books of architecture by P. Cataneio Senese.[9] Such – or even more extensive – libraries with architectural content probably existed elsewhere. Even the tiny estate of Nicholas Hood, a poor limner or painter who died in 1703, contained a library with books on perspective and also what appears to be volumes by Alberti and Vignola.[10] Ignorance of continental cultural movements cannot therefore have been behind Scotland's failure to conform to them.

Building was a principal means by which the Crown and magnates conveyed their cultural ambitions, and the agent was the designer or architect. The term architect, in its modern sense, was new to the Renaissance, another rediscovery of the ways of the Ancients – from Vitruvius through Alberti. In many ways comparable to our modern use, it required a knowledge of architectural principles, the ability to design and the ability to instruct and to control building work. The principal difference was that, in Alberti's terms, architecture was something that people did when they really *were* something else.[11] In the first instance, however, design was being given a theoretical foundation. It was not sufficient to be able to design buildings that were occupiable. Alberti believed that an architect had to aspire higher:

> I should explain exactly whom I mean by an architect; for it is no carpenter that I would have you compare to the greatest exponents of other disciplines; the carpenter is but an instrument in the hands of the architect. Him I consider the architect, who by sure and wonderful reason and method, knows both how to devise through his own mind and energy, and to realise by construction, whatever can be most beautifully fitted out for the noble needs of man, by the movements of weights and the joining and massing of bodies.[12]

So the use of the term 'architect' or (in Scotland 'architector') carried as much an implication of intellectual and cultural achievement as technical proficiency.

To describe the creation of Scottish Renaissance architecture, therefore, in terms of the *medieval* European pattern of 'a co-operative process between the patron . . . and the master mason, or other master tradesman'[13] goes against the perception of contemporaries. The Renaissance ideal was one in which the patron would be expected to be knowledgeable in architecture (*vide* the Earls of Bothwell and Huntly), advised and guided by the *conceiver* of the building.[14] Most of the buildings discussed in this book were conceived in three dimensions, and most of the designers were architects in the contemporary sense. It could be that the problem lies in our interpretation of the title.

Too sharp a distinction between architect and mason might be artificial, depending upon the definition of 'architect'. It now implies a lengthy and specific training in design, whether through apprenticeship in the early nineteenth-century model, or by attending an academic/vocational course. It was different three centuries ago. Such training as there was – even on the continental model – was reserved for craftsmen, of whom masons were the pre-eminent. Others learnt in other ways, usually by studying the Ancients or available publications. When William Schaw drew up the first Statutes for Freemasons in 1598, he laid down the expectation that the *Art of Memory* should be at the heart of the training of masons.[15] So masons were consequently expected to have knowledge and understanding of a highly charged symbolic language in which a building's significance extended far beyond a set of efficient chambers. Fixed with a twentieth-century conception, we tend to attribute the title only to those who 'might be called upon to supply plans and drawings and to exercise professional control over building operations'.[16] Since masons appeared to have had a similar duty, the distinction between them and architects remains cloudy, and it may be significant that it was in Scotland, following Schaw, that masonic lodges first welcomed non-mason members, to bring the two together.[17]

The unease at our using the word architect for those who conceived the Scottish château (an unease not shared by MacGibbon and Ross) probably has a cultural origin: namely that the buildings showed no evidence of the classical proportional systems and decorative approaches to architecture evident on the continent. Sir William Bruce's acceptance as an architect appears to have had little to do with his substantial construction, his planning innovation, his acts of patronage or directorship of works – for they were similar to many of his predecessors. It was linked to the fact that in three of his buildings – Holyrood, Kinross and Hopetoun – he used the international language of contemporary continental architecture (even if in a very particular way). The role ascribed to him within British architectural history was that he would 'design unfortified houses for the first generation of Scottish lairds to realise that the tower house was an anachronism, and to persuade them to abandon corbel and crowstep in favour of cornice and pediment'.[18] Scottish architecture, as this book has demonstrated, consisted of far more than fortified tower houses long before Bruce. The plan of the country house had evolved continuously, in the manner typical of northern Europe, to meet changing demands of hierarchy and privacy, and new concepts of the relationship between house, courts, yards, gardens and the countryside beyond. Indeed, most of Bruce's finest designs were not in the classical manner. The twentieth-century mindset has been that to earn the status of architect, a person would have to be able to demonstrate knowledge of buildings elsewhere, and show the influence of Renaissance architectural monographs – of Serlio, du Cerceau, Vignola or de l'Orme. It was too limited a perspective.

The habit specifying workmanship, dimensions or materials in contracts by reference to another building – the windows of Dreel to be as large and complete as those in the Hall of Kellie, for example[19] – has been taken as further proof of the absence of architects. Yet not only is specification by reference still practised nowadays, most surviving seventeenth-century drawings are too small in scale to contain exact dimensions of, say, windows. So specification by reference to another building could imply an increasing degree of precision sought by the designer rather than the converse.

If, however, the architect may be defined, *inter alia*, as a person with the ability to conceive an idea in three dimensions, draw it out, instruct the necessary tradesmen and, indeed, possibly supervise the work on site, what evidence can be inferred of such a role being exercised during this period in the absence of architectural drawings? The palace at Stirling, mostly built between 1538 and 1540, provides a good case study.[20] There was no designer officially identified at the time, and no drawing survives.

The principal mover was Sir James Hamilton of Finnart, who directed and paid for the works, and to whom contemporaries attributed the design. His role has been described as 'no different in kind from that of other patrons and leading officials of the day'.[21] When working at Linlithgow, he had evidently not been Master of Works for that was Sir Thomas Johnston,[22] 'oursear [overseer] to the work . . . wnder my maister Schir James Hammylton of Fynnart, knicht'.[23] A cleric and notary, Johnston was a close associate of Finnart, and the function of the Master of Works was primarily management and the keeping of accounts. When Finnart took responsibility for the palace at Stirling from Master of Works Sir James Nicholson in the summer of 1538, his remuneration was ten times greater – implying a role different in kind.[24] The distinction between Finnart and others is signalled by his title Master of Works *Principal*, less a technical appointment than an appointment in the royal household itself.

Finnart was far more intimately tied to the palace construction at Stirling than anyone else. If he was not the conceiver of the design, someone of high skill and knowledge surely was, and nobody else emerges from the records with remotely as good a claim. During 'the time he remained there upon the building of the new work at Stirling' he lodged with Mrs Atkins at a cost of £65, and contracted directly with suppliers and sub-contractors. He even pawned two of his silver flagons to Mungo Tennant for £56 to pay for some timber. On his death, money was outstanding to Walter Cousland for Eastland boards (Estonian timber), to the ironmaster William Hill for the balance for the ironwork delivered to the palace; and to a smith in Linlithgow for an iron window seemingly carried to Stirling by Finnart himself.[25]

The design of the palace required three-dimensional imagination and ingenuity. New levels and a new geometry had to be created from an extremely difficult, steep site cluttered with existing structures – all of which had to be concealed behind the appearance of order and symmetry. Its carved programmes required knowledge of contemporary European engravings, its façade composition may have been inspired by buildings in Italy and its ceiling decoration by work in Poland. In Alberti's terms, therefore, Finnart had carried out the role of architect.

Two charters, received in the last year of his life, imply that the king recognised Finnart in the role of Court architect. On 9 September 1539, Finnart was made 'Maister of Works Principal to our Soverane Lord of all his werkis within his realm now [building] or to be [built], and to have three or four deputies under him who shall answer to him'.[26] Foremost among those deputies must have been John Scrymgeour of the Myres (a laird), principal Master of Works at Falkland, Sir Thomas Johnston, Master of Works at Linlithgow (a cleric), and John Hamilton of Cragye (or Millburn), Finnart's successor in post (likewise a cleric).[27] Finnart received a further charter on 1 January 1540:

Ane letter made to James Hamilton of Finnart Knight, charging all the Captains, Constables and Keepers of our Sovereign Lord's castles, houses, places, palaces and fortalices wherever they be within the realm to suffer and let the said James, his servants and workmen, to enter in the same, as often as they please, for vysing [advice], seing [inspecting], mending, and biging [building] thereof where myster [need] is, and to lay sand, lime, stones, timber, and other stuff necessary therein, to the effect foresaid, under the pain of tinsale [loss] of their offices and punishment of their persons with all rigour etc.[28]

The charter implied a building team (not unlikely given that he had been paying for the design and construction of the Palace of Stirling out of his own pocket). Those 'servants and workmen' would probably have included the master masons with whom Finnart had worked such as John French, mason at Linlithgow, whom he proposed as king's master mason for life,[29] or John Kedder (or Cadder), master mason at Boghouse, on whom he settled land.[30] His team may also have included specialists and suppliers: Hill the ironmaster, Thomas Peebles the glassinwright (glasswright or glazier), or Walter Cousland, timber merchant.

The language of the second charter implies that Finnart had almost completed Stirling and was ready to move on. But its threat to punish the keepers of the royal properties 'with all rigour' implies ominous regal impatience with the lack of cooperation being experienced by Finnart. Captains and keepers were among the most responsible of royal officials, often noblemen, and should not normally require such minatory instruction. Finally, it implies that Finnart, his deputies, servants and workmen were being formed into something resembling a royal direct-labour organisation in place of the earlier casual arrangements. It confirms the king's ambition to use architecture as one of the principal symbolic activities of his reign.

Interpretations of Finnart's activities skate around his motivation. On the one hand, his role has been categorised as 'essentially that of a strong-minded private patron and of an energetic superior master of works for his monarch';[31] whereas, on the other, 'the job description sounds somewhat mundane for the son of the first Earl of Arran'.[32] Quite so – and Finnart had shown no propensity for the humdrum. His willingness to deviate from affairs of the realm or from controlling his burgeoning estates in order to spend time on site or pick up ironwork from Linlithgow only makes sense if Finnart was motivated by the role of devyser or architect (and we know he 'devised' or invented the machine that led to his execution). Whereas masters of works – the contract administrators – may have existed at individual projects, Finnart was awarded overall control and direction of the royal building programme throughout the country. Since the financial scrutineers or auditors were the comptrollers or the lords of Exchequer, Finnart occupied other ground. Given his birth and the cultural intentions of king and Court, it is plausible to conclude that his contribution was that of architect. It may, therefore, be taken as a distinctive feature of the Scots Court that in the immediate royal circle of both James V and James VI there was an architect – Sir James Hamilton of Finnart, and then William Schaw.

Contracts for lesser buildings might begin with a client statement of requirement, as may be judged from the contract to rebuild the House of Invermay, Perthshire, in May 1686. Invermay's rooms, storeys and

dimensions were first specified in broad terms, and the house thereafter –
seemingly at the builder's choice – was to be 'devised and contrived' by
Sir William Bruce of Kinross, Robert Mill (Mylne) 'or any other relevant
architect that the laird shall think fit'.[33] That is a narrower specification of
duties than, probably, those undertaken by Finnart at Stirling or Murray
at Linlithgow, and restricts the architectural function to that of applying
fashionable form, veneer and detail to a house already conceived.
Typically of these early contracts, it is for only part of the work.
Untypically, the contract is not with a mason or craftsman, but with a
neighbouring laird and social equal, John Craigie of Dunbarnie. So much
information is lacking from the contract that it would have been
impossible to build Invermay from it. Drawings and contracts with other
trades would also have been required. The width of the house was
calculated as three bays of 16 feet each (the same as Partick), with the
option for the architect to extend it by 6 feet more.

Renaissance contracting is far from a foreign country. Much of it –
down to the inclusion of liquidated damages[34] or the builder having to put
an inhibition upon the client's assets for non-payment (as appears to have
been the outcome at Invermay)[35] – has an unpleasantly contemporary ring.
The client generally made arrangements for the supply of the materials,
the bulk of which would be sought from as close by as possible – perhaps
from the laird's own quarries or plantations.[36] In Angus, for example,
slates for the more important buildings like Hatton were usually the heavy
brown crumbly sandstone ones from Carmyllie, and were likely to require
a sturdier roof structure to carry them. Wealthier clients who could afford
to select their materials indicate what was fashionable: French glass for
Scone Palace and Gallery House, blue (rather than local) slates from
Logiealmond for Invermay, very expensively imported Caithness slates for
Winton, or slates from Camstradden, Loch Lomond, for Linlithgow,[37] and
white stone from Queensferry for Gallery.[38] The regional descriptions
provided to Sir Robert Sibbald and Sibbald's own publications convey an
overriding sense of busyness in identifying existing or new sources of
building materials – such as 'here [Mountwhanie] is of late found good
slate for covering houses'[39] with the implication that it was better than the
local product.

Stone for Invermay was to come from the laird's own quarry, and lime
from the Lomond Hills or from Pitlessie, whereas timber and iron were to
be collected from Bridge of Earn, presumably off a boat. Timber joists,
coming through Dundee from Norway or the Baltic, may have arrived
already dressed and sized, since in several houses, they are numbered.[40]
Scotland's shortage of long-span timber is a primary cause of the distinctive
nature of its architecture – no wide spans, and none of the soaring
roofscapes of France. So timbers were very carefully selected for their
purpose, and imported even for humbler buildings in remote locations,
rather than just making do with what was available.[41] Clients allowed the
builder to retain whatever materials he took down on site – for example,
the materials resulting from the removal of the inner closes of Invermay or
of Kelburn,[42] or salvageable glass from Scone Palace – but made a suitable
deduction for it. Sometimes, lairds provided part of the labour. Invermay
contracted, for example, to supply 120 man-days of labour.

The contract between the 26-year-old George Hutcheson and William Miller, the master mason he brought all the way from Kilwinning in Ayrshire to Partick on the north bank of the Clyde, was for mason work only.[43] It gives no hint of the timberwork nor the interior or exterior finishes that would have been required. It is, indeed, more of a specification than a contract, and provides insufficient information even to draw out a floor plan. Since it is impossible to attempt elevations from it, drawings must have been imperative. Hutcheson was to provide all the materials (those from a villa formerly belonging to the Archbishops of Glasgow might have been on site) and Miller the 'layers, hewers and barrowmen'. Hutcheson had to provide sharp irons, and employ a wright to make a scaffold, with planks and walkways, centreing for both vaults and relieving arches above doors and windows. The contract provided for four stage payments: £120 up front, and £100 each upon the laying of the joists, reaching the wall-head, and completion. Hutcheson was also to provide meat and drink at the laying of the lintels (presumably an ancestor of the topping-out ceremony). When building Panmure, its earl had likewise to provide most of the materials, including iron, lead, lime, stone and material for the scaffolding. Milne's task as designer/contractor for Panmure was to provide the masons and erect the form and skeleton of the house. Panmure contracted separately with the wright and, presumably, with all other trades.[44]

Contract timescales were tight. Judging by the fact that many began in April, little external work may have been done over the winter. The house of Partick was to be complete within a year, with no variations permitted: 'Thair sall be na occasion of ony new task or new agriement [there] anent.'[45] The workmen needed remain on site only so long as Hutcheson kept them well supplied with the correct materials. Should either party break the contract, they or their cautioners (their guarantors or underwriters) were liable for £100 liquidate damages in addition to completion of the terms of contract, under threat of horning (outlawry), warding (imprisonment) and poinding (goods seized). Work proceeded surprisingly speedily, with the main structure complete within one or at most two seasons. So it would be wise to view all those extended dates given to the construction of the Scottish château with scepticism. Whereas construction might be interrupted by penury, feud, exile or death, building a country house need not extend to more than two years. Most of the Palace of Stirling was complete within two years – a programme that could not be achieved today.

That Hutcheson went to Kilwinning for his master mason implies that good tradesmen could command their own market, and this certainly appears to be the case for painters and decorators,[46] gardeners and plasterers. That John Melville (or Mellin) signed his initials on the 1590s painted ceiling in Delgaty implies a certain standing since most of the other transformers of the Renaissance interior remain unidentified.[47] Building accounts identify John White as the plasterer at Winton, but whether he was also responsible for the comparable work in Kellie and Edinburgh Castle remains unknown. Valentine Jenkin, who painted the frieze in the chapel in Stirling Castle, also worked at the Glasgow Tolbooth, Falkland Palace and at Hamilton and Kinneil Palaces.[48] The painter John Anderson was working at Huntly when he was summoned south to work on the palace in Edinburgh Castle in 1617. James Workman, a painter who was also appointed Marchmont Herald in 1597, owned a house in Burntisland (and hence may have been the author of the Rossend ceiling),[49] and worked on several notable royal projects, almost certainly with William Schaw and then with James Murray.[50]

The better records of the later seventeenth century make it much easier to follow plasterers, painters or wrights from one great project to the next. Jacob de Wet, summoned from Amsterdam by Sir William Bruce to paint in Holyrood, also worked at Balcaskie, Kellie, Hatton, Panmure and the chapel at Glamis.[51] The King's Wright, James Bain, worked at Stirling and Edinburgh Castles and at Ravelston, and acted in the role of timber contractor and supplier. The team of plasterers used by the Maitland family moved from Holyrood, Brunstane and Thirlestane to Hatton and Dudhope.

Of those who commanded their own market, masons were at the apex, and it is often only of the mason that the record speaks. Those who mutated from being a responsive tradesman to designer or architect were generally masons – with the possible exception of the Master of Works Drummond of Carnock who may have been related to the Drummond master wrights of the sixteenth century. Masons could be remarkably inventive when in their own element, but were very conservative when faced with new technologies. In modern parlance, the mason was the structural engineer, and greater ingenuities were being expected of him. Walls were getting much thinner – Partick's were under half the thickness of the typical fifteenth-century tower house – and skyline structural gymnastics that much more complicated. Yet there was very little creative exploitation of timber in Scotland and a distinct distrust of brick. Castle Hill House in Montrose, for example, contains brick cross-walls that are far thicker than they need be for brick, and thinner than they would have been in stone.

In conclusion, the twentieth-century perception of the sixteenth and seventeenth centuries has been fogged by a cultural presumption that the absence of classicism in their architecture implied the absence of people worthy of the title architect. That was not *contemporaries*' perception, and it should not be ours. There are many similarities between design and construction then and now. A re-evaluation of Scottish châteaux as deliberate cultural products, to which this book is just an introduction, is likely to reveal yet more surprises in how they were conceived, the proportional systems used, the symbolism inherent in their design, and in how they were built and fitted out.

Appendix 2
Scottish Monarchs, 1513–1689

Monarch		Exercise of Power
James IV, died 1513, at Flodden		
James V, 1513–42	1515–17	Regent Duke of Albany
	1517–20	Group led by 1st Earl of Arran
	1520–2	Regent Duke of Albany
	1522–3	Group led by Queen Margaret and 1st Earl of Arran
	1523–4	Regent Duke of Albany
	1524–5	Queen Margaret and 1st Earl of Arran
	1525–8	Earl of Angus
	1528–42	James V holds power
Mary I, 1542–67	1542–54	2nd Earl of Arran, later Duke of Châtelherault
	1554–60	Mary of Guise, Queen Regent
	1561–7	Mary I assumes power
	1567–8	Regent James, Earl of Moray
James VI, 1568–1625	1568–70	Regent James, Earl of Moray (assassinated)
	1570	Regent Matthew, Earl of Lennox (assassinated)
	1570–1	Regent John, Earl of Mar (died)
	1571–8	Regent James, Earl of Morton (deposed)
	1578–81	Regent James, Earl of Morton (executed)
	1581–2	Esme, Duke of Lennox (exiled)
	1582–3	William, Earl of Gowrie (executed)
	1584–5	James Stewart, Earl of Arran (deposed, assassinated)
	1585–1625	James VI holds power
	1603–11	Earl of Dunbar, Treasurer
	1611–25	Earl of Dunfermline, Chancellor
Charles I, 1625–49	1638–51	Covenanting regimes
Charles II, 1650–85	1651–60	Scotland under Cromwellian occupation
	1660–85	Charles II assumes power
	1660–3	Earl of Midlothian
	1663–7	Earl of Rothes
	1669–81	Duke of Lauderdale, virtual viceroy
	1679–82	James, Duke of York, virtual viceroy
James VII, 1685–9		

Glossary

This section is indebted to *A Dictionary of the Older Scottish Tongue*, ed. Sir W.A. Craigie (Edinburgh, 1937ff); *Dictionary of Scottish Building*, G.L. Pride (Edinburgh, 1996), and the *Oxford English Dictionary*.

aedicule	the framing of an opening, usually a window, by columns topped with a pediment so that it resembles a temple façade in miniature
aumbry	a wall recess; sometimes a cupboard for food. Particularly in a chapel or church for keeping sacramental vessels, etc.
barmkin	orig. a livestock enclosure, later legalese for walls of the inner or outer court or close
bartizan	projecting part of a battlement, usually corbelled out at the corners, and assumed to have had a defensive purpose
battaling	battlements, usually stone (sometimes implying crenellated) but occasionally a simple corbelled parapet
big, to	to build
biggins	buildings
caponier	a covered passage across a ditch, used militarily as a protected musketeer emplacement
clour, to	to hack out stone with hammer and chisel
chamber of dais (deas)	principal chamber, occasionally with a bed, considerably more private than the hall.
commendator	a person appointed to head a religious house not of that order. Post-reformation, a person appointed to enjoy the estates of a religious house
cottown (cottoun)	a group of cottages
châtelet	structure in the form of a miniature château, usually a gatehouse
couthy	homely, unpretentious, genial
corbel	projection from a wall-plane (usually stone, sometimes timber), intended to support a structure above
crowstep (corbie-step)	rectangular stones forming the gable of a building, each one stepped back from the one below
deidlie feid	feud which encompasses death
doocot yard	the walled enclosure near a country house containing the dovecote, usually in one corner
enceinte	the principal enclosing wall of a fortification, sometimes curtain-wall
enfilade	(domestic definition) a suite of rooms opening into each other (e.g. the state apartment), implying that the doors are all in the same location so that you can seen from one end through to the other
erchis	defies dictionary search: likely – an earth dyke, or unlikely – a hedgehog
fermtoun	collection of rural buildings including a farm
foreyard	the outer court
godbairne	godchild
glacis	a (usually artificial) defensive embankment designed to deflect cannonballs
indweller	resident
gunloop	opening in a wall for a firearm
harl	an external rough-cast coating of lime, sand and gravel
horning	being at the horn means outlawed. The threat of horning for malfeasance during a building contract was the useful threat of being outlawed for failure to fulfil its terms
intromittors	people interfering with the property of another whether or not they had right to do so
jamm (jamb)	(in reference to a house): a projecting wing
kirktoun	a small village around a kirk (church)
laigh	literally 'low'; by implication, lesser or less important. Examples are 'laigh biggins' – the lesser buildings (usually farm court) of a country seat; or 'laigh hall' – lower (always ground-floor) hall

lettermeit (lettermeat)	literally, the last or left-over meat hall, consequently the lower hall
lymmares	villains or malefactors
machicolations	openings between projecting parapet corbels through which objects may be dropped on invaders
multures	percentage of grain due to a miller or mill proprietor for having grain ground
neuk	corner or nook
osaris	osiers, a form of willow
policies	the estate lands of a country house, usually implying the improved or cultivated lands in its immediate neighbourhood
plenish	to furnish and fit out
poind	distrain, seize or impound
preclair	shining, lustrous, renowned, magnificent, splendid in the landscape
quhilk	which
re-entrant	the angle created between the main house and a projecting wing
roup	forced sale – usually through bankruptcy or forfeiture
rowme	an estate or farm (as well as a room).
sailzie	(i.e. sally): something that projects from a wall – corbel, battlement or oriel window
scale-and-platt stair	in contrast to the turnpike, a stair which rises in straight flights (scale) with platforms (platt)
smiddy	blacksmith's workshop
sowchis	haystacks (perhaps)
sustainit	sustained
squinch	arched support across a re-entrant carrying a structure above – in Scotland, usually a turnpike staircase (e.g. Luffness and Glenbuchat)
teind	(literally tenth) tithe.
tailledouce	a picture produced by line engraving on a metal plate
tholed	endured
trauchled	sore beset
transe	corridor or passage, usually vaulted, usually at ground level
turnpike	spiral staircase, and applied to varying degrees of grandeur
wall-walk	otherwise parapet-walk: outdoor passage at the head of the wall running between battlement and roof
ward	to put into custody
wrythen	ornately twisted
yards	walled enclosures in the vicinity of the mansion

For the sake of simplicity, the dates given in this book follow the conventions of the modern calendar.

Conversion Table

1 inch	=	2.54 centimetres
1 foot	=	0.3 metres
1 yard	=	0.9 metres
1 mile	=	1.6 kilometres

Notes

ABBREVIATIONS

APS	*The Acts of the Parliaments of Scotland*
HMC	Historic Manuscripts Commission
JSAH	*Journal of the Society of Architectural Historians*
MW a/c	*Accounts of the Masters of Works*
NAS	National Archives of Scotland
NTS	National Trust for Scotland
RIAS	The Royal Incorporation of Architects in Scotland
RMS/RGS	*Register of the Great Seal*
RSS	*Register of the Secret Seal*
RPC	*Register of the Privy Council*
TA	*Accounts of the Lord High Treasurer of Scotland*
PSAS	*Proceedings of the Society of Antiquaries of Scotland*
RCAHMS	Royal Commission on the Ancient and Historic Monuments of Scotland

1. CHANGING PERCEPTIONS

1. T. Pennant, *Tour through Scotland* (London, 1796), vol. ii, p. 200.
2. GD/120/20/ Box 1/16–1.
3. GD 314/579.
4. The pioneering work was D. Howard, *Scottish Architecture from the Reformation to the Restoration* (Edinburgh, 1995).
5. See L. Kanerva, *Defining the Architect in Fifteenth Century Italy* (Helsinki, 1998), p. 111.
6. D. Walker, 'The adaptation and restoration of tower houses', in M. Davis, ed., *Restoring Scotland's Castles* (Glasgow, 2000), p. 1. 'Until the restoration of Charles II to the throne in 1660, the tower house had been the universal landed proprietor's house type in Scotland.'
7. T.M. Devine, *The Scottish Nation* (London, 1999), p. xxi: 'the tower house, designed mainly for defence . . .'.
8. Howard, *Reformation to Restoration*, p. 7.
9. R. Sampson, 'The Rise and Fall of Tower-Houses in Post-Reformation Scotland', in R. Sampson, ed., *The Social Archeology of Houses* (Edinburgh, 1991), p. 224. 'Scotland lacked the requisite knowledge to build [classical architecture].'
10. H. Colvin, 'The beginnings of the architectural profession in Scotland', *Architectural History* 29 (London, 1986), pp. 173–4.
11. *Le Petit Robert* has several definitions for a château of which only the earliest is 'a fortified feudal dwelling defended by an enclosure . . .' etc. By the time of the Renaissance, the definition used in this book had become commonplace, military castles becoming increasingly referred to as 'châteaux-forts'.
12. In *Robert Adam and his Circle* (London, 1962) John Fleming quotes the 4th Lord Arniston's 1811 *Narrative of improvements at Arniston* of his grandfather that he 'either began to build the new house . . . or at least took down part of the old château with a view to preparing for it', p. 50. Arniston almost certainly contains fabric from the earlier château within the villa created by William Adam.
13. Sir William Brereton, quoted in P. Hume Brown, ed., *Early Travellers in Scotland* (new edn, Edinburgh, 1973), p. 148.
14. D. MacGibbon and T. Ross, *The Castellated and Domestic Architecture of Scotland* (Edinburgh, 1895).
15. D. Walker, 'The architecture of MacGibbon and Ross – the background to the books', in D. Breeze, ed., *Studies in Scottish Antiquity* (Glasgow, 1984).
16. Pitsligo in MacGibbon and Ross, *Castellated and Domestic*, vol. iv, p. 294.
17. MacGibbon and Ross, *Castellated and Domestic*, vol. i. Period 1 1200–1300; Period 2 1300–1400; Period 3 1400–1542; and Period 4 1542–1700.
18. R. Chambers, *The Domestic Annals of Scotland* (Edinburgh, n.d. – presumed *c.* 1842), p. 5.
19. Ibid., pp. 173 and 256.
20. Leaving aside references to monarchs and towns, the index shows that by far the most frequent subject was witchcraft, followed by pest and dearth (plague and famine), Presbyterians and Catholics. Architecture, music and art do not figure in the index at all.
21. Chambers, *Domestic Annals*, vol. i, pp. 521 and 550.
22. Quoted in Margaret Sanderson, *Robert Adam and Scotland* (Edinburgh, 1990), p. 88.
23. In East Lothian alone, Pinkie, Lennoxlove (Lethington) and Luffness. See photographic boxes in the Royal Commission on the Ancient and Historic Monuments of Scotland.
24. *Lennoxlove Guidebook* (Haddington, 1981).
25. T. Hannan, *Famous Scottish Houses* (London, 1928), pp. 119 and 27.
26. J. Warrack, *Domestic Life in Scotland, 1488–1688* (London, 1920), p. 99: 'But almost with the stroke of the new century there came a change.'

27. J. Zeune, *The Last Scottish Castles* (Leidorf, 1992), p. 13.

28. M. nan Rosenfeld, ed., *Serlio on Domestic Architecture* (New York, 1978), p. 50.

29. J. Lees-Milne, *Tudor Renaissance* (London, 1951), pp. 144–5.

30. P. Durand, *An Old Scottish Town House* (Glasgow, 1953).

31. T. Lugton, *The Old Ludgings of Glasgow* (Glasgow, 1901), photo facing p. 34. Also drawing by William Simpson in the Mitchell Library, reproduced in McKean, Walker and Walker, *Central Glasgow, an Illustrated Architectural Guide* (Edinburgh, 1990).

32. C. Innes, *Sketches of Early Scotch History* (Edinburgh, 1861), referring to the tastes of Sir Hugh Campbell of Cawdor and his wife Henrietta Stewart, pp. 425–6.

33. N. Tranter, *The Fortified House in Scotland* (Edinburgh, 1962–8).

34. A. MacKechnie, 'Design in early Post Reformation Scots Houses', in Gow and Rowan, eds, *Scottish Country Houses 1600–1914* (Edinburgh, 1995), pp. 15–35.

35. S. Cruden, *The Scottish Castle* (Edinburgh, 1963); A. MacKechnie, 'Design of post-Reformation Houses'.

36. D.J. Ross, *Musick Fyne: Robert Carver and the Art of Music in sixteenth-century Scotland* (Edinburgh, 1993).

37. R. Mason, 'Humanism and political culture', in R. Mason and N. Macdougall, eds, *People and Power* (Edinburgh, 1992), p. 131.

38. See E. Cowan, 'The darker version of the Scots Renaissance', in I. Cowan and D. Shaw, eds, *The Renaissance and Reformation in Scotland* (Edinburgh, 1983).

39. Giovanni Ferrario was in Kinloss. See C. Edington, *Court and Culture in Renaissance Scotland* (East Linton, 1995), p. 446. There are now many other books on aspects of Scottish Renaissance culture, for example, S. Mapstone and J. Wood, eds, *The Rose and the Thistle* (East Linton, 1998), Cowan and Shaw, eds, *Renaissance and Reformation*, R.A. Mason, *Kingship and Commonweal* (East Linton, 1998), and J.H. Williams, ed., *Stewart Style* (East Linton, 1996), *inter alia*.

40. 'I, Andrew de Cesize, of the Diocese of Orleans, but descended from a most noble family of Scots, was elected procurator of the said nation.' Quoted in 'The Scottish Nation in Orleans University', in *Scottish History Society Miscellany* (Edinburgh, 1904), pp. 70–102.

41. J. Wormald, *Court, Kirk and Community* (London, 1981), p. 71.

42. Sir John Scot of Scotstarvit, *The Staggering State of Scots Statesmen from 1550–1660* (Edinburgh, 1754).

43. Sir James Melvill of Hal-Hil, *The Memoires* (London, 1683), p. 182. James Melvill was the younger brother of Sir Robert Melville of Murdocairney and adopted son of the modernising reformer and royal servant Henry Balnaves. See also Sir W. Fraser, *The Melvilles* (Edinburgh, 1890), p. 117.

44. *Maitland Miscellany* (Edinburgh, 1834), pp. 351 ff.

45. HMC, *Second Report Appendix* (London, 1870), p. 168.

46. David Hume of Godscroft, quoted Chambers, *Annals*, vol. i, p. 98.

47. Patrick, 1st Earl of Strathmore, *Glamis Book of Record*, ed. A.H. Millar (Edinburgh, 1890), p. 19.

48. I. Campbell, 'A Romanesque Revival and the Early Renaissance in Scotland', in *JSAH* 54.3 (September 1995); and I. Campbell, 'Linlithgow's princely palace and its influence in Europe', in *Architectural Heritage* (Edinburgh, 1995).

49. See Chapter 11.

50. M.H.B. Sanderson, *Ayrshire and the Reformation* (East Linton, 1997), p. 108.

51. Revd C. Rogers, ed., *Estimate of the Scottish Nobility during the Minority of James VI* (London, 1873): the Earl of Rothes, for example, had 'many gentlemen of his surname of Lesleys', p. 14.

52. J. Wormald, *Lords and Men in Scotland* (Edinburgh, 1985).

53. See Chapter 7.

54. This suggestion came from Charles Wemyss, and the memorable phrase from Mark Girouard.

55. It is not known what murals may have adorned St Giles'. A similar church interior – the Friary Church in Konstanz – is adorned with beautiful paintings on the octagonal columns with saints rising above them. There is only scant record of the vividness of the interior of Scottish medieval churches, such as the painting of the window embrasure of Turriff Church (McKean, *Banff and Buchan*, Edinburgh, 1989).

56. Robert Lindsay of Pitscottie, *The History of Scotland* (Edinburgh, 1778), p. 325.

57. Chambers, *Annals*, vol. i, pp. 249, 260, 232.

58. M. Bath, *Renaissance Decorative Painting in Scotland* (National Museums of Scotland, forthcoming), Chapter 1.

59. Obviously intended, but other than being implied by the drawing on Timothy Pont's map, difficult to be certain that it was built.

60. Clearly visible on Pont's map.

61. Mason and Macdougall, eds, *People and Power*, p. 60.

62. HMC, *Appendix to the Second Report*, p. 102. This was Adam of Cologne. See M.R. Apted and S. Hannabuss, *Scottish Painters, 1400–1700* (Edinburgh, 1978).

63. *Black Book of Taymouth*, ed. C. Innes (Taymouth, 1855), p. 441.

64. For Balloch, *Black Book*, p. 350; for Castle Lyon and Glamis, Glamis Papers Inventory, 255/7/2; for Finavon, A. Jervise, *Land of the Lindsays*, ed. J. Gammack (Edinburgh, 1882), Appendix viii, p. 425; for Fetteresso, NAS/RH13.

65. MacGibbon and Ross, *Castellated and Domestic*, vol. ii, p. 1.

66. Howard, *Reformation to Restoration*, p. 3, quoting Benesch 'renascence . . . is independent of superficial imitation of ancient forms'.

67. Thomas Morer, in Hume Brown, *Early Travellers*, pp. 274–5.

68. Sir Anthony Weldon, in Hume Brown, *Early Travellers*, pp. 97–103.

69. John Taylor, 'The Pennyless Pilgrimage or the Moneylesse Perambulation', in Hume Brown, *Early Travellers*, pp. 104–31.

70. Ibid., p. 127.

71. Or they could be deliberately misleading, as were Sir Robert Lorimer's at Formakin.

72. *The Register of the Great Seal of Scotland*, J. Balfour Paul and J. Maitland Thomson, eds (Edinburgh, 1883), items 160 and 2350. This dating is a relief, for otherwise the tower would seem terribly anachronistic for the late sixteenth-century date customarily given. Although it is generally thought that charters used standard terminologies in their descriptions of estates and buildings, that was not always so.

73. These tables are based upon the dates of building and extension contained within Mike Salter's *Castles of Scotland* series (Malvern, 1993–6). For consistency's sake, the dates given by Salter are always used even where new evidence indicates otherwise. The figures distinguish between new-build and addition, the latter taken from dates on, for example, dormer windows. Those that are dated broadly into the early or late sixteenth century have been included in the composite graphs.

74. John Lesley, Bishop of Ross, *History of Scotland* (Edinburgh, 1830), p. 8.

75. Rogers, *Estimate of the Scottish Nobility*.

76. *Letters to James VI* (Edinburgh, 1835): 'Ayant entendu que la langue francaise est fort necessaire pour bien converser avec les nations estrangers les plus civilises, et sachant being que V. M^ie a grande envie que j'employe bien ma temps.'

77. See Chapter 9

78. M. Glendinning, R. MacInnes, A. MacKechnie, *A History of Scottish Architecture* (Edinburgh, 1996), pp. 50–4.

79. J. Dunbar, *The Historic Architecture of Scotland* (London, 1966), p. 52.

80. *Leonardo da Vinci – the Mystery of the Madonna of the Yarnwinder*, ed. M. Kemp (Edinburgh, 1992), p. 29.

81. Cruden, *Castle*, pp. 164–5.

82. Cited in A. MacKechnie, 'James VI's Architects', in J. Goodare and M. Lynch, *The Reign of James VI* (East Linton, 2000), p. 159.

83. Kanerva, *Defining the Architect*, p. 20.

84. This matter is much more fully developed in the Appendix on design and construction.

85. C.R. Mackintosh, *The Architectural Papers*, ed. P. Roberston (Wendlebury, 1990), p. 52.

2. SOURCES FOR REDISCOVERY

1. T. Garnett, *Tour through the Highlands* (London, 1800), p. 65.

2. *Geographical Collections relating to Scotland made by Walter Macfarlane*, eds Sir A. Mitchell and J.T. Clark (Edinburgh, 1906–8), pp. 351 and 353.

3. J.M. Leighton, *History of the County of Fife* (Glasgow, 1840), pp. 51–61.

4. J. Dunbar and K. Davies, 'Some late 17th century building contracts', in *Scottish Historical Review* XI (Edinburgh, 1990), pp. 269–324.

5. Etienne Perlin, 'Description of the Kingdoms of England and Scotland', in P. Hume Brown, *Early Travellers in Scotland* (reprint, Edinburgh, 1973), p. 73.

6. Hume Brown, *Early Travellers*, p. 82.

7. 'A Scottish Journie 1641', *Scottish History Society Miscellany* (Edinburgh, 1904), pp. 271–87.

8. Robert Lindsay of Pitscottie, *The History of Scotland* (Edinburgh, 1778), p. 250. It is now thought that Pitscottie may have got much of his information from Sir David Lindsay of the Mount, courtier, poet and herald.

9. C. Lowther, *Our Journall into Scotland* (Edinburgh, 1894), p. 18.

10. J. Goodare, 'James VI's English Subsidy', in J. Goodare and M. Lynch, *The Reign of James VI* (East Linton, 2000), pp. 110–25.

11. R. Grant, in Goodare and Lynch, *James VI*, p. 102.

12. The Pont maps are in the Map Library, the National Library of Scotland.

13. Macfarlane, *Collections*.

14. Ibid., vol. ii, p. 43.

15. Macfarlane, *Collections*, vol. ii, p. 12.

16. Sir W. Fraser, *Chiefs of Grant*, vol. i (Edinburgh, 1883), p. 22.

17. Sir James Melvil of Hal-Hil, *The Memoires* (London, 1683), p. 27.

18. K. Brown, *Bloodfeud in Scotland 1573–1625* (Edinburgh, 1986), Chapter 8.

19. P.D.A. Harvey, *Topographical maps* (London, 1980) and P.D.A. Harvey, *Maps in Tudor England* (London, 1993).

20. For further information on the cartographic and political context of Timothy Pont, and on the contents of the maps themselves, see *Timothy Pont*, ed. I. Cunninghame (East Linton, 2001).

21. Pont 34.

22. Ibid.

23. Pont's MS map of Linlithgow, on the rear of a map of South Uist. See J. Stone, *The Pont Manuscript Maps of Scotland* (Tring, 1989), pp. 204–9.

24. See Diana Webster, *Guide to Symbols on Pont Manuscript Maps* (National Library of Scotland pamphlet, Edinburgh, 2000).

25. Translation: Ibid.

26. Pont 23a.

27. Pont 34a.

28. Pont 19b.

29. Linlithgow MSS, National Library of Scotland.

30. Pont 34b.

31. There is reason to believe the Angus map was prepared 1586/7 because Claypotts is shown with its two round towers still incomplete. Since those round towers received their cappings in 1588, Pont probably drew them no later than 1587.

32. RCAHMS LA/412; supported by the painting by Robert Riddell of Glenriddell in the Riddell Manuscript Collection, Society of Antiquaries Library.

33. That is the date of the first bond of manrent issued from Balloch. Prior to that they were issued from his hall on the island in Loch Tay.

34. William Adam, *Vitruvius Scoticus*, ed. J. Simpson (Edinburgh, 1984).

35. Timothy Pont, *Cunninghame Topographized*, ed. J. Dobie (Glasgow, 1876), p. 7.

36. Pont 21b.

37. A. Hay, 'The Scottish Nobilitie in An. Dom. 1577', in Revd C. Rogers, *Estimate of the Scottish Nobility during the Minority of James VI* (London, 1873), p. 22.

38. Pont 26c. Kelly is customarily thought to have been a simple tower with enclosure until extended by James MacLaren in the mid-nineteenth century.

39. D. MacGibbon and T. Ross, *The Castellated and Domestic Architecture of Scotland* (Edinburgh, 1887–92), vol. iii, p. 596.

40. *Register of the Privy Council of Scotland*, vol. iv, ed. D. Masson (Edinburgh, 1881), pp. 781–7.

41. Information from Dr Allen Simpson.

42. A. McKean, 'The manuscripts of Timothy Pont: context and implications' (St Andrews University dissertation, 2000).

43. See K. Cavers, *A Vision of Scotland* (Edinburgh, 1993).

44. Collected as part of a much wider project to publish an illustrated description and atlas of the country. See Allen Simpson: 'John Adair, Cartographer, and Sir Robert Sibbald's Scottish Atlas', in *The Map Collector*, no. 62 (1993).

45. Captain John Slezer, *Theatrum Scotiae* (London, 1693 and reprinted).

46. Cavers, *A Vision*, p. 9. Someone other than Slezer undertook fifty-seven drawings in the project.

47. I am grateful to Peadar Callaghan for spotting this.

48. Board of Ordnance drawings, the Map Library, the National Library of Scotland.

49. Published in 1798. Three volumes of Nattes' manuscript drawings are in the National Library of Scotland. Some of these drawings were later published as J. Fittler and J.C. Nattes, *Scotia Depicta* (London, 1804).

50. R.W. Billings was later unnecessarily unkind in boasting of how he had made all his own drawings whereas Grose had

used his servant: 'his artists first corrected nature and he added to their inaccuracies by correcting them', R.W. Billings, *The Baronial and Ecclesiastical Antiquities of Scotland*, vol. i (Edinburgh, 1846–52), p. 3. It was not as clear-cut as that. Grose's original drawings show him to be pretty good, and much of the unreality in his books can be attributed to the engraver.

51. Fittler and Nattes, *Scotia Depicta*, Preface.

52. A. de Cardonnel, *Picturesque Antiquities of Scotland* (London, 1788).

53. Clerk was the brother-in-law to Robert Adam. *Views in Scotland* (Edinburgh, 1855) and his manuscript notebook of a journey through Scotland. NAS/GD18/2118.

54. W. Scott, *Border Antiquities* (Edinburgh, 1814).

55. Most of them in Edinburgh Central Library. See also the drawings of Sir T. Dick Lauder in Aberdeen Art Gallery.

56. In the National Monuments Record of Scotland.

57. C.A. McKean, Entry to the *New Dictionary of National Biography*: G.M. Kemp.

58. The publisher was possibly Lizars.

59. Billings, *Baronial and Ecclesiastical*.

60. See also I.B.D. Bryce, 'Craigievar: a fresh look at Scotland's premier tower house', in *Architectural Heritage XI* (Edinburgh, 2000).

61. In the standard histories or relevant guidebooks.

62. Broadly, from 6 feet plus in the fifteenth century to 4½ feet minus in the sixteenth, and to 3 feet to 3½ feet by the seventeenth century. There are significant variations, particularly where the wall contains chimney-stack.

63. Plans held by Lord Balfour of Burleigh in Brucefield.

64. Once the house reached its current state in the early seventeenth century, the dining-room moved east, and the kitchen with it to a location beside a more convenient stair.

65. E. Beaton, *Ross and Cromarty* (Edinburgh, 1992).

66. For Melgund, see R. Fawcett, *Scottish Architecture from the Accession of the Stewarts to the Reformation* (Edinburgh, 1994), pp. 220–1. For Carnasserie, see the Royal Commission on the Ancient and Historical Monuments of Scotland (RCAHMS), *Argyll Vol 7 – Mid Argyll and Cowal* (Edinburgh, 1992), pp. 214–26. RCAHMS admits the presence of some earlier residual structure, but does not accept that the hugely differing structure between the tower and the rest, different levels and blocked staircase imply a strange and needlessly expensive incompetence if it was all built at the same time.

67. *Ex info* Roger Curtis, Cumming & Co. contractors.

3. REAL OR FALSE FORTIFICATIONS?

1. *Calendar of State Papers, Scotland*, vol. i, p. 432, cited in A. Marshall MacKenzie, *The Medieval Castle in Scotland* (London, 1927), p. 80.

2. *The Glamis Book of Record*, quoted in A.H. Millar, *The Historical Castles and Mansions of Scotland* (Paisley, 1890), p. 227. The spelling of original quotations has been modernised where judged helpful.

3. Sir Lawrence Weaver, *The Scottish National War Memorial* (London, 1927).

4. J. Guillaume (translated) taking the example of the new royal lodging at Loches, to build which a heavy medieval fortification had had to be demolished; at *Vraie et Fausse Fortification Colloque*, Tours, 2000.

5. M. Howard, *Colloque*.

6. Information kindly supplied by M. Stewart.

7. Guillaume, *Colloque*.

8. S. Hoppé, *Colloque*.

9. Howard, *Colloque*.

10. M. Girouard, *Colloque*.

11. Ibid.

12. Weaver, *War Memorial*.

13. Sir John Scot of Scotstarvit, *The Staggering State of Scots Statesmen from 1550–1650* (Edinburgh, 1754), p. 163.

14. Information board on site.

15. Now in the Hill of Tarvit nearby.

16. T.G. Snoddy, *Sir John Scot of Scotstarvit* (Edinburgh, 1968), p. 11.

17. Sir Robert Sibbald, *History of Fife and Kinross* (new edn, Edinburgh, 1803), p. 361.

18. Savills' sales particulars, based to some extent upon Tranter's *Fortified House*.

19. W. Mackay Mackenzie, *The Medieval Castle in Scotland* (London, 1927), Appendix A.

20. G. Stell, 'Kings, nobles and buildings of the later Middle Ages, Scotland', in G. Simpson, ed., *Scotland and Scandinavia* (Edinburgh, 1992), p. 69.

21. Ibid.

22. *Register of the Privy Seal of Scotland*, vol. iv, ed. J. Beveridge (Edinburgh, 1952), p. 502.

23. *RSS*, vol. iv, 3239.

24. Stell, 'Kings, nobles', pp. 60–73. Maurice Howard has pointed out that far from being a control upon country house erection, the custom in England was for an ambitious landowner to write to the relevant Court of Requests to seek such a licence, almost as a fashion accessory (*Colloque*).

25. *APS* (12 June 1535), quoted in James Lord Somervill, *Memorie of the Somervills* (1679, reprinted Edinburgh, 1815), pp. 355–6; and taken by S. Cruden, *The Scottish Castle* (Edinburgh, 1963), to represent the wider state of affairs in the kingdom.

26. G. Buchanan, *The History of Scotland*, ed. Mr Bond (Glasgow, 1799), p. 137. 'Jedburgh (a town unfortified as the Scots custom is)'; and John Spottiswoode, in *The History of the Church of Scotland* (Menston, 1972) about Inverness p. 186: 'The town itself was unfenced with walls.'

27. Bishop Lesley, 'The manners of the rest of the people of the land here follow', in P. Hume Brown, ed., *Scotland before 1700* (Edinburgh, 1893).

28. Macfarlane, *Collections*, vol. ii, p. 638.

29. See C.A. McKean, 'The evolution of the European weather-protected city', in P. Dennison, ed., *Conservation and Change in Historic Towns* (York, 2000). When the Earl of Mar's 1572 palace in Stirling fell into ruin in the late eighteenth century, its façade was retained as a protection against the wind. W. Nimmo, *History of Stirlingshire* (Stirling, 1817), vol. i, p. 310.

30. M.H. Merriman, *The Forts of Eyemouth 1547–1559* (n.d.), and *The Rough Wooings* (East Linton, 2000).

31. R. Samson, 'The Rise and Fall of Tower-Houses in post-Reformation Scotland', in R. Samson, ed., *The Social Archaeology of Houses* (Edinburgh, 1991), pp. 197–241.

32. R. Knecht, *Colloque*.

33. K. Brown, *Bloodfeud in Scotland 1573–1625* (Edinburgh, 1986), pp. 276–9.

34. Ibid.

35. H. Burns, *Colloque*. See also M. nan Rosenfeld, *Serlio on Domestic Architecture* (New York, 1978).

36. *Border Minstrelsy* (Edinburgh, 1902), vol. i, p. 128, cited in Mackenzie, *Medieval Castle*, p. 200.

37. D. Baptie, *A Lairdship Lost* (East Linton, 2000), p. 17.

38. Samson's 'Tower Houses' was based upon a study of Brown, *Bloodfeud*.
39. G. Donaldson, *Scotland James V–James VII* (Edinburgh, 1987), p. 212.
40. *Diurnal of Occurrents* (Edinburgh, 1833), p. 133.
41. Brown, *Bloodfeud*, pp. 128–30, and Cowan, 'The dark side', pp. 133–4. Bothwell's actions provide a curious foretaste of the Earl of Essex's rebellion against Queen Elizabeth in 1600. Essex's aim, likewise, was to separate the monarch from a distrusted adviser.
42. *The Black Book of Taymouth*, ed. C. Innes (Taymouth, 1855), pp. 29 and 42.
43. I. MacIvor, 'Artillery and major places of strength in the Lothians', in D. Caldwell, ed., *Scottish Weapons and Fortifications 1100–1800* (New Jersey, 1981), pp. 94–122.
44. 'Muster-roll of the French garrison at Dunbar, 1553', ed. R.S. Rait, in *Miscellany of the Scottish History Society* (Edinburgh, 1904). It was part of James V's marriage negotiations that Francis I should compel Albany to gift Dunbar to the Scottish Crown, with all guns and ammunition within ten days of the consummation of his marriage (Hannay, *Letters*, p. 315). Its master mason, Mogin Martyne, entered royal service until his death some eighteen months later.
45. In the Scottish National Portrait Gallery. The attribution is presumed.
46. I am indebted to Denys Pringle for discussions and plans of Cadzow, albeit disagreeing with his analysis in '"Cadzow Castle" and "The Castle of Hamilton": an archaeological and historical conundrum', in *Château Gaillard* XV (Caen, 1992). See also MacIvor, 'Artillery'.
47. This suggestion is Iain MacIvor's. See also C.A. McKean, 'Craignethan, the house of the Bastard of Arran', in *PSAS* (Edinburgh, 1996).
48. Ibid. Zeune concurs in *The Last Scottish Castles* (Leidorf, 1992), p. 92 but claims that since attackers would not realise this, they would remain an effective deterrent against attackers. First, attackers have to be found, and they were not common; and where they were – like Gordon of Gight – they came from the same class and had buildings similarly equipped. The fanciful nature of Scottish gunloops cannot have been too well kept a secret.
49. C. Whatley has suggested that the intent of artillery was to wound rather than kill, and shot ricocheting off cobbles or aimed at ankles might be as much a sign of effectiveness as otherwise.
50. Zeune, *Last Scottish Castles*, p. 87.
51. See McKean, 'Craignethan'.
52. *Black Book*, p. 336.
53. Guthrie Smith, *Strathblane*, p. 327–8.
54. Baptie, *Lairdship*, p. 164.
55. To judge by what Queen Mary instructed her porters to carry off back to Edinburgh with her. *TA*, vol. xi, eds T. Dickson and Sir J. Balfour Paul (Edinburgh, 1877–1916), p. 213.
56. NAS RH 13/11/38.
57. Most accounts of the killing emphasise that he was fortifying it with new blockhouses when he was murdered by people who entered the castle in the guise of building workers.
58. John Knox, *The History of the Reformation in Scotland*, ed. C. Lennox (London, 1905), p. 98.
59. Sir R. Maitland, *The History of the House of Seyton* (Glasgow, 1829), p. 45.
60. Sir James Melvill of Hal-Hil, *The Memoires* (London, 1683), p. 85.
61. *Black Book*, p. 16.
62. Ibid., p. 22. After that, no charters appear to be signed from the island, and one presumes that it was eventually abandoned.
63. See Somervill, *Memorie*, pp. 353–8.
64. See Chapter 8, n. 33.
65. The researches of John Orr in Dollar (1.12.2000). While the evidence of damage to the tower is incontrovertible, it would be astonishing if the establishment could have done without the space and chambers provided by the tower, or that Argyll would have been prepared entirely to forfeit his highest vantage point.
66. See Figs 3.8 and 9.16.
67. I am grateful to James Brown of Baltersan for transcribing the original: NAS, Acts and Decrets of the Court of Session, 8 June 1559–11 March 1560 (CS 7 20).
68. Brown, *Bloodfeud*, p. 68.
69. As, for example, in Hills Tower, Dumfriesshire.
70. C.A. McKean, 'A plethora of palaces', in Gow and Rowan, eds, *Scottish Country Houses 1680–1914* (Edinburgh, 1995).
71. R.W. Billings, 'On certain features of the ancient architecture of Scotland', in *Transactions of the Architectural Institute of Scotland* (Edinburgh, 1853), pp. 27–39.
72. See A. Maxwell Irvine, 'Scottish yetts and window grilles', *PSAS* 124 (Edinburgh, 1994) for Italy. Such grilles are also commonplace in Germany and Denmark.
73. C. Graham, *Grampian, the castle country* (Aberdeen, n.d., c. 1980).
74. Cruden, *Castle*; W. Douglas Simpson, *Exploring Castles* (London, 1957); R. Clow, ed., *Restoring Scotland's Castles* (Glasgow, 2000); and the endless regional and local guides to historic country houses which interpret them in castle terms. Mike Salter acknowledges in correspondence that the term 'castle' in the title in his excellent series *The Castles of Scotland* (Malvern, 1993–6) was as much a marketing as descriptive matter.
75. Cited in J. Geddes, *Kincardine and Deeside* (Edinburgh, 2001).
76. J. Boswell, *Journal of a Tour to the Hebrides* (new edn, Oxford, 1979), p. 207.
77. *Correspondence of the Earls of Ancram and Lothian*, ed. D. Laing (Edinburgh, 1875), p. 64.
78. The process is very clear in the House of Innes, the reconstruction of which probably began in 1638. Drawings produced by Joe Innes, 1998 pers. comm. NTS quinquennial survey drawings reveal a similar structure underlying Castle Fraser and Craigievar.
79. A. Mussat, 'Château-miroir', in B. Kopeczi and E.H. Balàzes, eds, *Noblesse francaise, noblesse hongroise XVI–XIX siècles* (Budapest and Paris, 1981), p. 102.
80. As contemporaries called turrets. D. Calderwood, *A True History of the Church of Scotland, 1678* (facsimile reprint, Menston, 1971), p. 443, in his narrative of the Gowrie conspiracy.
81. Laing, *Correspondence*, p. 64.

4. THE SCOTTISH COUNTRY SEAT AND ITS SETTING

1. Quoted in C. Anderson, 'Pallaces of the poets'; an idea of the Tudor and Jacobean Country House', in M. Airs, ed., *The Tudor and Jacobean Great House* (Oxford, 1994).
2. *RSS*, 2900, p. 504.

3. R. Chambers, *Domestic Annals of Scotland* (Edinburgh, n.d.), vol. i, p. 365.

4. Guthrie Smith, *Strathblane*, p. 21.

5. RCAHMS, *Argyll, Vol ii, Lorn* (Edinburgh, 1975), pp. 180–1.

6. R. Marshall, *The Days of Duchess Anne* (East Linton, 2000), p. 40.

7. A.H. Millar, *The Historical Castles and Mansions of Scotland* (Paisley, 1890), p. 94.

8. The 2nd Earl of Wemyss, 'Diary', in J.G. Fyfe, ed., *Scottish Diaries and Memoirs* (Stirling, 1927), pp. 126–7. The figures are not entirely clear, and there could be both double counting or, more like, undercounting since, for example, £100 was paid to Will Brugh for paying his unlisted men – who appear to have been household servants.

9. C. Innes, *Sketches of Early Scotch History* (Edinburgh, 1861), p. 548.

10. Millar, *Castles and Mansions*, p. 225.

11. The woman house is never defined; but in some houses it included – or meant – the laundry; but increasingly it had bedchambers with several beds in each, implying it was where the female servants lived as well.

12. F. Grose, *Antiquities of Scotland* (London, 1797), vol. ii, p. 116. The spelling has been modernised from: IN DEV TYM DRAV YIS CORD YE BEL TO CLINC/QUHAIS MERY VOCE VARNIS TO MEAT & DRINC.

13. D. Moyses, *Memoirs of the Affairs of Scotland* (Edinburgh, 1755). See, for example, p. 10. Note: David Moyses was, in fact, Moysie, and his memoirs appear in original script published by the Bannatyne Club (Edinburgh, 1830). However, to make his record more easily understandable, the 1755 edition is used in this book, and in that edition he is called Moyses as he will be here, for the sake of consistency.

14. See J. Wormald, *Lords and Men in Scotland* (Edinburgh, 1985).

15. In November 1571. Chambers, *Domestic Annals*, vol. i, p. 77.

16. Ibid., p. 121.

17. *Diurnal of Occurrents* (Edinburgh, 1833), p. 77.

18. Ibid., pp. 267 and 320.

19. *Black Book*, p. 313.

20. See D. Stevenson, 'The English Devil of Keeping State', in R. Mason, and N. Macdougall, eds, *People and Power in Scotland* (Edinburgh, 1992).

21. Sir James Melvill of Hal-Hil, *The Memoires* (London, 1683), p. 50.

22. Patrick Gordon of Ruthven, *A Short Abridgement of Britane's Distemper* (Aberdeen, 1844), p. 76. See also Stevenson, 'English Devil'.

23. HMC, *Fourth Report*, Part 1 (London, 1874), p. 527.

24. *Maitland Miscellany* (Edinburgh, 1834), vol. i, pp. 165 ff.

25. A. Gibson and T.C. Smout, 'Food and hierarchy in Scotland 1550–1650', in L. Leneman, ed., *Perspectives in Scottish Social History* (Aberdeen, 1988), pp. 33–53.

26. G. Blakhall, *A Briefe Narration* (Aberdeen, 1844), p. 65.

27. See particularly Chapter 8.

28. W. Macfarlane, *Geographical Collections Relating to Scotland*, eds Sir A. Mitchell and J.T. Clark (Edinburgh, 1907–8), vol. ii, p. 10.

29. It was called St John's Well. Macfarlane, *Collections*, vol. iii, p. 105.

30. See Chapter 9.

31. Glamis Papers, 255/4 (1).

32. Or rejection, obviously. But given the extent to which these houses were surrounded by yards, refusal of entry would surely have taken place long before the inner close was reached.

33. Chambers, *Domestic Annals*, vol. i, p. 120.

34. See M. Bath, 'Alexander Seton's Painted Gallery', in L. Gent, ed., *Albion's Classicism* (New Haven, 1995).

35. M. Howard, reporting on a study of 120 early Tudor houses in 'The architecture and social history of the Tudor and Jacobean Great House', in Airs, *Great House*, p. 6.

36. Unusually thick walls in both Wollaton and Bolsover suggest that an explanation is needed.

37. See p. 177.

38. See p. 225.

39. G. Stell, 'The Scottish Tower', RIAS, *Prospect* (Edinburgh, 1983).

40. J. Reid, *The Scots Gard'ner*, ed. Annette Hope (Edinburgh, 1988), p. 2.

41. Timothy Pont's drawing implies that the original gardens went uphill immediately behind the house.

42. Quoted in Grose, *Antiquities*, vol. ii, p. 87.

43. Observation by James Simpson.

44. D. Howard, *Scottish Architecture from the Reformation to the Restoration* (Edinburgh, 1995), p. 68.

45. *MW a/c, vol. i, 1529–1615*, ed. H. Paton (Edinburgh, 1957) show that Eastland boards were specified for the palace at Stirling. 'Estland' was sometimes used to mean Estonia. The roof timbers in a house in Brechin's High Street had been dated to the fifteenth century and identified as Baltic pine (which is sturdier than Scots).

46. T.C. Smout, *Joan Auld Memorial Seminar* (Dundee, 1998).

47. See also Chapter 5, p. 88.

48. H.G. Slade, *Cromarty Castle* (Cromarty, 1993), citing Hugh Miller quoting an elderly lady who remembered it.

49. NAS RH 13/11/26.

50. As it did – and still does – in the Binns, for the chamber of dais is what they now call the King's Room. Sir J. Dalyell and J. Beveridge, 'Inventory of the Plenishing of the House of the Binns at the date of the death of General Thomas Dalyell', in *PSAS* (Edinburgh, 12.1.1924).

51. K. Brown, *Bloodfeud in Scotland 1573–1625* (Edinburgh, 1986), p. 121.

52. RH 13/11/34. Inventory of Sir A. Ramsay of Abbotshall, c. 1680.

53. Quoted in full in J. Napier, *Notes and Reminiscences Relating to Partick* (Glasgow, 1873), pp. 23–43.

54. Ibid., quoting from Craufurd's *Renfrewshire*, p. 42.

55. RCAHMS, *Lorn*, pp. 176–81. The inventory of Barcaldine mentions a pantry like Partick's, but it is not indicated on the plan.

56. Drawing of Kinnaird by Alexander Edward, 1697, published in D. Jones, 'A seventeenth-century inventory of furnishings at Kinnaird Castle, Angus', in Frew and Jones, eds, *Aspects of Scottish Classicism* (St Andrews, 1989), p. 50.

57. As also was Invermay in the late seventeenth century.

58. The stables at Fyvie have been coated in orange-tinted harling.

59. Sir Robert Sibbald, *History of Fife and Kinross* (new edn, London, 1803), p. 303.

60. W. Mackay Mackenzie considered that 'it is a crude delusion that the medieval builders liked rough stone surfaces. On the contrary, they were given over to plastering everything of the kind': *The Medieval Castle in Scotland* (London, 1927), p. 136. The Arts and Crafts among practising architects is represented by R.J. Naismith, pers. com., 'granite rubble walls are

particularly pleasing to see. . . . It would be an astonishing breach of sound conservation to cover them with harling. . . . There is no practical case for harling rubble sandstone walls' (23.5.1997). The evidence, on balance, does not sustain this view for buildings of the period 1500–1700.

61. *MW a/c, vol. ii, 1616–1649*, eds J. Imrie and J. Dunbar (Edinburgh, 1982), p. 50. It emphasises just how gorgeous the ashlar-faced Palace of Stirling must have appeared.

62. See, for example, National Art Survey Drawings/1838 building contract for George Heriot's/paintings in the Robert Riddell collection/painting at Pollok House.

63. Tim Meek's reharling of Brodie, Nairn, using fill and 'gallets' to flush out the surface, demonstrates just how high a quality of finish it could be, and how precisely geometric such houses were intended to appear.

64. Sir William Brereton in 1636, quoted in P. Hume Brown, ed., *Early Travellers in Scotland* (new edn, Edinburgh, 1973), p. 148.

65. Dunbar and Davies, 'Building Contracts'.

66. M. Bath, *Renaissance Decorative Painting in Scotland* (Edinburgh, forthcoming).

67. J. Geddes, *Kincardine and Deeside* (Edinburgh, 2001).

68. A. Jervise, *Memorials of Angus and the Mearns* (Edinburgh, 1851), p. 389.

69. NAS RH13/11 Inventories; Glamis Papers 255/7/2. So the 'Soft and Hairy House' recently built in Tokyo by an Angus architect had precedent.

70. Guthrie Smith, *Strathblane*, pp. 317–18.

71. 'My Lord's Lined Study' appears in the Abbotshall Inventory.

72. NAS RH13/11/67 and NAS RH13/11/34.

73. Dundee University Archives, Kelly Castle drawings.

74. A. Hutcheson, 'Inventory of the Goods and Plenishings . . . of Agnes Betoun', in *PSAS* (Edinburgh, 14.5.1917).

75. Sir W. Fraser, *Memorials of the Earls of Haddington*, vol. ii (Edinburgh, 1889), pp. 289–92.

76. C.A. McKean, 'The Chanonry of Dunblane', in *Journal of the Society of Friends of Dunblane Cathedral*, vol. XVII (Dunblane, 1996).

77. J. Gifford, *Buildings of Scotland – Highlands and Islands* (London, 1992), p. 111, considers this to be a defensive bretasche. Improbable since the storm-tossed rocks and cliffs below would have inhibited any invasion from that quarter.

78. Macfarlane, *Collections*, vol. ii, p. 634.

79. If the Long Room at Lochnaw was the gallery, all it contained at the roup of 1736 was a mirror. Abbotshall's contained eighteen chairs with red or silver velvet cushions and a single resting chair, and that at Balloch some wardrobes and chests. RHP 13/11/34 and 69.

80. There are many oddities in Craignethan's south-east tower. However, the recessed arch on the left (east) is not the entrance to a great fireplace (although it later became that): it is rather a burial niche still awaiting its occupant.

81. See M. Girouard, *Life in the French Country House* (London, 2000), pp. 79–83.

82. See Chapter 3, n. 74.

83. See Chapter 8.

84. Glamis Papers, 255/7/2.

85. NAS RH13 /11.

86. *The Library of James VI* (Edinburgh, 1893), p. liii.

87. There are references to golf and the purchase of golf clubs and balls far away from golf courses, implying that there was space in the policies for this pursuit. In 1628, John the Bairn charged five shillings for making a golf club – or perhaps for buying a golf club for the Dowager Countess

of Mar at Alloa (Chambers, *Domestic Annals*, vol. ii, p. 118), and Montrose had golf balls purchased for him at Mugdock (Guthrie Smith, *Strathblane*, p. 21).

88. See M-M. Fontaine, 'La vie autour du château', in J. Guillaume, ed., *Jardins, Chasses, Plaisirs* (Paris, 1999).

89. G. Blakhall, *Brief Narration*; indeed, it seems that Blakhall never entered the house.

90. See Chapter 10.

91. See T. Buxbaum, *Scottish Garden Buildings* (Edinburgh, 1989).

92. Patrick, 1st Earl of Strathmore, *Glamis Book of Record* ed. A.H. Millar (Edinburgh, 1890), p. 41.

93. As may have been the case at Dairsie. Ex info Edwina Proudfoot.

94. As stated of the House of Tyrie, Buchan in Macfarlane, *Collections*, vol. i, p. 54.

95. Buxbaum, *Garden Buildings*.

96. Pers. com. Kitty Cruft, 31.12.1994.

97. C. Innes, *Sketches of Early Scotch History* (Edinburgh, 1861), p. 445.

98. F. Jamieson, 'The Royal Gardens of the Palace of Holyroodhouse', in *Garden History*, vol. 22, no. i, 1994.

99. Macfarlane, *Collections*, vol. ii, p. 467.

100. Ibid., vol. iii, p. 105.

101. Dalyell and Beveridge, 'Plenishing of the House of the Binns', p. 368.

102. NAS GD112/20/Box1/27.

103. Perhaps the most comprehensive treatment of sundials remains D. MacGibbon and T. Ross, *The Castellated and Domestic Architecture of Scotland* (Edinburgh, 1887–92), vol. v. For a discussion of the freemasonry aspect, see D. Stevenson, *The Origin of Freemasonry – Scotland's Century 1590–1710* (Cambridge, 1988), Chapter 5.

104. See Chapter 8.

105. A.J. Warden, *Angus or Forfarshire* (Dundee, 1882), vol. iii, p. 223.

106. Macfarlane, *Collections*, vol. ii, p. 39.

107. Warden, *Angus*, vol. iii, p. 219.

108. There are several ways of spelling his name.

5. THE EARLY RENAISSANCE AND THE CHANGING TOWER HOUSE, c. 1500–c. 1542

1. G. Buchanan, *The History of Scotland*, ed. Mr Bond (Glasgow, 1799), vol. ii, p. 166.

2. J. Lesley, *The History of Scotland* (Edinburgh, 1830), p. 76; N. Macdougall, *James IV* (East Linton, 1997), p. 217.

3. Lesley, *History*, p. 76.

4. Ibid., pp. 217 and 288.

5. See p. 91 – James Hamilton of Finnart.

6. R.K. Hannay and D. Hay, eds, *Letters of James V* (Edinburgh, 1954), p. 129.

7. See Chapter 1, n. 38.

8. This table is based upon the dates given in the various volumes of M. Salter, *The Castles of Scotland* (Malvern, 1993–6).

9. I. Campbell, 'A Romanesque Revival and the Early Renaissance in Scotland, c. 1380–1513', in *Journal of the Society of Architectural Historians* 54 (1995).

10. Ibid.

11. J.G. Dunbar, *The Royal Palaces of Scotland* (East Linton, 1999), p. 90.

12. Macdougall, *James IV*, pp. 294–5.

13. M. Glendinning et al., *A History of Scottish Architecture* (Edinburgh, 1996), p. 14.

14. Lesley, *History*, p. 75.
15. Hannay and Hay, *Letters of James V*, p. 1.
16. Sir Thomas Dacre referred to himself as the 'fiddling stick to hold Scotland in cumber and business'. *Letters and Papers of Henry VIII*, ed. J.S. Brewer (London, 1867), vol. iii, part ii, 4217. Also intro, p. ccxcv.
17. J-F. Luneau, 'Les vitraux de la Sainte Chapelle de Vic-le-Comte', in *Revue de l'art* 107 (Paris, 1995).
18. It is the extent of the glass account that makes one suspect that the oriel windows might have been built at this time.
19. Buchanan, *History*, vol. ii, p. 132.
20. Information from Professor Robert Knecht.
21. Lesley, *History*, p. 109.
22. T. Dickson and J. Balfour Paul, eds, *TA*, vol. 5, p. 58; also Hannay and Hay, *Letters of James V*, p. 6.
23. For a more detailed study of Finnart's career and the many buildings that might be attributed to him see C.A. McKean, 'Craignethan, the house of the Bastard of Arran', in *PSAS* (Edinburgh, 1996), and also C.A. McKean, 'Sir James Hamilton of Finnart – a Renaissance Courtier Architect', in *Architectural History* (London, 1999). See also Lesley, *History*, p. 158; 11th Lord Somervill, *Memorie of the Somervills*, ed. Walter Scott (Edinburgh, 1804); Robert Lindsay of Pitscottie, *A History of the Stuart Kings of Scotland* (Edinburgh, 1778), p. 257.
24. J.M. Thomson et al., eds, *Registrum Magni Sigilii Regum Scotorum*, hereafter *RGS* (Edinburgh 1882–1914), ll 3803 and 3804; HMC, *Eleventh Report*, Appendix, Part VI, p. 53.
25. The legitimacy of the heir was disputed by the others in the line of succession to the Crown on the grounds that Arran's first divorce had not been legitimate.
26. For more on the many royal, military and judiciary appointments held by Finnart, see McKean, 'Bastard of Arran' and McKean, 'A Renaissance Courtier Architect'.
27. *RGS*, p. 983.
28. *TA*, vi, p. 179.
29. J.S. Brewer et al, *Letters and Papers of Henry VIII* (London, 1862–90), vol. vi, p. 332.
30. R. Lindsay of Pitscottie, *The History of Scotland* (Edinburgh 1778), p. 257. The three principal actors in Finnart's downfall were all Reformers, and Buchanan, who knew him, confirms the appointment – *History*, p. 167.
31. *Diurnal of Occurrents* (Edinburgh, 1833), p. 23.
32. A different perspective on Finnart's life is provided by J. Cameron, *James V* (East Linton, 1998).
33. Representing the Douglas family.
34. The description is Thomas Pennant's: *Tour in Scotland 1769*, vol. i, p. 174. 'The ruins of the old castle of Inchinnan, one of the principal mansion houses of the Earls of Lennox' were noted in W. Macfarlane, *Geographical Collections relating to Scotland*, eds Sir A. Mitchell and J.J. Clark (Edinburgh, 1907–8), vol. i, p. 424.
35. J. Dunbar, at the Buildings of Scotland Conference, Glasgow, autumn 1999.
36. Hannay and Hay, *Letters of James V*, p. 425.
37. Somervill, *Memorie*, pp. 354–6.
38. A. Thomas, 'Renaissance Culture at the Court of James V' (PhD thesis, University of Edinburgh, 1997).
39. C. Edington, *Court and Culture in Renaissance Scotland* (East Linton, 1994).
40. Ibid., p. 103.
41. Hannay and Hay, *Letters of James V*, p. 388.
42. Initially the lands of the Earl of Angus and his brothers. See Jamie Cameron, *James V – the personal rule* (East Linton, 1998).
43. R. Mason, *Kingship and the Commonweal* (East Linton, 1998), p. 104.
44. Mason, *Kingship*, p. 125.
45. Pitscottie, *History*, p. 238.
46. Thomas, 'Renaissance Culture', p. 41.
47. Ibid.
48. Edington, *Court and Culture*, pp. 92, 96–8.
49. It was part of the attenuated negotiations for a pre-marital settlement for Queen Madeleine, and transferred to Mary of Guise in her turn. Hannay and Hay, *Letters of James V*, pp. 314 and 341.
50. Lesley, *History*, p. 55.
51. Pitscottie, *History*, p. 250.
52. In the Map Library, the National Library of Scotland.
53. Linlithgow, Blackness, Stirling and Boghouse of Crawfordjohn.
54. See Leslie, *History* and Somervill, *Memorie*.
55. *MW a/c, vol. i, 1529–1615*, ed. H. Paton (Edinburgh, 1957), p. 115.
56. Dunbar, *Royal Palaces*, pp. 138–40.
57. *MW a/c, vol. i*, pp. 115–31.
58. For a more detailed analysis of the Stirling Palace see McKean 'A Renaissance Courtier Architect'. The creation of a level platform was exactly the approach he had taken at his own house of Craignethan, and, in reality, the palace is three-storeyed.
59. Probably a private garden with a fountain.
60. *MW a/c, vol. i*, p. 310.
61. Neil Cameron drew this to my attention. *MW a/c*, vol. ii, p. 256.
62. The focus of the carved heads has always been on the King's Presence Chamber; but c. 1662, John Ray referred to 'very good carved wood-work' on *many* of the ceilings, and this observation was echoed by others including John Taylor when visiting in 1618. P. Hume Brown, ed., *Early Travellers in Scotland* (new edn, Edinburgh, 1973), pp. 118 and 236. Pennant observed two rooms called the Queen's and the nursery with 'roofs of wood divided into squares *and other forms* [my italics], well carved (*Tour*, 1769, Part ii, p. 223. See also J.G. Dunbar, *The Stirling Heads* (Edinburgh, 1975).
63. S. Mossakowski, 'Ethos of the Royal Palace in Cracow', in *Polish Art Studies* III (Warsaw, 1982), pp. 35–45.
64. Ibid.
65. When the palace was first built, only one façade could be seen at a time.
66. D. Bentley-Cranch and R. Marshall, 'Iconography and literature in the service of diplomacy', in J. Hadley Williams, ed., *Stewart Style 1513–1542* (East Linton, 1998), p. 288.
67. RCAHMS, *Stirlingshire* (Edinburgh, 1963).
68. H. Shire, 'The King in his House', in Hadley Williams, ed., *Stewart Style*, pp. 76–8.
69. Most commentators have followed *Stirlingshire*, p. 220.
70. On 2 November, he received full letters of legitimisation, *RSS* II, 3196, and on the following day he was granted a quitclaim and discharge for £4,000 owed for the previous day's charter, on the understanding that he completed the work at Stirling 'which he hes begun', *RSS* II, 3199.
71. Lesley, *History*, p. 157.
72. Ibid., p. 158.
73. Late eighteenth-century drawing by P. de la Motte, reproduced in A. Macdonald, *Linlithgow in Pictures* (Edinburgh, 1932).
74. *RGS*, 1885.
75. Ibid.

76. This interpretation differs entirely from the received one contained in the guidebook. There are indications that there may have been an entrance directly in front of the Lodging. The northern gatehouse is small – and no gunloop in the Lodging gives it any cover.

77. As in the palace of Edinburgh Castle.

78. Taken to the apex of the barrel-vaulted ceiling. The western façade of the Lodging below the corbel table appears to be to the Fibonacci proportions.

79. The chapel is the resting place for dismembered and displaced antelopes and their limbs.

80. See J. Lewis, E. Cox and H. Smith, 'Excavations at Craignethan Castle, 1984 and 1995', *PSAS* 128 (Edinburgh, 1998), pp. 923–36.

81. *TA*, vii, p. 397.

82. Ibid., pp. 383, 397 etc.

83. *Diurnal of Occurrents*, p. 71.

84. The junction is visible within the tower. This analysis differs radically from the accepted interpretation of Kinneil in both Colin McWilliam's *Buildings of Scotland – Lothian* and John Gifford's presentation at the Buildings of Scotland Conference, Glasgow, 1999. The west-facing gunloops, indeed, were too high to be effective. I am very grateful to Bob Hislop for letting me explore the building in such detail in his company.

85. Hereditary Masters of the Household – Inveraray (demolished); Masters of the Household – Pittencrieff and Dairsie (altered beyond recognition); Marshall of Scotland – Inverugie (blown up), Fetteresso (remodelled) and Dunnottar; Great Constable – Slains (demolished); Great Chamberlain – Cumbernauld (demolished); Justice Clerk – Pitgormo (vanished); Principal Sewers – Grange and Cleish (residual); Principal Carvers – Methven (disappeared – see Chapter 12); Cupbearer – Cessford (in ruins); Chief Janitor – Kincavil (possibly embedded within Champfleurie); Masters of the Wine Cellar – Drumlanrig (reformatted) and Sauchie (ruined).

86. Who was charged with counting the gold coin which Finnart had stored at Craignethan.

87. This interpretation differs from that of Ian Bryce, 'Craig Castle' (unpublished), and is based upon the different cellar construction of the different portions, substantial variations from the norm and the customary collection of peculiarities remaining in the walls.

88. Thomas, 'Renaissance culture', pp. 387–423.

89. See Chapter 4.

90. J. Zeune, *The Last Scottish Castles* (Leidorf, 1992), p. 141.

91. See the engravings in F. Grose, *Antiquities of Scotland* (London, 1797) and J. Clerk of Eldin, *Views in Scotland* (Edinburgh, 1855) for Culzean.

92. Cameron, *James V*, p. 263. It is not certain that Thomaston in Ayrshire was his house.

93. See Chapter 3, n. 70.

94. Originally from Tournai, but later from Scottish manufactories of Dornick, such as set up in Dunfermline.

95. Judging by surviving towers, or walls of such towers embedded within later structures.

96. Illustrated in M. Davis, *The Castles and Mansions of Ayrshire* (Ardrishaig, 1991), p. 181.

97. Macfarlane, *Collections*, vol. ii, p. 12.

98. Tam Ward, presentation at the Pont Conference, New Lanark, March 2000.

99. Boghall was drawn by Timothy Pont, Robert Riddell, John Clerk of Eldin and Francis Grose. This interpretation is based upon the information in those drawings.

100. The group of lords removed by the Earl of Angus in 1525 as being an unwholesome influence upon the young James V.

101. Quoted in D. MacGibbon and T. Ross, *The Castellated and Domestic Architecture of Scotland* (Edinburgh, 1887–92), vol. ii, p. 484.

102. *RGS*, iii, 1407–11; J.B. Greenshields, *Annals of the Parish of Lesmahagow* (Glasgow, 1864).

103. The rear wall is much thicker than the others, and has traces of connection to buildings on both sides. However, archaeology has not so far found evidence to support the illustrations.

104. A. de Cardonnel, *Picturesque Antiquities of Scotland* (London, 1788).

105. Thomas, 'Renaissance culture', pp. 387–423.

6. ENTER THE CHÂTEAU: ARCHITECTURE OF THE MARIAN PERIOD, c. 1542–c. 1568

1. A.J. Warden, *Angus or Forfarshire* (Dundee, 1882), vol. iii, p. 273.

2. This memorable phrase of David Beaton's was recorded by Sir James Melvill, *The Memoires* (London, 1683), p. 14.

3. J. Wormald, *Court, Kirk and Community* (London, 1981), p. 117.

4. R.K. Marshall, *Mary of Guise* (London, 1977), p. 72.

5. *Maitland Folio Manuscript*, ed. W.A. Craigie (Edinburgh, 1919) – spelling modernised.

6. There was an original tower to which the twin round towers and the ashlar façade were added in 1536, offset against the building behind. Consistently referred to as 'the old tower of Falkland' by Sir James Melvill (e.g. p. 26), it would not have been called that if built only twenty years before. The king's tower at Holyrood earned no such description.

7. S. Cruden, *The Scottish Castle* (Edinburgh, 1963), p. 149.

8. A. Thomas, 'Renaissance Culture at the Court of James V' (University of Edinburgh, 1997), p. 69.

9. The Treasurer's Accounts show that at her death in 1561, the majority of her household had non-Scots and probably French names. See also Marshall, *Mary of Guise*, p. 70.

10. See J.G. Dunbar, *The Royal Palaces of Scotland* (East Linton, 1999), p. 33. *MW a/c, vol. i, 1529–1615*, ed. H. Paton (Edinburgh, 1957), p. xxxvi (Mansioun); pp. 254–5 (Roy).

11. Pitscottie, quoted in A.M. Mackenzie, *Scottish Pageant, 1513–1625* (Edinburgh, 1948), p. 155.

12. See p. 52.

13. J. Lesley, *The History of Scotland* (Edinburgh, 1830), p. 194. See also S. Harris, 'The fortifications and siege of Leith', in *PSAS* 121 (Edinburgh, 1991), pp. 359–68.

14. *TA*, x, p. 22.

15. Ibid., p. 207.

16. J.S. Richardson, 'Mural Decorations at the House of Kinneil, Bo'ness', *PSAS* (Edinburgh,1940–1), pp. 184–204. The Treasurer's Accounts record money expended on those who laid the ground stones of the palace of Kinneil (*TA*, x, p. 207) but do not state which part of the palace was then being new built. That it is the north block that we now call the palace is pure supposition.

17. David Beaton had never been a monk, nor – for over half of his life with Marion Ogilvy – was he in full priest's orders. He was a skilled clerical administrator with a postgraduate degree in civil law. See Margaret Sanderson, 'Marion Ogilvy', in *Mary Stewart's People* (Edinburgh, 1987), p. 5.

18. *RSS*, vol. iii, p. 50.
19. J. Zeune, *The Last Scottish Castles* (Leidorf, 1992), p. 61.
20. Lesley, *History*, p. 296.
21. Marshall, *Mary of Guise*, pp. 187–9.
22. Ibid., p. 23.
23. R. Knecht, 'Noblesses anglaise et française: une comparaison', Tours *Colloque*, 2000.
24. J-P. Babelon, *Châteaux de France au siècle de la Renaissance* (Paris, 1989), Chapter 4, pp. 313–403.
25. Information from Pamela Ritchie.
26. Lesley, *History*, p. 243.
27. There are many examples in *RSS*, vol. iv.
28. Zeune, *Castles*, p. 111.
29. *Correspondence of the Earls of Ancram and Lothian*, ed. D. Laing (Edinburgh, 1875), p. 52.
30. A. Jervise, *Memorials of Angus and the Mearns* (Edinburgh, 1851), pp. 7–8.
31. It was in full use in the mid-1560s. See Melvill, *The Memoires*, p. 85.
32. N. Haynes, *Perthshire – an illustrated architectural guide* (Edinburgh, 2000); M. Swain, 'The Loch Leven and Linlithgow hangings', in *PSAS* 124 (Edinburgh, 1994), pp. 455–66.
33. The date of the first charters being issued from it. Previously they had been issued from Glenorchy's island in Loch Tay.
34. Inventories of Balloch, a late sixteenth-century elevation by Timothy Pont, the elevation and plan by William Adam in *Vitruvius Scoticus*, and the splendid landscape painting by James Norie senior undertaken to celebrate the completion of Adam's work, reproduced in M. Macdonald, *Scottish Painting* (London, 2000).
35. The Adam plan indicates a rebuilt stairtower.
36. J.C. Nattes, *Sketchbook*, in the manuscripts collection, the National Library of Scotland.
37. 1736 drawing of Blair by C. Frederick, courtesy of Sarah Troughton.
38. *Black Book*, p. 23.
39. Marshall, *Mary of Guise*, pp. 203–4.
40. *MW a/c, vol. i, 1529–1615*, ed. H. Paton (Edinburgh, 1957), p. xxxiv. *TA*, vol. xi, pp. 21 ff.
41. Published in D. Wilson, *Memorials of Edinburgh* (Edinburgh, 1891), vol. i, plate 15.
42. *Exchequer Rolls*, ed. G.P. McNeill (Edinburgh, 1898), vol. xix, pp. 252, 236; and also *TA*, vol. x, pp. 240, 296, 409, 418, 434.
43. Within three years they were to be at war with each other. Lesley, *History*, p. 287.
44. The guidebook suggests that the refitting took place from 1548. The dramatic change to the Scottish tower format that it exemplified argues for a powerful motive: and one could well have been to construct in Scotland an echo of what Huntly had seen in France in order to please the queen dowager.
45. W. Douglas Simpson, 'Further notes on Huntly Castle', in *PSAS* (Edinburgh, 9.1.1933).
46. W. Douglas Simpson, 'The Architectural History of Huntly Castle', in *PSAS* (Edinburgh, 13.2.1922).
47. Alterations to the lower floors reveal the tower to have been added, rather than being part of the original hall house as is thought. The entrance passage to the prison at the base of the tower is squint, and the current kitchen and its chimney singularly ill-fitting. The probability is that the original kitchen fireplace and chimney would have been against the western gable wall. When the round tower was added, the only possible access to the prison at its base was by cutting through the kitchen fireplace and creating a corridor through it. The kitchen was then inserted into pre-existing chambers along the southern wall.
48. Information from Alan MacDonald, based on eighteenth-century Gordon estate papers.
49. *Memoriales of George Bannatyne* (Edinburgh, 1829), pp. 333–8.
50. In the Drum, beside Edinburgh, however, Lord Somervill's bed was within the great chamber, or chamber of dais, itself. R. Chambers, *Domestic Annals of Scotland* (Edinburgh, n.d.), p. 191.
51. The fact that the narrator thought it worth mentioning that he was sitting – the others presumably standing – reflects an aspect of social hierarchy.
52. Chambers, *Domestic Annals*, p. 105.
53. Lesley, *History*, p. 257.
54. Huntly also enjoyed the revenues of the earldoms of Mar and Moray. Simpson, 'The Architectural History', p. 156.
55. Ibid.
56. Chroniclers like Spottiswoode have the execution in Aberdeen, Sir John Gordon 'pitifully mangled by an unskilful executioner' whereas the Treasurer's Accounts reimburse the tailor Alexander Schaw for clothing Gordon while he was imprisoned in Edinburgh's Tolbooth before his execution (*TA*, xi, p. 245).
57. Huntly had anticipated Mary visiting Strathbogie, failing to appreciate the deep offence his family's behaviour had given the queen. Spottiswoode thought that his wife, Elizabeth Keith, daughter of the Earl Marischal, 'a woman of haughty disposition, wise and crafty withal in sifting the minds of others', had been instrumental in pushing Huntly to the offensive. See Sanderson, *Mary Stewart's People*, p. 37.
58. *Inventaires de la Royne Descosse Douairière de France, 1556–1569* (Edinburgh, 1863), pp. 49–57. Also discussed in Swain, 'Lochleven hangings', p. 460.
59. I. Shepherd, *Aberdeen and North-East Scotland* (Edinburgh, 1996), pp. 105–6.
60. W. Douglas Simpson, 'Balvenie Castle', *Transactions of the Banffshire Field Club*, 16 July 1938.
61. Therefore rather more slender than Huntly's whopping 38 feet diameter tower: but it was probably a matter of proportion since Balvenie's is two storeys lower than Huntly's.
62. A larger version of a very similar design at Esselmont.
63. They can, or could, be seen at Ballindalloch, Kininvie, the Bishop's Palace and some of the High Street houses in Elgin. See C.A. McKean, *Banff and Buchan* (Edinburgh, 1989) and *The District of Moray* (Edinburgh, 1987).
64. Simpson, 'Balvenie'.
65. John Spottiswoode, *The History of the Church of Scotland 1655* (Menston, 1972 reprint), p. 95.
66. W. Douglas Simpson and D.J. Breeze, *Bishop's Palace and Earl's Palace* (Edinburgh, 1986).
67. M.R. Apted and S. Hannabuss, *Painters in Scotland, 1301–1700* (Edinburgh, 1978), p. 25; Wormald, *Court, Kirk and Community*, p. 84.
68. One of the few lesser houses following the pattern of the dominant round tower is Beldorney, Aberdeenshire, above the Deveron about midway between Balvenie and Huntly. Its tower has lost perhaps two storeys. See H.G. Slade, 'Beldorney Castle, Aberdeenshire: an early Z plan tower house', in *PSAS* 105 (Edinburgh, 1975),

pp. 262–81, albeit its evolution might not have followed the description therein – and the alphabetical designation Z-plan covers at least two totally different building periods.

69. *APS*, vol. ii, pp. 400–500, cited in M.H.B. Sanderson, *Ayrshire and the Reformation* (East Linton, 1997), p. 77.

70. *Maitland Quarto Manuscripts*, ed. W.A.C. Craigie (Edinburgh, 1920), p. 229.

71. Marshall, *Mary of Guise*, p. 211.

72. Lesley, *History*, p. 251.

73. Melvill, *Memoires*, p. 27.

74. Brought about by Henry II's penury. Knecht, 'Noblesses anglaise et française'.

75. Ibid.

76. D. Calderwood, *A True History of the Church of Scotland, 1678* (Menston, 1971 reprint), p. 11.

77. *The Warrender Papers*, vol. i, ed. A.I. Cameron and R.S. Rait (Edinburgh, 1931–2), p. 265.

78. Brantôme, cited in Mackenzie, *Scottish Pageant*, pp. 166–7; and D. Angus, 'Mary's Marginalia', in *Review of Scottish Culture* 3 (Edinburgh, 1987), pp. 9–13.

79. *TA*, xi, pp. 110 and 154.

80. Ibid., p. 373.

81. Ibid., p. 392.

82. Ibid., p. lx.

83. Melvill, *The Memoires*, p. 76.

84. *TA*, xi, p. 440.

85. Ibid., pp. 79, xxxi and xxxvii.

86. Ibid., p. 109.

87. Melvill, *The Memoires*, p. 54. In fact, being Italian, Riccio was useless at French letters, and the queen often had to redo them herself, but that did not impede the growth of his influence over her.

88. *TA*, xi, p. 158.

89. E.M. Furgal, 'The Scottish Itinerary of Mary Queen of Scots 1542–8 and 1561–8', *PSAS* 117 (Edinburgh, 1987), pp. 219–31. This valuable analysis should be treated with great caution when it comes to buildings and the cultural quality of Scotland, for he appears to regard most of the Scottish country houses of the time as 'medieval fortress buildings'.

90. W. Nimmo, *Stirlingshire* (Stirling, 1817), vol. ii, p. 457.

91. Craigcrook is generally thought to be early seventeenth century but, called Graycrook, it already existed in 1568. Chambers, *Domestic Annals*, p. 55; William Gordon, who built Terpersie, fought at the Battle of Corrichie in 1562.

92. *The Black Book of Taymouth*, ed. C. Innes (Aberdeen, 1864), p. 22.

93. Cruden, *Scottish Castle*, pp. 157–8.

94. M.R. Apted, *Claypotts Castle* (Edinburgh, 1957), p. 13.

95. M. Salter, *The Castles of Grampian and Angus* (Malvern, 1995), p. 118.

96. The bases of the pilasters which framed the dormer window are just visible below the eaves.

97. Cruden, *Scottish Castle*, p. 157.

98. W. Douglas Simpson, 'Two Donside Castles', *PSAS* (Edinburgh, 1942).

99. *Inter alia*, Inverugie, Ardmillan, Monklands, Kinnaird, Dudhope, Bedlay, and Nisbet.

100. *RSS*, p. 412.

101. Warden, *Angus*, vol. i, p. 360.

102. Ibid., vol. iii, p. 235.

103. D. Jones, 'A seventeenth century inventory of furnishings at Kinnaird Castle, Angus', in J. Frew and D. Jones, eds,

Aspects of Scottish Classicism (St Andrews, 1989), pp. 49–65.

104. Ibid., p. 57.

105. W. Boyd, cited in MacGibbon and Ross, *Castellated and Domestic*, vol. iii, p. 151.

106. McKean, *Banff and Buchan*, p. 149.

107. *Warrender Papers*, p. xxvii, also *Diurnal of Occurrents* (Edinburgh, 1833), p. 133.

108. *Bannatyne Miscellany*, vol. i. (Edinburgh, 1827), pp. 23–9.

109. MacGibbon and Ross, *Castellated and Domestic*, vol. iii, p. 143.

7. EARLY JACOBEAN MANSIONS, c. 1568–c. 1600

1. 29 January 1580–1. D. Calderwood cited in R. Chambers, *Domestic Annals of Scotland* (Edinburgh, n.d.), vol. i, p. 142.

2. Revd C. Rogers, *Estimate of the Scottish Nobility during the Minority of James VI* (London, 1873), p. 69.

3. Ibid., p. 45.

4. Ibid., pp. 63–72.

5. M. Lynch, *Scotland, a New History* (London, 1991), p. 232.

6. Illustrated in F. Grose, *Antiquities of Scotland* (London, 1797). Gowrie's new gallery in his town house in Perth may be dated to approximately the same date.

7. Bonds of manrent were mutual defence and support agreements, usually between superiors and inferiors, and often involved some tribute. See K. Brown, *Bloodfeud in Scotland 1573–1625* (Edinburgh, 1986) and J. Wormald, *Lords and Men in Scotland* (Edinburgh, 1985).

8. John Knox, *The History of the Reformation of Religion within the Realm of Scotland*, ed. C. Guthrie (London, 1898), p. 23.

9. See R.J. Lyall, 'James VI and the Sixteenth-Century Cultural Crisis', in J. Goodare and M. Lynch, eds, *The Reign of James VI* (East Linton, 2000), pp. 55–71.

10. Rogers, *Estimate of the Scottish Nobility*, p. 48.

11. James V, of course, had James Hamilton of Finnart. For Schaw, see Chapter 10.

12. Morton is normally credited with the elaborate entrance in the Portcullis Gate and the Half-Moon Battery, but since the walls of the castle were still ruined after his death, the latter seems unlikely.

13. *MW a/c, vol. i, 1529–1615*, ed. H. Paton (Edinburgh, 1957), pp. 301 ff.

14. There was no longer any mention of Boghouse of Crawfordjohn as one of the principal royal hunting seats, as there had been during the reign of James V.

15. Drummond recommended the rebuilding of the chapel further back to make a larger and more regular Upper Square: as was indeed done ten years later.

16. *MW a/c, vol. i*, p. 313.

17. Ibid.

18. The king took personal charge of overseeing the chapel's construction and convened all the crafts necessary. William Fowler cited in A. Mackechnie, 'James VI's Architects', in Goodare and Lynch, *James VI*, p. 164.

19. D. Moyses, *Memoirs of the Affairs of Scotland* (Edinburgh, 1755), pp. 110 and 204.

20. Ibid., p. 209.

21. Ibid., p. 189.

22. Ibid., p. 43.

23. A. Thomas, 'Renaissance Culture at the Court of James V' (PhD thesis, Edinburgh University, 1997).

24. This version is that of David Moyses, published alongside his memoirs, pp. 265–308.

25. Calderwood claimed that some leading Presbyterian divines like Robert Bruce found the story too incredible to merit giving thanks for the king's salvation, but he exaggerated (D. Calderwood, *A True History of the Church of Scotland, 1678* (facsimile reprint, Menston, 1971), p. 443).

26. Châtelherault's heir, Earl of Arran, once even thought a contender for Mary Queen of Scots' hand, had been confined in Craignethan by reason of lunacy.

27. Morton undertook another harrying in 1579, and on 19 May, the 'Castle of Hamilton' was rendered and was ordered to be demolished. It is likely that this refers to what we now call Cadzow, in view of Hamilton town's harrying eight years earlier, and the fact that this particular castle was fortified with men and victual, and only surrendered because of a mutiny (Moyses, *Memoirs*, pp. 33–4). The palace in the haugh would not have been so defensible.

28. *Diurnal of Occurrents* (Edinburgh, 1833), p. 177.

29. The castle, and palace and town of Hamilton; the place of Roploch; the place of Stanehouse; the place of Pedderisburne; the place of Laichope; Garing; the Haggs; the place of Orbistoun; the Torrence, Silvertonhill, with diverse other places pertaining to the said Hamiltons and their adherents. *Diurnal of Occurrents*, pp. 177–8.

30. Almost certainly Finnart's town house.

31. *Diurnal of Occurrents*, p. 287.

32. The Clydesdale map is the only one dated – 1596, whereas that of Angus can be dated by the unfinished state of Claypotts to 1586–7.

33. Sir John Scot of Scotstarvit, *The Staggering State of Scots Statesmen from 1550–1600* (Edinburgh, 1754), p. 2.

34. Possibly. There are some oddities in Drochil if it were built from scratch, not least variable and rather too thick walls.

35. Sanderson, *Mary Stewart's People*, p. 61, See also RCAHMS, *Peeblesshire 2* (Edinburgh, 1967), pp. 223–31.

36. M. Glendinning et al., *A History of Scottish Architecture* (Edinburgh, 1996), p. 37. The plan could also derive from that of Castle Lachlan, which had parallel chambers facing across a narrow rectangular court, joined by a timber stair and gallery. Once the chapel was added, Chernonceau lost its symmetry, and its staircase was to one side and not in the centre.

37. The engraving Slezer erroneously ascribed to Glamis has been suggested as Dalkeith. The landscape does not fit Dalkeith's position on the River Esk, and Slezer is usually reliable, despite his engravers.

38. M.R. Apted, *Aberdour Castle* (Edinburgh, 1985), particularly p. 20.

39. That they once had them is implied in the footings of a magnificent aedicular window below the pyramid roof of the little closet tower opening to the north.

40. There were numerous examples of this design approach. See Gylen in the next chapter.

41. RCAHMS, *Argyll Vol 7* (Edinburgh, 1992), pp. 214–26 admits the existence of older masonry but believes that substantially Carnasserie is all of one period – like Melgund, and, like Melgund, inconvenient walls, differing floor levels and other peculiarities imply otherwise.

42. C. Lowther, *Our Journall into Scotland* (Edinburgh, 1894), 'it having at each corner 4 pyramidal turrets, they call them pricks', p. 16.

43. Or, to judge from their walls, two separate towers, like Kellie, for the current stairtower looks from the plan as though it predates its adjacent chambers.

44. 'Chronical of Fortingall', in *The Black Book of Taymouth*, ed. C. Innes (Taymouth, 1855), p. 114.

45. The walls of the south-west tower differ greatly in thickness at ground level, but are consistent in the top two storeys. Moreover, the rear wall of the new main house is substantially thinner in the upper storeys than its front wall, implying two different periods of building.

46. Rogers, *Estimate of the Scottish Nobility*, p. 64.

47. Judging by the great thickness of the walls and its old-fashioned mural chambers on the upper floors.

48. Rogers, *Estimate of the Scottish Nobility*, p. 18.

49. D. MacGibbon and T. Ross, *The Castellated and Domestic Architecture of Scotland* (Edinburgh, 1887–92), vol. iv, p. 48.

50. I am grateful to David Walker for this information.

51. The turnpike in the north-east angle of Hatton is clearly a later interpolation in that location. It is too large and blocks pre-existing windows on two of the floors, and it hits the kitchen at the wrong level. David Walker points out that a scale-and-platt stair is attributed to the 1570s in Carnousie. The 1618 date of alteration, J. Zeune, *The Last Scottish Castles* (Leidorf, 1992), p. 256.

52. I am grateful to Charles Wemyss for this information.

53. The original courtyard wall and the remains of the south-western tower are clearly visible in the west façade, as are the joints between the various phases of construction.

54. Information from Cathy Sayer, National Trust for Scotland.

55. Misleadingly called a crypt.

56. That it was earlier, perhaps co-aeval with a very similar insertion at Elcho, is implied by the fact that the walls of the main house have been thinned on the *piano nobile*, presumably when Oliphant's large first-floor windows were inserted, and remain thicker upstairs. The floor levels between the bedrooms are different, those at the west end having to be reached up a short flight of steps.

57. *MW a/c, vol. ii, 1616–1629*, eds J. Imrie and J. Dunbar (Edinburgh, 1982), p. 79.

58. The western gable fills in the space between the two medieval towers with a fine seventeenth-century edged crowstepped gable capped by chimneys: yet look from the other side (the east) and you will see that it is not a gable, for the roof is much lower. It is a screen required for the composition of the west façade.

59. MacGibbon and Ross, *Castellated and Domestic*, vol. iii, p. 478–84.

60. Ibid.

61. Dormer windows currently flank the stairtower but according to MacGibbon and Ross, the left-hand one is a later addition. That may be the case, but the windows on the storey below imply that they are set symmetrically around that stairtower, and the idea of framing such a tower between dormers was carried through in Newark, Port Glasgow, and in the east wing of Seton.

62. MacGibbon and Ross, *Castellated and Domestic*, vol. iii, p. 481.

63. The first bond was signed there in May 1587: *Black Book*, p. 241.

64. For it was erected by the second Sir Colin of Glenorchy who died in 1523: *Black Book*, pp. 17 and 35.

65. Ibid., p. 37.

66. Ibid., pp. 60 and 45.

67. Ibid., p. 192: Bond of manrent with James Stewart and Alexander Drummond, to pursue to the death Duncan Laudosach McGregor.

68. C. Innes, *Sketches of Early Scotch History* (Edinburgh, 1861), pp. 329 and 334.

69. I am grateful to Allan Macinnes for this.

70. MacGibbon and Ross, *Castellated and Domestic*, vol. iii, pp. 583–4. The only recording *by the Campbells* of the Campbells beheading people is on the green at Kandmoir which Pont's maps show to be at the east end of the Loch rather than by Finlarig.

71. *Black Book*, Household Books, pp. 309–10. The inventory of wine for Balloch is more detailed: white wine, Spanish wine, old Spanish wine, and new claret – pp. 300–2.

72. Ibid., p. 331.

73. C. Tabraham, *Kildrummy Castle and Glenbuchat Castle* (Edinburgh, 1995).

74. Contained in his collection of drawings in Aberdeen University's manuscripts collection.

75. James Giles' painting shows the same detail at Balfluig.

8. *EARLY JACOBEAN TALL SMALL HOUSES, c. 1570–c. 1600*

1. Quoted in P. Hume Brown, ed., *Early Travellers in Scotland* (new edn, Edinburgh, 1973), p. 159.

2. Information from Alan MacDonald. See *APS*, vol. iii, p. 145 against 'destroyers of trees'.

3. See Chapter 4.

4. Balbegno's hall has very similar dimensions to the vaulted hall in Towie Barclay.

5. J. Sutherland, 'The Heraldic Ceiling of Balbegno Castle', in *Aberdeen University Review* XLVI (Aberdeen, 1976), pp. 268–73.

6. A. Jervise, *Epitaphs and Inscriptions* (Edinburgh, 1875–9).

7. Pers. com S. Mitchell, 28.7.1998, and genealogical research by D. Baptie in National Register of Archives.

8. Bryce and Roberts, 'Catholic Houses', pp. 366–7.

9. The great garden was probably completed in 1604, the date above its gate, implying that the other works were of the previous few years.

10. S. Mitchell.

11. See A.T. Maxwell-Irving, *The Border Towers of Scotland – the West March* (Blairlogie, 2000), pp. 57–64.

12. The Amisfield door, in the Museum of Scotland, portrays Hercules fighting the Nemean lion 'most barbarously carved in basso relievo, and most tawdrily painted' (F. Grose, *Antiquities of Scotland* (London, 1797), vol. i, pp. 159–60). It may have been part of a partition (Maxwell-Irving, *Border Towers*, p. 63).

13. Maxwell-Irving, *Border Towers*, p. 61.

14. Plans in Maxwell-Irving, *Border Towers*, p. 58.

15. Grose, *Antiquities*, vol. i, p. 159.

16. Drawn by William Brown, 1891, published in the *National Art Survey*, vol. 1 (Edinburgh, 1921).

17. It is a very modern conception: rather like Mies van der Rohe affixing steel columns to the exterior of the Seagram Tower in New York to represent the hidden steel structure within.

18. Shown in both Grose, *Antiquities* and John Clerk of Eldin, *Views in Scotland* (Edinburgh, 1855). Although the drawings are sketchy, those of the 1631 house imply that the ornate carvings in the Nithsdale apartments in Caerlaverock should not be treated as unique.

19. Ibid.

20. See H. MacDougall, *Island of Kerrera* (Oban, 1979) to which I am much indebted. See also RCAHMS, *Argyll, vol. ii, Lorn* (Edinburgh, 1975), pp. 217–23.

21. Most unlikely to have been a watchtower, as suggested by Leslie Grahame MacDougall in his restoration plans.

22. RCAHMS, *Argyll, vol. ii*, p. 291. The phrase 'let them say' in Gylen, is the last line of the Earls Marischal motto: 'They say, What say they, Let them say'.

23. The form of its pediment cannot be surmised. See D. MacGibbon and T. Ross, *The Castellated and Domestic Architecture of Scotland* (Edinburgh, 1887–92), vol. ii, pp. 71–4.

24. It will not do to suggest, as did MacDougall, that the kitchen shared the same tiny space on the first floor as the hall – unless to emphasise the extent to which this was a holiday house.

25. MacGibbon and Ross, *Castellated and Domestic*, vol. iii, p. 606.

26. Not unlike those in Castle Stewart.

27. Hume of Godscroft, quote in R. Chambers, *Domestic Annals of Scotland* (Edinburgh, n.d.), vol. i, p. 120. The name implies that this was a timber building.

28. The phrase used was 'to keep a good neighbourhood'. A. Warden, *Angus or Forfarshire* (Dundee, 1882), vol. iii, p. 563.

29. See plan in MacGibbon and Ross, *Castellated and Domestic*, vol. ii, p. 82.

30. Hume of Godscroft, *A History of the Houses of Douglas and Angus* (Edinburgh, 1648), p. 259.

31. See Maxwell-Irving, *Border Towers*, pp. 235–8. The medieval walls were on average 9 feet thick, and the superstructure 3 feet 2 inches thick.

32. Published in Reid and Scott, *Interesting Views in Scotland* (Edinburgh, 1802).

33. E. Proudfoot and C. Aliaga-Kelly, 'Excavations at Niddry Castle, West Lothian, 1986–90', in *PSAS* 127 (Edinburgh, 1997), pp. 783–842.

34. Ibid.: they suggest Valençay and Montsoreau as possible sources.

35. MacGibbon and Ross, *Castellated and Domestic*, vol. i, p. 325: 'When increased accommodation was wanted at Niddrie, security from attack was evidently of greater consequence than convenient arrangement of plan.' Rather, the provision of additional height must have been regarded as an ennobling feature.

36. Marooned corbels on the entrance façade suggest Monymusk was likewise heightened, possibly in the early seventeenth century to judge from the slender viewing platform at the apex of the design.

37. It is a very similar device to the one later used by William Adam in the creation of Châtelherault.

38. Implied by MacGibbon and Ross, *Castellated and Domestic*, vol. iii, p. 546.

39. Similar examples are Pinwherry, Ayrshire, where the corbelled stair is rectangular, Galdenoch, Wigtownshire, and Jerviston, Lanarkshire.

40. See MacGibbon and Ross, *Castellated and Domestic*, vol. iii, pp. 542–7.

41. J. Zeune, *The Last Scottish Castles* (Leidorf, 1992), p. 77.

42. Walls 4 feet thick (Ibid.).

43. Records discovered by James Brown as part of his project to restore Baltersan.

44. Testament of Egidia Blair, Lady Row, 31.8.1530. I am grateful to James Brown for this and the other information about Baltersan.

45. James Brown, 'Baltersan, a stately tower house in Ayrshire', unpublished, 1998. He researched the following information as part of his restoration project. Nearby Killochan, and the very similar Castle of Park, Wigtownshire, shares the same inscription as Baltersan.

46. Revd William Abercrummie, 'Description of Carrict', in W. Macfarlane, *Geographical Collections Relating to Scotland* (Edinburgh, 1907–8), vol. ii, p. 21.

47. Chambers, *Domestic Annals*, vol. i, p. 366. To judge from eighteenth-century engravings, the new late sixteenth-century house was a large building separate from the original tower and environed in yards.

48. J. Brown, pers. com.

49. Many of these smaller houses were the earliest to vanish. None the less, similarities can be found in Greenknowe, Dounreay, Whitefield, Lordscairnie, Plunton, Park, Sorbie, Kirkhill, and Pinwherry.

50. 1699 drawing by Alexander Edward of the 'south façade of the gallery' copied and contained in the W. Douglas Simpson collection of drawings in Aberdeen University Archives.

51. As MacGibbon and Ross call it, *Castellated and Domestic*, vol. ii, p. 499.

9. THE SCOTTISH RENAISSANCE PALACE

1. R. Lindsay of Pitscottie, *The History of Scotland* (Edinburgh 1778), pp. 227–8. Pitscottie dated this hunting trip to 1529 erroneously. David Lindsay, as Lyon Herald, might well have been the man to whom the Pope's Legate would have made such confidences, which he then passed on to Pitscottie.

2. See J. Wormald, *Court, Kirk and Community* (London, 1981), p. 173.

3. See W. Macfarlane, *Geographical Collections Relating to Scotland* (Edinburgh, 1907–8). Although the term is used sometimes loosely, the various authors who contributed distinguished between house, palace and place, and castle in a way that implies the form of a courtyard was indicated.

4. W.M. MacKenzie, *The Medieval Castle in Scotland* (London, 1927), p. 144.

5. 11th Lord Somervill, *Memoir of the Somervills*, 1679, ed. W. Scott (Edinburgh, 1815), p. 322.

6. See Chapter 5. Red Bag Somervill, a principal supporter of the Douglas faction, used the periods of Angus domination to obtain the lands and inheritance for himself. When the Douglases lost, so did Red Bag.

7. This depiction of Couthally is compiled from Somervill's *Memoir*. Only some mounds remain.

8. Guthrie Smith, *Strathblane*, pp. 72–126.

9. G. Blakhall, *A Briefe Narration* (Aberdeen, 1844), p. 124.

10. *RPC*, vol. iv, pp. liii, 214 and 610.

11. Improvements were carried out to the east wing at least, and to the building currently called stables. The seeming horseshoe above the door more resembles a vesica, or oval window, whose bottom stones have fallen out, implying it was once a chapel prior to subsequent enormous reworking.

12. It could equally have been inspired by the sixteenth-century Casa dei Diamante in Segovia, Casa dos Bicos, Lisbon, the fifteenth-century *diamante* work in the Kremlin, the *diamante* design in Serlio's *Third Book of Architecture*, or even by the comparable painted decoration which was still widespread in Denmark, Germany and Poland. A façade with carvings in relief could take other forms: the mansion built beside the Sainte Chapelle in Paris some decades earlier was decorated with stone fleurs-de-lys and some contemporary palaces in Spain with stone sea shells.

13. Schaw added a wing – or perhaps two wings – to Seton Palace from about 1585. See p. 176.

14. See next chapter, pp. 190–2.

15. 39 James IV, 1489.

16. Castle Campbell *Guidebook* considers that the southern wing was the first extension, but the wall thicknesses in the eastern block are greater, implying that it was first, but later refashioned *c.* 1595.

17. Ibid.

18. *Scottish Historical Review*, vol. x, p. 301.

19. D. MacGibbon and T. Ross, *The Castellated and Domestic Architecture of Scotland* (Edinburgh, 1887–92), vol. i, p. 202.

20. Based on the inventory published in F. Grose, *Antiquities of Scotland* (London, 1797), vol. i, pp. 166–70.

21. It could be risky to assume that the furniture within was in its usual place, because the inventory was prepared after siege and capitulation. Indeed, of the building's three halls, both the new and the long halls were being used for storage.

22. Grose, *Antiquities*, vol. i, pp. 166–70.

23. The term used is two-handed swords.

24. Plans of Branxholme and of The Dean, Kilmarnock, imply that the first lodging additional to the original tower was a separate, narrower tower at the far end of the enclosure.

25. Visible in John Clerk of Eldin's etching of Laurieston.

26. It was the property of Margaret Livingstone of Easter Wemyss, wife of Sir James Hamilton of Finnart. The exchange happened in the early 1530s when Colville sat on many commissions with Finnart. It is possible that Finnart may have had a hand in Colville's improvements.

27. R.D. Pringle, *Huntingtower* (Edinburgh, 1989).

28. *Diurnal of Occurrents* (Edinburgh, 1833), p. 133.

29. See the engravings in Grose's *Antiquities*.

30. Seton, Grandtully, Drum, Fordell, Dalgety and Craigmillar for example.

31. See p. 84.

32. MacGibbon and Ross, *Castellated and Domestic*, vol. iv, pp. 384–5.

33. Sir Richard Maitland of Lethington, continued by Alex, Viscount of Kingston, *The History of the House of Seyton* (Glasgow, 1829), p. 39.

34. Ibid., p. 42.

35. See J.S. Fleming, *Ancient Castles and Mansions of the Stirling Nobility* (Paisley, 1902), p. 348 for Touch, and MacGibbon and Ross, *Castellated and Domestic*, vol. iv, p. 186, for Saltcoats. Note, however, that the latter's unusual trefoil gunloop is to be found on Drochil.

36. J.G. Dunbar, *The Royal Palaces of Scotland* (East Linton, 1999), p. 25.

37. J. Macky, *Journey Through Scotland* (London, 1723), p. 173.

38. D. Hume of Godscroft, *A History of the Houses of Douglas and Angus* (Edinburgh, 1648), p. 377.

39. C.A. McKean, 'The Chanonry of Dunblane', *Journal of the Society of Friends of Dunblane Cathedral*, XVII (Dunblane, 1996), pp. 78–83.

40. D. Moyses, *Memoirs of the Affairs of Scotland* (Edinburgh, 1755), p. 43.

41. Macfarlane, *Collections*, vol. iii, p. 233 and vol. ii, p. 341.

42. NAS RH 13/11/38. Dunnottar was occupied more as a fortress than a house, and one gallery chamber was full of the earl's luggage. Windows of some of the rooms lacked glass, several chambers were locked, the keys were lost and could not be inventoried, and the whole place was decrepit. But it contained a prodigious amount of weaponry.

43. See Chapter 10.

44. NMRS LA/412.

45. For a fuller description of Pitsligo, see C.A. McKean, 'The House of Pitsligo', *PSAS* 121 (Edinburgh, 1991), pp. 369–90.

46. See pp. 181–2.

47. The same detail as was found at Glenbuchat.

48. Simon Montgomery, based on computer survey drawings by Douglas Forrest Architects and analysis by the author.

49. W. Douglas Simpson, 'Tolquhon Castle and its builders', *PSAS* 11.4.1938 (Edinburgh, 1938), pp. 248–70.

50. The Tolquhon *châtelet*, on its own, is not unlike that of Les Réaux and that formerly in the château du Bury, both in Touraine.

51. If it were a Leiper trademark, then we should also be looking to the Menzies lodging in Fordyce, at Schivas, the lower part of the round tower at Fraser, Arnage and the great garden at Edzell – at the very least – as also being Leiper's work. See Chapter 11.

52. See p. 190.

53. Simpson, 'Tolquhon Castle', p. 252.

54. See J. Giles, *Castles of Aberdeenshire* (Aberdeen, 1836), illustrations 23–5; and also C.A. McKean, *Banff and Buchan* (Edinburgh, 1989), p. 149.

55. The opinion of John Keith in the late seventeenth century. Macfarlane, *Collections*, vol. iii, p. 233.

56. Ibid., p. 234.

57. Ibid. Keith confirms the sequence by referring to the east block with its large chambers and library as being between the chapel and the *New Work*.

58. His chair was carefully if ignominiously preserved in the pantry three decades later. NAS RH/13/11/38 Inventory.

59. A corbelled staircase took the occupant to a chamber in the second floor, making this little tower the tallest building of the palace.

60. Ibid.

61. This interpretation differs from that of Simpson and others. If the gallery had been built second, how to explain the fact that the main house blocked its doors and windows, if not that the main house was only extended over the sea gate *after* the gallery had been completed.

62. *Fraser Papers* (Edinburgh, 1924), p. 57.

63. The inventory was published in Sir W. Fraser, *The Lords Elphinstone of Elphinstone* (Edinburgh, 1897), vol. 1, pp. 271–3.

64. Ibid.

65. A. MacKechnie, 'Scots Court Architecture of the early 17th century' (PhD thesis, University of Edinburgh, 1993), p. 38.

66. Kingston recorded that George, 4th Lord, had been offered an earldom by Mary Queen of Scots, but that he had refused it as premature. The queen then penned a verse based on the celebrated Sieur de Coucy rhyme of the Middle Ages (roi ne suis, ni duc aussi/Je suis Sieur de Coucy). For Seton it ran:

> Il y a des comtes, des rois, des ducs; aussi
> C'est assez pour moi d'être seigneur de Seton.

Friendly, perhaps, but terrible scansion.

67. In reality rhomboid, since there appears to have been four, rather than three, quarters. After Winton's forfeiture, post-1715, it fell to the York Buildings Company, and the tack was taken by William Adam. First-hand knowledge of Seton's ruins may have been a strong influence upon the young Robert Adam and it was upon his brother-in-law, John Clerk of Eldin, who recorded them. See W.R.M. Kay, 'Would the real William Adam please stand up?', *Architectural Heritage* 1 (Edinburgh, 1990), p. 55.

68. Their loyalty was to their long-term disadvantage, for the Earl of Winton came out for the Old Pretender in 1715, his estates were forfeited and fell to the notorious York Buildings Company. Winton only just survived, being lived in by a gardener (Macky, *Journey*), but Seton fell into total ruin, and was eventually replaced by a castellated villa designed by Robert Adam in 1790 for Alexander MacKenzie.

69. Macky, *Journey*, p. 43.

70. In the Scottish National Portrait Gallery.

71. Maitland of Lethington, *History of the House of Seyton*, p. 44.

72. Macky, *Journey*, p. 39.

73. Ibid.

74. Maitland of Lethington, *History of the House of Seyton*, pp. 60 and 75.

75. See Chapter 10.

76. M. Glendinning, R. MacInnes and A. MacKechnie, *A History of Scottish Architecture* (Edinburgh, 1996), pp. 42–3.

77. Building accounts in NAS/GD 137/4138/1–32. The mason was D. Milne, the wright R. Crystall, the slaters J. and W. Guild, and at the time, Dudhope had a gallery.

78. MacGibbon and Ross, *Castellated and Domestic*, vol. ii, p. 304.

79. Mary Beaton had not been Alexander Ogilvy's first choice. His childhood sweetheart was Huntly's sister Jane, who had had to marry the recidivist Earl of Bothwell (who divorced her to marry Mary Queen of Scots), then the sickly Earl of Sutherland, whose estate she managed and whom she outlived. Only then could they get married. M. Sanderson, *Mary Stewart's People* (Edinburgh, 1987), pp. 34–55.

80. Grose, *Antiquities*, vol. ii, p. 103.

81. Quoted in J. Spence, *Ruined Castles in Banff* (Edinburgh, 1873), pp. 49–50.

82. P.D. Anderson, *Robert Stewart, Earl of Orkney, Lord of Shetland* (Edinburgh, 1982), p. 73.

83. See Fig. 3.8.

84. Ibid., p. 135.

85. See n. 45, Chapter 3.

86. HMC II *Report, Appendix, Part IV*, p. 66.

87. Riddell manuscripts.

88. See R. Marshall, *The Days of Duchess Anne* (East Linton, 2000).

89. NAS (Scot)/05231. For more about Seton, see pp. 183–9.

90. See pp. 190–2.

91. L. Kanerva, *Defining the Architect in Fifteenth Century Italy* (Helsinki, 1998), p. 15.

92. Plan 10b of Fyvie by MacCombie and Mennie, 1993, the National Trust for Scotland. The chapel is referred to by Sir Andrew Hay, cited in A.M.W. Stirling, *Fyvie Castle* (London, 1928), p. 131. There is no obvious location for a gallery. The two 1733 drawings, identified by Richard Emmerson as by William Adams, published by Douglas Simpson in *PSAS* 73 are not **survey** drawings – albeit they indicate the ruinous north and east wings. They represent modest proposals to regularise the south façade.

93. That Schaw was the designer, see M. Glendinning *et al*, *A History of Scottish Architecture*, p. 42.

10. LATER JACOBEAN COURT ARCHITECTURE, c. 1590–c. 1640

1. Quoted in G. Seton, *Memoir of Alexander Seton, Earl of Dunfermline* (Edinburgh, 1882), p. 39.
2. J. Wormald, *Court, Kirk and Community* (London, 1981), p. 156.
3. G. Donaldson, *Scotland James V–James VII* (Edinburgh, 1987), Chapter 13.
4. His title seems to have been inspired by an oppressed stanza in Alexander Montgomerie's 1597 poem *The Cherrie and the Slae* which runs thus:

As scorn comes commonly with skaith	[harm]
So I behoved to endure tham baith,	
O! What a staggering state!	
For under cure I got such check	
That I might not remove nor neck	[chess terms]
But either stale or mate.	[chess terms]
My agony was so extreme	
I swelt and swooned for fear:	[became faint]
Only before I wakened of my dream,	
He spoiled me of my gear.	[plundered]

   A. Montgomerie, *The Cherrie and the Slae*, ed. H.H. Wood (London, 1937), words modernised.
5. Sir John Scot of Scotstarvit, *The Staggering State of Scots Statesmen from 1550–1600* (Edinburgh, 1754).
6. Loans obtained on the security of property.
7. Brother of Sir John Seton of Barnes, builder of Barnes, brother-in-law of Lord Claud Hamilton, rebuilder of Hamilton Palace, uncle of 3rd Earl of Winton, builder of Winton.
8. *History of the House of Seyton*, p. 63, quoted in Seton, *Memoir*.
9. Seton, *Memoir*, p. 122. The work was entitled *Rabdologie sive numerationis per virgulas*, Book Two.
10. Somervill, *Memoir*, pp. 459–60. Quoted in D. Stevenson, *The Origin of Freemasonry – Scotland's Century 1590–1710* (Cambridge, 1988), p. 29.
11. From Fyvie Charters, quoted in A.M.W. Stirling, *Fyvie Castle* (London, 1928), p. 158.
12. Seton, *Memoir*, p. 176.
13. In his will, he requires others to finish the building in accordance with plans which he had drawn up. Ibid., p. 158.
14. The square turrets or pricks that Lowther had seen at Gala House may still be seen at Kilbryde and Meggernie.
15. That the bay window and gallery were added to an existing building is indicated by the crowsteps of a lower gable which have been fossilised into the wall to the west of the bay's top storey.
16. A similar one may have existed in New Slains, Buchan.
17. A. MacKechnie, 'Scots Court Architecture of the early 17th century' (PhD thesis, University of Edinburgh, 1993), p. 207.
18. Such ornamental cappings were customary in Europe – some surviving in the Danish Renaissance mansion of Egeskov. Slezer's engraving of the East Lothian coast shows Pinkie's dormer windows quite distinctly. MacGibbon and Ross concluded that the roof had been raised at a later date.
19. Quoted in M. Bath, *Renaissance Decorative Painting in Scotland* (National Museums of Scotland, forthcoming), Chapter 4, p. 11.
20. This description of the long gallery owes much to Chapter 4 of Bath, *Renaissance Decorative Painting*. But see also M.R. Apted, *The Painted Ceiling in Scotland* (Edinburgh, 1966).
21. An early seventeenth-century date would be far more appropriate for some of its details than late seventeenth-century rebuilding after riot damage by Sir Alexander Dick, as is currently surmised. Prestonfield's dormer windows and – in particular – its buckle-quoins (see later) seem very 1620s–'30s.
22. Scotstarvit, *Staggering State*, p. 24.
23. *Staggering State*, p. 72.
24. Illustration reproduced from MS in Crawford and Balcarres Muniments in John Rylands Library, Manchester, by F. Bardgett, *Scotland Reformed* (Edinburgh, 1989), p. 152.
25. *HMC Appendix to the Fourth Report* (London, 1874), p. 457.
26. W. Macfarlane, *Geographical Collections Relating to Scotland* (Edinburgh, 1907–8), vol. i, p. 389.
27. Patrick, 1st Earl of Strathmore, *Glamis Book of Record*, ed. A.H. Millar (Edinburgh, 1890), pp. 55–63.
28. R. Chambers, *Domestic Annals of Scotland* (Edinburgh, n.d.), vol. i, p. 432.
29. *Correspondence of the Earls of Ancram and Lothian*, ed. D. Laing (Edinburgh, 1875), pp. 63–76.
30. Ibid., p. 69.
31. See p. 57 for the full instruction and reasoning.
32. Sir James Melvill, *The Memoires* (London, 1683), p. 162.
33. He was appointed in December 1583, replacing Sir Robert Drummond of Carnock who was meant to have held the post for life. See Stevenson, *Freemasonry*, Chapter 3. In a 1616 charter, Schaw was posthumously delineated 'regius architectus'. Quoted in D. MacGibbon and T. Ross, *The Castellated and Domestic Architecture of Scotland* (Edinburgh, 1887–92), vol. v, p. 547.
34. D. Stevenson, *Scotland's Last Loyal Wedding* (Edinburgh, 1997), pp. 50–1.
35. Christian imported into Denmark the Dutch architect Hans Steenwinckel, who designed, *inter alia*, the handsome brick palace of the Rosenberg now in Copenhagen, 1613–35 (completed by his son Hans), and refashioned Fredericksborg to the north-west in the 1620s. His father Frederick II had earlier employed Flemish architects Hans van Paeschen and Antonius van Opbergen to construct the Kronborg at Helsingor. In certain respects, there are strong similarities of form between the Rosenberg and George Heriot's Hospital, Edinburgh.
36. Quoted in *RPC*, vol. iv, 1589–9, p. 470.
37. Schaw had at least the £1,000 provided by Edinburgh Town Council. Ibid., p. 471.
38. M. Lynch, 'Court Ceremony and Ritual', in M. Lynch and J. Goodare, *The Reign of James VI* (East Linton, 2000), pp. 71–93.
39. Inscribed on his tombstone in Dunfermline Abbey. See later.
40. Lynch, 'Court Ceremony and Ritual', p. 85.
41. Ibid., pp. 88–9.
42. He designed a cradle, timber bed, chair, seat and four stools costing £118 for which his fee was £16. (*Letters to James VI* (Edinburgh, 1835), p. lxxiii).
43. See Howard, *Renaissance to Reformation*, pp. 28–9. The description is John Taylor's, in P. Hume Brown, ed., *Early Travellers in Scotland* (new edn, Edinburgh, 1973), p. 115. That it was Charles I's birthplace, Macfarlane, *Collections*, vol. 1, p. 288.
44. Translated from the inscription contained in J. Jamieson, *The Royal Palaces of Scotland* (Glasgow, 1840), p. 90.

45. Which probably explains the long, low roof running across the front in Slezer's drawing.

46. As recorded on the monument itself. The entire text is transcribed in Stevenson, *Freemasonry*, p. 26.

47. *RPC, vol. iv, 1585–1592*, ed. D. Masson (Edinburgh, 1881), p. 89.

48. D. Howard, *Scottish Architecture from the Reformation to the Restoration* (Edinburgh, 1995), p. 32.

49. Stevenson, *Freemasonry*, pp. 34–51.

50. Thus named in the charter of 1612 conveying to him the lands of Kilbaberton. Quoted in MacGibbon and Ross, *Castellated and Domestic*, vol. v, p. 547.

51. Much of this account of Murray is indebted to MacKechnie, 'Scots Court Architecture'.

52. Ibid., p. 176.

53. Ibid., p. 162–3.

54. MacGibbon and Ross, *Castellated and Domestic*, vol. ii, p. 526.

55. MacKechnie, 'Scots Court Architecture', p. 119.

56. Ibid., p. 403.

57. *MW a/c*, vol. ii, p. 269.

58. As stated by MacKechnie, 'Scots Court Architecture', p. 193.

59. N. Hynd, 'The representation of the royal apartments within Edinburgh Castle' (unpublished paper, 1995), p. 5.

60. A. MacKechnie, 'Evidence of a post-1603 Court Architecture in Scotland', *Architectural History* 31 (London, 1988), pp. 107–19, suggests that buckle-quoins form a principal motif of Court architecture between *c*. 1619 and 1657.

61. MacGibbon and Ross, *Castellated and Domestic*, vol. iv, pp. 67–8.

62. As does MacKechnie, 'Scots Court Architecture', p. 376.

63. The house was demolished in 1800. For more details of the house see C.A. McKean, 'The Wrichtishousis – a very curious edifice', *Book of the Old Edinburgh Club*, new series, vol. 3 (Edinbugh, 1994), pp. 113–22.

64. Its substantial structure can still be read from the plans.

65. This analysis is based upon the Inventory of Tyninghame drawn up in 1635 as the Earl of Haddington was preparing to hand it all over to his son, Lord Binning. Sir W. Fraser, *Memorials of the Earls of Haddington* (Edinburgh, 1889), pp. 300–2.

66. The titles and the houses have caused confusion. Manerstoun, a small old house, has been assumed to be the original seat; but the Binns contains clear pre-sixteenth-century structures. Perhaps the clue lies in one of the charters' directions: To Thomas Dalyell *of Manerstoun at* Binns (Binns Papers, Part 1, 122): i.e. the original title was that of Manerstoun but the location was the Binns. *Binns Papers 1320–1864*, eds Sir J. Dalyell and J. Beveridge (Edinburgh, 1938), no. 101.

67. Ibid., nos 89 and 90 for example; and 110.

68. Largely imperceptible from the outside, these towers are very clear from the plan.

69. The older house behind, indicated in Slezer's drawing, is dated to 1590 in the sketch plan in the Revd John Sime's *Memorabilia* notebook in RCAHMS. Sime's recording of an elaborate plaster ceiling in the form of a large oval implies that the new house was completed.

70. Brereton, in Hume Brown, *Early Travellers*, p. 133.

71. Quoted in M. Girouard, *Robert Smythson and the Architecture of the Elizabethan Era* (London, 1966), p. 34.

72. Scotstarvit, *Staggering State*, p. 35.

73. The orientation in MacGibbon and Ross is inaccurate. The processional pattern is that of the palace in Edinburgh Castle.

74. Hynd, 'Royal apartments'. The Bromley ceiling is now in the Victoria & Albert Museum, and the plaster figures of the Bow Worthies appear in at least Thirlstane, Balcarres, Muchalls and Craigievar.

75. See Seton, last chapter.

76. Motifs on the painted ceiling formerly in Gardyne's Lodging, Dundee, can be traced to Francis Quarles' book of emblematics, published in 1637. See Bath, 'Francis Quarles goes north', in 'Scottish Applications of the *Emblemes* (1635)' in W. Harms and D. Peil, eds., *Tagundsbandes 5 Internationale Emblem – Kongresses 1999 in München* (Bern, 2000).

77. C. Gapper, 'Chastleton House: the Decorative Plasterwork in context', in M. Airs, ed., *The Tudor and Jacobean Great House* (Oxford, 1994), p. 107.

78. Hynd, 'Royal apartments'.

79. *MW a/c, vol. ii, 1616–1629*, eds J. Imrie and J. Dunbar (Edinburgh, 1982), p. 79.

80. N. Pattullo, *Castles, Houses and Gardens of Scotland Vol ii* (Edinburgh, 1974), p. 139.

81. HMC, *Appendix to Vol. ii* (London, 1870), p. 190.

82. MacKechnie, 'Scots Court Architecture', p. 367.

83. Ibid., p. 291.

84. Visible in Slezer's aerial view of the castle. British Library, Ktops 49 74a.

85. MacGibbon and Ross, *Castellated and Domestic*, vol. ii, p. 545 say 1615 onwards, MacKechnie the previous year.

86. MacKechnie, 'Scots Court Architecture', p. 94.

87. That there was an existing structure is implied by the squint corridor cut through from the new staircase into the service corridor.

88. MacGibbon and Ross, *Castellated and Domestic*, vol. ii, p. 538.

89. W. Nimmo, *History of Stirlingshire*, vol. ii, p. 488.

90. Scotstarvit, *Staggering State*, p. 123.

91. Ibid., p. 63.

92. E.M. Cox, O. Owen, D. Pringle, 'The discovery of medieval deposits beneath the Earl's Palace, Kirkwall', *PSAS* 128 (Edinburgh, 1998), pp. 567–80.

93. Chambers, *Domestic Annals*, vol. i, p. 460.

94. Laird of Grant's piper: early eighteenth-century portrait by Richard Waitt in the Museum of Scotland.

95. Sir W. Fraser, *Chiefs of Grant* (Edinburgh, 1883), vol. i, p. 32.

96. Most people assume that the initials IB stand for John Bel, but it could as well be Ian.

97. For a fuller discussion of Drum, see H.G. Slade, 'The Tower and House of Drum, Aberdeenshire', *PSAS* 115 (Edinburgh, 1985), pp. 297–356, although there are some differences in interpretation of how the house grew.

98. For a fuller discussion, see H.G. Slade, 'Craigston Castle, Aberdeenshire', *PSAS* 108 (Edinburgh, 1976), pp. 262–300.

99. A.J. Warden, *Angus or Forfarshire* (Dundee, 1882), vol. i, p. 328.

100. From Ochterlony of Guynd's description of Angus, quoted in A. Jervise, *Land of the Lindsays*, ed. J. Gammack (Edinburgh, 1881), p. 291.

101. Warden, *Angus or Forfarshire*, vol. iii, pp. 77–80.

102. See J.G. Dunbar and K. Davies, 'Some late seventeenth-century building contracts', *Scottish History Society Miscellany XI* (Edinburgh, 1990), pp. 269–323.

103. Dunbar and Davies, 'Building contracts', p. 278.

104. T. Garnett, *Observations on a Tour of the Highlands* (London, 1800), vol. ii, p. 119.

105. F. Grose, *Antiquities of Scotland* (London, 1797), vol. ii, p. 148. Also Riddell MSS.

106. J. Gifford *et al*, *Buildings of Scotland – Edinburgh* (London, 1984), p. 544.

107. Good drawings of *c*. 1808 exist in the *Memorabilia* of the Revd John Sime, in the National Monuments Record, which show that the current pointed crowsteps of the flanking towers are nineteenth-century additions, replacing the equally unrealistic late eighteenth-century cappings with their Venetian windows.

108. George Dundas of Dundas chose to build a mansion detached from his tower (like Amisfield and Eglinton). George Dundas of Duddingston may have reformatted his house about the same time. Thomas Dalyell had reformatted the Binns. They were all leading heritors of Abercorn parish implying that some competitive architecture was under way in early seventeenth-century Abercorn.

109. They appeared, for example, in Drum (Aberdeenshire), Pilrig (Edinburgh) and Bonhard (Linlithgow).

11. LATER JACOBEAN NATIONALISM, *c. 1590–c. 1640*

1. R. Franck, *Northern Memoirs*, ed. Sir W. Scott (Edinburgh, 1821), pp. 221–2.

2. It is implied that they were open to inducement to change sides in the histories of Spalding, Blakhall and Gordon of Ruthven. See particularly Gordon of Ruthven, *A Short Abridgement of Britain's Distemper* (Aberdeen, 1844), p. 85, G. Blakhall, *A Briefe Narration* (Aberdeen, 1844), p. 80, and J. Spalding, *The History of the Troubles* (reprint, Aberdeen, 1830), p. 226.

3. Board of Ordnance drawing, Z2/82ff, National Library of Scotland.

4. *Bannatyne Miscellany* (Edinburgh, 1827), vol. i, p. 55 and vol. ii, p. 21.

5. R.J. Lyall, 'James VI and the cultural crisis', in J. Goodare and M. Lynch, *The Reign of James VI* (East Linton, 2000), pp. 67–9.

6. Melvill, *Memoirs*, cited in R. Chambers, *Domestic Annals of Scotland* (Edinburgh, n.d.), p. 184.

7. D. Moyses, *Memoirs of the Affairs of Scotland* (Edinburgh, 1755), p. 137.

8. R. Grant, 'The Brig o'Dee Affair: the sixth earl of Huntly and the politics of the Counter-Reformation', in Goodacre and Lynch, *James VI*, pp. 93–109.

9. Pers. com. Alan MacDonald.

10. Spalding, *History*, p. 38.

11. Ibid.

12. The existence of the first, probably late fifteenth-century tower may be inferred from the Gordon Castle Drawings in West Register House. Confirmation of the Slezer drawing can be made to a large extent, although most of the inner court buildings have gone. NAS RHP 2379 (1–6), RHP 2381–2, RHP 1075.

13. P.F. Tytler, *History of Scotland* (new edn, London, *c*. 1880), vol. iii, p. 251. The first bond of manrent issued from Bog was on 28.10.1586. (J. Wormald, *Lords and Men in Scotland* (Edinburgh, 1985), p. 292.)

14. D. Defoe, *A Tour through Great Britain* (London reprint, 1983), vol. ii, p. 288.

15. Thus resembling the first addition to Castle Fraser. This analysis is based upon the Gordon Castle Plans NAS/RH 2372, 2379, 2381–2, largely prepared by J. Baxter and A. Roumieu prior to substantial remodelling. Baxter's were built.

16. Slezer has a drawing of Bog mistitled Inveraray Castle by his engravers – thus deceiving many publishers into continuing the error even now.

17. See, for example, the Infanta's Palace in Guadalquivir.

18. NAS/RHP 1075.

19. Ibid. The drawing shows only the south façade, and there is no record of the eastern one. The inscription, at least, or perhaps much of the new arcading etc, was added after 1599.

20. Tytler, *History of Scotland*. Also, that is the first date that bonds begin to be issued from Bog.

21. Pers. com. A. MacDonald, 'Anent the demolition of the old tower at Huntly Castle', NAS/GD44/33/18/3/8/1725.

22. Easily discernible from the wall thickness and the change to the windows of the north façade.

23. W. Douglas Simpson, 'The architectural history of Huntly Castle', *PSAS* 13.2.1922 (Edinburgh, 1922), p. 158.

24. Changing perceptions can be seen in W. Douglas Simpson's two *PSAS* papers on Huntly. The first refers to the palace as a keep because Huntly was known to have had a medieval tower. Since it had not yet been discovered by excavation, Simpson presumed the palace was it and referred to it as a keep. The excavation of the tower's foundations impelled a reinterpretation. Those seeking castles find them.

25. All this can be seen in the 1798 sketches by J.C. Nattes held in the National Library of Scotland manuscripts.

26. Grant, 'Brig o Dee', p. 97.

27. C.J. Burnett and M.D. Dennis, *Scotland's Heraldic Heritage* (Edinburgh, 1997), p. 67.

28. Red sandstone is not the natural material of Huntly. It has been suggested by Alistair Urquhart (pers. com.) that it was used because the granite of the day would have been far too coarse and difficult to work to achieve the same effect. That implies a 'platt': an *a priori* design for which special materials had to be imported.

29. M.R. Apted and S. Hannabuss, *Painters in Scotland, 1301–1700* (Edinburgh, 1978), p. 23.

30. C. Cordiner, *Antiquities and Scenery of the North of Scotland* (London, 1780), pp. 9–10.

31. Sir Robert Gordon, *Genealogical History of the Earldom of Sutherland*, quoted in Chambers, *Domestic Annals*, vol. ii, pp. 91–2.

32. Blakhall, *Brief Narration*, p. 170.

33. Spalding, *History*, p. 304.

34. Judging by the form and the gunloop at its base.

35. The House of Schivas has the same plan as the Tolquhon laird's lodging. That particular gunloop type may also be seen at Arnage, Edzell, the town house of Menzies of Durn in Fordyce, possibly early Muchalls and Lesmoir. Leiper was still in business in 1600, working on Udny kirk.

36. H.G. Slade, 'Castle Fraser', *PSAS* 109 (Edinburgh, 1977), p. 255. Seventeenth-century building legislation clearly has something to teach the twenty-first century.

37. H.G. Slade, 'Midmar Castle, Aberdeenshire', *PSAS* 113 (Edinburgh, 1983), pp. 594–620.

38. *RSS*, vol. viii, p. 635.

39. Crathes, 1596; Knock 1596; Birse late sixteenth century; Balfluig late sixteenth century; Tillycairn after 1590; Fyvie from 1596; Balbithan *c*. 1600; Westhall 1600; Midmar 1603–9; Cluny 1604; Craigston 1607; Barra 1614–18;

Drum 1615–23; Fraser 1617; Muchalls 1619–27; Craigievar 1626; Lickleyhead 1629.

40. From contemporary descriptions of the Gowrie conspiracy, it is clear that the perception of what we now call turrets was that they were studies.

41. Dundee University Archives, Kelly Castle no. V.MS 105P/562, *c.* 1860.

42. See D. MacGibbon and T. Ross, *The Castellated and Domestic Architecture of Scotland* (Edinburgh, 1887–92), vol. ii, pp. 108–11. Also Bath 'Renaissance Decoration'. The dated ceiling is in the Muses' Room.

43. M. Bath, *Renaissance Decorative Painting* (Edinburgh, forthcoming).

44. Ibid., chapters eight and nine.

45. Slade, 'Midmar'.

46. Illustrated in ibid., plate 43a.

47. Slade calls them 'trompes' because one side is expressed as a corbel and the other fades away into the wall: 'Midmar', p. 611. Squinches, however, were not unusual in Scotland, as may be seen in Pitsligo, Muckrach, Kellie and Glenbuchat.

48. M. Salter, *The Castles of Grampian and Angus* (Malvern, 1995), p. 37.

49. J. Skene of Rubislaw, quoted in MacGibbon and Ross, *Castellated and Domestic*, vol. ii, p. 235.

50. Ibid., p. 237.

51. There are some curious wall thicknesses and squint junctions and changes to floor level that argue the existence of an earlier building.

52. Slade, 'Castle Fraser', p. 252.

53. H.G. Slade, 'Craigston Castle, Aberdeenshire', *PSAS* 108 (Edinburgh, 1976), pp. 262–300. Slade also considers the planning to be much less advanced than its contemporaries. p. 271.

54. NTS, McCombie and Mennie, east elevation/section, 1968.

55. MacGibbon and Ross, *Castellated and Domestic*, vol. ii, p. 105 disagree utterly, but clearly did not have the time to study the oddities of the plan in much detail. I.B.D. Bryce has suggested that the earlier house of the Mortimers of Craigievar, described as Flemish, was in fact a house of the Towie and Craig School – see pp. 144–8, 'Craigievar: a fresh look at Scotland's premier tower house', *Architectural Heritage* XI (Edinburgh, 2000). Yet it lacks their characteristic plan and does not explain why the entrance should be several steps above all the cellars.

56. I am indebted to Ian Gow, 'Craigievar Castle' guidebook for much of what follows.

57. Ibid.

58. Quoted in MacGibbon and Ross, *Castellated and Domestic*, vol. ii, p. 113.

59. MacGibbon and Ross, *Castellated and Domestic*, vol. ii, p. 125, suggest that the designer might have been William Schaw. If so, it could only have been by a drawing, for he had died by 1602.

60. H.G. Slade holds that this wing represents a building anterior to the tower. Judging by the construction and the wall thicknesses, that seems extremely unlikely, although parts of it almost certainly embrace remains of an inner close – in the corner of which the round tower was probably first begun.

61. Patrick, 1st Earl of Strathmore, *Glamis Book of Record*, pp. 37–40.

62. Patrick, *Glamis Book of Record*, quoted in A.H. Millar, *The Historical Castles and Mansions of Scotland* (Paisley, 1890), p. 92.

63. Ibid., p. 215.

64. Hollow newels for holding lanterns or perhaps even for heating purposes were once widespread in Scotland.

65. The courtyard is several steps higher than the ground floor within.

66. Millar, *Castles and Mansions*, p. 216.

67. A hundred years ago, Glamis' Lower Hall was called the Great Hall, and was used for guests and hosts to meet before moving into the dining-room in the west wing (Ibid., p. 216). The hall above was the Drawing Room. Since the new stair is aligned with the upper hall rather than the one below, it does not seem likely that that was the plan in 1621. The upper one has much larger windows and the heraldic fireplace.

68. R.W. Billings, *The Baronial and Ecclesiastical Antiquities of Scotland* (Edinburgh, 1852), vol. ii, has an excellent drawing of this.

69. *Ane Account of the Family of Innes*, ed. C. Innes (Aberdeen, 1864), p. 266. Sir Robert Innes has quarriers working on the project from 1 January 1639. It is curious that Ayton is paid five years later. Either Innes brought him in later once dissatisfied with how the work was going, or he was a slow payer.

70. MacGibbon and Ross, *Castellated and Domestic*, vol. ii, p. 203.

71. Spalding, *History*, p. 26.

72. Hosted by Hermione Tennant, and stimulated by Joe and Carole Innes and Blair Brooks, and by their surveys, plans and sections, the study was undertaken in April 1998 by the author, Neil Grieve, James Simpson, Ian Davidson, Bob Heath, Peter Donaldson, Ted Ruddock and Kitty Cruft.

73. Spalding, *History*, p. 26.

74. Almost certainly replacing an earlier one approximately in this location.

75. That certainly appears to be the case in the ground level – now the dining-room.

76. Clearly revealed in the sections prepared by Joe Innes.

77. J.G Dunbar and K. Davies, 'Some late seventeenth-century building contracts', in *Scottish History Society Miscellany* XI (Edinburgh, 1990), pp. 269–332.

78. Ibid., p. 293.

79. Drawing by Brigadier Petit when it was still complete, National Library of Scotland Map Library, Board of Ordnance drawing Z3/27a, National Library of Scotland.

12. WAR AND PEACE, 1641–84

1. J. Spalding, *The History of the Troubles* (reprint, Aberdeen, 1830), pp. 74–5.

2. G. Blakhall, *A Briefe Narration* (Aberdeen, 1844), pp. 80–1.

3. Patrick Gordon of Ruthven, *A Short Abridgement of Britane's Distemper* (Aberdeen, 1844).

4. Spalding, *History*, p. 194.

5. Quote in A.M. Mackenzie, *Scottish Pageant 1625–1707* (Edinburgh, 1949), p. 189.

6. Quoted in A J. Warden, *Angus or Forfarshire* (Dundee, 1883), p. 355.

7. Henry Guthrie, 'Memoirs', in J.G. Fyfe, *Scottish Diaries and Memoirs* (Stirling, 1927), p. 143.

8. Spalding, *History*, p. 180.

9. Ibid., p. 183.

10. Ibid., p. 492.

11. D. Stevenson, *Highland Warrior* (Edinburgh, 1980), p. 148.

12. Spalding, *History*, p. 494.

13. Ibid., p. 490.

14. W. Nimmo, *History of Stirlingshire* (Stirling, 1817), p. 532.

15. Spalding, *History*, p. 494.

16. This analysis differs entirely from the accepted history of the house as stated, for example, in MacGibbon and Ross and RCAHMS, *Peeblesshire* (Edinburgh, 1963), pp. 311–25. The latter finds only the diminutive western tower old, but the plan of the house reveals a standard sixteenth-century palace block extending westwards from a much thicker-walled, earlier, probably L-plan tower at the east. The dormer windows are dated 1642, and the lowering of the east wing clearly predated James Smith's 1695 proposals to replicate it at the west end.

17. See pp. 144–5.

18. Patrick Gordon, quoted in R. Chambers, *Domestic Annals of Scotland* (Edinburgh, n.d.), vol. ii, p. 203.

19. Chambers, *Domestic Annals*, p. 211.

20. Robert Baillie, 'Memoirs', in Fyfe, *Scottish Diaries*, pp. 173–4.

21. *Letters and Journals of Robert Baillie*, ed. D. Laing (Edinburgh, 1842), p. 357.

22. Sir Archibald Stewart in 'Coltness Collections', quoted in Chambers, *Domestic Annals*, vol. ii, p. 245–7.

23. Macky, *Journey*, p. 285.

24. Stewart, 'Collections', Chambers, *Domestic Annals*, vol. ii, p. 256.

25. Ex info C. Wemyss.

26. R.S. Milne, *Master Masons to the Crown* (Edinburgh, 1893), p. 185.

27. See p. 197.

28. J. Guthrie Smith, *Strathblane*, pp. 135 and 315–17.

29. Just as the Earl of Mar recommended his son to spend August and September at the Mar seat of Braemar. ('Lord Mar's legacy to his son', in *Wariston's Diary and other papers*, ed. G.M. Paul (Edinburgh, 1896), p. 183).

30. *Glamis Book of Record*, quoted in A.H. Millar, *The Historical Castles and Mansions of Scotland* (Paisley, 1890), pp. 92–6.

31. Ibid., p. 94. 'No access there was to the upper pairt of the house without goeing through the hall, even upon the most undecent ocasions of drudgery, unavoidable to be seen by all who should happen to be in that room.'

32. Ibid., p. 95.

33. Inventory, *c.* 1680, Glamis Papers, 255/7/2.

34. Ibid.

35. A. Jervise, *Land of the Lindsays*, ed. J. Gammack (Edinburgh, 1881), p. 170.

36. Ibid., p. 192.

37. Ibid., p. 426: the description of the nursery lists the children who slept in it as well as the maids.

38. W. Macfarlane, *Geographical Collections Relating to Scotland* (Edinburgh, 1907–8), vol. i, pp. 50–1.

39. There are countless examples of this process over the next 150 years, from Philpston, West Lothian, in 1676 (see C. McWilliam, *Lothian* (Edinburgh, 1978), p. 388) to William Burn's reformatting of Invergowrie and John Smith's of Slains in the nineteenth century.

40. Walter Scott, *Waverley* (Edinburgh, 1829), vol. i, p. 82.

41. RCAHMS, *Edinburgh* (Edinburgh, 1951), p. 228.

42. There is not enough detail to form a picture of the house from the accounts. There was certainly a hall, several bedrooms, an east chamber and a writing chamber.

43. Information A. MacDonald, 'The navy, the palace and the pinewoods of Ross: a case study in the long-distance Scottish timber trade in the seventeenth century', in T.C. Smout, A.R. MacDonald, F. Watson, eds, *The Native Woodlands of Scotland: an Environmental History* (Edinburgh, forthcoming).

44. Marbling – the painting of wood or stone as imitation marble – had long been fashionable in expensive houses, beginning with the officials' apartments above the state apartments in the palace of Stirling.

45. 'The transe' in the original.

46. *The Account Book of Sir John Foulis of Ravelston*, ed. A.W.C. Hallen (Edinburgh, 1893), particularly pp. 1–80.

47. See, most recently, M. Glendinning *et al.*, *A History of Scottish Architecture* (Edinburgh, 1996), p. 90.

48. 'Lord Mar's Legacy to his son', in *Wariston's Diary*, p. 182.

49. See R.S. Mylne, *The Master Masons to the Crown of Scotland* (Edinburgh, 1893), pp. 161–200.

50. Described thus by the Earl of Kincardine to Lauderdale 9.3.1671, cited in Mylne, *Master Masons*, p. 165.

51. D. Calderwood, *A True History of the Church of Scotland, 1678* (facsimile reprint, Menston, 1971), p. 310 claimed that on his deathbed, Maitland murmured that he would have done better to have spent the money on a hospital.

52. Mylne, *Master Masons*, p. 168.

53. Now all missing thanks to David Bryce's mid-nineteenth-century reworking. See the 1794 drawing by James Denholm in Reid and Scott, *Interesting views in Scotland* (Edinburgh, 1802).

54. I am greatly indebted to Margaret Stewart's unpublished essay for an extended discussion on imagery and ancestors in relation to the architect Earl of Mar and his house at Alloa.

55. Millar, *Castles and Mansions*, p. 232; 'Architecturs' is a misspelling of 'architector', the normal seventeenth-century term for an architect, lifted directly from Latin.

56. The only change was that the roof of the new west wing had a flat balustraded viewing platform. See Fig. 4.3.

57. It was very similar to a comparable wing at Dunglass which likewise appeared to be enfolding a staircase (a rectangular one) at the centre of a triangular composition. (Reid and Scott, *Interesting Views*).

58. Millar, *Castles and Mansions*, p. 289 states that Panmure was on a new site. It was certainly some way away from the extensive, towered courtyard castle of Panmure which the earl had quit for the house of Bowshen after its destruction by the English during their occupation of Broughty *c.* 1549. Millar thought Bowshen distant from the new site, but the plan in *Vitruvius Scoticus* shows some enormously thick walls in the east of the new building, implying that Millar was mistaken. R.S. Mylne states that Panmure was building at, rather than near to, Bowshen (*Master Masons*, p. 155).

59. J. Gifford, *Fife* (London, 1988), pp. 84–7. This pattern of extension by a balancing addition, most evident in Holyrood, became quite common. Another, now invisible, was the extension of a 1595 L-plan house by doubling at nearby Balcarres, Fife, in 1662 (Gifford, *Fife*, pp. 80–1).

60. See J. Simpson, 'William Adam's design for Gladney', in Gow and Rowan, *Scottish Country Houses*. Generally Simpson views this type of house as rather later, into the early eighteenth century, but its ancestry is indubitable.

61. See RCAHMS, *Peeblesshire* (Edinburgh, 1967), pp. 283–5.

62. For example, Macfarlane, *Collections*, vol. i, pp. 93 and 123.

63. Ibid., pp. 171 and 58.
64. I am indebted to Charles Wemyss for most of this information from his researches into the seventeenth-century country house in Strathearn and, in particular, from the Smyth Papers in Perth Museum, and from GD 190 in the NAS.
65. Smith, newly back from an education in Rome, is generally associated with compact 'classical' houses whose pediments are framed by tall chimney-stacks, like Strathleven House or Rait. Accepted as an architect by his contemporaries, he was certainly at Kinross. There was no sharp break with the Scottish tradition in Smith's work, as there was not with Bruce. Melville House, for example, with its tall compact form, corner towers and cupola, has all the nobility of height and skyline of earlier generations of Scottish seats.
66. Sime, *Memorabilia* (National Monuments Record).
67. *Collections for a History of the Shires of Aberdeen and Banff* (Aberdeen, 1843), vol. iv, p. 449.
68. Macfarlane, *Collections*, vol. i., p. 54.
69. Macky, *Journey*, p. 14.
70. A painting by Robert Riddell *c.* 1780 shows Drumlanrig with tall harled towers flanking lower blocks.
71. See John Gifford, *Dumfries and Galloway* (London, 1966), pp. 222–30.
72. RCAHMS, *Peeblesshire*, plate 89.
73. This differs from J. Macaulay, *The Gothic Revival* (Glasgow, 1975), p. 50.

EPILOGUE: THE CASTLE OF DREAMS

1. 'Lord Mar's Legacy to his son', in *Wariston's Diary and other Papers*, ed. G.M. Paul (Edinburgh, 1896).
2. C.R. Mackintosh 'Untitled paper on Architecture', 1892, in *The Architectural Papers*, ed. P. Robertson (Wendlebury, 1990), p. 196.
3. Burns, *Colloque*, Vrais et fausses fortifications, Tours 2000.
4. Guillaume, *Colloque*, Vrais et fausses fortifications, Tours 2000.
5. In addition to a number of papers in books by MacKechnie, the author, and others, the principal change was heralded by the *Architecture of the Scottish Renaissance* exhibition in 1990 by the Royal Incorporation of Architects in Scotland curated by Deborah Howard, and Howard's subsequent volume *Scottish Architecture from the Reformation to the Restoration* (Edinburgh, 1995).
6. Maitland, p. 138, spelling partially modernised.
7. 'Legacy', p. 179.
8. Graham explained this – and claimed to have invented the term 'baronial' – in a letter to the Grand Duke of Russia in February 1848. NAS/GD/121/67/1/409.
9. Mackintosh, *Architectural Papers*, p. 63.
10. See F.A. Walker, 'Scottish Baronial Architecture', in C.R. Mackintosh, *Architectural Papers*, ed. P. Robertson (Wendlebury, 1990), pp. 29–65. All but the first four pages and the final page of Mackintosh's notes for his 1891 lecture on Scotch Baronial Architecture were extracted, more or less verbatim, from D. MacGibbon and T. Ross, *The Castellated and Domestic Architecture of Scotland* (Edinburgh, 1887–92), which therefore puts far more weight upon the introductory and concluding pages that represent Mackintosh's own views.
11. *Architectural Papers*, p. 52. See also C.A. McKean, 'The Début', in the *CRM Newsletter*, 60 (Winter, 1992).

12. S. Cruden, *The Scottish Castle* (Edinburgh, 1963), pp. 164–5.
13. The legacy may be seen in the fact that in R. Fawcett, *Scottish Architecture from the Accession of the Stewarts to the Reformation 1371–1560* (Edinburgh, 1994), the question of whether there was an architect with an *a priori* design is scarcely raised; and the architecture of 1500–50 is discussed almost entirely in terms of masons on the one hand, and foreign influences imported by patrons on the other.
14. See Appendix.
15. As MacGibbon and Ross believed. *Castellated and Domestic*, vol. v, pp. 515–69.
16. See p. 104.
17. J-P. Babelon, *Châteaux de France au siècle de la Renaissance* (Paris, 1989), pp. 313–17.
18. Bishop John Lesley, in P. Hume Brown, *Scotland before 1700 from Contemporary Documents* (Edinburgh, 1893), p. 171, spelling modernised.
19. Sir R. Maitland, *Quarto Manuscript*, ed. W.A. Craigie (Edinburgh, 1920), pp. 216–22, spelling partially modernised.

APPENDIX 1: DESIGN AND CONSTRUCTION

1. S. Cruden, *The Scottish Castle* (Edinburgh, 1963), p. 165.
2. See n. 5.
3. J.G. Dunbar and K. Davies, 'Some late seventeenth-century building contracts', *Scottish History Society Miscellany* XI (Edinburgh, 1990), pp. 272–3 in reference to Tobias Bauchop of Alloa.
4. D. MacGibbon and T. Ross, *The Castellated and Domestic Architecture of Scotland* (Edinburgh, 1887–92), vol. v, p. 567.
5. Deborah Howard, in *Scottish Architecture from the Reformation to the Restoration* (Edinburgh, 1995), nails this neatly by commenting on the pleasing seventeenth-century paradox of someone being an architect, and capable of great aesthetic imagination, and having high craft skills at the same time. Sir Philip Dowson, founder of Arup Associates, regarded his training as a cabinet-maker as invaluable.
6. R. Samson, 'The Rise and Fall of Tower-Houses in post-Reformation Scotland', in R. Samson, ed., *The Social Archaeology of Houses* (Edinburgh, 1991), p. 224.
7. M. Bath, *Renaissance Decorative Painting in Scotland* (National Museums of Scotland, forthcoming).
8. D. Calderwood, *A True History of the Church of Scotland, 1678* (facsimile reprint, Menston, 1971), pp. 44 and 46.
9. *Warrender Papers*, eds A.I. Cameron and R.S. Rait (Edinburgh, 1932), pp. 19–20. See also D. Shaw, 'Adam Bothwell, a Conserver of the Renaissance in Scotland', in I.B. Cowan and D. Shaw, eds, *The Renaissance and Reformation in Scotland* (Edinburgh, 1983), pp. 141–70.
10. NAS RH 13/11, no. 64. Amongst the books, 'Albert to Mr Hue' and 'Vigoli to Mr Kenneth' who also received 'Livres de Perspective'.
11. L. Kanerva, *Defining the Architect in Fifteenth-Century Italy* (Helsinki, 1998), p. 142.
12. Cited in ibid, p. 20.
13. J.G. Dunbar, *The Royal Palaces of Scotland* (East Linton, 1999), p. 236. Dunbar sees no change between the patterns in the reign of James I and James VI in this respect.

14. Kanerva, *Architect*, p. 15.
15. D. Stevenson, *The Origin of Freemasonry – Scotland's Century 1590–1710* (Cambridge, 1988), Chapter 5.
16. Dunbar and Davies, 'Building contracts', pp. 272–3.
17. For the significance of this see Stevenson.
18. H. Colvin, 'The beginnings of the architectural profession in Scotland', *Architectural History* 29 (London, 1986), pp. 173–4.
19. MacGibbon and Ross, *Castellated and Domestic*, vol. v, p. 555.
20. Much of the following section first appeared in C.A. McKean, 'Sir James Hamilton of Finnart – a Renaissance Courtier-Architect', *Architectural History* (London, 1999).
21. Dunbar, *Royal Palaces*, p. 237.
22. *RSS*, vol. ii, 2147.
23. *MW a/c, vol. i, 1527–1615*, ed. H. Paton (Edinburgh, 1957), p. 131.
24. *TA*, vol. vii. £200 for Finnart as Master of Works Principal, and £20 for Sir James Nicholson. The crucial post of Wardens of the March earned only £100, and Sir John Scrymgeour of Myres, 'principal master of works' at Falkland, £80.
25. Ibid., pp. 482, 393, 456, 471.
26. *RSS*, vol. ii, 3144.
27. *RSS*, vol. iii, 283. 'On 13 May 1543, John Hamilton of Cragye was made Master of Work of all our Sovereign Lady's palaces and places within the realm for all the days of his life.'
28. *RSS*, vol. ii, 3245.
29. *MW a/c, vol. i*, p. xxxiii, 30 April 1535.
30. Ibid., p. 228.
31. R. Fawcett, *The Architectural History of Scotland 1371–1560* (Edinburgh, 1994), p. 295.
32. J. Cameron, *James V – the Personal Rule* (East Linton, 1998), p. 202.
33. NAS RD/DAL/879. I am very grateful to Charles Wemyss for this and for sharing his researches about Invermay and seventeenth-century houses in the Earn valley.
34. J. Napier, *Notes and Reminiscences Relating to Partick* (Glasgow, 1873), p. 39.
35. NAS RD/MACK/70/42.
36. Ben Tindall and Ian Cumming have suggested that vernacular may be defined by all the materials having been obtained from within 400 yards of the site – unless a river were nearby.
37. MacGibbon and Ross, *Castellated and Domestic*, vol. v, p. 550.
38. Dunbar and Davis, 'Building contracts', pp. 278, 297–8.
39. Sir Robert Sibbald, *A History of Fife and Kinross* (new edn, Edinburgh, 1803), p. 411.
40. See T. Addyman and W. Kay, 'Archeological report on Old Auchentroig, Stirlingshire' for the NTS, and N. Grieve, report on Gardyne's Land, High Street, Dundee.
41. See R. Turner on archeology in the NTS, on Moirlannich ('Understanding the Scottish Home', forthcoming). Timbers in a roof of a house facing in Brechin's High Street are medieval Baltic pine. (N. Grieve, Tayside Building Preservation Trust).
42. MacGibbon and Ross, *Castellated and Domestic*, vol. iv, pp. 30–1.
43. Napier, *Partick*, pp. 23–43.
44. A.H. Millar, *Castles and Mansions*, pp. 288–91.
45. Ibid., p. 27.
46. M.R. Apted and S. Hannabuss, *Painters in Scotland 1301–1700* (Edinburgh, 1978), Introduction.
47. Ibid., p. 65.
48. Bath, *Decorative Painting*, p. 7.
49. Now in the Museum of Scotland.
50. Apted and Hannabuss, *Painters*, pp. 108–10.
51. Ibid., pp. 105–7.

Bibliography

PRIMARY SOURCES

The largest category of primary sources used for this book are the buildings themselves. In addition to visits, they can also be accessed through photographic collections at, for example, the Royal Commission on the Ancient and Historic Monuments of Scotland, or through drawings – at the National Monuments Record, or other collections such as the National Archives of Scotland at West Register House, Edinburgh University's Special Collections, or provided by owners such as the National Trust for Scotland. Some of the principal manuscript sources for the book are as follows:

Aberdeen University Archives

W. Douglas Simpson's collection of drawings and notes

Dundee University Archives

Kelly Castle drawings no.V.MS 105P/562
Glamis Papers MSS 255/7

Edinburgh University Special Collections

Rowand Anderson collection which includes William Burn's drawings of Hoddam, and several by Brown and Wardrop for *châteaux* alterations
The William Playfair collection contains some of Playfair's drawings for *châteaux* alterations, particularly Craigcrook, Prestongrange, and the House of Grange

Map Library, National Library of Scotland

Manuscript maps of Timothy Pont
Maps by John Adair
Board of Ordnance drawings

Mitchell Library, Glasgow

William Simpson drawings, *Views and Notices in Glasgow* – manuscript collection of Simpson's early nineteenth-century drawings and watercolours

National Archives of Scotland

Plans from the Gordon Castle Muniments RHP 2379 (1–6), RHP 2381–2, RHP 1075
The Book of Inventories NAS RH 13/11/38
Breadalbane Muniments NAS/GD/112
Fyvie Castle Muniments NASS/05251
NAS GD 237/262/3
Invermay contract. NAS – RD/DAL/879
NAS RH/6/1121B
John Clerk of Eldin, *Sketchbook* NAS/GD18/2118

National Library of Scotland

Major General John Brown, *Sketchbook*

Hutton Collection
J.C. Nattes, *Sketchbook*

National Monuments Record

Revd J. Sime, *Memorabilia*

National Museums of Scotland Library/Society of Antiquaries Library

Robert Riddell of Glenriddell, *Manuscript Collections*

National Trust for Scotland

Quinquennial Survey Plans for Brodie, The Binns, Leith Hall, Fyvie, Drum, Kellie, Crathes and Craigievar

Perth Museum

Smyth Papers

Household inventories

Household inventories form a coherent body of primary information about the way in which a house was used in addition to its furnishings. This list has been arranged in date order.

1558 Kelly Castle, Angus: *PSAS* (Edinburgh, 14.5.1917)
1559 Sanquhar-Hamilton, Ayr: NAS Court of Session Decrets 1559/60 (CS 7 20)
1562 Huntly: *Inventaires de La Royne Descosse Douairiere de France 1550–1569* (Edinburgh, 1863); *Collection of the Inventories of Mary Queen of Scots*, ed. T. Thomson (Edinburgh, 1815)
1595 Castle Campbell: *Scottish Historical Review*, vol. x, 1905, p. 301
1598 1600/04/09 Finlarig and Balloch: in *Black Book*, pp. 346–91
1604 Kenmure (Kenmore): in *Reliquae Antiquae Scotica*
1611 Byres: Fraser, *Earls of Haddington*, pp. 289–92
1612 Dunnottar: *Scottish Historical Review*, vol. ii (Glasgow, 1905)
1621 Barcaldine: RCAHMS *Argyll*, vol. ii, pp. 176–80
1633 Tyninghame: Fraser, *Earls of Haddington*, pp. 300–2

1640   Caerlaverock: Grose, *Antiquities*, vol. i, pp. 166–70
1647   Hamilton Palace in Marshall, *Duchess Anne*, pp. 234–46
1648   Floors: NAS/RH 13/11/12
1660   Dunnottar: *Scottish Historical Review*, vol. ii (Glasgow, 1905)
1667   Craigbarnet: Guthrie Smith, *Strathblane*, pp. 317–18
1680   Abbotshall: NAS/RH 13/11/34
1682   House of the Binns: *PSAS* (Edinburgh, 12.1.1924)
1684   Glamis: Glamis Papers, 255/7/2
1684   Castle Huntly: Glamis Papers, 255/7/2
1689   Fedderate: NAS/RH 13/11/26
1690s Kinnaird: Jones, 'A seventeenth century inventory', pp. 56–64
1699   Dunnottar: NAS/RH 13/11/38
1712   Finavon: Jervise, *Lindsays*, p. 426
1722   Fetteresso's pictures: Fraser, *The Lords Elphinstone*, pp. 271–3
1732   Westertown (packing for travel): NAS/RH 13/11/51
1736   Lochryan: NAS/RH 13/11/69

Printed primary sources

This section contains official documents, memoirs and topographical writing. The latter qualify as primary sources in that the authors record (or draw) what they themselves could observe, and frequently reprint original documents.

Account Book of Sir John Foulis of Ravelston, ed. A.W.C. Hallen (Edinburgh, 1893)
Accounts of the Lord High Treasurer of Scotland, eds T. Dickson and Sir J. Balfour Paul (Edinburgh, 1877–1916)
Accounts of the Masters of Works Vol. I 1529–1615, ed. H. Paton (Edinburgh, 1957)
Accounts of the Masters of Works Vol. II 1616–1649, eds J. Imrie and J. Dunbar (Edinburgh, 1982)
The Acts of the Parliaments of Scotland 1509–1603, eds T. Thomson and C. Innes (Edinburgh, 1833)
Adam, W., *Vitruvius Scoticus*, ed. J. Simpson (Edinburgh, 1980)
Ane Account of the Family of Innes, ed. C. Innes (Aberdeen, 1864)
Bannatyne Miscellany (Edinburgh, 1827)
Billings, R.W., *The Baronial and Ecclesiastical Architecture of Scotland* (Edinburgh, 1852)
Binns Papers 1320–1864, eds Sir J. Dalyell and J. Beveridge (Edinburgh, 1938)
The Black Book of Taymouth, ed. C. Innes (Taymouth, 1855)
Blakhall, G., *A Briefe Narration* (Aberdeen, 1844)
Boswell, J., *Journal of a Tour to the Hebrides* (new edn, Oxford, 1979)
Buchanan, G., *The History of Scotland*, ed. Mr Bond (Glasgow, 1799)
Calderwood, D., *A True History of the Church of Scotland, 1678* (facsimile reprint Menston, 1971)
Calendar of State Papers 1547–53, ed. W.B. Turnbull (London, 1861)
Calendar of State Papers Scotland, ed. M.J. Thorpe (London, 1858)
Campbell, A., *Journey from Edinburgh* (London, 1802)
Cardonnel, A. de, *Picturesque Antiquities of Scotland* (London, 1788)
Chambers, R., *Domestic Annals of Scotland*, three volumes (Edinburgh, n.d.)
Chronicles of the Atholl and Tullibardine Families (private, 1908)
Clerk of Eldin, J., *Views in Scotland* (Edinburgh, 1855)
Collection of the Inventories of Mary Queen of Scots, ed. T. Thomson (Edinburgh, 1815)
Collections for a History of the Shires of Aberdeen and Banff (Aberdeen, 1843)
Cordiner, C., *Antiquities and Scenery of the North of Scotland* (London, 1780)

Correspondence of the Earls of Ancram and Lothian, ed. D. Laing (Edinburgh, 1875)
Defoe, D., *A Tour through Great Britain* (reprint London, 1983)
Diurnal of Occurrents (Edinburgh 1833)
Dobie of Cumnock, J., *Cuninghame Topographized by Timothy Pont A.M.* (Glasgow, 1878)
Exchequer Rolls of Scotland, eds J. Stuart, et al. (Edinburgh, 1878–1908)
Franck, R., *Northern Memoirs*, ed. W. Scott (Edinburgh, 1821)
Fraser Papers (Edinburgh, 1924)
Fraser, Sir D., ed., *The Christian Watt Papers* (Collieston, 1988)
Fyfe, J.G., ed., *Scottish Diaries and Memoirs* (Stirling, 1927)
Garnett, T., *Observations on a Tour of the Highlands* (London, 1800)
Giles, J., *Castles of Aberdeenshire* (Aberdeen, 1936)
Gordon of Gordonstoun, Sir R., *A Genealogical History of the Earldom of Sutherland* (Edinburgh, 1813)
Gordon of Ruthven, P., *A Short Abridgement of Britain's Distemper* (Aberdeen, 1844)
Grose, F., *Antiquities of Scotland* (London, 1797).
Hamilton of Wishaw, W., *Descriptions of the Sheriffdoms of Lanark & Renfrew compiled c. MDCCX* (Glasgow, 1831)
Historic Manuscripts Commission, *Appendix to the Second Report, Part IV* (London, 1887)
——, *Appendix to the Fourth Report* (London, 1874)
——, *Appendix to the Eleventh Report Part VI*, 'The manuscripts of the Duke of Hamilton' (London, 1887)
——, *Appendix to vol. 12* (London, 1870)
Hume, D., of Godscroft, *A History of the Houses of Douglas and Angus* (Edinburgh, 1648)
Hume Brown, P., ed. *Early Travellers in Scotland* (new edn, Edinburgh, 1973)
——, *Scotland before 1700 from Contemporary Documents* (Edinburgh, 1893)
Illustration of the Reign of Mary Queen of Scots (Glasgow, 1837)
Innes, C., *Sketches of Early Scotch History* (Edinburgh, 1861)
Inventaires de La Royne Descosse Douairiere de France 1550–1569 (Edinburgh, 1863)
Knox, J., *The History of the Reformation in Scotland*, ed. C. Lennox (London, 1905)
——, *The History of the Reformation of Religion within the Realm of Scotland*, ed. C. Guthrie (London, 1898)
Lesley, J., Bishop of Ross, *The History of Scotland* (Edinburgh, 1830)
Letters and Journals of Robert Baillie, ed. D. Laing (Edinburgh, 1842)
Letters of James V, eds R.K. Hannay and D. Hay (Edinburgh, 1954)
Letters to James VI (Edinburgh, 1835)
Letters and Papers of Henry VIII Foreign & Domestic 1500–1547, eds J.S. Brewer et al. (London, 1864–98)
The Library of James VI (Edinburgh, 1893)
Lindsay, R., of Pitscottie, *The History of Scotland* (Edinburgh, 1778)
Lowther, C., *Our Journall into Scotland* (Edinburgh, 1894)
Macfarlane, W., *Geographical Collections Relating to Scotland*, eds Sir A. Mitchell and J.T. Clark (Edinburgh, 1907–8)
Mackenzie, A.M., *Scottish Pageant 1513–1625* (Edinburgh, 1948)
——, *Scottish Pageant 1625–1707* (Edinburgh, 1949)
Mackintosh, C.R., *The Architectural Papers*, ed. P. Robertson (Wendlebury, 1990)
Macky, J., *A Journey through Scotland* (London, 1723)
Maitland Folio Manuscript, ed. W.A. Craigie (Edinburgh, 1919)
Maitland Miscellany (Edinburgh, 1834)
Maitland Quarto Manuscript, ed. W.A. Craigie (Edinburgh, 1920)
Maitland, Sir R., *The History of the House of Seytoun* (Glasgow, 1829)

Melvill, Sir James, of Hal-Hil, *The Memoires* (London, 1683)

Memorials of George Bannatyne (Edinburgh, 1829)

Miscellenea Antiqua (London, 1910)

Montgomerie, A., *The Cherrie and the Slae*, ed. H.H. Wood (London, 1937)

Moyses, D., *Memoirs of the Affairs of Scotland* (Edinburgh, 1755)

National Art Survey, three volumes (Edinburgh, 1921–33)

Nattes, J.C., and Fittler, J., *Scotia Depicta* (London, 1804)

Nimmo, W., *History of Stirlingshire* (Stirling, 1817)

Pitcairn, R., *Criminal Trials in Scotland*, vol. 1, part 1 (Edinburgh, 1833)

Register of the Privy Council of Scotland, eds J.H. Burton et al. (Edinburgh, 1878–1902)

Register of the Privy Seal of Scotland, ed. J. Beveridge (Edinburgh, 1952)

Registrum Magni Sigilii Regum Scotorum, eds J.M. Thomson et al. (Edinburgh, 1882–1914)

Registrum Secreti Sigilii Regum Scotorum, eds J.H. Burton et al. (Edinburgh, 1908)

Reid, J., *The Scots Gard'ner*, ed. A. Hope (Edinburgh, 1988)

Reid and Scott, *Interesting Views in Scotland* (Edinburgh, 1802)

Reliquae Antiquae Scoticae (Edinburgh, 1848)

Rogers, Revd C., *Estimate of the Scottish Nobility during the Minority of James VI* (London, 1873)

Scot of Scotstarvit, Sir John, *The Staggering State of Scots Statesmen from 1550–1600* (Edinburgh, 1754)

Scott, W., *Border Antiquities* (Edinburgh, 1814)

Scott, Sir W., *Waverley* (Edinburgh, 1829)

Scottish History Society Miscellany (Edinburgh 1904)

'A Scottish Journie 1641', in *Scottish History Society Miscellany* (Edinburgh 1904)

Sibbald, Sir R., *History of Fife and Kinross* (new edn, London, 1803)

Slezer, Captain J., *Theatrum Scotiae*, ed. J. Jamieson (London, 1693, reprint Edinburgh, 1874)

Somervill, 11th Lord, *Memoir of the Somervills*, 1679, ed. W. Scott (Edinburgh, 1815)

Spalding, J., *The History of the Troubles* (reprint, Aberdeen, 1830)

Spottiswoode, J., *The History of the Church of Scotland 1655* (facsimile reprint, Menston, 1972)

Strathmore, Patrick, 1st Earl of, *Glamis Book of Record*, ed. A.H. Millar (Edinburgh, 1890)

Two Missions of Jacques de la Brosse, ed. G. Dickinson (Edinburgh, 1942)

Wariston's Diary and Other Papers, ed. G.M. Paul (Edinburgh, 1896)

Warrender Papers, eds A.I. Cameron and R. Rait (Edinburgh, 1931)

SECONDARY SOURCES

Broader histories, cultural and historical issues

Angus, D., 'Mary's Marginalia', *Review of Scottish Culture 3* (Edinburgh, 1987)

Bentley-Cranch, D. and Marshall, R.K., 'Iconography and literature in the service of diplomacy', in J. Hadley Williams, ed. *Stewart Style 1513–1542* (East Linton, 1998)

Broun, D., Finlay R.J., and Lynch, M., eds, *Image and Identity* (Edinburgh, 1998)

Brown, K., *Bloodfeud in Scotland 1573–1625* (Edinburgh, 1986)

——, *Noble Society in Scotland* (Edinburgh, 2000)

Cameron, J., *James V – the Personal Rule* (East Linton, 1998)

Clark, A.M., *Murder Under Trust* (Edinburgh, 1981)

Cowan, E.J., 'The Darker Version of the Scottish Renaissance', in I.B. Cowan and D. Shaw eds, *The Renaissance and Reformation in Scotland* (Edinburgh, 1983)

Cowan, I.B., and Shaw, D., eds, *The Renaissance and Reformation in Scotland* (Edinburgh, 1983)

Devine, T.M., *The Scottish Nation* (London, 1999)

Dodgshon, R., *From Chiefs to Landlords* (Edinburgh, 1998)

Donaldson, G., *James V–James VII* (Edinburgh, 1987)

Edington, C., *Court and Culture in Renaissance Scotland* (East Linton, 1994)

Emond, W.K., 'The minority of King James V' (PhD thesis, University of St Andrews, 1988)

Federov, D.G., 'Russia's Scottish clans', *Scottish Records Association Conference Report 1993*

Furgal, E.M., 'The Scottish Itinerary of Mary Queen of Scots 1542–8 and 1561–8', *PSAS* 117 (Edinburgh, 1987)

Gibson, A., and Smout, T.C., 'Food and hierarchy in Scotland 1550–1650', in L. Leneman ed., *Perspectives in Scottish Social History* (Aberdeen, 1988)

Goodare, J., and Lynch, M., *The Reign of James VI* (East Linton, 2000)

Hadley Williams, J., ed., *Stewart Style 1513–1542* (East Linton, 1998)

Harvey, P.D.A., *Topographical Maps* (London, 1980)

——, *Maps in Tudor England* (London, 1993)

Hewitt, G., 'Reformation to Revolution', in I. Donnachie and C. Whatley eds, *The Manufacture of Scottish Identity* (Edinburgh, 1992)

Hume Brown, P., *Surveys of Scottish History* (Glasgow, 1919)

Kelley, M.G., 'The Douglas Earls of Angus' (PhD thesis, University of Edinburgh)

Lee, M., 'King James' Popish Chancellor', in I.B. Cowan and D. Shaw eds, *The Renaissance and Reformation in Scotland* (Edinburgh, 1983)

Leneman, L., ed., *Perspectives in Scottish Social History* (Aberdeen, 1988)

Lynch, M., *Scotland, a New History* (London, 1991)

Macdonald, M., *Scottish Painting* (London, 2000)

Macdougall, N., *James IV* (East Linton, 1997)

Macinnes, A.I., *Clanship, Commerce and the House of Stuart* (East Linton, 1996)

MacKenzie, R., *A Scottish Renaissance Household* (Darvel, 1990)

McNeill, P.G.B. and MacQueen, H.L., eds, *Atlas of Scottish History to 1707* (Edinburgh, 1996)

Mapstone, S., and Wood, J., eds, *The Rose and the Thistle* (East Linton, 1998)

Mason, R., *Kingship and the Commonweal* (East Linton, 1998)

——, and Macdougall N., *People and Power in Scotland* (Edinburgh, 1992)

Mathew, D., *Scotland under Charles I* (London, 1955)

Mitchison, R., *Lordship to Patronage* (London, 1983)

Sanderson, M.H.B., *Scottish Rural Society in the Sixteenth Century* (Edinburgh, 1982)

——, *Ayrshire and the Reformation* (East Linton, 1997)

The Scottish Historical Review, vols 10 and 11 (Glasgow, 1905 and 1913)

Simpson, G.G., ed., *Scotland and the Low Countries* (East Linton, 1996)

Smout, T.C., *A History of the Scottish People 1560–1830* (London, 1969)

Stevenson, D., 'The English Devil of Keeping State', in R. Mason and N. Macdougall eds, *People and Power in Scotland* (Edinburgh, 1992)

——, *Scotland's Last Loyal Wedding* (Edinburgh, 1997)

Stone, J., *The Pont Manuscript Maps of Scotland* (Tring, 1989)

Tytler, P.F., *History of Scotland* (new edn, London, c. 1880)

Whatley, C., *Scottish Society 1707–1830* (Manchester, 2000)

Whyte, I., *Agriculture and Society in Seventeenth Century Scotland* (Edinburgh, 1979)

——, 'Poverty or Prosperity? Rural Society in Lowland Scotland in the Late Sixteenth and Early Seventeenth centuries', *Scottish Economic and Social History* (Edinburgh, 1998)

Wormald, J., *Court, Kirk and Community* (London, 1981)

——, *Lords and Men in Scotland* (Edinburgh, 1985)

Biographies and genealogies

Aiton, W., *Enquiry into the Pedigree (etc.) of the Hamilton Family* (Glasgow, 1822)

Anderson, J., *Historical and Genealogical Memoirs of the House of Hamilton* (Edinburgh, 1825)

Anderson, P.D., *Robert Stewart, Earl of Orkney, Lord of Shetland* (Edinburgh, 1982)

Balfour Paul, Sir J., *The Scots Peerage* (Edinburgh, 1905)

Finnie, E., 'The House of Hamilton', *Innes Review*, no. 36 (1985)

Fraser, Sir W., *Chiefs of Grant* (Edinburgh, 1883)

——, *Memorials of the Earls of Haddington* (Edinburgh, 1889)

——, *The Lords Elphinstone of Elphinstone* (Edinburgh, 1897)

Hamilton, Lt Col G., *A History of the House of Hamilton* (Edinburgh, 1933)

McFarlane, I.D., *Buchanan* (London, 1981)

Marshall, R.K., *The Days of Duchess Anne* (East Linton, 2000)

——, *Mary Queen of Scots* (Edinburgh, 1986)

——, *Mary of Guise* (London, 1977)

Sanderson, M., *Mary Stewart's People* (Edinburgh, 1987)

——, *Cardinal of Scotland David Beaton* (Edinburgh, 1986)

Seton, G., *Memoir of Alexander Seton, Earl of Dunfermline* (Edinburgh, 1882)

Snoddy, T.G., *Sir John Scot of Scotstarvit* (Edinburgh, 1968)

Stevenson, D., *Highland Warrior* (Edinburgh, 1980)

Regional histories and topography

Baptie, D., *A Lairdship Lost* (East Linton, 2000)

Greenshields, J.B., *Annals of the Parish of Lesmahagow* (Glasgow, 1864)

Jervise, A., *Land of the Lindsays*, ed. J. Gammack (Edinburgh, 1881)

——, *Memorials of Angus and the Mearns* (Edinburgh, 1851)

Leighton, J.M., *History of the County of Fife* (Glasgow, 1840)

Macdonald, A., *Linlithgow in Pictures* (Edinburgh, 1932)

MacDougall, H., *Island of Kerrera* (Oban, 1979)

Napier, J., *Notes and Reminiscences Relating to Partick* (Glasgow, 1873)

Smith, J. Guthrie, *The Parish of Strathblane* (Glasgow, 1886)

Walker, N.H., *The Seven Castles of Kinrosshire* (Kinross, 1993)

Warden, A.J., *Angus or Forfarshire*, five volumes (Dundee, 1882)

Architecture, painting and interiors

Airs, M., *The Tudor and Jacobean Country House* (Stroud, 1995)

Anderson, C., 'Pallaces of the poets'; an idea of the Tudor and Jacobean Country House', in Airs, M., ed., *The Tudor and Jacobean Great House* (Oxford, 1994)

Anderson, W.J., *The Architecture of the Renaissance in Italy* (London, 1901)

Apted, M.R., *Aberdour Castle* (Edinburgh, 1985)

——, *Claypotts Castle* (Edinburgh, 1957)

——, *Painted Ceilings of Scotland* (Edinburgh, 1966)

——, and Snowden, R., 'The De Wet paintings at Glamis Castle', in D. Breeze, ed., *Studies in Scottish Antiquity* (Edinburgh, 1984)

——, and Hannabuss, S., *Painters in Scotland 1301–1700* (Edinburgh, 1978)

Babelon, J-P., *Châteaux de France au siècle de la Renaissance* (Paris, 1989)

Bath, M., 'Alexander Seton's Painted Gallery', in L. Gent, ed., *Albion's Classicism* (Yale, 1995)

——, *Renaissance Decorative Painting in Scotland* (National Museums of Scotland, forthcoming)

Bentley-Cranch, D., 'An early sixteenth-century French Architectural Source for the Palace of Falkland', *Review of Scottish Culture* 2 (Edinburgh, 1986)

——, and Marshall, R., 'Iconography and literature in the service of diplomacy', in J. Hadley Williams, ed., *Stewart Style 1513–1542* (East Linton, 1998)

Billings, R.W., 'On certain features of the ancient architecture of Scotland', *Transactions of the Architectural Institute of Scotland* (Edinburgh, 1853)

Breeze, D., *A Queen's Progress* (Edinburgh, 1987)

Bryce, I.B.D., and Roberts, D., 'Post Reformation Catholic Houses', *PSAS* 123 (Edinburgh, 1993)

——, 'Craigievar: a fresh look at Scotland's premier tower house', *Architectural Heritage* XI (Edinburgh, 2000)

Burnett, C.J., and Dennis, M.D., *Scotland's Heraldic Heritage* (Edinburgh, 1997)

Buxbaum, T., *Scottish Garden Buildings* (Edinburgh, 1989)

Caldwell, D.H., ed., *Scottish Weapons and fortifications 1100–1800* (New Jersey, 1981)

Campbell, I., 'A Romanesque Revival and the Early Renaissance in Scotland', *JSAH* 54.3 (September 1995)

——, 'Linlithgow's princely palace and its influence in Europe', *Architectural Heritage* (Edinburgh, 1995)

Cavers, K., *A Vision of Scotland* (Edinburgh, 1993)

Clow, R., ed., *Restoring Scotland's Castles* (Glasgow, 2000)

Colvin, H., 'The beginnings of the architectural profession in Scotland', *Architectural History* 29 (London, 1986)

Cox, E.M., Owen, O., and Pringle, D., 'The discovery of medieval deposits beneath the Earl's Palace. Kirkwall', *PSAS* 128 (Edinburgh, 1998)

Cruden, S., *The Scottish Castle* (Edinburgh, 1963)

Davis, M., *The Castles and Mansions of Ayrshire* (Ardrishaig, 1991)

Dehn-Nielsen, H., *Slotte og Herregarde – set fra luften* (Viborg, 1996)

Dewar, A., *Castle Menzies* (Pilgrim Press, 1992)

Dunbar, J.G., *The Historic Architecture of Scotland* (London, 1966)

——, 'French influence in Scottish Architecture during the Sixteenth Century', in SRA Conference Report (September 1989)

——, 'Some 16th century French parallels for the Palace of Falkland', *Review of Scottish Culture* 7 (Edinburgh, 1991)

——, *The Royal Palaces of Scotland* (East Linton, 1999)

——, and Davies, K., 'Some late seventeenth-century building contracts', *Scottish History Society Miscellany* XI (Edinburgh, 1990)

Durand, P., *An Old Scottish Town House* (Glasgow, 1953)

Emmerson, R., 'The Building of Fyvie Castle' in *Treasures of Fyvie* (Edinburgh, 1985)

Erlande-Brandenburg, A., and Jestaz, B., *Le Château de Vincennes* (Paris, 1989)

Fawcett, R., *The Castles of Fife* (Glenrothes, 1993)

——, *The Architectural History of Scotland 1371–1560* (Edinburgh, 1994)

——, *Stirling Castle* (London, 1995)

Fenwick, H., *Architect Royal* (Kyneton, 1970)

——, *Scottish Baronial Houses* (London, 1986)

Fiore, F.P., and Tafuri, M., *Francesco di Giorgio Architetto* (Milan, 1993)

Fleming, J., *Robert Adam and his Circle* (London, 1962)

Fleming, J.S., *Ancient Castles and Mansions of the Stirling Nobility* (Paisley, 1902)

Fontaine, M-M., 'La vie autour du château', in J. Guillaume, ed., *Jardins, Chasses, Plaisirs* (Paris, 1999)

Geddes, J., *Kincardine and Deeside* (Rutland Press, forthcoming)

Gifford J., McWilliam, C., and Walker, D., *Buildings of Scotland – Edinburgh* (London, 1984)

Gifford, J., *Buildings of Scotland – Fife* (London, 1988)

——, *Buildings of Scotland – Highlands and Islands* (London, 1992)

——, *Buildings of Scotland – Dumfries and Galloway* (London, 1996)

Gillespie, J., *Details of Scottish Domestic Architecture* (new edn, Edinburgh, 1992)

Girouard, M., *Robert Smythson and the Architecture of the Elizabethan Era* (London, 1966)

——, *Life in the English Country House* (New Haven, 1978)

——, *Life in the French Country House* (London, 2000)

Glendinning, M., MacInnes, R., and MacKechnie, A., *A History of Scottish Architecture* (Edinburgh, 1996)

Gow, I., *Craigievar Castle* (Edinburgh, 1999)

——, and Rowan, A., *The Scottish Country House 1600–1914* (Edinburgh, 1995)

Graham, C., *Grampian, the Castle Country* (Aberdeen, n.d.)

Grodecki, C., *Les travaux de Philibert Delorme pour Henri II* (Nogent le Roi, 2000)

Hannan, T., *Famous Scottish Houses* (London, 1928)

Harris, S., 'The fortifications and siege of Leith', *PSAS* 121 (Edinburgh, 1991)

Hay, G., 'Scottish Renaissance Architecture', in D. Breeze, ed., *Studies in Scottish Antiquity* (Edinburgh, 1984)

Haynes, N., *Perthshire – an Illustrated Architectural Guide* (Edinburgh, 2000)

Hein, J., and Kristiansen, P., *Rosenborg* (Copenhagen, 1999)

Hill, O., *Scottish Castles of the Sixteenth and Seventeenth Centuries* (London, 1953)

Howard, D., *Scottish Architecture from the Reformation to the Restoration* (Edinburgh, 1995)

——, 'Chasse Sport et Plaisir: autour des châteaux de la renaissance en Ecosse', in J. Guillaume, ed., *Jardins, Chasses, Plaisirs* (Paris, 1999)

Howard, M., 'The architecture and social history of the Tudor and Jacobean Great House', in Airs, M., *The Tudor and Jacobean Great House* (Oxford, 1994)

——, 'Inventories, surveys and the histories of great houses 1480–1640', *Architectural History* (London, 1998)

Hutcheson, A., 'Inventory of the Goods and Plenishings . . . of Agnes Betoun', *PSAS* (Edinburgh, 14.5.1917)

Hynd, N., 'Towards a study of gardening in Scotland from the sixteenth to the eighteenth centuries', in D. Breeze, ed., *Studies in Scottish Antiquity* (Edinburgh, 1984)

——, 'The representation of the royal apartments within Edinburgh Castle' (unpublished paper, 1995)

Jamieson, F., 'The Royal Gardens of the Palace of Holyroodhouse', *Garden History*, vol. 22, no. i (1994)

Jamieson, J. *The Royal Palaces of Scotland* (Glasgow, 1840)

Jones, D., 'A seventeenth-century inventory of furnishings at Kinnaird Castle, Angus', in J. Frew and D. Jones, eds, *Aspects of Scottish Classicism* (St Andrews, 1989)

Kanerva, L., *Defining the Architect in Fifteenth Century Italy* (Helsinki, 1998)

Kay, W., 'Would the real William Adam please stand up?', *Architectural Heritage* 1 (Edinburgh, 1990)

Kemp, M., ed., *Leonardo da Vinci – the Mystery of the Madonna of the Yarnwinder* (Edinburgh, 1992)

Knecht, R., 'Noblesses anglaise et française: une comparaison', at the *Colloque* (Tours, 2000)

Leask, H.G., *Irish Castles and Castellated Houses* (Dundalk, 1999)

Lees-Milne, J., *Tudor Renaissance* (London, 1951)

Levron, J., *The Royal Châteaux of the Île de France* (London, 1965)

Lewis, J., Cox, E., and Smith, H., 'Excavations at Craignethan Castle 1984 and 1995', *PSAS* 128 (Edinburgh, 1998)

Lugton, T., *The Old Ludgings of Glasgow* (Glasgow, 1901)

Luneau, J-F., 'Les vitraux de la Sainte Chapelle de Vic-le-Comte', *Revue de l'Art* no. 107 (Paris, 1995)

Macaulay, J., *The Gothic Revival* (Glasgow, 1975)

MacGibbon, D., and Ross, T., *The Castellated and Domestic Architecture of Scotland*, five volumes (Edinburgh, 1887–92)

MacIvor, I., 'Artillery and major places of strength in the Lothians', in D. Caldwell, ed., *Scottish Weapons and Fortifications 1100–1800* (New Jersey, 1981)

——, 'Sir James Hamilton of Finnart and the Palace at Stirling Castle' (unpublished, 1992)

——, 'Craignethan Castle, Lanarkshire', in *Ancient Monuments and their Interpretation* (Edinburgh, 1977)

McKean, C.A., *The District of Moray* (Edinburgh, 1987)

——, *Banff and Buchan* (Edinburgh, 1989)

——, 'Finnart's Platt', *Architectural Heritage* 2 (Edinburgh, 1991)

——, 'The House of Pitsligo', *PSAS* 121 (Edinburgh, 1991)

——, 'Hamilton of Finnart', *History Today* (January 1993)

——, 'The Wrichtishousis – a very curious edifice', *Book of the Old Edinburgh Club*, new series, vol. 3 (Edinburgh, 1994)

——, 'Sir James Hamilton of Finnart', Thomas Ross Prize Dissertation in RIAS Library, 1994

——, 'A plethora of palaces', in I. Gow and A. Rowan, eds, *The Scottish Country House 1600–1914* (Edinburgh, 1995)

——, 'The Chanonry of Dunblane', *Journal of the Society of Friends of Dunblane Cathedral* XVII (Dunblane, 1996)

——, 'The re-evaluation of Scottish Renaissance Architecture', *Architectural Heritage* VI (Edinburgh, 1996)

——, 'Craignethan, the house of the Bastard of Arran', *PSAS* (Edinburgh, 1996)

——, 'The Palace at Edinburgh Castle', *Book of the Old Edinburgh Club* (Edinburgh 1998)

——, 'Sir James Hamilton of Finnart – a Renaissance Courtier-Architect', *Architectural History* (London, 1999)

——, 'The Evolution of the European Weather-protected City', in P. Dennison, ed., *Conservation and Change in Historic Towns* (York, 2000)

——, Walker D., and Walker, F.A., *Central Glasgow, an Illustrated Architectural Guide* (Edinburgh, 1990)

MacKechnie, A., 'Scots Court Architecture of the early 17th century' (PhD thesis, University of Edinburgh, 1993)

——, 'Evidence of a post-1603 Court Architecture in Scotland', *Architectural History* 31 (London, 1988)

——, 'Design in early Post Reformation Scots Houses', in I. Gow, and A. Rowan, *The Scottish Country House 1600–1914* (Edinburgh, 1995)

——, 'James VI's Architects', in Goodare and Lynch, *James VI* (East Linton, 2000)

MacKenzie, W.M., *The Medieval Castle in Scotland* (London, 1927)

——, 'Old Cromarty Castle', *PSAS* (Edinburgh, 1947–8)

McNeill, T., *Castles in Ireland* (London, 1997)

McWilliam, C., *Lothian* (London, 1978)

Marshall, R.K., 'The plenishings of Hamilton Palace in the seventeenth century', *Review of Scottish Culture* 3 (Edinburgh, 1987)

Mason R., 'Humanism and political culture', in R. Mason, and N. Macdougall, eds, *People and Power* (Edinburgh, 1992)

Maxwell-Irving, A.T., 'Hoddam Castle – a re-appraisal of its architecture and place in history', *PSAS* 117 (Edinburgh, 1987)

——, 'Scottish yetts and window-grilles', *PSAS* 124 (Edinburgh, 1994)

——, *The Border Towers of Scotland – the West March* (Blairlogie, 2000)

Merriman, M.H., *The Forts of Eyemouth 1547–1559* (n.d.)

——, *The Rough Wooings – Mary Queen of Scots 1542–1551* (East Linton, 2000)

Millar, A.H., *The Historical Castles and Mansions of Scotland* (Paisley, 1890)

Mossakowski, S., 'Ethos of the Royal Palace in Cracow', *Polish Art Studies* iii (Warsaw, 1982)

Mussat, A., 'Château-miroir', in B. Kopeczi and E.H. Balàzes, eds, *Noblesse française, noblesse hongroise XVI–XIX siècles* (Budapest and Paris, 1981)

Mylne, R.S., *The Master Masons to the Crown of Scotland* (Edinburgh, 1893)

Myrtue, A., *Castles and Manor Houses of Funen* (Odense, 1997)

Neilsen, G., *Peel, its Meaning and Derivation* (Glasgow, 1893)

Pattullo, N., *Castles, Houses and Gardens of Scotland*, two volumes (Edinburgh, 1974)

Pedretti, C., *Leonardo, Architect* (London, 1986)

Prentice, A.N., *Renaissance Architecture and Ornament in Spain*, ed. H.W. Booton (London, 1970)

Pringle, D., '"Cadzow Castle" and "The Castle of Hamilton": an archeological and historical conundrum', *Château Gaillard XV* (Caen, 1992)

Proudfoot, E., and Aliaga-Kelly, C., 'Excavations at Niddry Castle, West Lothian, 1986–90', *PSAS* 127 (Edinburgh, 1997)

Richardson, J.S., 'Mural Decorations at the House of Kinneil, Bo'ness', *PSAS* (Edinburgh, 1940–1)

——, *The Medieval Stone Carver in Scotland* (Edinburgh, 1964)

——, *Stirling Castle* (Edinburgh, 1972)

Richens, R., 'History of the Hamilton Lands in Lesmahagow' (unpublished)

Robertson, F.W., *Early Scottish Gardeners and their Plants* (East Linton, 2000)

Rosenfeld, M. nan, *Serlio on Domestic Architecture* (New York, 1978)

Royal Commission on the Ancient and Historic Monuments of Scotland, *Argyll Vol. 2 – Lorn* (Edinburgh, 1975)

——, *Argyll Vol. 7– Mid Argyll and Cowal* (Edinburgh, 1992)

——, *County of Dumfries* (Edinburgh, 1920)

——, *Fife, Kinross and Clackmannon* (Edinburgh, 1933)

——, *Peeblesshire* (Edinburgh, 1967)

——, *Stirlingshire* (Edinburgh, 1963)

Salter, M., *The Castles of Scotland*, six volumes (Malvern, 1993–6)

Samson, R., 'The rise and fall of tower-houses in post-Reformation Scotland', in R. Samson, ed., *The Social Archaeology of Houses* (Edinburgh, 1991)

——, 'Tower houses in the sixteenth century', in S. Foster, A. Macinnes, R. MacInnes, eds, *Scottish Power Centres* (Glasgow, 1998)

Sanderson, M., *Robert Adam and Scotland* (Edinburgh, 1990)

Shepherd, I., *Aberdeen and North-east Scotland* (Edinburgh, 1996)

Shire, H., 'The King in his House', in J. Hadley Williams, ed., *Stewart Style 1513–1542* (East Linton, 1998)

Simpson J., 'William Adam's design for Gladney', in I. Gow, and A. Rowan, *The Scottish Country House 1600–1914* (Edinburgh, 1995)

Simpson W. Douglas, 'Notes on Five Donside Castles', *PSAS* (Edinburgh, 14.2.1921)

——, 'The Architectural History of Huntly Castle', *PSAS* (Edinburgh, 13.2.1922)

——, 'Edzell Castle', *PSAS* (Edinburgh, 8.12.1930)

——, 'Further notes on Huntly Castle', *PSAS* (Edinburgh, 9.1.1933)

——, 'Invermark Castle', *PSAS* (Edinburgh, 11.12.1933)

——, 'Balvenie Castle', *Transactions of the Banffshire Field Club* (16.7.1938)

——, 'Tolquhon Castle and its builders', *PSAS* (Edinburgh, 1938)

——, 'Fyrie Castle', *PSAS* (Edinburgh, 1939)

——, 'Two Donside Castles', *PSAS* (Edinburgh, 1942)

——, *Exploring Castles* (London, 1957)

——, 'The Northmost Castle of Britain', *Scottish Historical Review* (Edinburgh, 1959)

——, and Breeze, D.J., *Bishop's Palace and Earl's Palace* (Edinburgh, 1986)

Slade, H.G., 'Beldorney Castle, Aberdeenshire: an early Z plan Tower House', *PSAS* 105 (Edinburgh, 1975)

——, 'Craigston Castle, Aberdeenshire', *PSAS* 108 (Edinburgh, 1976–7)

——, 'Castle Fraser', *PSAS* 109 (Edinburgh, 1977)

——, 'Midmar Castle, Aberdeenshire', *PSAS* 113 (Edinburgh, 1983)

——, 'Fyvie Castle, Aberdeenshire', *Château Gaillard XII* (Caen, 1984)

——, 'The Tower and House of Drum, Aberdeenshire', *PSAS* 115 (Edinburgh, 1985)

——, *Old Cromarty Castle* (Cromarty, 1993)

Smith, J.S., *North East Castles* (Aberdeen, 1990)

Spence, J., *Ruined Castles in Banff* (Edinburgh, 1873)

Stell, G., 'The Scottish Tower House', *RIAS Prospect* (Edinburgh, 1983)

——, 'The Scottish Medieval Castle', in K.J. Stringer, ed., *Essays on the Nobility of Medieval Scotland* (Edinburgh, 1985)

——, 'Kings, nobles and buildings of the later Middle Ages, Scotland', in G. Simpson, ed., *Scotland and Scandinavia* (Edinburgh, 1992)

Stevenson, D., *The Origin of Freemasonry – Scotland's Century 1590–1710* (Cambridge, 1988)

Stewart, M., 'The Earl of Mar and Scottish baroque', *Architectural Heritage IX* (Edinburgh, 1998)

Stirling, A.M.W., *Fyvie Castle* (London, 1928)

Sutherland, J., 'The Heraldic Ceiling of Balbegno Castle', *Aberdeen University Review XLVI* (Aberdeen, 1976)

Swain, M., 'The Loch Leven and Linlithgow hangings', *PSAS* 124 (Edinburgh, 1994)

Tabraham, C., *Kildrummy Castle and Glenbuchat Castle* (Edinburgh, 1995)

——, *Scottish Castles* (London, 1997)

Thomas, A., 'Renaissance Culture at the Court of James V' (PhD thesis, University of Edinburgh, 1997)

Thomson, D., *Renaissance Paris* (Berkeley, 1984)

Thurley, S., 'Henry VIII and the building of Hampton Court', *Architectural History* (London, 1988)

——, *The Royal Palaces of Tudor England* (New Haven, 1993)

Tranter, N., *The Fortified House in Scotland* (Edinburgh 1962–8)

Urquhart, E.A., *Castle Huntly – its History and Development* (Dundee, 1956)

Walker, D., 'The architecture of MacGibbon and Ross – the background to the books', in D. Breeze, ed., *Studies in Scottish Antiquity* (Edinburgh, 1984)

——, 'The adaptation and restoration of tower houses', in R. Clow, ed., *Restoring Scotland's Castles* (Glasgow, 2000)

Walker, N.H., *Kinross House* (Kinross, 1990)

Ward, T., *Glenochar Castle House and Fermtoun* (Lanark, 1998)

Ward, W.H., *The Architecture of the Renaissance in France* (London, n.d.)

Warrack, J., *Domestic Life in Scotland, 1488–1688* (London, 1920)

Weaver, Sir L., *The Scottish National War Memorial* (London, 1927)

Wilson, D., *Memorials of Edinburgh*, (2nd edn, Edinburgh, 1891)

Zeune, J., *The Last Scottish Castles* (Leidorf, 1992)

Guides and series

The two prominent series of volumes introducing Scottish architecture are the Penguin *Buildings of Scotland*, general editor John Gifford, and the RIAS/Landmark illustrated architectural guides. There are countless guidebooks to Scotland's Renaissance country houses under the disguise of castles, even in addition to those produced by their owners – e.g. Historic Scotland. Most are regionally based. The only ones that have been included in this bibliography are those to which specific attention is drawn. For the others, consult the current version.

Index

Numbers in *italics* denote illustrations.